D1499577

STAFF DEVELOPMENT AND INSTRUCTIONAL IMPROVEMENT

Plans and Procedures

Leslee J. Bishop

University of Georgia

Allyn and Bacon, Inc. Boston · London · Sydney

Library of Congress Cataloging in Publication Data

Bishop, Leslee J
Staff development and instructional improvement.

Includes bibliographical references and index.
1. Teachers—In-service training. I. Title.
LB1731.B53 371.1'46 75-43746

ISBN 0-205-05470-6

Fourth printing . . . June, 1979

Contents

STAFF DEVELOPMENT
AND
INSTRUCTIONAL IMPROVEMENT
Plans and Procedures

Introduction

In-service education and staff development desperately need to be given a higher priority. Since these activities function in the improvement as well as the routine operation of a school system, they must be integral to the career experience of every staff member. This can be facilitated by showing how such efforts can resolve basic problems and result in desired outcomes. Planning is the critical ingredient in this process and, in all phases of education, must be considered a more necessary element. The ideas presented in this guide are proposals for action. They are open-ended agendas for use in planning and decision making; they are meant to be resources, not prescriptions.[1-3]

Good staff development, in-service education, and instructional change programs are intensely human and personal processes. Well-drawn and well-conceived plans for such development are the most conclusive commitment that a school system can exhibit towards its personnel and their achievements. If humaneness is not included in the conceptualizing and structuring of these plans, it is unlikely that it will surface in the implementing and evaluating phases. The human element will be emphasized in the suggested approaches of this guide, based on the premise that plans for development are integral to other continuing processes, plans are adequately delineated and reviewed, and plans are a part of a communication and sharing enterprise.[4,5]

This book has been structured as a guide to accommodate a number of purposes:

1. A planning tool for those charged with the responsibility of planning in-service and staff development activities for their school or system, such as lead teachers, department chairpersons, subject area consultants, and principals.
2. A guide to product and process quality for those who are charged with the responsibility for supervising in-service and staff development activities.
3. A resource for those who plan major curricular or instructional change and who assist in the building of the personnel competencies and components for that change.

4. A basis of study for those who wish to analyze the process of in-service planning, staff development, instructional improvement, and implementation; i.e., to review basic procedures, assumptions, and specific techniques.
5. A reference for those charged with the improvement of system policy, procedure, structure, or leadership, who can use the guide ideas as a basis for conceptualizing and developing their own approaches and competencies.

The text is organized in a functional sequence. Chapters 1-6 include standard process stages used in planning or problem solving; namely, rationale, diagnosis, design, development, implementation, and evaluation. Guidelines, process and product models, and elements are to be considered for each of these chapters. Chapters 7 and 8 deal with managing and organizing the necessary activities. Many of the concepts and techniques are amplified in the appendix, which also introduces various approaches for use according to the orientation and competencies of the leadership persons. Each chapter emphasizes a particular stage or process; however, each is dependent upon the total context and substance provided by other sections of the book.

In the past, improvement has depended too much upon good will, professional zeal, and generalized approaches. Developments such as teacher negotiations, criticisms of educational processes and the resulting learner roles and achievements, and expanded media (especially new management approaches aided by computers) are added dimensions to education, the handling of which will require precision and comprehensiveness. Television has yet to fulfill its rightful place in programs for change or staff development utilizations, but it may when video cassettes, video disks, holeographic video and film cartridges, plus cable and telephone communications and feedback systems contribute more flexibility, more individualization. Supplementary content materials now supplied in curricular packages are being developed to meet many in-service requirements. Some examples include audio cassettes and related competency modules containing related print materials, models, relevant follow-up readings, and individualized evaluation and implementation. More precise instructional objectives require more specific responses and expertise by teachers and support personnel. Community and year-round learning arrangements need to be made. Planning and budgeting, along with demands for explicit "accountability," require more detailing of program thrusts and related needs and services. New time frames for the work day, work week, and even the school year are upon us. Population mobility requires more adequate diagnosis and particularized experiencing by learners and professionals. Performance criteria and related competencies are replacing credentials as prerequisites. Demands for institutional openness, along with new psychological, technological, and chemical mediations, require the inclusion of different and non-school personnel and agencies. New problems and themes such as resource utilization, population, environment, urbanization, technology, changing life styles, and value ambiguities need incorporation into curricular planning. These new demands and dimensions now make professional renewal and quality education imperatives rather than recommendations.[6-11]

The processes that we invoke in response to the current challenges should not be viewed as ends in themselves, but rather, as the means by which we may accomplish more than in the past—when we focused upon the tasks to be done with little else to assist us save dedication and hard work. The approaches to be presented not only can facilitate the continual development of more competent personnel, but it also can provide concurrently a vehicle through which extensive substantive, instructional, and organizational change may be accomplished. As a result, issues and skills can be anticipated as well as belatedly included or remediated.

Complexity is one reason that staff development has an unimpressive record. Even a small system would be hard-pressed to document, much less organize, all the shades and varieties of efforts that comprise the procedures of staff development. For this reason, priorities must be identified to organize processes and to agree on a structure. Without definition, virtually any activity can be called in-service or staff development. Without clarification, no line separates in-service from supervisory activities. However, definitions and clarifications by themselves do not obtain results. Policy decisions, personnel assignment, resources, authorization, program, participation, and implementation are required.[12,13] The design and management of the staff development program and its resultant complexity are what this "guide" is all about.

Those who seek a single solution, a "package panacea," will not find it here. Rather, they will find suggestions for means through which to develop improved personnel responses and program quality. Moreover, this "guide" seeks to assist primarily in the conceptualizing and planning phases of staff development and instructional improvement, not in the total range of in-service activities.

System "leadership style" is not prescribed except as philosophy and approach are included in such items as guidelines and as possible options to be selected in planning. It is hoped that developmental, human-related, participatory modes will be chosen, but that is also a system/project decision. The guidelines and check items chosen for inclusion here should be rewritten by local school district personnel in order to spell out the desired orientation or stance, which will operationally affect the nature of the activities undertaken. Consideration must also be given such factors as the organizational climate, the type of management system to be selected—its resources and constraints, the relationship of the desired program to other processes in operation, and the extent of interaction with administrative levels at the various process phases.

Courage, caution, consensus, and size factors will determine the extent and speed with which a given program can (or should) be initiated. These decisions will be reflected in the means, formats, budget, personnel allocations, and other system considerations. It is an open-end, sub-system plan. Decisions by roles or hierarchical levels are not indicated. In a local situation, however, it would be desirable to indicate points and persons to be incorporated into the planning sequences. In any case, these materials assume that the planning described here will exist within some larger context for system policy, personnel, and procedure.

Technologies and structures can be dangerous and frightening unless and until they are mastered. A half-mastered technology imposes its own constraints; it forces persons to conform. For example, early computer "down times," including errors, were blamed on computer characteristics rather than upon the inadequacies/inaccuracies of the programmers. Given a naive planner, devices for performance objectives can be destructive and debilitating rather than useful for focusing instructional resources and strategies. The technologies of the system's approach, even of such participatory approaches as *organization development* or *clinical supervision*, become humanized and personalized only when thoroughly understood by both leadership and participants. Value considerations must be incorporated within the application of the processes; they cannot be part-time, ancillary, or hoped-for adjuncts. Technologies can provide alternatives and divergencies, not needing to be fixed or convergent. This is the challenge to the planner, the administrator, the supervisor, and even the lay decision-maker.

Many illustrations (visualizations) are used throughout the text. These sketches are designed to facilitate an understanding of the possible dimensions, the structure, and the consequent interrelationships of a concept. As "hilltop" views, they have the advantages of overview and analogy, enabling one to perceive the field. However, the disadvantage of appearing mechanical is inherent, depending upon a few key words or over-simplications. In such visualizations, it is difficult to convey personal dimensions, the dynamics of process, and the intricacies of communication and detail. Like roadmaps or musical scores, they need not be dehumanizing or impersonal.

The intent of illustration is to build the desired outcomes, qualities of experience, and direction into a form that can be examined and implemented; they should present generative beginnings and alternatives, not cause closure. While many design elements are believed compatible in the context presented, obviously, no single design or process approach is adequate to the organism that is the school system and its environment or even to a particular situation. Whatever elements are chosen, it is hoped that the advantages mentioned above will prevail and that the ideas will aid clarification of the personal and process dimensions as well as of the concepts, relationships, and overall perspective intended.

While it is true that any plan may fall short of its intended potential in clarity or usefulness; it is equally true that it may be unfulfilled operationally if care is not exercised at its initiation and implementation, i.e., by the leadership who will work directly with it. Certain cautions appear worthy of mention:

1. Strong consideration should be given to involving qualified, experienced personnel from outside the system in which the program is to be attempted. Their responsibility would be to assist in providing the background mentioned above, to give specific assistance in the initial steps of the planning (that could very well include training in human relations), and to participate in a periodic review of progress at identified check points throughout the process period.
2. It is proposed that the ideas included here be presented to teachers and to leadership, along with the preparation, study, and orientation in its use and implementation. This is a guide with many alternatives, not a "fait accompli."

More is gained with professionals by building upon strengths than by always searching for inadequacies or by utilizing remedial approaches. When improvement projects stem from publicized deficiencies, a negative and self-fulfilling "destruct" process is created. If in-service is a synonym for failure, then such activities will be viewed as punishment, not advancement. For innovative instructional programs or significant learner achievement to be built and maintained, both the context (the system, structure, and routines) and the personal commitment (values and operational implementation) of the staff must be emphasized. This posits an affirmative stance.

This is a personal document; e.g., the writer acknowledges a struggle in maintaining a balance between some items that are very specific and others that are general considerations. Also, questions of balance arise between desired task outcomes and personal-process considerations; and between the need to have intermediate closures for sensing and achieving progress and for opting for openness, serendipity, and flexibility when this may not always be the desired system stance. These tensions, however, are believed to be both realistic and productive, if they are recognized and kept in perspective by the reader. Likewise, redundancy occurs in some of the concepts that are used because many of the ideas recycle within the various developmental stages and program operations.

This "guide" is also a translation document, attempting to utilize the technologies of many design and planning schemes and delivering them in practitioner terms, and hopefully in a practical synthesis. It is the writer's belief that planning is not a neutral enterprise; the development and selection of alternatives proposes value orientations. Thus, the approaches carry many injunctions, many "shoulds." This strong language is intended only for worthy procedural approaches. If this causes discomfort, the reader is invited to recall the admonition of Portia:

> "If to do were as easy as to know what were good to do, chapels had been churches, and poor men's cottages princes' palaces. It is a good divine that follows his own instructions: I can easier teach twenty what were good to be done, than be one of the twenty to follow mine own teaching." (*The Merchant of Venice*, Act 1, Scene 2.)

RELATED REFERENCES

1. Rubin, Louis J., *A Study on the Continuing Education of Teachers.* Santa Barbara: Center for Coordinated Education, University of California, 1969.
2. Meade, Edward J., "No Health in Us." In *Improving In-Service Education,* edited by Louis J. Rubin. Boston: Allyn and Bacon, 1971.
3. Davis, Russell C., *Planning Human Resource Development.* Chicago: Rand McNally, 1966.
4. Downey, Lawrence W., "Organizational Theory as a Guide to Educational Change." *Educational Theory,* 11:38 (1961).
5. Howey, Kenneth R., "Preconditions for Education Renewal and Reform." *Journal of Teacher Education,* 26:1 (1975): pp. 6–11.
6. Bourgeois, Donald A., "Mass Living: Impact on Man and His Environment." In *Curriculum Decisions and Social Realities,* edited by Robert R. Leeper. Washington, D.C.: Association for Supervision and Curriculum Development, 1968.
7. Ellul, Jacques, *The Technological Society.* New York: Alfred A. Knopf, 1964.
8. Hellman, Hal, *Biology in the World of the Future.* New York: Evans and Company, 1971.
9. Shane, Harold, "Looking to the Future: Reassessment of Educational Issues of the 1970's." *Phi Delta Kappan,* 54:326 (1973).
10. Shane, Harold. "The Educational Significance of the Future." *Phi Delta Kappan,* Bloomington, Indiana (1973).
11. Sciara, Frank, and Jantz, Richard K., *Accountability in American Education.* Boston: Allyn and Bacon, 1972.
12. Watson, Goodwin, and Glaser, Edward M., "What We Have Learned about Planning for Change." *Management Review Magazine,* 54:34 (1965).
13. Chin, Robert, "Models of and Ideas about Changing." In *Media and Educational Innovation,* Lincoln: University of Nebraska, 1963.

1

Renewing and Changing

Staff development and program improvement activities are the career counterparts of pre-service education. And as such, they provide for change, renewal, quality education, and professional competence. What they seek is an affirmative response to the changing social and political scene and to criticism that curricula are not relevant, that professionals are not adequate, and that educational institutions represent lag rather than progress. Such efforts are important ingredients of the continuing curriculum for every career teacher and supervisor.[1,2]

Staff development and in-service education bear the brunt for continuity in program quality, for responsiveness to educational needs, for the initiation of programs for change, and for the opportunity for individuals to engage in self examination and renewal.

Staff development focuses upon professional growth rather than upon credentialing or maintaining. It assumes the need for change and renewal.[3] Staff development has personal, role, and institutional dimensions, all of which are critical to effective functioning. Thus, many kinds of activities that are called in-service education are not included in this account. Rather, the emphasis here is upon those attitudes, competencies, and knowledges that enhance learning, program effectiveness, and professional adequacy. These are related to systematic efforts to improve the conditions, objectives, resources, and processes that are the responsibility of the school district.[4]

This focus requires sensitivity to individual needs and to developments in society, whether within the field of education or in a particular school system. Expectations for education change as new media, new technologies, new life styles, new political, social, international, and economic forces surface as priorities or potentials. The number of imperatives is as great as there are points of view. The function of leadership is to determine which are educational and which are school responsibilities and to contend with them.[5-7]

Administrators, supervisors, and curriculum workers are aware that staff development and in-service education programs generally are considered "disaster areas," that is, often poorly done and considered ineffective.

> . . . In-service education has indeed been virtually a lost cause . . .; teacher professional growth has not been taken seriously, it lacks systematic methodology, and it has been managed with astonishing clumsiness. It is not surprising, therefore, that teachers have grown accustomed to its impotence and that administrators have come to regard it as a routine exercise in futility. (Rubin, 1971, p. 245.)[8]

It need not be this way. This document neither laments the weaknesses nor defends such practices. Rather, it considers some basic propositions and approaches that may help improve the situation with desired outcomes from workable processes.

The best catalyst for staff development is a relevant, need-oriented, well-conceived, and organized, instructional improvement program. To this must be added the importance of personal involvement, consensus, and commitment. Hopefully, these are also reasons *for* and products *of* the change effort. Educational planning for change and renewal must achieve new dimensions.[9-11] Credibility must be restored through response and quality. Community, regional, professional, consortia, and media developments create a different locus for planning, representation, and implementation. New research and recommendations about the nature and role of youth and the schools will also lend to the final shape of changes. The pressure will continue for programs to be more efficient, more effective, more open, and more integral to every time and every individual, now and in the future.[12-16] The horizon has moved.

In-service projects, staff development, and instructional improvement efforts can no longer be isolated events. Not only must they be compatible with the ongoing context of the school system, but they also must include mass media, community personnel, non-educational agencies, and a variety of learning sites. The community concept must include related institutions such as colleges and schools of education, business and industrial facilities, regional agencies, and other schools.[17-19] Educational goals are too complex, means are too expensive, outcomes are too important, and lead time is too precious to stop short of this larger perspective.

Major shifts in power have resulted as: (1) community persons, roles, sites, and decisions become more explicit and involved; (2) teachers and other professional groups negotiate for autonomy, access to decision making, and resources; (3) individual learners and student groups delineate rights and engage in more significant decisions regarding objectives, aspirations, and learning alternatives; (4) technology and media including new techniques and processes restructure or realign the elements of education; and (5) as governments and agencies at all levels joust for the power to allocate resources and affect the nature and quality of life.[20-30] A leveling population has decreased the need for "anyone" who will teach. It has increased the competition for available jobs, changed the criteria as to what is a competent professional, and contributed to the struggle as to who will control teacher education, certification, and tenure.[31-35]

Cooperation and coordination of a different order will be required. If the necessary improvements cannot be made by the institutional agencies and processes of education, then likely, other means will be found to achieve them. It is the function and responsibility of educators to make the educational experience relevant, renewing, and qualitative for all learners, i.e., our youth, our professionals, and our citizens. This "guide" addresses itself to the challenge of providing a framework within which may be realized new content for learners, new expertise for professionals, and new involvements and understandings for citizens. Whatever the focus, it should be recognized that every change, whether it be in programs or competencies, is basically a change in attitude.[36-38]

Many other objectives or emphases are possible, but these few point to certain high priority tasks and to alternative methods and combinations of methods by which these tasks can be achieved. The national call for systematic planning, achievement, and accountability should alert leaders to exhibit the same attention at system and planning levels (to sharpened objectives and particularized content and strategies) that are expected of other educational staff in the classroom and instructional level.[39,40]

What change is desired should be a determining factor as to which of the alternatives in the "guide" are to be selected; for its purpose is to facilitate the change whether it be organizational, substantive, or instructional in nature.[41,42] For example, a plan to provide for greater utilization of technology would likely stress the use of facilities and media and the opportunity to gain competence and skill. On the other hand, a plan to modify instructional practices would require more prolonged and interactive experiencing, during which period changes could occur in the value orientation of the staff. Skills might be developed via actual practice/simulation, and support features would be installed as needed.

One suitable opportunity for long term and perhaps large group involvement would be activities that necessarily accompany an instructional change, whatever the grade levels or the content area. Related and ongoing staff development results as this change idea is developed into a program. The form of involvement might vary from individual consultation and small group dialogue to course work in highly structured group sessions.[43,44] As a matter of fact, variety would not only help such a change, but would be welcome relief from the stereotyped gatherings that characterize most efforts. Some possibilities are included later in the text.

The following representation, Figure 1.1, reflects the basic design that is used and amplified throughout the "guide." Assuming that a change is desired in curriculum or instruction, it would be necessary to

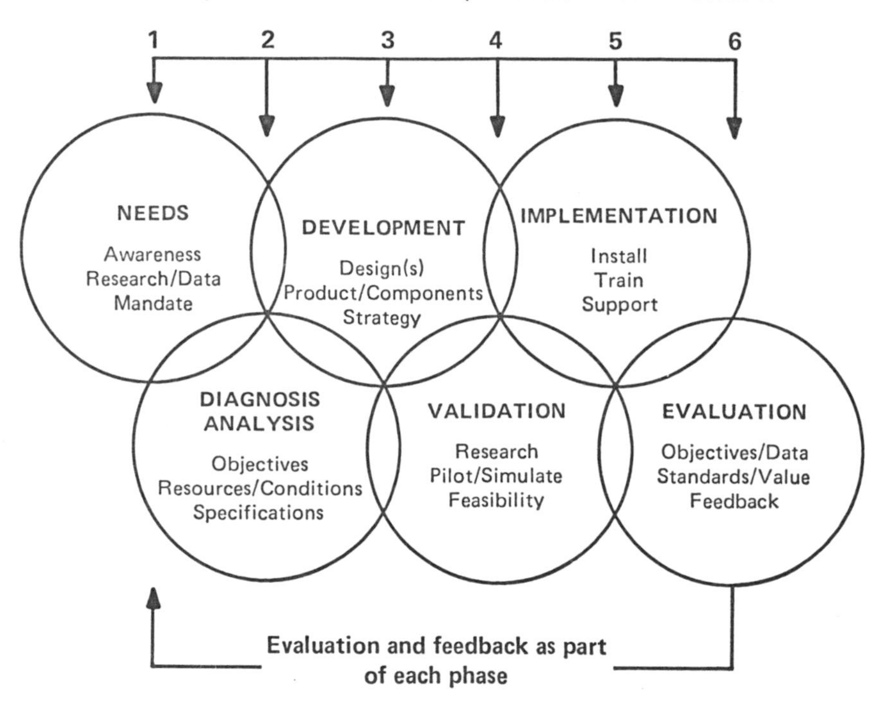

FIGURE 1.1 Instructional Change Model.

design and institute a sequential and comprehensive plan. The elements presented in Figure 1.1 are basic to any such plan. They are the substantive elements and procedural phases to be considered as a checklist of tasks rather than a format of linear or discrete operations. In addition to presenting possible change phases and tasks, the figure illustrates the need to have a developed strategy to which involved persons can relate—as both a total process and as intermediate terminal points. These can contribute to a basic understanding of what will transpire, as well as to assist personnel in both knowing that progress is occurring and in contributing to the gains that are made.

Other change sequences that could be used depending on the effort undertaken are presented later. One example of these is the Initiation, Design, Transaction, Evaluation sequence. Also, in order to simplify the design, additional tasks have been omitted, although they are addressed later in the text. Arrows could be inserted on the figure to show that each change phase recapitulates all the others. Each involves decision making, management, feedback, evaluation, and recycling. Likewise, each phase is dependent upon others, and each has subordinate elements. The latter are only indicated here but would need to be explicated in a fully developed plan or graphic representation.

Three versions of this model are presented in later chapters:

1. The instructional change phases, Chapter 2, which emphasize the basic elements to be considered.

2. The staff development design agenda, Chapter 3, which highlights the elements and tasks that maximize staff renewal.
3. The management plan, Chapter 7, which features management tasks essential to the initiation and operation of either a staff development or instructional change program. The relationships and emphases of the two approaches are indicated in connection with the management plan.

In the following visualization and discussion, only key activities are indicated. They suggest what can or should be done and introduce ideas that will be expanded later.

NEEDS, for example, can arise from a variety of sources and can exist in a variety of forms. In the model above, "awareness" indicates those needs that are sensed and more or less agreed upon but for which no supporting data of any consequence exist. General goal statements tend to fall in this category. In this case, the related staff development activities would need to be of an interactive, involving type, since one function of the needs analysis would be to clarify both the needs and the perceptions of the related personnel. If a need is clearly delineated as the result of studies or "research" and exists in clear-cut evidence or objectives, the consequent program then can be more easily perceived and structured. Where the need (and/or related objectives) are "mandated," i.e., made imperative by powers such as the board of education or the state legislature, the direction of the program response then likely will be indicated by the mandate.[45,46]

Once needs are identified or delineated, teachers, counselors, supervisors, principals, and community people must all participate in the search for program focus and direction. The tendency to minimize this phase of program building should be avoided, and all personnel and faculty should be involved appropriately in the analysis of system needs. Actually, once clear purpose exists, especially one that has general understanding and agreement, a major portion of the desired change already has been achieved.

During the DIAGNOSIS-DESIGN phase, procedures must be established to allow input for program development from all professionals in accordance with their expertise and responsibility. Goal setting, identification of objectives, and production of specifications have their

staff-related components. Leaders at each level of education, e.g., classroom, school, system, and region, should be qualified to exert leadership at this juncture with appropriate assistance from specialists in structuring the design.[47,48]

At the point of **PROGRAM DEVELOPMENT,** teachers especially are needed for their experience, knowledge, and peer impact on other staff members. Direction and leadership can come from other sources

DEVELOPMENT

Design(s)
Product/Components
Strategy

such as consultants, research, and model programs tried elsewhere, but the participation in selection, adaption, and commitment must come from staff who will be involved intimately in the program. Alternative program approaches need to be built in at this point.

VALIDATION through a procedure such as pilot testing can be a most exciting though painful process, e.g., experimenting, experiencing, researching, and monitoring. The staff that is selected and involved in

program piloting is usually critical to an assessment of appropriateness and adequacy and offers a unique and an important contribution in identifying the problems as well as determining the impact, soundness, and efficiency of the proposed solutions.

IMPLEMENTATION demands full commitment by the total district and especially those who are directly involved in the new program. Once staff commitment and competency are achieved, the worthwhile

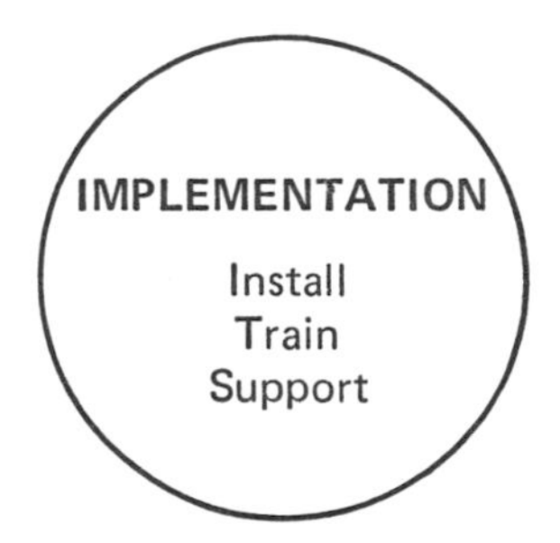

program efforts at this juncture of process are: (1) Superintendents and boards of education provide policy and budgetary/personnel support. (2) Supervisors help in the development and support of the new educational design and structure, providing the needed assistance to produce results. (3) Building principals provide professional climate, process, time, operational leadership, and immediate ongoing support. (4) Instructional staff members give necessary help to their peers in acquiring new knowledge and skill. (5) Learners know the rationale, sense the commitment, and participate fully and willingly. (6) Parents and other members of the community see results, which match their program expectations. A whole new array of organizational and procedural support systems are crucial to program survival. They cannot be emphasized too strongly.

Finally, the formative and summative **EVALUATION** procedures that have monitored installation, collected data, and assessed discrepancies should involve the entire staff in diagnostic, development, research, and evaluation activities. As the data are evaluated and communicated through related activities, implications for staff review and growth will emerge.[49-52]

As the cycle is completed, the program and its staff will mature in their understanding and performance due to the fact that all participants and educational segments are vital to the process and are held accountable in accordance with their responsibility and contribution. The most creditable results will be evidenced by learner gain, staff adequacy and community acceptance. Such achievement must include process as well as product modifications. Important objectives cannot be delivered by a single segment of the operation; no one can be excluded. The real challenge of instructional change and staff development is to make a difference happen and to enable all contributors to be instrumental in the program making it possible.

Where staff development is the intent, those involved in the problem-solving must understand how the proposed response will resolve the issue. In the course of a project's operations, the problem becomes reclarified and the objectives become internalized. The resolution often results from these transactions rather than from a yet-to-be achieved product at some designated future date. Stated differently, planning schemes organize the environment and its resources to facilitate the process of resolution, rather than producing an absolute outcome. The solution may defy the time frame by serendipitous achievements; likewise, the time frame may indicate the duration of attention to the problem rather than the achievement of the solution. Thus, whether a partial solution exacerbates the issue or provides a stepping stone to the next attempt is a critical judgment. These discrepancies and repercussions provide data for the leadership to make decisions regarding further plans and interventions. In any case, the credibility of the effort is a significant concern.

OPPORTUNITIES FOR IMPROVEMENT

A responsive school operation will be alert to many possibilities for growth and change. The many routines of a school or system provide opportunities that can be made more interactive and more productive in connection with staff meetings, teacher-supervisor conferences, work with new teachers or the paraprofessionals, informal sharing through intervisitation or demonstrations of work, participation in grade level or content area committee activities, and new contacts and relationships with parents and community agencies. Such efforts will be more productive if given purpose and recognition, and if allied with the known curriculum development and staff development emphases.[53-58]

Other possibilities include professional days, institute days, workdays, and in-service days. Whatever they may be called locally, they provide opportunities for both bringing together the many threads of improvement efforts and also for focusing on particulars that need review or emphasis. Professional libraries that contain research and references related to the staff projects as well as to ongoing programs should be established. "Peer power" suggests the use of existing teachers who, given time and help, can become more effective as leadership persons and ad hoc change agents, thus retaining their teaching roles and furthering their influence with other teachers. Professional associations and subject matter organizations, university course work, U.S. State Department consultants, publisher representatives, and consortium efforts with similar school systems where teams of teacher-experts share talents and experience, all have potential. As changes are made in standards, in content, in expectations, and in social and technological developments, they should be reviewed and incorporated into the stream of instructional change and staff development objectives and activities.[59,60]

HUMAN RELATIONS AND STAFF DEVELOPMENT

Instructional improvement and staff development activities at their best are very personal enterprises involving professionals who, as a result of their experience and training, have acquired strong feelings, individual styles, and commitments. By implication, such programs often threaten persons who feel that any improvement effort represents a criticism of their contribution (and such may be the case). The press for program and teacher evaluation also contributes to this tension and discomfort.[61-65] Some approaches to evaluation, competence, accountability, and change appear to be mechanistic, production/output oriented; more compatible with industrial or military processes than with personalized, localized, or professionally directed approaches. Further, to many people design efforts such as systems analysis, PPBES, PERT, MBO, and CPM* and means such as television, computer, cassettes, and programmed modules appear depersonalized, authoritarian, and contrary to a developmental, humane "democratic" philosophy (see Appendix E). These conflicts in perception or process must be reconciled.

This text assumes that measures in themselves are neutral. As extensions of purpose, they can be rigid or flexible; they can be impersonal or personal. The determining factor is their use, the extent to which they become the techniques and means to facilitate the desired goals, not the ends to be achieved. The textbook is an oft-cited example, for it can serve either to determine or to assist learning. The media center can be a rigid, storage-retrieval facility or it can be a center for individualizing and learning. Hopefully, we recognize that *education is not merely a building function, that learning is not exclusive to the school, that teaching is more than directing and telling, and that in-service, staff*

*PPBES—Planning, Programming, Budgeting, Evaluation System, Appendix E.
PERT—Program Evaluation and Review Technique, p. 225.
CPM—Critical Path Method, p. 233.
MBO—Management by Objectives, Chapter 7.

development and instructional improvement are interactive processes and not a schedule, a day so-assigned, or a non-personalized intervention.

A plea here or at a faculty meeting for good human relations, for involvement, or for individualization is not enough. These elements need to be built into operational procedures that demonstrate commitment and that utilize such relationships. The uses of individual contracts/process agreements—of working groups and instructional councils and of methods that incorporate the power and perceptions of the involved persons—are as crucial to systematic and comprehensive approaches as are sophisticated means for planning, costing, or transmitting information.[66] As an objective is pursued throughout the selected design elements that the text proposes, each phase presents a growth opportunity for those who plan, interact, decide, adapt, appraise, and relate. Thus, the process of involvement becomes an important contributor to the personal and professional gains desired.

Structure may be imposed or it may be developed mutually. The structures suggested here are recommended as resources and alternatives from which to draw, not as predetermined sets. In any case, the planners and the system decision-makers will determine how open or how closed the objectives and procedure will be; this responsibility cannot be relegated to technicians. The process should be a blend of personal involvement and organizational definition.

Either a highly structured "systems" approach or a more developmental process can be used. If the latter is preferred, it would be appropriate to consider *clinical supervision* techniques, or for groups, the *organization development* approach.[67-69] These seek to maximize trust and communication, to minimize personal risk taking by emphasis on goal clarification and sharing, and to use outside assistance to provide action interventions and training, along with clarification and feedback regarding actions. The intent is a decentralization of decision making through collaboration, consensus, and role clarification, and a development of acceptable alternatives for proceeding. Analysis and evaluation are approached as broadly shared processes, with self-corrective mechanisms and interactions rather than arbitrary or punitive uses of data. Many ideas from new planning schemes and from comprehensive and systematic approaches are built into the recommendations, although they are not presented in terms of any one precise "technology."

A number of questions are relevant to this issue. At what point does structure surface—is it predetermined, does it emerge as a result of consultation and feedback, or is it a selective process in which alternatives are examined? Who makes the decisions and what processes are employed to arrive at "fix" points and change interventions? What is the attitude of top leadership toward other participants—is it that they are resistant, indifferent, and rigid or that they are self-motivating, responsible, and capable? What are the processes for sharing decisions, data, recognition, and competencies? Are the operational goals perceived to be primarily products and materials rather than professional gains and skills? How hierarchical or how goal related are the procedures? These and other considerations are environmental, morale, leadership, and style questions that require resolution.

LEADERSHIP AND DIALOGUE

An obvious implication is the need for perceptive, organized leadership.[70-72] It may be that the first task in any sustained staff development or change program is the development of leadership capabilities within the administrative/supervisory staff, as well as a strong leadership cadre within the teacher group. This can be developed functionally—in process—or as an initial training effort.

Leadership and planning capabilities should mark the central office staff. Their responsibility is to know the community, to be familiar with the powers and constraints with which to work and contend, and to be ready to choose the processes and change mechanisms most appropriate for a given circumstance. A small school system needs to rely on its principals and lead teachers for the same functions. Teachers should know the learners and their problems and what changes would make the learning situation more productive.

Whatever the initiating source is for staff development or instructional change objectives, strong school units and involved local leadership must implement and maintain the thrust. Schools can be linked within a system, with regional agencies, or with university-school agreements.[73] The power of any sustained effort must include the operating school unit(s) as a major organizing center. Otherwise, the improvement projects are minimized or aborted at the very places where they should be strongest.

Therefore, the maintenance of dialogue between the planning center and the operating centers is critical. This dialogue will need reinforcement from continuous and concrete evidences of support. "Management" and plan are not enough; there also must be concern for relationships as they relate to both means and ends, to individual and professional concerns.

Some persons find design efforts frustrating and "unnecessary." They prefer to strike out in a particular direction and develop activities as the need arises, solve problems as they become intrusive, and rely upon experience, serendipity, and intuition. This heuristic or creative-expanding approach has validity. It can be made to work if the drive and the power exist; in fact, it may be the only tenable approach when personal risks are high, when objectives, variables, and structure are not clarified by leadership (or participants). Such a procedure places a higher premium on the various interactions that may occur in the course of the activity than upon certain outcomes or products. (However, this style has limitations where long-range, multiple, or complex projects are underway, and where policy and decision making require more definition regarding plans, personnel, costs, and outcomes.) The "guide" is written for these persons also, for its information is not a matter of "either/or." Leaders who prefer this style can use the proposed design elements when they reach certain developmental points; they can select those planning and structuring elements that relate to the problems encountered. As a matter of fact, both the logical and the empirical approaches must be flexible. The logical, pre-structured plan must change as new inputs modify the initial conditions and assumptions. The empirical approach tends to move toward structural elements as recurring data and experiences provide useful constructs. Whatever the preferred approach, textual suggestions are proposed as possibilities and alternatives. In no case would all the included elements be used in a single project, however complex.

Structuring (planning, designing) and developing personalized and localized alternatives represent the focus of this guide. As indicated, such assistance should not be the only support. Professionals resent being streamed into pre-existing decisions or actions; therefore, the ground rules should be made clear. If a given effort is a mandated change, that should be communicated. If the effort is a cooperative venture to mobilize competence, with form and process emerging from the contributions of an involved staff, that should be evident. A dialogue with structure is not the same as a pre-determined means and ends stance. Good design should facilitate, not inhibit, collaboration. Charisma and inspiration are not enough.

Improvement programs are intended to build staff competencies and to enhance the learning process and environment. They must be integral to the continuing operation and program, and they must be based on validated needs, resulting in effective joint implementation. Success is measured to the degree that staff morale and competencies are enhanced, as well as good feelings and substantive gains for learners. As the career counterpart of pre-service education, both present and future programs posit the need for more comprehensive and effective approaches.

A critical purpose of dialogue is to develop mutual understanding, personal and cognitive, as a way of minimizing "static" regarding individual values, intent, problems, or life-style considerations. Freedom to express views and to place one's ideas "on the line" for use or rejection requires a high level of trust and self-confidence. Without psychological comfort and esteem, "hidden agenda," piecemeal specifics, and convergent ideas will develop to restrict both change and personal involvement.[74-77]

PROCESS IS PARAMOUNT

In an era of increasing professionalism, in an educative enterprise seeking staff renewal and curricular gain, process considerations are of major concern. Media and technology can capture and store the basic elements of any product outcome. Structure has utility and can be generative. However, the significant gains are in staff competencies and attitudes, in developing ways to manage, perform, and participate more effectively.

A simple listing may be adequate to make the point. New curricular programs rely heavily upon appropriate process skills and "modes of investigation" by the learner and teacher.[78,79] Great concern exists for humaneness, for the integrity of each person, for authenticity, for alternative life styles (and school programs), for awareness, for sensitivity, for individualization at all levels, and for self, criterion, or domain-referenced measures.[80-85] New organizational procedures include clinical supervision, intervention strategies, systems approach, organization development, and group procedures that facilitate communication. Classroom interaction research seeks patterns of response—verbal and nonverbal (see Appendix E). Linguistic efforts stress precision, but also more respect for dialect and patterns of usage. Feedback and accountability are processes as well as products. Social transactions seek involvement, decentralization, and heightened levels of awareness. Ecologists have helped make concern for environment, as well as production and output, factors with which to contend.[86-90]

Not to be minimized, even in rational and complex enterprises, is the joy of the journey.[91] Ends, products, and outcomes are important, but their importance must be viewed in relationship to larger schemes and purposes. In so many developments and situations, the most forceful and durable consequences are those that relate to processes and means, especially those that contribute to a basic understanding of how events and outcomes can be achieved, how change can be managed within a given context, and how the necessary considerations and relationships can be developed.

The hypothesis presented here is that outcomes such as personal and professional growth, adequacy in coping, and the reconsideration of meaning and values are not achieved by highly constrained, pre-determined or externally controlled requirements. Rather, dialogue, inquiry, and emergent and successive approximations are more likely to achieve the larger ends. Also, these gains can be facilitated by planning designs and organizational structures that build in flexibility, choice-making, exceptions, and a host of other humane dimensions. The intention of the design, then, is to rationally map out directions and domains for exploration, to incorporate alternative routes and style possibilities, to consciously deal with contingencies and constraints, and to be willing at all times to recast the original structure or elements. This complicates project decision making and includes more persons in the consideration of exceptions. But, in the long run, such a stance can also accommodate more ambiguities and modifications, thus enhancing the durability and regard for the program effort. The principles of a humane, professional, personalized, and synergistic approach cannot flourish in a simplistic, linear, or mechanistic operation.[92] Even science is seeking new potentials within people as well as in technology, i.e., new insights from intuition, contemplation, and conjecture, also a broader interpretation of rationality. Research for new energy sources should not exclude human aspirations and talents (see Appendix E).

A process orientation does not infer an exclusive commitment to "methods" or to activities unrelated to objectives. Staff competencies and instructional change are evolutionary and developmental, not only for organized groups but for individuals as well. Process, as used here, is the mode for achieving an outcome, wherein the "outcome" is the extent of progress made toward the desired objective at any given time. It expresses a concern for a long range goal achievement that is interwoven with more specific and more terminal objectives.

In this context, processing and process evaluation become more strategic. Many issues need resolutions: How clearly are *goals perceived?* How well are they accepted and reconciled within each participant? Are they large enough to challenge, specific enough to be achieved? Is the *system for involvement* adequately representative? Is it collegial or status-bound; is it accessible? Is it appropriate to the tasks? Is *decision making* speedy and fair; does it facilitate or slow progress? Are the persons, agencies, and processes delineated? Is *communication and feedback* evident among individuals and organizational elements? Is time sufficient for the *achievement of tasks*, the accommodation of ideas, the rearrangement of policies and procedures? Is there *a support system* with developed *procedures and resources;* are there places to work as well as powers at work? Does evidence exist of increased *commitment and gain in necessary skills?* Is there an adequate understanding and application of concepts? Is *power* distributed according to tasks and responsibilities; does it move up as well as down the hierarchy? Who can *influence* what happens and what does not happen? Is the *atmosphere* conducive to productivity and morale, or to disunity and deliberation? Is the system *adaptive* and flexible, or is it rigid and unresponsive? Is *risk-taking* worth the personal and professional price?[93,94]

Phrased here as questions, these items are reconstructed as objectives or criteria later on, see pages 79-82 and 121-122, and as specific procedures throughout. These process elements are as critical to progress as are task achievements. To regard them as concomitants or side issues is to ignore the power of personal involvement, dedication, and the need for continuity beyond direct program emphasis. Both individual and group development processes are appropriately built into the ongoing operation.[95-97] Data needs include these concerns and relationships. Structure can facilitate, but it cannot successfully replace affirmative human interactions. These factors need to be as rigorously applied and inspected as the artifacts of progress, with process and product dependent on each other. The starting place is the needs of the learners and staff.

STAFF DEVELOPMENT AND INSTRUCTIONAL CHANGE

Improvement and renewal activities continue to be one of the major responsibilities of those charged with leadership functions in education.

The superintendent, curriculum director, principal, supervisor, consultant, and curriculum worker must share in this leadership responsibility, which encompasses more than just a "some time" leadership role; for it involves a professional-career function as well. And, as such, it must include all related personnel. Each individual, whatever his role, has the obligation to engage in improvement activities.[98-103]

Staff development and instructional change activities can range widely from ad hoc and individual involvement to highly organized and large group activities. Every element of the educational enterprise possesses in-service and staff development implications that demand not to be viewed as an add-on to the present program. As indicated, they must be considered as an integral feature, not one that occurs a few days before the regular school year, after school day classes, or during the summer vacation. They must be woven into the ongoing substantive, procedural, and organizational fabric of the system.

General Objectives of Staff Development

If staff development is to be vital to quality education, increased attention must be given to its relationship to program adoption and implementation. These should be the processes by which needs become objectives and objectives become programs, facilitating the growth of those charged with meeting the various responsibilities and the learners for whom they are responsible.

Improvement efforts have various objectives or emphases, each requiring its own unique mode.[104-107] For example, one important, general objective is to convey *knowledge* or information about new ideas and an intended change, including the rationale, concepts, objectives, and strategies involved. Information transmittal can be achieved by telling via film, video, learning modules, general meetings, lectures, publications, programmed instruction, or other like communication processes.

A second objective involves the development of *competency*. Competency involves a combination of information and related skills. For competency to exist there must be not only the opportunity to observe, to practice, to experiment, to prepare, to transact, and to evaluate, but also a situation to receive prompt feedback and reinforcement regarding style and effectiveness, followed by the opportunity to try again. For example, open education, individualizing, and using learning centers or diagnostic approaches require more than resources and knowledge about them if they are to succeed.

A third purpose is to seek *commitment*, a personal attitude that is necessary if knowledge is to be used correctly. A positive attitude cannot be secured by obtaining knowledge alone; it needs interaction, involvement, participation, identification, and support. Thus, techniques such as the discussion group, the seminar, the visit, the laboratory experience, and a multi-sensory proprietorship become essential.

Figure 1.2 is a simple delineation of these objectives and activities, plus their related groupings. Such generalized objectives and approaches require more specific development and detail. These considerations are the subject of Chapter 2, Diagnosing, and Chapter 3, Designing.

CHANGE AND TIME

Time is a potential resource as well as a critical dimension.[108] Time (sufficient time) is needed within the working day; an adequate time span must be available for the accommodation of new ideas or skills in addition to completion of the necessary tasks. The use of time must be creative, participatory, and integral to the individual and school system operation. Time is only one of many desirable "trade offs" or incentives. Others can be additional pay, leadership status, in-service credits, scholarships for graduate courses, staff recognition procedures, professional counseling services, secretarial assistance, teacher aides, parent volunteers, student teachers, and so forth.

Inertia and conflicts towards in-service and staff development activities have existed because the pressures too often have been for routine concerns; these have elicited passive compliance. Program assignments have tended to be fixed, not flexible, with teachers both insulated and isolated. Lacking priority and budget, staff development has been consigned to non-classroom times—an indication that it was *extra*, not *integral* to the instructional program.

A school district committed to program quality will also be committed to staff renewal and change. Time should be allocated for personnel to engage in productive and growth activities as a regular part of the work day and year. The production of learner resources and materials, research, evaluation, mutual assistance, and self-improvement programs should be a standard expectation for *all* instructional personnel. Participation in change and growth activities, however, would not be exclusive to school personnel but would involve parents, agency groups, community resource personnel, and others engaged in various and related phrases of the educational enterprise.[109-112]

A policy is needed that establishes staff development as an ongoing priority of the *total* instructional program. Staff development and instructional improvement efforts emerge most effectively from the workers working and learners learning. Such efforts are the responsibility of both the individual and the system, and therefore, should be incorporated into the planning of each. Every major professional operation of the system has staff development dimensions; every assignment and professional aspiration of individual staff members can have its in-service component. Operationally, these should be joined for maximum impact and effectiveness.

With clearer rationale, higher priority, greater flexibility, and imagination, standard practices can be utilized and improved. Examples can

MAJOR OBJECTIVE(S)	*GROUP SIZE*		
	Individual	*Small Group*	*Large Groups*
1. Knowledge Transmission-Information	Reading Modules Audio Tape Mediated, Programmed Materials	Study Group Case Study	Lecture Film-TV
2. Skill Development-Competency	Directed Practice	Simulation Laboratory Exercises Training Sessions	Demonstration
3. Understanding-Commitment	Visitation Internship Interview Research Utilization	Discussion Gaming Real Situation Human Relations Training	Field Trip Feedback Groups

Adapted from a similar display in Ben Harris, *Supervisory Behaviors in Education*, Prentice-Hall, Inc., Englewood Cliffs, N.J., 1963, p. 71.

FIGURE 1.2 Activities Regarding Objectives and Group Size.

be found in professional journals, ERIC reports, funded projects, and commercially operated programs. What follows is a list of employable possibilities for in-service and staff development activities. To provide specific examples for review, each practice has been keyed to models presented in the October and December, 1972 issues of *Theory Into Practice.*

STANDARD STAFF DEVELOPMENT PRACTICES

1. School Related Courses, Seminars, Institutes, Conferences, and Workshops. This category refers to professionally endorsed activities that may or may not be directly under the aegis of a school or school district. Participation in the activities may be voluntary or compulsory, carry university and/or certification credit, and involve some monetary remuneration. The time when these activities occur may vary: in the summer, during the school year before or after class work, and just prior to or following the school year. Provisions also can be made for personnel to be released periodically from regular duties so that they can engage in the designated activities.[113]

2. Inter- and Intra-School Programs, Activities, and Projects. Staff development practices included in this category are designed to occur on the school-building or district level. Specific practices may involve providing opportunities for planning periods, team and committee meetings, in-service programs, and differentiated team assignments and projects. All of these may occur within the "normal" school day by lengthening it or reshuffling student schedules on a weekly, monthly, or quarterly basis.

Other provisions may occur as a part of regular duties. Examples of these include planning projects, participating on instructional councils, performing action-research, making community and parental contacts, and observing teaching. At times, interclass and interschool demonstrations can be given that involve all segments of the school community. Another possibility within this category is a visitation program that is within the same school or district, or one that can be extended to other schools and districts where innovative or desirable program ideas are in operation.[114]

3. Consultant Directed Programs. Staff development programs may employ persons with expertise in a desired area to work on a continuing basis with school personnel. Persons who may be considered for consultant work are university personnel, professional resource specialists, curriculum specialists, commercial representatives, and supervisory personnel. Consultants may come from within or outside the system utilizing their services.[115]

4. Production and Use of Instructional Media, Resources, and Materials. Programs of this type make primary use of verbal, audio, visual, and nonelectronic/electronic technologies. Mediated instruction, learning packets, and modules are among the resources available for use in these programs. In a staff development operation, these technologies may be used individually or collectively at designated times, or at the convenience of the staff.

The development and use of professional libraries, media centers, exhibits, professional journals, reports, outdoor labs, and community excursions are additional considerations for use in resource and media programs.[116]

5. Individual Centered Personal and Professional Growth Plans. Plans comprising this category may stress individually targeted activities where teachers identify objectives and work with supervisors or peers regarding means, progress, standards, and evaluation. Internship programs and individual growth projects, often self-designed and self-coordinated by the participants, are other possibilities.[117,118]

6. School or Regional Consortia Programs. Programs in this category emphasize a professional partnership among schools, districts, or regional facilities. Their major program priority is to provide occasions for participating schools or districts to trade and share ideas, staff, and development tasks.[119]

7. Extended Year Programs and Assignments. This category covers programs and assignments that may extend beyond the usual school year. One such example is a full-year contract in connection with a four-quarter school year or a continuous school program. Summer employment, with or without pay, in academic or enrichment programs can also be considered in this category.

Whatever the focus or organizing scheme for the instructional improvement project, alternatives are needed to accommodate the range of individual perceptions, abilities, and style preferences. No one pattern will achieve the desired end except in very limited or specialized situations. Complex or multiple program objectives will require a variety of approaches, some individualized, some group-oriented. In total, the approaches are designed to facilitate the desired gains in staff attitudes and competencies. The same holds true for organizational, curricular, and instructional changes.[120]

ACTION GUIDELINES

Staff development and program improvement activities are keys to positive action in education. They are critical means for responding to the changing political and economic situation, as well as to the needs of the educational enterprise. Planning for educational change should utilize both structural and heuristic approaches. The use of models, i.e., conceptual schemes, combined with the considerable body of knowledge about change can assist in this effort. Staff development programs can maximize their impact by providing a variety of options for growth and change. These should be integral to the ongoing program and activities of the agency or system. Committee work, consultant-oriented approaches, individual plans, and inter-school and inter-agency events are among those to be considered.

Instructional improvement and staff development require personal as well as professional commitment. Thus, good human relations, participant involvement, and individualization are crucial. Leadership must be sought from all segments of the system; experienced teachers constitute a major resource that should be utilized because of their peer power, their familiarity with needs, and their expertise.

Experience and research emphasize the importance of means and processes. Personal, professional, and program outcomes are best achieved through collegial and developmental approaches, rather than highly contrived, pre-determined, and externally controlled procedures.

RELATED REFERENCES

1. Edmonds, Fredrick, Ogletree, James, and Wear, Patricia, *In-Service Education: Crucial Process in Educational Change.* Lexington, Kentucky: Bulletin of the Bureau of Services, University of Kentucky, 1966.
2. Rubin, Louis J., ed., *Improving In-Service Education.* Boston: Allyn and Bacon, 1971.
3. Gardner, John, *Self Renewal: The Individual and the Innovative Society.* New York: Harper, 1963.
4. Henry, Nelson, ed., *In-Service Education for Teachers, Supervisors, and Administrators.* Fifty-Sixth Yearbook of the National Society for the Study of Education. Chicago: University of Chicago Press, 1957.
5. Association for Supervision and Curriculum Development, *Life Skills in School and Society.* Yearbook. Washington, D.C.: author, 1969.
6. Piele, Philip K., et al., *Social and Technological Change: Implications for Education.* Eugene, Oregon: The Center for the Advanced Study of Educational Administration, 1970.
7. Toffler, Alvin, *Future Shock.* New York: Random House, 1970.
8. Rubin, Louis J., ed., *Improving In-Service Education. op. cit.*
9. Howey, Kenneth R., "The Context and Potential of Teacher Centers." *Education Digest,* 40:2 (1974), p. 20.
10. Fibkins, William, "The Whys and Hows of Teachers' Centers." *Phi Delta Kappan,* 55:567 (1974).
11. Estell, Lucile, "Regional Service Centers: Impetus for Change." *Educational Leadership,* 29:543 (1972).
12. Fabun, Donald, *The Dynamics of Change.* Englewood Cliffs, New Jersey: Prentice-Hall, 1970.
13. Frymier, Jack R., *A School for Tomorrow.* Berkeley, California: McCutchan Publishing, 1973.

14. Leonard, George B., *Education and Ecstasy.* New York: Dell, 1968.
15. Toffler, Alvin, ed., *Learning for Tomorrow: The Role of the Future in Education.* New York: Random House, 1974.
16. Wirth, Arthur G., *Education in the Technological Society.* Scranton, Pennsylvania: International Textbook Co., 1972.
17. Havighurst, Robert J., "Educational Leadership for the Seventies." *Phi Delta Kappan,* 53:403 (1972).
18. Models of Staff Development I, *Theory Into Practice.* Entire issue, 11:205 (1972).
19. Models of Staff Development II, *Theory Into Practice.* Entire issue, 11:273 (1972).
20. Association for Supervision and Curriculum Development, *Freedom, Bureaucracy, and Schooling.* Yearbook. Washington, D.C.: author, 1971.
21. Bagdikian, Ben H., *The Information Machines: Their Impact on Men and the Media.* New York: Harper and Row, 1971.
22. Clark, Walter E., *Community Power and Decision Making: A Selective Bibliography.* Council of Planning Librarians. Post Office Box 229, Monticello, Illinois.
23. Frey, Sherman H., "Policy Formulation—A Plan Involving Teachers." *The Clearing House,* 43:259 (1969).
24. Gross, Neal, "Who Controls the Schools?" In *Education and Public Policy,* edited by Seymour Harris. Berkeley, California: McCutchan Publishing Corp., 1965.
25. Hart, Richard, and Saylor, J. Galen, eds., *Student Unrest: Threat or Promise?* Washington, D.C.: Association for Supervision and Curriculum Development, 1970.
26. Marburger, Carl L., *School and Community: The Need for a New Relationship.* Los Angeles, California: American Educational Research Association, 1969.
27. Masters, Nicholas A., *Political Power: Impact on Educational Direction.* In *Curriculum Decisions and Social Realities,* edited by Robert R. Leeper. Washington, D.C.: Association for Supervision and Curriculum Development, 1968.
28. McCarty, Donald, and Ramsey, Charles, *The School Managers: Power and Conflict in American Public Education.* Westport, Connecticut: Greenwood Publishing Corp., 1971.
29. Stemnock, Suzanne K., *Framework for Student Involvement.* Washington, D.C.: National Education Association, 1970.
30. National Education Association, *Negotiating for Professionalization.* National Commission on Teacher Education and Professional Standards. Washington, D.C.: author, 1970.
31. Bishop, Leslee J., *Collective Negotiation in Curriculum and Instruction—Questions and Concerns.* Washington, D.C.: Association for Supervision and Curriculum Development, 1961.
32. *Competency Assessment, Research, and Evaluation.* Report of a National Conference, University of Houston. Syracuse: National Dissemination Center for Performance Based Education, 1974.
33. Koerner, James D., *Who Controls American Education?* Boston: Beacon Press, 1968.

34. Regier, Herold, "Too Many Teachers: Fact or Fiction?" *Phi Delta Kappan*, Bloomington, Indiana, 1972.
35. Stinnett, Timothy M., *Professional Negotiation in Public Education*. New York: Macmillan, 1966.
36. Benne, Kenneth, and Muntyan, Bozidar, *Human Relations in Curriculum Change*. Illinois Secondary School Curriculum Program Bulletin No. 7. Springfield, Illinois: Office of the State Superintendent of Public Instruction, 1949.
37. Miel, Alice, *Changing the Curriculum*. New York: Appleton-Century-Crofts, 1946.
38. Hipple, Theodore W., ed., "The Money Game and Educational Accountability." Chapter 4 in *Crucial Issues in Contemporary Education*. Pacific Palisades, California: Goodyear Publishing Co., 1973.
39. Harris, Ben M., Bessant, Wailand, and McIntyre, Kenneth, *In-Service Education: A Guide to Better Practice*. Englewood Cliffs, New Jersey: Prentice-Hall, 1969.
40. Newbury, D. N., and Wells, D. W., "Staff Development Through Association." *Theory Into Practice*, 11:258 (1972).
41. Miller, Richard I., ed., *Perspectives on Educational Change*. New York: Appleton-Century-Crofts, 1967.
42. "Sharing in Change." *Educational Leadership*. Entire issue. 27:326 (1970).
43. Allen, Dwight W., "In-Service Teacher Training: A Modest Proposal." In *Improving In-Service Education*, edited by Louis J. Rubin. *op. cit.*
44. Trump, J. Lloyd, "Illustrative Models for Evaluating School Programs." *Journal of Research and Development in Education*. 8:3 (1975), p. 16.
45. Fitzgerald, Peter, "Assessing the Perceived Educational Needs of Students." *Education*, 2:3 (1972), p. 13.
46. Westinghouse Learning Corporation, *Educational Needs Assessment*. Iowa City, Iowa: author, 1973.
47. Avis, Warren E., *Shared Participation*. Gordon City, New Jersey: Doubleday, 1973.
48. Mager, Robert F., *Goal Analysis*. Belmont, California: Fearon Publishers, 1972.
49. Guba, Egon G., "Problems in Utilizing the Results of Evaluation." *Journal of Research and Development in Education*, 8:3 (1975), p. 42.
50. Provus, Malcolm, *Discrepancy Evaluation*. Berkeley, California: McCutchan Publishing Corp., 1971.
51. Stufflebeam, Daniel E., et al., "Educational Evaluation and Decision Making." *Phi Delta Kappan*, Bloomington, Indiana, 1971.
52. Talmage, Harriet, "Evaluation of Local School/Community Programs: A Transactional Evaluation Approach." *Journal of Research and Development in Education*, 8:3 (1975), p. 32.
53. Davis, John B., "A Case Study: Change in a Big City School District." *Journal of Teacher Education*, 26:1 (1975), p. 47.
54. Bennis, Warren G., Benne, Kenneth D., and Chin, Robert, eds., *The Planning of Change*. 2nd ed. New York: Holt, Rinehart, and Winston, 1969.
55. Griffiths, Daniel E., "The Elementary School Principal and Change in the School Systems." *Theory into Practice*, 2:278 (1963).

56. Harnack, Robert S., *The Teacher: Decision Maker and Curriculum Planner.* Scranton, Pennsylvania: International Textbook Co., 1968.
57. Miles, Matthew B., ed., *Innovation in Education.* New York: Bureau of Publications, Teachers College, Columbia University, 1964.
58. Rubin, Louis J., ed., *Improving In-Service Education. op. cit.*
59. Broudy, Harry S., Smith, Othanel B., and Burnett, Joe R., *Democracy and Excellence in American Secondary Education.* Chicago: Rand McNally, 1964.
60. Kneller, George F., ed., *Foundations of Education.* 3rd ed., New York: John Wiley and Sons, 1971.
61. Brubaker, Dale L., and Nelson, Roland H., "Pitfalls in the Educational Change Process." *Journal of Teacher Education,* 26:1 (1975), p. 63.
62. Carlson, R. O., et al., *Change Processes in the Public Schools.* Eugene, Oregon: Center for the Study of Educational Administration, University of Oregon, 1965.
63. Eye, Glenn G., and Netzer, Lanore A., *Supervision of Instruction—A Phase of Administration.* New York: Harper and Row, 1965.
64. Fordyce, Jack K., and Well, Raymond, *Managing with People.* Reading, Massachusetts: Addison-Wesley, 1971.
65. Stanford, G., and Roark, A. E., *Human Interaction in Education.* Boston: Allyn and Bacon, 1974.
66. Neagley, Ross L., and Evans, N. Dean, *Handbook for Effective Supervision of Instruction.* 2nd ed. Englewood Cliffs, New Jersey: Prentice-Hall, 1970.
67. Cogan, Morris L., *Clinical Supervision.* Boston: Houghton Mifflin, 1973.
68. Goldhammer, Robert, *Clinical Supervision.* New York: Holt, Rinehart, and Winston, 1969.
69. Schmuck, Richard A., Runkel, Philip J., Stauren, Steven L., Martell, R. J., and Derr, O. B., *Handbook of Organization Development in Schools.* Palo Alto: National Press Books, 1972.
70. Bishop, Leslee J., "Identifying Leadership Competencies for Staff Development." In *Procedures and Patterns for Staff Development Programs,* Georgia Department of Education and the Center for Curriculum Improvement and Staff Development. Athens, Georgia: The Center, Department of Curriculum and Supervision, University of Georgia, 1975.
71. Harrison, Raymond H., *Supervisory Leadership in Education.* New York: American Book Company, 1968.
72. Wiles, Kimball, *Supervision for Better Schools.* 3rd ed., Englewood Cliffs, New Jersey: Prentice-Hall, 1967.
73. Kirby, Paul W., "In-Service Education: The University's Role." *Educational Leadership,* 30:431 (1973).
74. Bush, Robert N., "Curriculum-Proof Teachers: Who Does What to Whom." In *Improving In-Service Education.* Edited by Louis J. Rubin. *op. cit.*
75. Horvat, John J., *Content and Strategies of Communication in Current Educational Change Efforts.* National Institute for the Study of Educational Change, 1967.
76. Jackson, Philip W., "Old Dogs and New Tricks: Observations on the Continuing Education of Teachers." In *Improving In-Service Education.* Edited by Louis J. Rubin. *op. cit.*

77. Lippitt, Ronald, and Fox, Robert, "Development and Maintenance of Effective Classroom Learning." In *Improving In-Service Education.* Edited by Louis J. Rubin. *op. cit.*
78. Crary, Ryland W., *Humanizing the School: Curriculum Development and Theory.* New York: Alfred A. Knopf, 1969.
79. Parker, J. Cecil, and Rubin, Louis J., *Process as Content: Curriculum Design and the Application of Knowledge.* Chicago: Rand McNally, 1966.
80. Association for Supervision and Curriculum Development, *Perceiving, Behaving, Becoming.* Yearbook. Washington, D.C.: author, 1962.
81. Association for Supervision and Curriculum Development, *To Nurture Humaneness.* Yearbook. Washington, D.C.: author, 1970.
82. Bruner, Jerome S., et al., *Studies in Cognitive Growth.* New York: John Wiley and Sons, 1966.
83. Havighurst, Robert J., *Developmental Tasks and Education.* 3rd ed., New York: David McKay, 1972.
84. Macagnoni, Virginia, *Social Dimensions of the Self as an Open System: A Curriculum Design.* Research Bulletin, Florida Educational Research and Development Council. 5:2 (1969), p. 1.
85. Panel on Youth of President's Science Advisory Committee, James S. Coleman, Chairman, *Youth: Transition to Adulthood.* Washington, D.C.: Government Printing Office, 1974.
86. Amidon, Edmund J., and Hough, J. B., eds., *Interaction Analysis: Theory, Research, and Application.* Reading, Massachusetts: Addison-Wesley, 1967.
87. Beagle, Charles, and Brandt, Richard, *Observational Methods in the Classroom.* Washington, D.C.: Association for Supervision and Curriculum Development, 1973.
88. Ewald, William R., ed., *Environment for Man: The Next Fifty Years.* Bloomington, Indiana: Indiana University Press, 1967.
89. Flanders, Ned A., *Analyzing Teaching Behavior.* Reading, Massachusetts: Addison-Wesley, 1970.
90. Shores, David L., ed., *Contemporary English: Change and Variation.* Philadelphia: Lippincott, 1972.
91. Davies, Ivor K., "Some Philosophical and Psychological Dimensions of Competency-Based Education." Paper presented at the Conference on Competency-Based Education, University of Georgia. Athens, Georgia: May 1975.
92. Rubin, Louis J., "Synergetics and the School." In *Contemporary Thought on Public School Curriculum.* Edited by Edmund C. Short and George D. Marconnit. Dubuque, Iowa: William C. Brown Publishers, 1968.
93. Gibson, James L., Ivancevich, John M., and Donnelly, James H., *Organizations: Structure, Process, Behavior.* Dallas: Business Publications, 1973.
94. Schmuck, Richard A., and Miles, Matthew B., eds., *Organization Development in Schools.* Palo Alto, California: National Press Books, 1971.
95. Burgoon, Michael, Heston, Judee K., and McCroskey, James, *Small Group Communications: A Functional Approach.* New York: Holt, Rinehart, and Winston, 1974.
96. Kemp, C. Gratton, *Perspectives on the Group Process.* Boston: Houghton Mifflin, 1970.
97. Savage, William W., *Interpersonal and Group Relations in Education Administration.* Glenview, Illinois: Scott, Foresman, 1968.

98. Association for Supervision and Curriculum Development, *Role of the Supervisor and Curriculum Director in a Climate of Change.* Yearbook. Washington, D.C.: author, 1965.
99. Bishop, Leslee J., and Perry, Ione, *Staff Development: Sources and Resources.* Georgia Department of Education and the Center for Curriculum Improvement and Staff Development. Athens, Georgia: The Center, Department of Curriculum and Supervision, University of Georgia, 1973.
100. Dionne, Joseph L., "To Encourage Teacher Growth." *Educational Leadership,* 24:264 (1966).
101. Spears, Harold. *Curriculum Planning Through In-Service Programs.* Englewood Cliffs, New Jersey: Prentice-Hall, 1957.
102. Miel, Alice, and Lewis, Arthur J., *Supervision for Improved Instruction.* Belmont, California: Wadsworth Publishing Co., 1972.
103. Yarger, Sam J., and Mallow, John T., "Articulating the Bits and Pieces for Productive Change." *Journal of Teacher Education,* 26:1 (1975), p. 12.
104. Bare, I. L., et al., *The Ann Arbor Public Schools Participative Model In-Service Staff Development Project.* Ann Arbor: The Ann Arbor Public Schools, 1971.
105. Franseth, Jane, *Supervision as Leadership.* Evanston, Illinois: Row, Peterson Co., 1961.
106. Harris, Ben M., *Supervisory Behavior in Education. op. cit.*
107. Lavin, R. J., and Schuttenberg, E. M., *An Innovative Approach to Public School Staff Development: A Collaborative Mode.* Chelmsford, Massachusetts: Merrimack Education Center, 1973.
108. Bishop, Leslee J., "Time and the Supervisor." In *Improving Supervisory Competencies.* Edited by Leslee J. Bishop. Georgia Association for Supervision and Curriculum Development and the Center for Curriculum Improvement and Staff Development. Athens, Georgia: The Center, Department of Curriculum and Supervision, University of Georgia, 1973.
109. Estes, Nolan, "Marshalling Community Leadership to Support the Public Schools." *Phi Delta Kappan,* Bloomington, Indiana, 1974.
110. Foshay, Arthur W., "The Problem of Community." *Education Digest,* 40:1 (1974), p. 50.
111. Goldhammer, Keith, *Issues and Strategies in the Public Acceptance of Educational Change.* Center for the Advanced Study of Educational Administration. Eugene, Oregon: University of Oregon, 1965.
112. Wilhelms, Fred J., *Supervision in a New Key.* Washington, D.C.: Association for Supervision and Curriculum Development, 1973.

The bibliography for all but one of the following seven notes refer to material taken from the November and December 1972 issues of *Theory into Practice.* Each notation includes: (1) the name of the person(s) who described the model, (2) page number of the issue in which the description is given, and (3) month and year of the journal entry.

113. Adams, J. A., Sinclair, R., and Storm, H., 307, December 1972.
Bentley, E. L., 262, October 1972.
Jirik, E. F., 291, December 1972.
Locke, C., 321, December 1972.

Mason, T., and Rohde, F., 236, October 1972.
Mulhern, E. F., and McKay, A. B., 245, October 1972.
Stinson, R. H., 267, October 1972.
Unruh, G., 239, October 1972.

114. Adams, J. A., Sinclair, R., and Storm, H., 307, December 1972.
Bentley, E. L., 262, October 1972.
Clothier, G. M., 252, October 1972.
Finnegan, H., 215, October 1972.
Goodlad, J. I., 207, October 1972.
Jirik, E. F., 291, December 1972.
Locke, C., 321, December 1972.
Mason, T., and Rohde, F., 236, October 1972.
Mulhern, E. J., and McKay, A. B., 245, October 1972.
Mullins, M. U., 232, October 1972.
Newberry, D. N., and Wells, D. W., 258, October 1972.
Olson, R. F., and Millgate, I. H., 299, December 1972.
Unruh, G., 239, October 1972.

115. Finnegan, H., 215, October 1972.
Jirik, E. F., 291, December 1972.
Loadman, W. E., and Mahan, J. M., 329, December 1972.
Mason, T., and Rohde, F., 236, October 1972.
Mullins, M. W., 232, October 1972.
Perritt, M. C., 324, December 1972.
Stinson, R. H., 267, October 1972.

116. Adams, J. A., Sinclair, R., and Storm, H., 307, December 1972.
Bentley, E. F., 262, October 1972.
Finnegan, H., 215, October 1972.
Jung, C., 276, December 1972.
Mason, T., and Rohde, F., 236, October 1972.
Moon, J. B., Morrison, R. R., and Sims, E. H., 296, December 1972.
Mulhern, E. J., and McKay, A. B., 245, October 1972.
Mullins, M. U., 232, October 1972.
Stewart, C. E., and Hart, H. A., 285, December 1972.
Stinson, R. H., 267, October 1972.
Unruh, G., 239, October 1972.

117. Felix, J. L., and Jacobs, J. N., 225, October 1972.
Finnegan, H., 215, October 1972.
Locke, C., 321, December 1972.
Perritt, M. C., 324, December 1972.
Stewart, C. E., and Hart, H. A., 285, December 1972.
Unruh, G., 239, October 1972.

118. English, F. W., "Teacher Competencies in the Public School Setting: Paradoxes and Problems." *Journal of Collective Negotiations*, 2:294 (1973).

119. Chothier, G. M., 252, October 1972.
Goodlad, J. I., 207, October 1972.
Sankowski, E., 314, December 1972.

120. Mulhern, E. J., and McKay, A. B., 245, October 1972.
Unruh, G., 239, October 1972.

2

Diagnosing

The needs and objectives for staff development and instructional improvement are unlimited. They arise from every segment of the school or system operation, every propensity or problem regarding learners, every instructional element with which the educational enterprise is concerned, and every staff member as a concern of his personal and professional role responsibilities. Community expectations and national imperatives also dictate renewal needs. Obviously, difficulty is encountered in isolating from this range those objectives that have greatest need and impact in terms of instructional improvement, or those objectives that have highest priority in terms of policy and practice considerations.[1-3]

The problem of selecting objectives becomes the critical issue in initiating decision making and providing for leadership. The "guide" provides assistance for this selection process through a description or outline of each integral part of the planning process. Included are the processes by which needs are translated into objectives and into design (see pp. 62-65), the explication of the developmental phase (Chapter 4), the checklists dealing with operational procedures (pp. 79-82 and 121-122), and the planning sequences for instructional change (p. 4). A generalized text cannot provide for the policy, perspective, or priority that must be the determination of the particular school, system, or locale. If a school system does not have adequate and established procedures for such determination, their absence should signal those charged with staff development and instructional improvement to make provision for such parameters and processes as a high priority target.

Goals as starting points for in-service staff development and program renewal have the advantage of being "worthy"; their disadvantage is that of being general or unachievable. Usually, they are unrelated to a particular time frame and have no criterion or placement; e.g., see *Goals for Georgia* or *Goals for Education in Florida.*[4-8] Statements of system goals, state department goals, or content-area goals do present, however, focusing points for many related activities. Focus is essential. Otherwise, random and unrelated responses will result from efforts to reconcile new demands for creativity, for competence and performance adequacy, for new instructional materials and tools, for more effective instructional strategies and modes of investigation, and for a continuous effort to individualize instruction and satisfy basic human needs. Goals, however worthy, also require system decisions as to priority and functional implementation. Because education is a public enterprise, goal statements arise from many sources, and they often have contradictory intent. This diffusion and contradiction is less of a problem at the goal level than at the operational level where translation and specificity are required. Similarly, in some sensitive areas it is possible to tolerate a generalized statement, but, not a particularized expression of that idea.[9]

DETERMINING NEEDS AND OBJECTIVES

Neither general goal statements nor discrepancies in data necessarily identify "needs," *per se*, especially when they have been identified by single or simple measures. Such data can be misleading as a basis for analysis, "solution," or program decision making. For example, pupils scoring lower than anticipated (discrepancy) on a mathematics test may be said to need more instruction in mathematics. Perhaps. However, they also may need help with reading skills, with test taking, or with basic concepts other than numeration and computation. Pupils scoring lower than expected (discrepancy) on a reading test may be "analyzed" as needing remedial reading. Maybe. Perhaps the better solution is to place these students with someone who cares, who can translate their school tasks into relevant situations, or who can reinforce progress rather than categorize failure. The need may be improved staff competencies rather than learner placement.

With younger learners or professionals, the point is the same: programs built upon an inadequate data base are prone to treat symptoms and surface evidences of need rather than basic problems or causes. The reshuffling of pupils or the addition of remedial or specialist personnel may, in fact, exacerbate the basic problems by providing an "out," or a limited response. Attention should be given to the factors that contribute to the deficiency or failure to deliver the desired program objectives. To always "add on" a course or specialist is not an adequate program response to a general or pervasive problem. The real need may be for program review and revision, for development of staff adequacies in instructional skills and content at particular grade levels or in content areas, or for other related efforts aimed at eliminating the basic causes and *maintaining* improved learning and growth. Indicators of problems are neither causes nor solutions.

Institutional requirements or organizational solutions are not needs. For example, team teaching may be listed as a need, but upon analysis, it clearly is an hypothesized solution instead. The need may be for better utilization of superior teacher talents. Or, it may be necessary to provide support for ineffective persons, offering interaction of learners with certain skilled persons as a regular part of their instruction. The tentative solution may appear to be some form of team teaching or staff differentiation. To be adequately treated, such a "need" statement would begin better as an item to be researched, then moved through all the change stages; or, it could be assigned to the development stage, then worked toward delineation and implementation.

Most need statements assume that a gap exists between a standard as to what *is* and what *ought* to be, between the existing situation and the desired condition. The need may be expressed in learner terms: information, skill, or attitude; or, it may deal with the more involved concepts: teaching competency, program adequacy, system process, structure, facility, or readiness for change.

Need determination is a process of focusing, assessing, and modifying.[10-13] Needs arise from *valued* discrepancies or goals, assessment having been made that something must change. Not all needs can be addressed and not all needs can be a school or school system responsibility.

A Review of Selected Variables That Affect Strategy

One recognized problem in planning for instructional outcomes is the large number of variables to be considered—human dimensions, task dimensions, and institutional dimensions, among others. These complicate and compound the planning, implementing, and evaluating responsibilities. Figure 2.1 includes a number of these variables, although it is admittedly incomplete. Therefore, many of the items can be considered as generalized placeholders for the detailed areas, which they can only suggest. Six categories are proposed:

1. *Need Arenas.* Needs have multiple origins. This summary includes seven general arenas that have utility in planning.

Information. Some needs can be met by providing data relevant to the situation. This is especially true when a base exists for performance; therefore, information will provide an adequate response to the need and is so used as the justification for many meetings, bulletins, and presentations.

Content/Skills. These are basic responsibilities of the school and are applicable to either staff or learners. Content is information about program areas, delineating and detailing the data to be learned. Skills are the performance or processes that evidence gain in the defined fields and in the modes essential to produce or utilize the phenomena of that area.

Competencies. These are considered here as generalized and clustered behaviors that incorporate both knowledge and skills. In context, competencies are denoted in relationship to the professional staff and their ability to deliver instruction, leadership, classroom or program management, and personal-instructional facilitation.

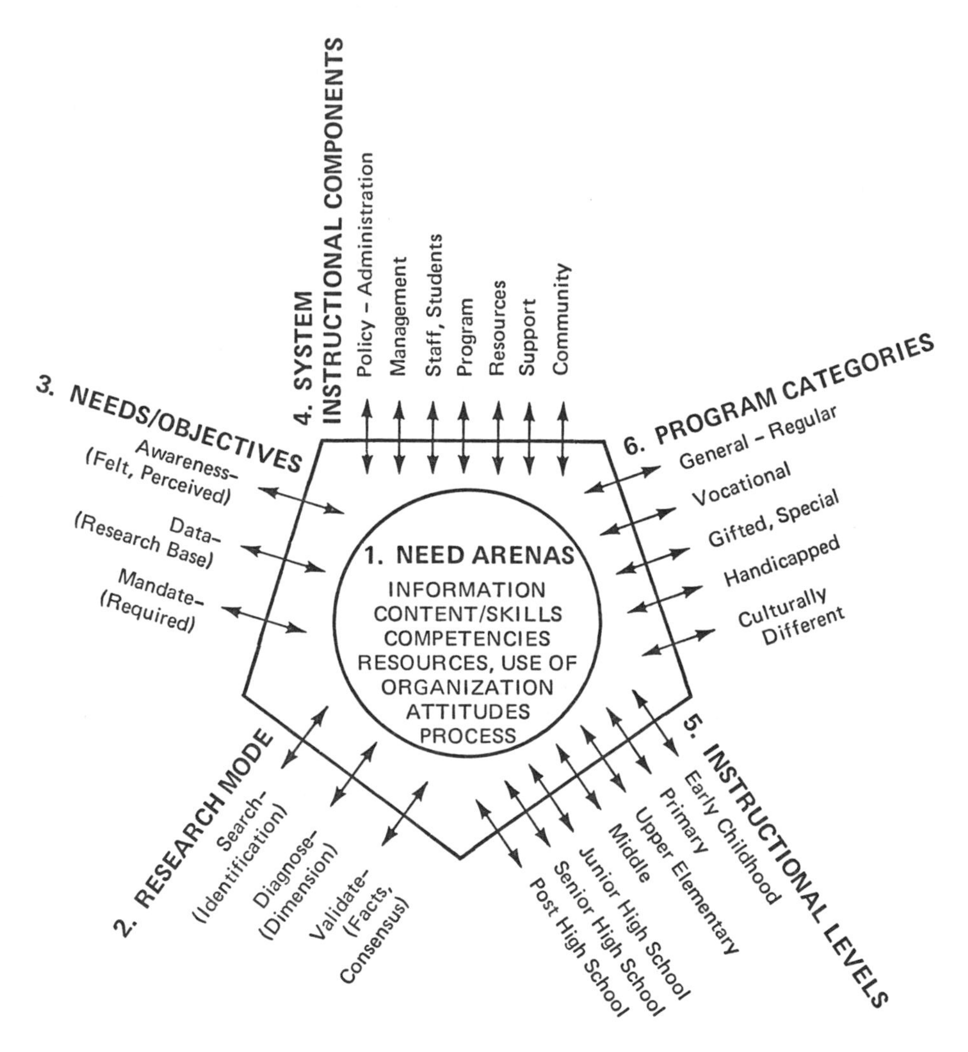

FIGURE 2.1 Selected Variables That Affect Strategy.

Resources and their use. These assume the need for both adequacy and quality in the resources required for instruction and experiencing. Such considerations include books, audio visual materials, computers, textbooks, typewriters, instructional supplies, personnel, and the like. Special facilities such as classrooms, shops, laboratories, and community sites are additional examples.[14]

Organization. This is a necessity involving many persons, objectives, and resources. This need arena can refer to the organization of a classroom, department, and service agency, or of the school district. It may suggest organization of goals and objectives, teaching or instructional teams, and of groups such as a curriculum committee. If these elements are inadequately structured for deployment, decision making, program implementation, and access or service, many needs can arise that need resolution.[15-17]

Attitudes. These refer to the commitments and feelings of the persons who are involved, whether they arise in learners, professional staff, service personnel, or community and parents. Attitudes suggest the motivation—the willingness/reluctance to engage in the necessary operations and activities—and the concerns for self-worth or role adequacy. However difficult to determine or plan, they are too seldom addressed adequately or systematically.[18]

Process. This refers to the mode of operation, the style existing within any segment of the school enterprise. Included are the ways of working, the nature and flow of decision making, the teaching and learning approaches that give life to the curriculum, and the transactions of the organizing elements. Processes are critical to implementing any plan or idea at all levels and with all persons.[19-21]

2. *Research Mode.* The purpose and timing of the research effort may be referred to as research modes. They are directly related to the kinds of needs or objectives already established.[22,23]

Search. In the early stages of need definition, it is sometimes necessary to select those needs that have not been identified adequately from the many possibilities. Certain needs are believed to exist, but provision must be made for them to surface, to become recognized, and, if desired, subsequently built into program designs. Questionnaires, tests, or check lists are common devices.

Diagnose. Need areas may have been identified, yet may exist in general statements of undefined dimension. Weaknesses may have been identified by low test scores, specifically in reading or mathematics. But what elements of reading/math need specific instruction or reinforcement? Where staff are involved, what particular skills in teaching or leadership would likely produce better results? What specific content requires diagnosing so that curriculum can be developed? Diagnosis is a necessary follow-up when a generalized need has been identified.

Validate. The effectiveness of previous efforts may need to be confirmed to establish a data base upon which to communicate and build. Sometimes, this can be a research approach that establishes priority or consensus, ranging from a program action to a particular learning. Many feasibility studies fall within this category, as are data collections that ratify or "justify" a particular approach or program. Research for verification can relate very well to formative evaluation. In any case, it must be continuous.

3. *Needs/Objectives.* Needs surface with varying degrees of impact. Some seem to demand immediate attention; others require that they be teased out and given identification (see also discussion in Chapter 1).[24-26]

Awareness. Given the opportunity, parents, learners, or professional staff members will identify certain items as "needs." These persons will tell you quite confidently that they exist and that something must be done about them; their existence derives from concerns, circumstances, contexts, or constraints. They are perceived or felt. Yet, upon examination, very little research data or "hard facts" may exist to define them. Therefore, the task of the planner may be to accept them as real; however, the necessity exists to establish their nature and extent before they can be built into program objectives. (See related research modes.)

Research data. Some needs are well-defined, sometimes too obviously. They are clearly established by definitions (a discrepancy between objectives and outcomes), such as lower-than-expected test scores or issues that are evident in the achievement or growth data (for example, developmental tasks). The temptation exists to move directly upon them, i.e., add a course or a special teacher. establish a remedial section, or set up a task force. However, once accepted as a need, they can readily be framed as objectives. And since needs have a clear rationale, design efforts can usually proceed with dispatch.

Mandate. Some needs exist because groups or persons in power say that they do. They may take the form of board of education or administrative injunctions to do something—from a state department or federal well-funded priority, from a status or political impetus demanding attention, or from an issue arising from citizen concern. Clarification or validation may be needed before objectives or program can be developed, but planners and participants sometimes have little choice but to provide a reasonable response, to get going. . . . Such directives often contain a rationale or charge. The need or problem may be clearer than the desired objectives, so an appropriate research mode must be determined in order to proceed correctly.

4. *System Instructional Components (or Sub-Systems).* Every school district has an organizational structure that must be reoriented and recast to be effective and supportive of the desired program. These component areas are listed on pp. 75-76 and 230, 232, and are built into the various models throughout the text.[27]

5. *Instructional Levels.* Most school districts still use traditional grade and age levels as placement areas for learners. They may be further subdivided by grouping procedures or specialized course designations (regular, honors, advanced, etc.). However, the literature of nongrading, of individualized instruction, and of flexible scheduling have proposed that learners be organized by achievement levels. These would be determined by ratings and tests and by student-counselor selections in regard to educational objectives.[28] Related to age and maturity levels in the lower schools, no such restrictions would be necessary in collegiate or adult programs. These are more sophisticated and viable determinants for placement and are indicated on the model in clusters (early childhood, elementary, etc.).

6. *Program Categories.* Program areas arise from goal statements; they are sustained by the traditional practices that assign objectives and goal achievements to content/discipline areas or to special program configurations (culturally different, special education, vocational, etc.). They offer the desirable qualities of ease in assignment, existing organizational features, and funding possibilities, which are reflected in the central office positions, the consultant assignments, and budget

categories. The pattern used reflects both the size and the philosophy of the school or school district.

This model, especially useful at the needs analysis stage, suggests six clusters of variables. Many others could be added; for example, demographic data regarding learners or community, style items regarding the school or district, and organizational and process elements might also be incorporated. The purpose of the model is to suggest options that can be major considerations for planning, especially at the beginning phases. When determinations are made as to the placement and configuration of these items, it then becomes easier to specify and communicate objectives, targets, support elements, and the like. Also, by analyzing various program efforts in such a fashion, it is more likely that adequate provision is made for balance and representativeness in planning. A number of these considerations are discussed later in this chapter in regard to "Determining the Target."

Very often, the initial needs are identified by gross data that need sharpening. This, too, is a refining process that requires sensitivity and accurate perception. Preliminary need identification can be followed by validation procedures such as the following:

1. Data collection, using standardized or developed instruments such as the questionnaire, test, or checklist.
2. Interview schedules during which selected or random personnel are consulted.
3. Small group sessions, tape recorded and analyzed for key ideas, concerns, and possible courses of action.
4. Observer reports involving visitation by skilled observers. These may be from other school systems, universities, or the community, depending upon the nature of the need.
5. Intervisitation schedule to observe schools, processes, and personnel in the designated areas of activity, with reports of features and factors to be used in modifying the desired objectives.
6. Analysis of case studies, logs, diaries, anecdotal records, critical incident reports, or follow-up studies.
7. Weighing and considering with representative or concerned personnel goal statements, objectives, and achievement data to arrive at consensus or focus.
8. Depth study by existing or task groups, such as an instructional council or steering committee.
9. Use of a modified Delphi technique, where selected individuals respond to original data and to subsequent interactions.

Procedures as above contribute to a more accurate diagnosis of need, to validation, and to priority setting. Relevance for the target group and impact on professional or instructional gain are more likely when the rationale has consensus and is supported by data.

Validation of Needs and Objectives

Validation requires more than process considerations. It also requires checking the need in terms of large system goals and priorities; it means checking in terms of substantive, instructional, or contextual programs and purposes; i.e., areas of content, instructional objectives and levels, existing materials, resources and facilities, and staff competencies.[29,30]

As indicated by Figure 2.2, validation also seeks consensus among staff, administration, program design, community and learners, or those who will be directly affected. Validation and consensus-seeking techniques are plentiful; two such "kits" in print are:

Center for the Study of Evaluation. *The CSE School Evaluation Kit: Needs Assessment.* Boston: Allyn & Bacon, 1973.

Northern California Program Development Center. *Educational Goals and Objectives.* ESEA, Title III. Bloomington, Indiana: *Phi Delta Kappa,* 1972.

Other approaches and programs are in preparation. Establishing priorities and validating are important operations if the needs and objectives are significant and if the program is to receive acceptance, support, and successful implementation.[31-33] Needs data are those permitting a qualitative, valuing selection. They provide insights as to appropriate and possible objectives, as an important link between purposes and processes. Neither group agreement nor logical data are adequate by themselves. Consensus is critical for understanding and commitment. Data and a sound conceptual base are essential for quality and balance. Together these elements provide the ingredients for negotiation and decision making, and for reconciling a theoretical or logical stance with a common viewpoint.

Need *identification* can be an analytic process; but need *selection* is a "political" process. For a discrepancy to be valued or for a need to become a program, persons, powers, and priorities must be clearly aligned.[34,35] In many situations, this results in a kind of manipulation of initial data while the lines of force are being tested (attitude of the superintendent or principal, stance of the board of education, community expectations, staff priorities, and so forth). If these support elements are lacking, the needs data tend to remain in the discussion-study stage, or become a single, perhaps abortive, effort. This hypothesis acknowledges the fact that education is public, expensive, and complicated. It is in accordance with experience that an extensive program requires consensus, validity, and authorization if it is to have impact and durability.[36,37]

Needs data that are implicitly designed to justify a pre-determined course of action are likely to be viewed cynically and be self-defeating. For example, included are those designed to "justify" the installation of a career education emphasis or to rationalize the "need" for additional personnel or particular media. Such investigations are worthy, but they should not parade under the needs banner. Rather, they should be developed as data bases or supporting feasibility data for an acknowledged program effort. If the intent is a particular project and if the needs step is a screen for an impending program thrust, the staff is likely to engage then in delaying tactics until it can ferret out the

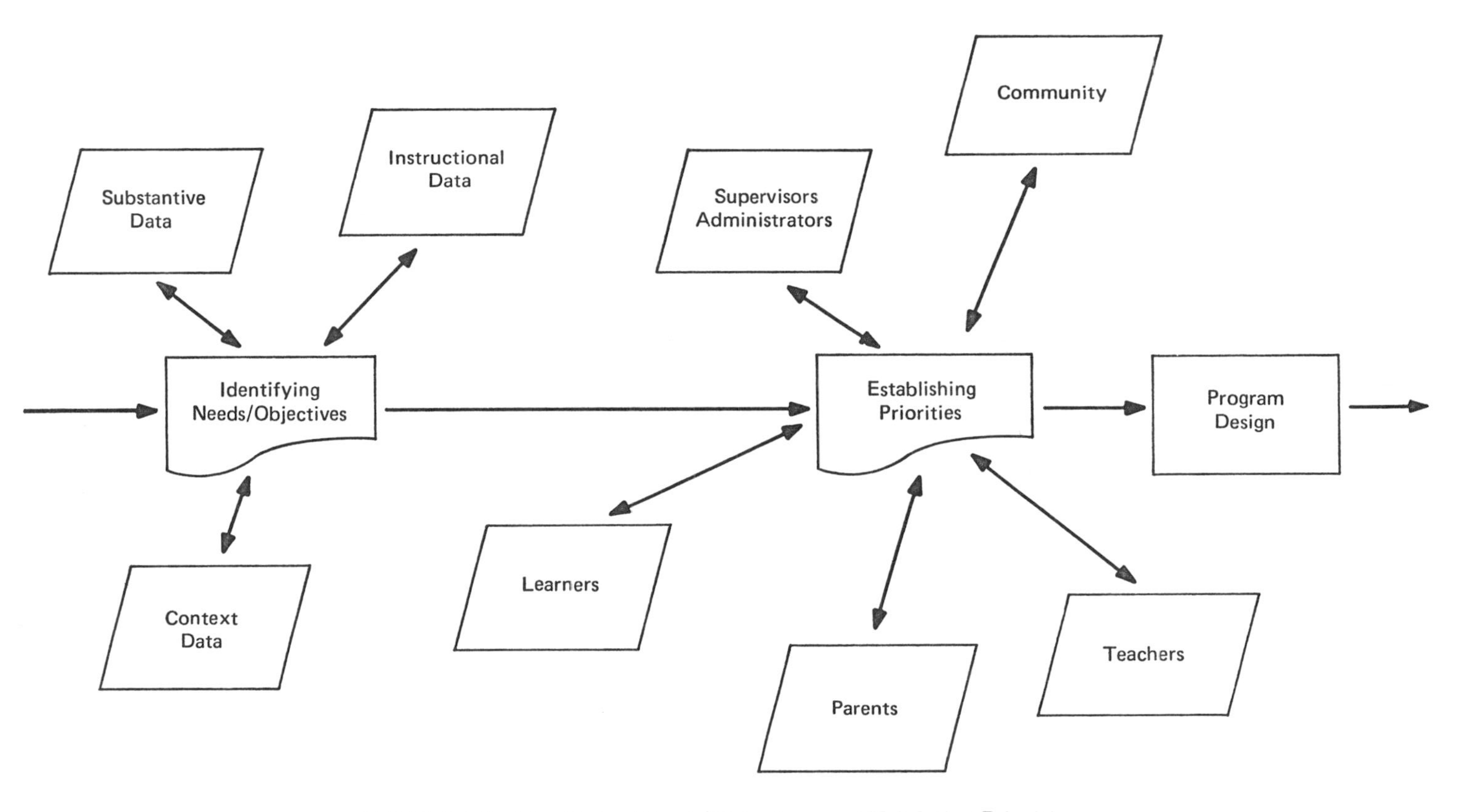

FIGURE 2.2 Identifying Needs/Objectives and Validating Priorities.

intent. An experienced staff can quickly spot a hidden agenda. Therefore, the posture and intent of leadership personnel, as well as staff members, are critical elements in the initial stage of a developing project.

Needs, Objectives, and Program Levels

Needs can exist at various levels. Each level has its own pattern and design needs. Needs at a high (institution or goal) level tend to be complex and long range in impact and implementation. Very likely, what will be required is the development of a large number of sub-needs and objectives that can be structured, sequenced, and managed so that, in a calculated time, the larger need will have been resolved. Needs at the learner performance level (teacher or student) can be managed more quickly and with less complex organizational efforts.[38,39]

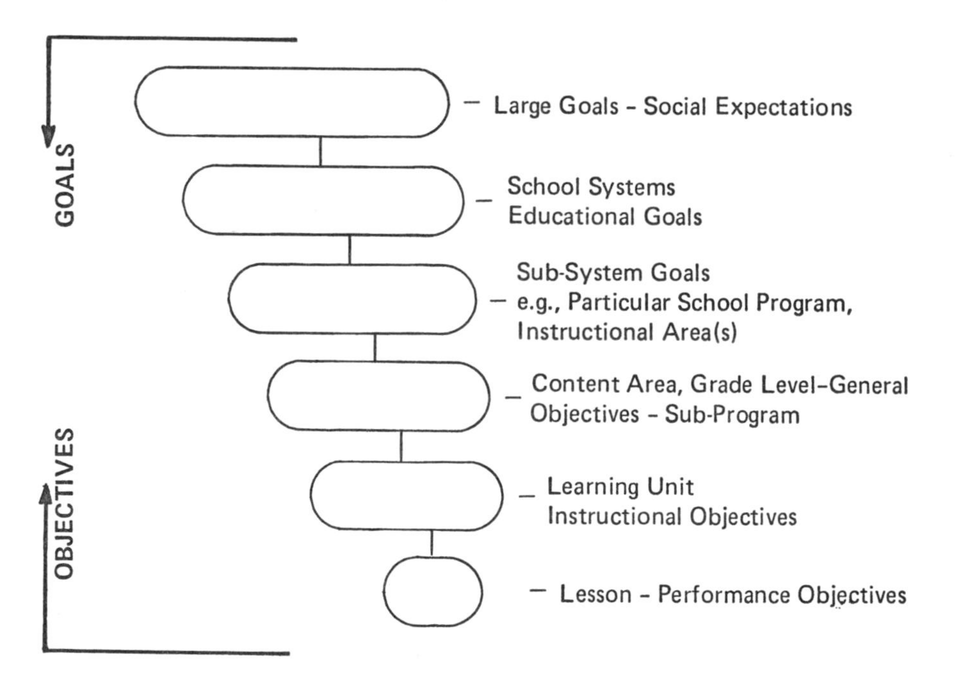

FIGURE 2.3 Needs, Goals, and Objectives.

As instructional needs are translated into program objectives, it is important to make a distinction between those that are general statements and those that are more specific. For example, goals are usually considered to be general statements of intent that provide for direction but do not specify a particular time frame and do not designate program level or task responsibility. Although outcomes are suggested, measurement or standards of achievement are seldom provided. In many cases, achievement of goals often requires non-school experiences and learnings. They are framed in such terms as fundamental processes, general citizenship competencies, and abilities.

Program objectives define broad areas of school responsibility, often stated in program areas such as social studies, mathematics, or special education. Broad responsibilities are assigned to departments or service agencies within the school district. They imply organized sequences and defined program efforts that include related content achievement and skill acquisition.

Interim or enabling objectives indicate more specific tasks and gains. These may be assigned to developmental levels, departments, grade levels, teacher teams, and to more specific segments of the goal and program objectives. These can be framed as computational skills, sequences in composition or science, and concepts to be implemented in courses—such as American history, general music, or commercial art. These objectives indicate how program areas will be organized and translated into learning segments. Areas of responsibility will be indicated, but the achievement of these objectives can be acquired in various situations or modes of learning.[40,41]

Instructional or performance objectives are well defined in the literature of instruction. They incorporate performance indicators or criteria, conditions, standards, and target personnel, and are considered to have test item utility. They are usually combined into units, packages, or kits. Such objectives can be written at various taxonomic or sophistication levels, and include such domains as the cognitive (knowing), the affective (feeling), and the psychomotor (neuro-muscular or physical). The determination and use of goals and objectives is an important decision to be made by each school district. Definitions differ among authors. Similarly, another concern is whether or not all goals can be, or should be, translated into performance outcome statements, and if so, whether these performance objectives should represent the totality *or* the focus for a course or grade level.[42–44]

Figure 2.4 provides one example of various goal statement levels and objectives. It illustrates the derivation of objectives based on a goal statement and the usefulness of generating sub-objectives that show implications and objectives as they relate to program objectives, learner performances, and related staff competencies. Also, they show that the resolution of the goal might be framed quite differently. However, it should be clear that before learner achievement or teacher performance can be planned or implemented, both clarity and explicitness are needed in the subsequent statement of objectives. More specific examples are provided in Appendix B.

NEEDS ANALYSIS AND BASELINE DATA

During the early stages of a staff development project or an instructional change, relevant base line data must be collected, it being essen-

Program Levels	*Goals (i.e., all levels, all subject areas)*	*Program Objectives (i.e., math, science, social studies, grades 7–9)*	*Course Objectives (i.e., science–9th grade 6 units)*	*Unit Objectives—Motion (one of six units)*	*Instructional Objective—for a Unit on Motion in a 9th Grade Science Class*
Learner Performance	Every child should be given the opportunity to be creative in various fields of endeavor	Student demonstrates creative problem-solving techniques as an alternative strategy for dealing with problem situations	Student employs creative problem-solving techniques as one strategy for investigating scientific concepts	Student designs an experiment employing creative problem solving techniques to test a scientific principle relating to energy	The individual learner will brainstorm and record for 5 minutes on possible variables to be controlled in investigating the factors effecting the period of a pendulum. Acceptable performance will be at least 15 responses
Teacher Performance	Teacher accepts responsibility for fostering creative opportunities for the learners, as an alternative and appropriate procedure for facilitating intellectual growth	Teacher provides learning situations where students are encouraged to provide input Teacher develops a classroom environment where student ideas are accepted and used	Teacher introduces learners to scientific concepts by employing inquiry and concept formation techniques	Teacher provides stimulus situations designed to encourage divergent thinking about designing experiences to investigate scientific principles relating to motion, i.e., questions, demonstrations, etc. Teacher accepts and uses all learner responses to stimulus situations	Teacher assesses learned performance in terms of quantity and originality. Teacher provides an opportunity for student to justify brain storming session Teacher accepts and uses all inputs of learners to assist in further designing their experiments to investigate the period of a pendulum

FIGURE 2.4 Goals and Levels of Objectives.

tial to subsequent processes and evaluation. They are also critical to the development of realistic assumptions regarding the needs to be addressed and the resources to be utilized. While they are not the same, a reciprocal impact does exist between needs data and baseline data; therefore, they are considered here together because they affect the development of specific objectives, the determination of targets, and the appropriate means.[45] Along with the checklists and guidelines that have been included, even a partial delineation of possible concerns would suggest the following items for consideration:

Content—Substantive Areas

- Objectives and related instructional resources.
- Achievement data including standardized testing and teacher input data (reading, math, etc.).
- Staff preparation in instructional areas, qualifications.
- Vocational, interest inventories, and other growth and developmental evidence.
- Content options for learners, balanced and comprehensive.
- Basic content literacies, themes, concepts, structures, skills, and sequences.
- New or needed program areas, content relevance, and adequacy.
- Congruence with established or expected standards for area, state, region, or nation.
- Follow-up or longitudinal study regarding program effectiveness.

Instructional Areas

- Instructional or learning levels, criteria and use.
- Needed training or recruitment of personnel.
- Sociometric, participation, self concept, attitude, and role data.
- Learning, teaching styles, and relationship to instructional objectives and means.
- Psychological testing and observational data.
- Relationship to established, state or school system goals.
- Classroom management and planning skills, class load.
- Shadow study, logs, or diaries.
- Validity and use of pre- (diagnostic) and post- (achievement) inventories, tests, and related staff skills.
- Drop out, dismissal, attendance data.
- Self inventories by teachers, learners, anecdotal records.
- Grouping, pacing, promotion procedures, and requirements.
- Teacher or learner competencies as observed, evaluated, and recorded.
- Availability, accessibility, flexibility, and adequacy of related instructional materials, published or produced locally.
- Availability and use of consultants and teacher aides.
- Development of test instruments and procedures for assigning, diagnosing, and evaluating.
- System and classroom decision-making practices and persons, levels of autonomy or requirements, involvements, nature, and levels of participation.

- Teacher and learner access to resources/materials, media, both school and community.

Context Areas

- School or system climate, organizational health, morale, reinforcement practices.
- Community, demographic data—developments and likely impact.
- Parent-patron expectations, goals, concerns, and values.
- School system structure, policies, procedures, and goal statements.
- Community, school readiness—constraints—involvements as organizations or individuals.
- Readiness for change among teachers, learners, and administrators.
- Time frames, timing regarding schedules and planning; flexibility or rigidity.
- Management structure, organization, capability, and impact—planning and intervention strategies and policies—provisions for change and renewal.

Any given instructional change or staff development program will require checking out the initial and subsequent status of these or similar, representative items. An accurate assessment will enhance adequacy and implementation. Foundation data are too often ignored and the significance of this omission is attested by the failure rate of in-service, staff development and change programs.[46] One temptation is to reach closure too soon, i.e., leap to a ready "solution," cutting off consideration of likely or innovative possibilities rather than making the research effort necessary for extracting adequate data. A second typical problem is to shape the determination of needs in such a way as to justify previously held opinions or favored courses of action. The research effort should not be an ad hoc function that surfaces only when pressures are acute or when special funds become available.

Need Bases and Research

Since program improvement and staff development efforts are a continuing responsibility of leadership, it is important that a means be established to review constantly the ongoing program and to propose improvement possibilities. In addition, the importance of "touching all bases" constantly reinforces the usefulness of considering the essential operating components, i.e., structural elements and processes. The following list is representative.

1. The climate, standards, data flow, organizational adequacy, reward system, involvement, professionalism, and leadership of the organism we call a *school* or school system.
2. The adequacy of a school/systems *program*—curricular plans, materials, media, facilities, resources, and support features—to provide a sufficient base to deliver the goals and objectives desired.
3. The competency of the *staff* to handle the concepts, knowledge, resources,

skills, and modes of investigation appropriate to a given content, context, instructional level, and number of learners.
4. The aspirations, energy level, determination, ability, attitude, and readiness of the *learners* to achieve reasonable gains assuming that other elements provide adequate access and opportunity.
5. The level of expectations and support by the parents and *community* as reflected in inputs to individual students, cooperation with the school, and financial and policy backing.[47]

For these and related elements, ways are needed to determine the current status and level of operation, but also for a more critical review that delineates the discrepancies between *what is* and what *should be.* These responsibilities demonstrate the need for:

- *Data bases* about each program area or element as to current status and related contextual information.
- *Programs* for each area, i.e., objectives, content and skills, personnel, structure, resources, and delivery/maintenance systems.
- *Instruments* to ascertain existing levels of adequacy, (learner achievement and staff competency), quality of processes being used, and a research and review capability.
- Realistic *plans* for the improvement of each, including evaluation and restructuring.

Thus, the collection of data is not the point. The important issue is the use of such information for identifying need areas and for establishing agreement as to needs and priorities. Also, it is necessary to establish professional, learner, or system entry levels so that subsequent research can indicate the nature and extent of gain considered important. This is the function of the diagnosis-design stage.

Different persons and different groups should participate in the development of data and in the agreements of its relevance. The relationship of these different perceptions to the central needs and objectives is essential data. It is the responsibility of the planners to ascertain which items and which priorities are strategic and to build this knowledge into the designed program, its implementation, evaluation, and related program plans.[48] These considerations are also discussed as strategy matters regarding an analysis of the "force field," p. 135, and in regard to management activities, pp. 184-194.

Translating Goals and Needs into Objectives

Goal definition and accuracy in needs analysis is central to all other stages and processes. Relevant, targeted, and authentic assists are much more likely to achieve the desired outcomes. Evaluation as both in-process and summative procedures, monitoring as concurrent and coordinating functions, and planning as explication of objectives; all these require that the means and the ends be congruent. Staff members are the most fundamental sources of data about needs. They are also most critical agents in the shaping of needs statements and, obviously, essential to the adequate response to the personal, instructional, or contextual needs that have been identified. *Analyzing needs data and defining objectives is the first step in the problem solving/planning process.*

The Critical Nature of Objectives

The last decade has seen an almost frantic search for improved statements of objectives. Greater precision has been prompted by concerns for organizing the related elements, that is, instructional strategies, media and resources, learner experiences, content, and especially evaluation. Similarly, the pressures for effectiveness and adequacy have resulted in measures for accountability, structuring, budgeting, reporting, programming, and planning.[49,50]

Objectives are the counterpart of needs; they are the reverse side of the coin but with a difference. A need statement by itself is inert; you can talk, worry, or create turbulence. But, planning for staff development or instructional gain requires that the need be translated into objectives. Statements of objectives indicate value positions. The restatement process is thus critical, since the data—now worded in a different way—should carry the same meaning and the same feeling. Otherwise, inadequacy, distortion, or deliberate modification will occur at this critical stage.

From these objectives, program elements can be developed to help manage the necessary activities. In any systematic approach, a needs analysis is followed closely by the delineation of objectives that provide clarification of intent, focus for development, and criteria for evaluation. It is realistic to assume that, no matter how well written or extensive, objectives cannot be written that will, or should, represent the total effect. They can, however, be the means for providing an acknowledged emphasis. As such, it is easier to plan for appropriate resources and methodologies, to structure evaluative measures, and to prepare for a common core of activities and outcome(s).

The conversion of goals and needs into objectives should encourage creativity as well as quality. Even as needs are assessed and objectives written, the next series of tasks are being considered. What are the constraints? The resources? What must be the strategy for the change, for the particular elements of the plan? What activities represent landmarks or progress toward the desired objectives? How extensive or intensive shall the experiences be? And what of time, leadership, and pressure to move or hold? How simple or complex can the program be, and who will do the required work? Is a strong mandate needed because of the nature of the needs, or is the project one that requires a careful walk in delicate territory? Who or what forces are the opposition; who or what forces are proponents? Where is the commitment or the power to proceed? What other pressures will likely modify the desired plan?

And so it goes, but always inherent is the realization that any given structure can only key upon a limited number of activities.

OBJECTIVES AND PLANNING

Every objective that has been given a priority should have a program response. It may be possible to cluster objectives or to generalize the program content and activities in such a way that multiple objectives will be served. However the planning is done, every objective should be developed into program activities and materials. This is necessary to achieve each objective; it is also critical in the subsequent monitoring or auditing and in the formative and summative evaluation. Objectives represent the intent and the focus of the project. In any case, side-effects and unforeseen happenings occur, hopefully fortuitous. However, work flow and progress are enhanced by clear purpose and direction, especially in a comprehensive project and a complex situation.[51,52]

Objectives are the key to translating problems into program. Without going through this translation, it is likely that the response to a problem or need will be stereotyped, i.e., that adding a course, adding a remedial teacher, or holding in-service days deal with the problem rather than with possibilities and desired outcomes. However, once objectives are written that can be restated as program and outcome objectives for staff or learners, appropriate action then can flow more productively with minimum time used in the design phase or in initial activity. Generating appropriate objectives is the key to variety, adequacy, and appropriateness of response; it is a way of transferring the needs from learner or program, making both the responsibility of the professional.

Since major program elements should not exist unrelated to program objectives, these become the basis for the development and implementation phase. Thus, objectives calling for the acquisition or sharpening of skills will require opportunities for practice and for feedback as to quality. Broad competencies will require laboratory experiences via simulations—micro, "in place," and "hands on" encounters. Even the demonstration of new knowledge will necessitate situational transactions that are observed and evaluated. Both unattended objectives and programs without direction are evidence of inadequate planning and are invitations to failure.

Many planning and development schemes such as MBO (management by objectives), PPBES (planning, programming, budgeting, and evaluation), and PERT (program evaluation and review technique) have from three to five levels of goals and objectives (see Appendix E). By so-ordering the plans, it is possible to organize, specify, and develop; it is also possible to develop alternatives at each level, to prepare cost estimates, to allocate staff and materials, to develop appropriate evaluation measures, and to assign specific accountability measures at each level of operation. In such program planning, the supervisor, principal, and involved staff identify and delineate the layers of responsibility that need to function for particular outcomes. Auditing, accountability, management, and evaluation techniques require these definitions of program responsibility; also, they contribute to the development of the necessary support system and facilitate planning for a longer time frame.

Comprehensive planning involves a number of elements. These usually include: (1) developmental phases or stages, (2) a management plan (including monitoring and evaluation) built expressly to achieve the desired objectives, program levels of development, and events (work packages), (3) a 3-5 year time span, (4) the involvement of more persons in the total system, and (5) systematic process.

Factors to Consider in Developing Objectives

As a result of these developments and concerns, a number of factors should be considered when objectives are being identified and explicated. While no list can be complete, the following items are representative:

1. *Relationship to broad goals of society:* expressed in such statements as the Seven Cardinal Principles (1918), the NEA-Educational Policies Commission publications, state goals, presidential commissions, and other expressions of social aims and priorities.[53–57]
2. *Congruence with ongoing system-policy statements:* determining the relationship of the new objectives to the existant aims and objectives, establishing the placement in relationship to existing course offerings and units as reflected by scope and sequence considerations, and relating to the baseline or system data to established need or discrepancy.
3. *Response required from school district organizational and program levels:* for central office personnel, including the administration, business, personnel, etc.; program areas such as math, science, English or others, which will be involved or affected; particular grade levels or courses; and classroom-teacher materials including specific units and lessons.
4. *Balance among domains and taxonomies:* maintaining a balance among cognitive, psychomotor, and affective areas; a balance among the taxonomic, competency, or instructional levels.
5. *Degree and nature of specification:* the extent to which objectives delineate conditions, target, performance level, outcome, and other behavioral or non-behavioral criteria; the extent to which any combination of sub-objectives do, in fact, "deliver" the prioritized goal; the extent to which they are measurable and achievable; and their brevity and range, long or short.
6. *Impact upon instructional strategies:* methodology, instructional materials, or system organization (staff), cost, and compatibility; acceptability, amount and nature of the change required in the classroom or system operation in order to implement the objectives; product or process; and learner or staff orientation.
7. *Validity in terms of the above factors:* objectives may arise from many sources whether they are purchased, developed as a response to an instructional need,

grow out of a data discrepancy, or become mandated by a board of education or the state department. Their validity must also be viewed in terms of student perceptions, and teacher/parent perceptions. Validation also involves a process whereby the decision makers can decide upon priorities, policies, and appropriate resources.

By whatever methods done, and to whatever degrees specified, the development of statements for *program*, *enabling*, and *performance* objectives are critical to the design process and to subsequent objectives and related activities. Each planned activity, long or short in range, should be so delineated that the "mission" can be planned, implemented, and evaluated. Further, the desired consequences and the nature of the impending program should be known to the participants. This is crucial to progress, process, and morale. The translation of needs into objectives is not only a valuing and shaping process, it is also *predictive*. The act of recasting the needs into objectives identifies the target group. Data from staff members regarding their feelings and their competencies and their relating to these objectives can be ascertained at this time. It is then built into the selection and designation of those persons who will be most affected. Such considerations should include leadership and supervisory personnel.

The Target—Impact and Ripple Effect

Problem solution, instructional change, and professional renewal require careful consideration of the target individual(s) and groups.[58-60] Targeted projects assume a precise or narrow gauge impact in contrast to the general "shotgun" approach so often used. In visualizing the target group, it is important to consider both the impact point and the desired and likely repercussions. In most instructional change efforts, the ultimate target is the learners; but for a particular staff development or instructional change effort, it may be more effective to concentrate upon one of the various organizational or staff units. However, at the same time the planning of activities and the shaping of objectives must be done in such a way that the result will be an improvement in learner gain.

In any given project, a need is to consider the various system *possibilities* and areas, as well as to make a decision regarding the specific *focus*. Figure 2.5 shows representative organizational elements and pressure points. The circle lines represent different organizational levels, beginning with the learner and moving outward. Three outside forces are suggested: (1) community, (2) society, and (3) professional and commercial. Lines from these elements intersect with the circle lines to suggest concerns and inputs that are likely to determine or modify the program being developed.

Realistically, these elements all operate constantly. The need to make target decisions regarding program focus often causes leadership to neglect these larger or related concerns and input possibilities. This we do at our peril. As an open and public enterprise, the school system cannot function realistically or effectively unless the total "field" is factored into planning and operation.

The intersecting circles and arcs produce segments that are useful to consider in discussions, decisions, and plans. These segments could be numbered to produce cells for systematic review. It is sometimes as instructive to decide consciously what to exclude as well as what to include. The intent of the figure is to suggest one possible way of visualizing the potential targets. While organizational elements are shown, it should be recognized that there are also personal, process and product elements that can also be reviewed using the same sketch.

Another purpose of the figure is to encourage conscious attention being given to the ripple effect of any given program. The target is the focus, not the end of the process. If the instructional change or the staff development project is important, many side-effects will be present that may be affirmative or negative. If third grade teachers become more competent in some skill, the results will have impact on the subsequent grades. If selected teachers use a new technique or resource

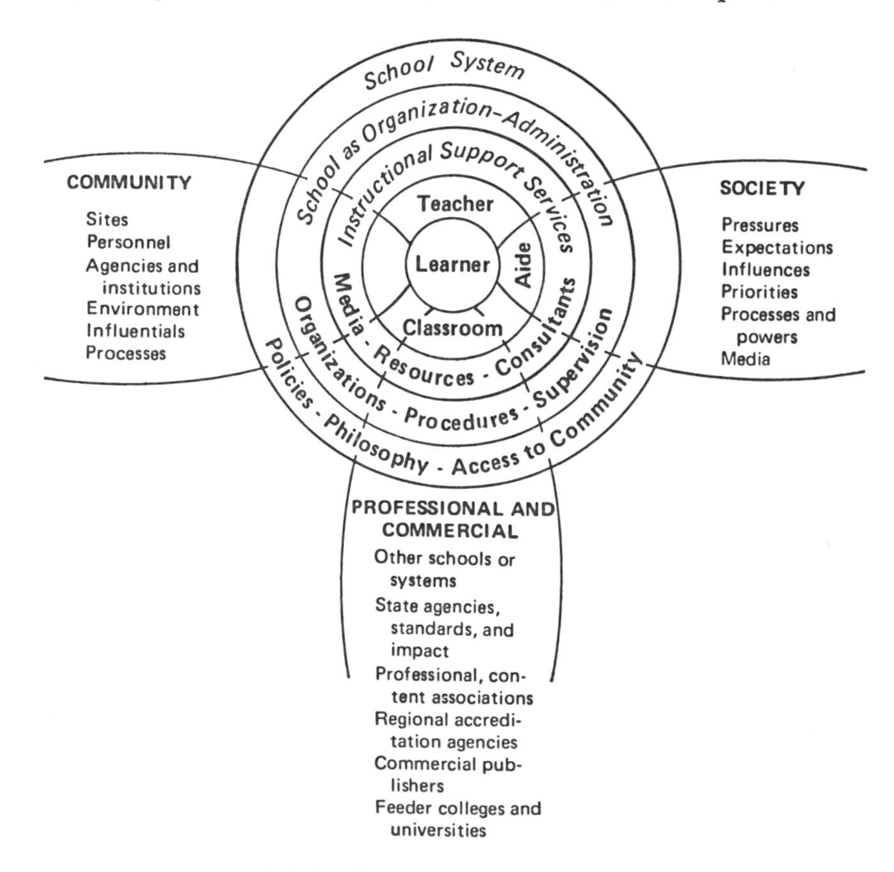

FIGURE 2.5 Determining the Target.

with success, others will likely want the same help. The installation of new objectives will likely require new materials. Teachers who are encouraged and instructed to use materials or resources will affect the library and media facilities. If content is changed, then a change should be considered in the testing program, course structures, and sequences. If the new curriculum calls for field trips or use of community resources, budget, busing, and policy changes then may be required. The possibilities are endless, but the decision to focus objectives and activities at some particular point does not mean that other points and processes are not affected. This factor has to be built into planning, coordinating, and evaluating. Side effects and unexpected results often constitute the significant gains (or losses) in achievement or commitment. Comprehensive planning also must include these considerations.

These target and strategy considerations are important in developing the definition, design, and rationale. Likewise, as program activities and implementation are achieved, deliberate attention must be given to the relationships between the program impact, personal powers (status and competencies of individuals), and the desired affect upon instructional improvement. An allied need is a review and reconstitution of the *support system*—those elements of operation and program that relate to the new product or proposal. Support features include such factors as consultant help, adequacy of appropriate media and materials, schedules and assignments that provide assistance, evaluative measures that emphasize rather than disregard the desired change, attention, and status procedures. In short, they are the reinforcement and response factors that exist in the system. In any case, a ripple effect will result, but the aim is a causal change, not a casual result. Target considerations are integral to both the shaping of objectives and the decisions regarding program. Representative target groups are considered in the next chapter in connection with panel 3 of the design agenda, see p. 62. Similar considerations should be given to the force field idea (see Chapter 5, p. 135) and related strategies. Figure 2.6 summarizes progress toward a program design that should be evident at this point in planning.

Other Utilizations of Objectives

The importance of objectives does not end with statements of program or performance objectives, or an equivalent. It is not enough to capture the statements of mission and purpose and to identify target personnel. Curriculum development as advocated by Taba, Tyler, Herrick, and others have stressed repeatedly the need for precision and clarity as the basis for *subsequent* planning in curriculum and staff development. More recently, calls have been made for competency-based instructional approaches, for assurances regarding learner gait, for criterion or domain-referenced testing, and for both formative and summative evaluation.

Objectives have also become the central element in a number of management schemes. For example, MBO (management by objectives) is a process for working with staff or with product outcomes. PPBES (planning, programming, budgeting, and evaluation system) requires specification of objectives on a number of program levels in order to plan, program, budget, and evaluate.[61-63]

Process approaches such as organization development or clinical supervision require clear statements of intent as essential beginning and process points. Evaluation as decision making, "systems" approaches, intervention strategies and changes, monitoring, auditing, and performance contracting have similar requirements.

Visual display techniques such as PERT (program evaluation and review technique) and CPM (critical path method) have objectives as the key to the determination of product packages (events), activities, time, and resource allocations. Management involving the computer and other technological applications relies upon objectives and criteria for data and decision making. Other illustrations could be cited, but the point is that skill in the development, validation, and use of objectives has become an expected competency for persons in a responsible or decision making role. It has become a necessary preliminary to the development of comprehensive and systematic planning at all levels and in all areas (see Appendix E).

Coping with Constraints

Supportive data include the basic assumptions or "givens" considered by those who are involved in a project. Too often in planning, there is little possibility or encouragement to rethink basic elements such as teacher-pupil ratios, schedules of staff or students, time assignments, the use of buildings or community learning sites and personnel, the roles of those charged with instruction, or the type of resources that may be used. If these items are always considered "fixed," then many exciting or useful alternatives never surface for consideration or restructuring. Bureaucratic processes or organizations by their very nature too often preclude the possible emergence of new and creative approaches. Understandings regarding time, cost, personnel, policies, and facilities are essential. The more it is that fixed constraints exist or are perceived to exist, the less likely it is that variety or innovations will emerge as viable program options.

It, therefore, behooves leadership to clarify its stance in these matters. "They won't let us . . ." is a too-familiar charge; responsibility should be clear at the outset. A useful procedure would be to list so-called "fixed" assumptions or constraints that are not to be amendable to challenge. As a departure point for discussion, the consideration of such items is one way to widen (or narrow) the range of options. In the same vein, past practices, traditional modes, professional standards, learner characteristics, and community expectations also may need clarification or reconsideration.

New developments provide new dimensions and resources (remote terminals, cassette and cable television, and pocket electronic calcu-

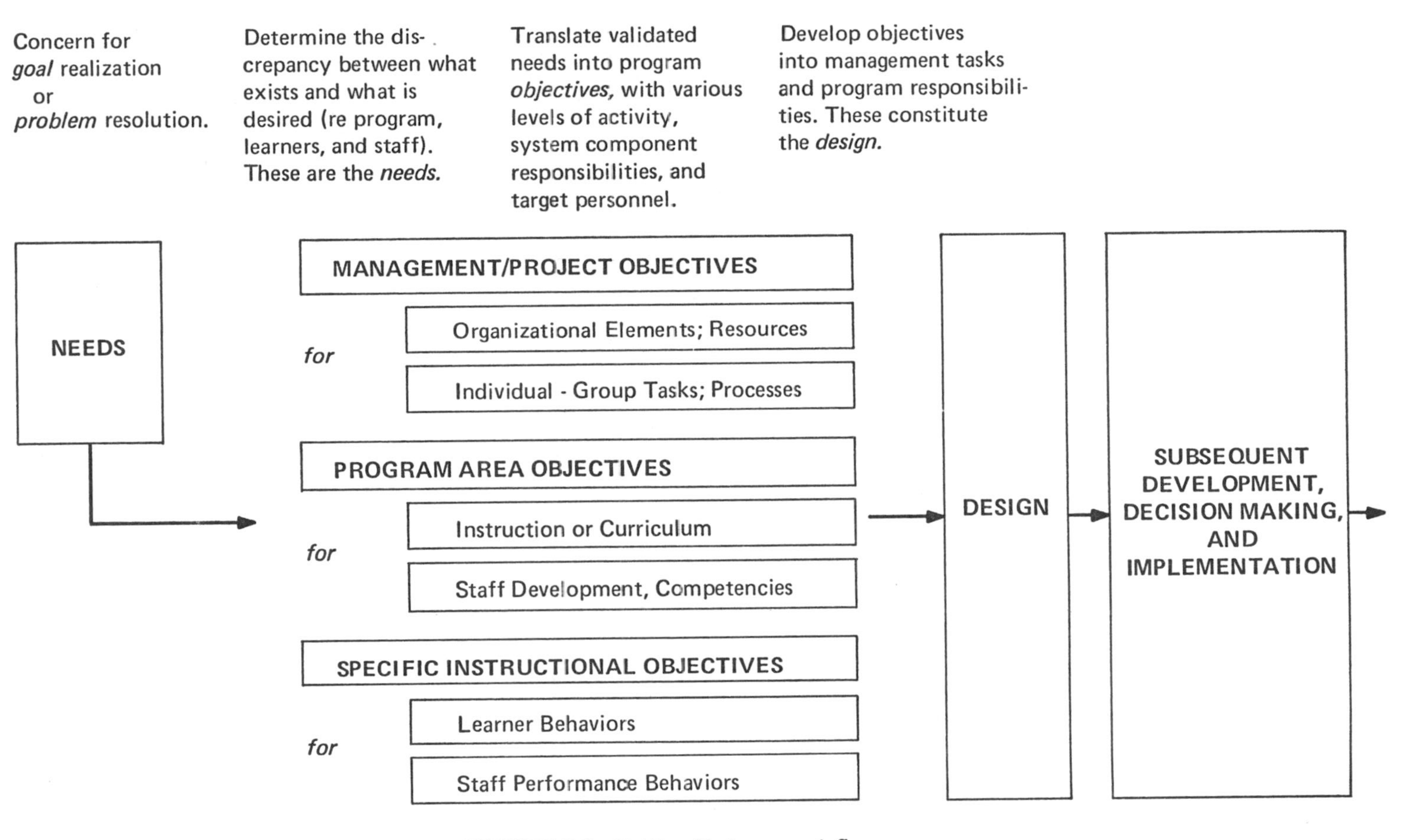

FIGURE 2.6 Getting Underway—A Summary.

lators); new responsibilities and freedoms (professional negotiations, lowered age for contracts, student rights, and student power at the polls or in business enterprises); the emergence of different life styles and life coping skills (choosing, inter-relating, changing, and decision making); plus ever newer, emerging techniques and technologies. A clear need exists to invent new responses, to modify willingly all routines, to learn to unlearn and relearn, to develop possibilities for openness and new criteria, and to respect the primacy of purposes and persons as well as the principles of the past.[64-73]

Program design has its genesis in issues and problems that surface as needs. Needs must be translated into objectives, which become the base for subsequent planning. These steps are preliminary elements in the development of a program design for staff or for learners, hopefully both. Too many proposals for change end with the statement of objectives and target personnel; these are important beginning steps, but they are not sufficient in themselves without further delineation as to how they will be developed and implemented. These design considerations are discussed in the following chapter.

ACTION GUIDELINES

Needs and objectives have multiple origins. Their determination is a critical phase in planning for program improvement and staff development. Needs analysis and assessment can be best achieved through comprehensive and systematic approaches. The use of conceptual models can assist in this effort.

Goals are general statements that are useful as departure points for planning. However, they are often nebulous and unachievable as stated, and it is necessary to develop sub-objectives for which specific plans, activities, and outcomes can be arranged. These specific intents also provide a structure that will enhance evaluation, accountability, and on-going review.

In addition to needs data, the collection and consideration of relevant baseline data is essential. These data can include information regarding content, instruction, context, and management. Comprehensive and valid data are best achieved through involvement of a wide range of individuals and groups within the system. Involvement should not be ended with such decisions, but should be maintained through subsequent deliberations and activities. Converting goals and needs into achievable objectives is a critical step in planning. This honing, targeting, and deciding process requires the consideration of constraints, resources, and consequences. Process and product criteria are useful in keeping these translation efforts realistic, manageable, and valid.

A continuing research and evaluation capability is essential in a dynamic and changing milieu. Experience and data can suggest bases for a program planning that moves continuously from initial diagnosing through the various stages of designing, developing, implementing, and evaluating.

RELATED REFERENCES

1. Association for Supervision and Curriculum Development, *Education for an Open Society*. Yearbook. Washington, D.C.: author, 1974.
2. Association for Supervision and Curriculum Development, *A New Look at Progressive Education*. Yearbook. Washington, D.C.: author, 1972.
3. Williams, Charles, and Nusberg, Charlotte, *Anticipating Educational Issues Over the Next Two Decades: An Overview Report of Trends Analysis*. Menlo Park, California: Stanford Research Institute, 1973.
4. Alaska Department of Education, *Directions '70: An Assessment of Educational Needs in Alaska*. Juneau, Alaska: author, 1971.
5. Brown, Leslie M., *Aims of Education*. New York: Teachers College Press, 1970.
6. Bucks County Public Schools and the Pennsylvania Department of Education, *Quality Education Program Study. Booklet A: Program Description*, Philadelphia: Project Coordinator, 1971.
7. Florida Department of Education, *An Assessment of Educational Needs for Learners in Florida, 1970*. Bureau of Research, Tallahassee: Florida Department of Education, 1970.
8. Georgia Department of Education, *Goals for Education in Georgia*. Atlanta, Georgia: Department of Education, Division of Planning, Research, and Evaluation, 1970.
9. Pharis, William L., Robinson, Lloyd, and Walden, John, *Decision Making and Schools for the 70's*. Washington, D.C.: National Education Association, 1970.
10. Lee, Walters, "The Assessment Analysis and Monitoring of Educational Needs." *Educational Technology*, 13:4 (1973), p. 28.
11. Lindvall, C. M., *Defining Educational Objectives*. Pittsburgh: University of Pittsburgh Press, 1964.
12. Stake, Robert E., and Gooler, Dennis, "Measuring Educational Priorities." *Educational Technology*, 11:9 (1971), p. 44.
13. Eisele, James E., et al., *Computed-Assisted Planning of Curriculum and Instruction*. Englewood Cliffs, New Jersey: Prentice-Hall, 1973.
14. Weisgerber, Robert, ed., *Instructional Process and Media Innovation*. Chicago: Rand McNally, 1968.
15. Goodlad, John I., *School, Curriculum, and the Individual*. Waltham, Massachusetts: Blaisdell Publishing Co., 1966.
16. Morphet, Edgar L., Johns, Roe L., and Reller, Theodore L., *Educational Organization and Administration*. 2nd ed., Englewood Cliffs, New Jersey: Prentice-Hall, 1967.
17. Umans, Shelley, *The Management of Education*. New York: Doubleday, 1970.
18. Downey, Lawrence W., *The Task of Public Education: The Perceptions of People*. Chicago: University of Chicago, 1960.
19. Doll, Ronald C., Curriculum Improvement: *Decision-Making and Processes*. 2nd ed., Boston: Allyn and Bacon, 1970.
20. Feyereisen, Kathryn V., Fiorino, A. John, and Nowak, Arlene T., *Supervision and Curriculum Renewal: A Systems Approach*. New York: Appleton-Century-Crofts, 1970.
21. Immegart, Glenn, and Pilecki, Francis J., *An Introduction to Systems for the Educational Administrator*. Reading, Massachusetts: Addison-Wesley, 1973.

22. Anderson, Richard, ed., *Current Research on Instruction.* Englewood Cliffs, New Jersey: Prentice-Hall, 1969.
23. Travers, Robert M. W., ed., *Second Handbook of Research on Teaching.* Chicago: Rand McNally, 1973.
24. Bradley, P. A., and Wooley, D., *Making Better Decisions on Assessed Needs: Differentiated School Norms.* New York: Paper presented at the Annual Meeting of the American Educational Research Association, February 1974.
25. Taba, Hilda, "The Objectives of Education." In *Contemporary Thought on Public School Curriculum,* edited by Edmund C. Short and George D. Marconnit. Dubuque, Iowa: William C. Brown Publishers, 1968.
26. Tyler, Ralph W., "Some Persistent Questions on the Defining of Objectives." In *Contemporary Thought on Public School Curriculum,* edited by Edmund C. Short and George D. Marconnit. Dubuque, Iowa: William C. Brown Publishers, 1968.
27. Taba, Hilda, "Translating General Objectives into Specific Ones." In *Contemporary Thought on Public School Curriculum,* edited by Edmund C. Short and George D. Marconnit. Dubuque, Iowa: William C. Brown Publishers, 1968.
28. Goodlad, John I., *School, Curriculum, and the Individual. op. cit.*
29. Deck, L. Linton, *Educational Needs Assessment: Priorities for Education in the Public Schools of Orange County, Florida.* Orlando, Florida: Orange County Board of Education, 1973.
30. Woodbury, C. A., *Research Model for State Educational Needs Assessment.* Paper presented at the Annual Meeting of the American Educational Research Association. Minneapolis, Minnesota, 1970.
31. Morrissett, Irving, "Accountability, Needs Assessment and Social Studies." *Social Education,* 37:271 (1973).
32. Mullen, David J., and Mullen, Rosemary C., "A Principal's Handbook for Conducting a Needs Assessment Using the School Program Bonanza Game." *Georgia Association of Elementary School Principals Quarterly,* Athens, Georgia: 11:1 (1974).
33. Trull, J. R., "A Proposal for the Implementation of the Needs Assessment Model." *EDRS,* 1973.
34. Nunnery, Michael Y., and Kimbrough, Ralph B., *Politics, Power, Polls, and School Elections.* Berkeley, California: McCutchan Publishing Corp. 1974.
35. Stake, Robert E., *Priorities Planning: Judging the Importance of Individual Objectives.* Los Angeles: Instructional Objectives Exchange, 1972.
36. Bowers, C. A., Housego, I., and Dykes, D., eds., *Education and Social Policy.* New York: Random House, 1970.
37. Kimbrough, Ralph B., *Political Power and Educational Decision-Making.* Chicago: Rand McNally, 1964.
38. Killman, Caroline, and Rahnlow, Harold, *Writing Instructional Objectives.* San Francisco: Fearon Publishers, 1972.
39. Kebler, R. J., Larker, L. L., and Miles, D. T., *Behavioral Objectives and Instruction.* Boston: Allyn and Bacon, 1970.
40. Gronlund, Norman E., *Stating Behavioral Objectives for Classroom Instruction.* New York: MacMillan, 1970.
41. Popham, W. James, and Baker, Eva L., *Establishing Instructional Goals.* Englewood Cliffs, New Jersey: Prentice-Hall, 1970.

42. Bloom, Benjamin, et al., *Taxonomy of Educational Objectives, Handbook I: Cognitive Domain.* New York: McKay, 1956.
43. Harrow, Anita, *A Taxonomy of the Psychomotor Domain.* New York: McKay, 1972.
44. Krathwohl, David R., Bloom, Benjamin, and Masia, Bertram, *Taxonomy of Educational Objectives, Handbook II: Affective Domain.* New York: McKay, 1964.
45. Campbell, Vincent N., and Mark, D. G., *Identifying and Formulating Educational Problems.* Palo Alto: American Institutes for Research, 1967.
46. Sweigert, R. L., "Assessing Educational Needs to Achieve Relevancy." *Education,* 9:315 (1971).
47. Welty, Gordon, "Evaluation and Planning in Education: A Community Concern." In *Readings in Curriculum Evaluation,* edited by Peter A. Taylor and Doris M. Cowley. Dubuque, Iowa: William C. Brown Publishers, 1972.
48. Stake, Robert E., ed., *Instructional Objectives.* Chicago: Rand McNally, 1969.
49. Bishop, Leslee J., "The Centrality of Objectives." In *Improving Supervisory Competencies,* edited by Leslee J. Bishop. Georgia Association for Supervision and Curriculum Development and the Center for Curriculum Improvement and Staff Development. Athens, Georgia: The Center, Department of Curriculum and Supervision, University of Georgia, 1973.
50. Whitner, John A., and Antin, Arthur P., *Program-Planning-Using MBO in School Administration.* Englewood Cliffs, New Jersey: Prentice-Hall, 1972.
51. Banghart, Frank W., and Trull, Albert, *Educational Planning.* New York: Macmillan, 1972.
52. Stake, Robert E., *Priorities Planning. op. cit.*
53. French, Will, et al., *Behavioral Goals of General Education in High School.* New York: Russell Sage Foundation, 1957.
54. Educational Policies Commission, *The Central Purpose of American Education.* Washington, D.C.: author, 1961.
55. U.S. Office of Education, *Cardinal Principles of Secondary Education.* Washington, D.C.: Government Printing Office, 1918.
56. Educational Policies Commission, *The Purpose of Education in American Democracy.* Washington, D.C.: author, 1938.
57. National Commission on the Reform of Secondary Education, B. Frank Brown, Chairman, *The Reform of Secondary Education.* New York: McGraw-Hill, 1973.
58. Luft, Joseph, *Of Human Interaction.* Palo Alto, California: National Press Books, 1969.
59. Runkel, Philip J., and McGroth, Joseph E., *Research on Human Behavior: A Systematic Guide to Method.* New York: Holt, Rinehart, and Winston, 1972.
60. Stanford, G., and Roark, A. E., *Human Interaction in Education.* Boston: Allyn and Bacon, 1974.
61. Boston, Robert E., "Management by Objectives: A Management System for Education." *Educational Technology,* 12:5 (1972), p. 49.
62. Churchman, Charles W., *The Systems Approach.* New York: Dell, 1968.
63. Hartley, Harry J., *Educational Planning-Programming-Budgeting: A Systems Approach.* Englewood Cliffs, New Jersey: Prentice-Hall, 1968.
64. Hipple, Theodore W., ed., *The Future of Education: 1975–2000.* Pacific Pali-

sades, California, Goodyear Publishing Co., 1974.

65. Joyce, Bruce R., *Alternative Models of Elementary Education.* Waltham, Massachusetts: Blaisdell Publishing, 1969.
66. Leeper, Robert, ed., *Curriculum Change: Direction and Process.* Washington, D.C.: Association for Supervision and Curriculum Development, 1966.
67. Macdonald, James B., Anderson, Dan W., and May, Frank B., eds., *Strategies of Curriculum Development. Selected Writings of the Late Virgil E. Herrick.* Columbus, Ohio: Charles E. Merrill, 1965.
68. Roszak, Theodore, *The Making of a Counter Culture.* Garden City, New York: Doubleday, 1969.
69. Saylor, J. Galen, "What is Relevant for Today's Students?" *Educational Leadership*, 31:41 (October 1973).
70. Saylor, J. Galen, and Alexander, William, *Planning Curriculum for Schools.* New York: Holt, Rinehart, and Winston, 1974.
71. Taba, Hilda, *Curriculum Development: Theory and Practice.* New York: Harcourt, Brace, and World, 1962.
72. Toffler, Alvin, *Future Shock.* Random House, 1970.
73. Tyler, Ralph W., *Basic Principles of Curriculum and Instruction.* Chicago: University of Chicago Press, 1950.

3

Designing

The task of the design phase is threefold: to describe the instructional strategy that is used in the attainment of the desired objectives, to lay out the conceptual pattern, which includes the work segments and processes of the project undertaken, and to show this pattern within the context in which it will operate. The design may not include all the details, but it must explicate the major elements, i.e., those ingredients that have evolved from the planning sequence.[1,2]

This configuration of concepts constitutes the design. As such, the design elements are those built into the necessary tasks and program formats, and subsequently delineated for decision making as the specifications—logistics and alternatives. This organization of ideas facilitates planning and decision making in regard to the particulars that are to be developed and the program elements that are to be implemented. Good design provides new insights as to strengths, weaknesses, and possible omissions or duplications of significance. Elements of support or resistance, relationships to ongoing programs and established personal roles, and estimations of impact upon the targeted persons and programs, as well as those indirectly related, all should become more evident as a result of the design effort.

The clarity of purpose (needs and objectives) and its incorporation into design contributes to the quality of the decision making, which must follow the design phase. The quality of decision making and development is enhanced if the problem or need has dimension and validity, if the objectives are clear and ordered in priority, if the appropriate personnel are identified, and if the mode of solution is calculated and the alternatives indicated. The impact and intended consequences will be evident and much more likely to eventuate as planned. The design, therefore, represents the climax of the *analysis* phase.

SELECTING THE BEST MEANS

Objectives need a means, a way by which they can be achieved. The methods that are selected become an extension of the desired objectives and the most viable methodology available to the planner. Since the means have both substantive and procedural impact, they deserve conscious and critical attention. Means are the "hows"—the media, vehicles, instruments, agents, or agencies that are employed to effect the intended purposes. These are suggested on panel 4 of the Design Alternatives, p. 63. Haste "to get on with the job" often results in planners ignoring the relationship between means and ends. This decision or lack of consideration may "simplify" the selection of means, but it also endangers the desired outcome. Objectives and means interact with each other, thus become determining factors in any plan of action. Means should be selected for their potential efficiency to promote the desired results.

Administrators and supervisors tend to standardize their responses to problems or situations, that is, fall into the same decision patterns. For example, for a project the stock response is appoint a director; for a problem, appoint a committee; for a decision, establish a study group; or for promoting an idea, use the context of a general meeting. It would be worthwhile to check the impulse to proceed as usual and to consider the available options in order to have a different, qualitative, multiple, and creative approach.[3-6]

For planning purposes, system means have been consolidated into five categories; each will be considered briefly as follows:

1. Media. To surround participants with relevant materials and artifacts. Almost any educational objective can be facilitated by providing books, films, realia, film strips, VTR or audio tapes, exhibit situations, and related materials. Bulletin boards, library displays, and illustrations of student work are other examples. The existence and availability of these items provide a reference base, as evidence of intent, alternative ideas, and modes of sharing. The provision for such resources and activities usually requires the involvement of library, materials, and support personnel who become functionally related to the activity. Also, once obtained and used, these resources provide a residue of stimuli for related or subsequent efforts.[7-12]

This approach, although often stimulating and self generating, may lack directionality or task definition. It is not a good technique for meeting deadlines, but it is a fine way to share ideas and build resources.

2. Processes or Organizations. To establish a process or to create an organizational unit to do the work. Objectives, such as improved human relations, a more open climate, and problem solving or inquiry usually require a number of persons, a particular approach, and a span of time. In many school systems, it is possible to assign responsibility to standing committees (or councils). These have a knowledge and experience background that makes them the natural agency to provide leadership and planning regarding the in-service or change objective. Alternatives include central office committees, the instructional or school-community council, a university-school or state department group, a local school committee, and others.[13-18]

It may be desirable to establish a special group to be responsible for action or to contract with an outside agency who would organize, consult, train, or assist as needed. Very often, special projects require the establishment of an ad hoc structure or organization, which is dissolved once the project time elapses. This may be desirable, but without conscious effort to integrate the project achievements into the system operation, the gains may "disappear" along with the project leadership.

The process approach is increasingly employed. For example, human relations outcomes can be sought as the product of working together in special ways on particular targets. When results are viewed in terms of skills to be learned, commitments to be made, perceptions to be strengthened, and so forth; process then becomes more important than a particular artifact or structure. In any case, the procedures used carry a significant message as to the objectives to be achieved and the philosophy of those responsible for the mission.

This approach seldom yields a quick response or solution; its purpose is change among the participants as well as in the situation. It is harder to fix schedules, complete specific tasks, or assign a clear-cut outcome. The process or organization approach depends upon the composition of the group and the leadership. It is most useful where value questions, awareness, and interactions are also objectives in the search.[19]

3. *Information.* To provide a continuous flow of research and data. Examples include professional reports or bulletins; informative presentations made by consultants or staff persons who are prepared to make recommendations based on reading, research, and experiences; an in-service speaker; a faculty meeting presentation; or a professional meeting focused on the topic. Generally, the assumption is made that if people are informed, if they know the objective, the rationale, and the substance, then the desired consequence will occur. This is basically a one-way information flow.[20,21]

This approach is a low impact procedure, despite its overuse. Its greatest utility occurs when used in connection with other means, but as a single approach it lacks durability.

4. *Facilities and Resources.* To develop a facility that will enhance the function or task to be achieved. Thus, we build media, reading, staff renewal, or learning centers. We identify and use laboratories, community sites, or museums. The conference center and the community room also are examples as are the purchases of offset printing presses, electric typewriters, transcription equipment, system-wide TV, and computers. These are environmental, instrument, and utilization concerns. Likewise, a place that is too hot, too cold, too noisy, too drab, or

too busy detracts from the task at hand. Without books, tables, tools, and resources, the tasks seem more onerous and the results are less likely. Some settings are more inspirational, more helpful, than others. The leadership responsibility is to provide the contextual support for the activity, to provide the necessary equipment and environment.[22-24]

In addition, the development of physical and technological resources and facilities can enhance productivity. With enabling personnel, a well-equipped media center gives impetus to media development and use. A new, accessible duplicating machine usually results in more teacher produced materials. A sound-conditioned room contributes to control and concentration. Many routine functions can be handled by technology; thus, every new task does not necessarily require more people, but it may require resources or facilities. These, in turn, provide assists that are extensions of purpose as well as provisions to be considered.[25]

Administrators often use this technique to establish a situational and continuous need for activities, personnel, or budget support, and a place or thing to have "when the grant expires." This means is powerful when operated by persons who facilitate its proper use. It is expensive and useless when not supported by program, leadership, policy, or procedure.

5. *Personnel.* To select a person to perform the desired task and make him responsible for its execution. Persons may achieve the expected outcomes as the result of leadership ability, expertise, persuasion, or consultative talent. This may result in an ad hoc or a continuing responsibility for the designated inside or out-of-the-system change agent.

Designating specific personnel for tasks or processes is a common approach and it provides for easy accountability. Used singly, the means is defective in not providing: (1) an opportunity for other persons to learn, or (2) for a support system to be installed, or (3) for an established process to continue the task. It is often a quick and easy response, and care must be taken that the function or program does not disappear when the assignment is changed or the person leaves. Also, it often places emphasis on the role, not on the objective to be achieved. Sometimes, a continuing status role must be found for someone effective in a specialized but not continuing leadership position.[26]

Responsibility for achieving an objective need not be confused with actually performing the objective/achieving work. Conversely, a faceless, unaccountable responsibility has little likelihood of being met. It may be more productive to train and use teacher leadership, to have certain functions performed by teaching rather than supervisory or administrative personnel, and to clarify the ad hoc or continuing assignment. To always import competence is short-sighted because it deprives the local professionals from gaining experience and competence in the areas of concern. To never involve outside persons as consultants or leadership can be stultifying and making for the routine.

These, then, are generalized means. In a particular situation, decisions must be made regarding the specifics. A configuration of such agents, agencies, instrument, or media can represent power and variety. The supervisor, council, or administrator who desires to make an impact uses them for their inherent and complementary values. Any significant question or issue deserves a consideration of the various utilizations and combinations. Most importantly, means must be considered in terms of ends (objectives) and must be in harmony with them.

In summary, these strategy considerations involve financial, policy, and priority decisions. A change recommendation—is it best done from within or from outside? A quick job—if no system competency exists, then an imported assist may be best. Is it a sensitive or delicate task? Perhaps a non-school or non-system person would be more likely to elicit the feeling or make the point. The key is to determine critical competencies, to obtain and train personnel for these tasks, and to use the best means available from inside or outside the system.

These design decisions become critical to the subsequent pattern and process. They are impact, effectiveness, and status matters of consequence. It is the hypothesis of this "guide" that deliberations on these alternatives are necessary. The configuration of means has been incorporated into the subsequent *format* and strategy decisions (see Panel 4, p. 63).

DEVELOPING THE DESIGN

The brief flow chart, Figure 3.1, suggests possible steps and sequences in planning staff development and instructional change activities. This is a summary of the more complete agenda given on pp. 62–65. The intention of the visual summary is to list the desired phases in a likely sequence and, hopefully, to contribute to a better analysis and perspective of the total process.

Planning Agenda and Alternatives

Figure 3.2, which follows, contains a more complete listing of the various elements needing consideration by a systematic approach and encompasses any staff development or instructional improvement program. The total scheme is divided into eight panels and ten steps. These sequences are used throughout the text in various flow charts and visuals. Likewise, the chapters that follow (Designing, Developing, etc.) deal more specifically with the elements that are listed. The chart section is two-dimensional:

1. The *horizontal* dimension lists component areas that need to be considered, e.g., needs, objectives, targets, means, etc.
2. The *vertical* dimension suggests alternatives for each component area.

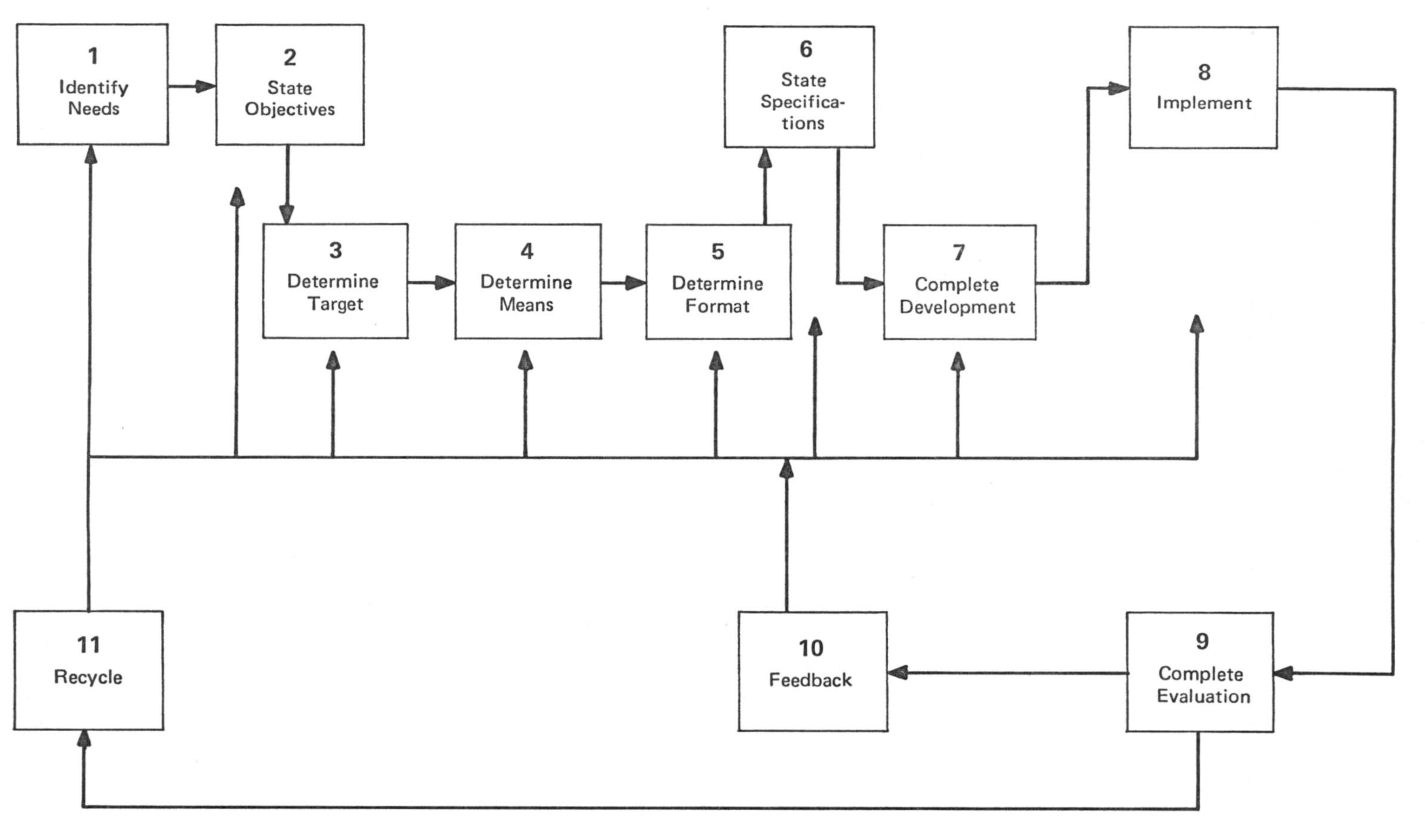

FIGURE 3.1 Project Tasks

It is not expected that every option will be utilized in each case. This is particularly true for the first five columns.

It will be noted in Panels 1–5 that the first four columns provide for *analysis*, for a systematic consideration of elements that are involved. For these segments, suggested options are listed. The task of the developer would be to translate these general items into program specifics as necessary in a given situation.

Panel 6, *Specification*, provides for a statement of the specifics selected for a particular staff development or instructional change event or series of events. The range of specifications to be utilized will depend upon the nature of the need, the objectives to be sought, and the size and nature of the system undertaking the project(s)—and similar considerations.

The last four columns in the chart, Panels 6–10, *Synthesis*, provide for synthesizing and implementing the plan for action. When all columns are delineated, system and systematic planning will be evident that will enhance the likelihood of worthwhile products and experiences.

It will be noted that the first panel is numbered 1 and 2 (1–2). This has been done because it is advantageous to make Needs Analysis one event and the Determination of Objectives another event in developing a project of any size. Thus, these functions are separated in developing flow charts or PERT diagrams (see pp. 60, 225–228). The same is true of the Evaluation panel because it is likely that Evaluation (9) and Feedback (10) will be separate events, decisions, and processes.

In addition to presenting a planned sequence of events and representative elements for consideration,* each panel segment also indicates the basic tasks to be achieved. For example, Panel No. 1 (Needs/Objectives) proposes two such tasks: (1) the identification of needs, and (2) the translation of needs data into program objectives. In the chapters that follow, notably Chapter 7, Managing, many other sub-tasks are discussed. Obviously, the nature and dimension of the project will greatly influence the type of tasks necessary for program achievement.

The second panel (Targets) proposes the determination of specific target(s) appropriate to the identified objectives as a major task. A related or subordinate task is the consideration and analysis of the constraints and resources that will affect the structuring and priority of the program. At this point, mention should be made that baseline data in some situations are best collected in connection with the needs analysis, especially where program standards indicate discrepancies that are to be addressed. In other cases, perhaps where staff development factors are considered, it may be advisable to collect baseline data *after* the target area or personnel have been determined. This will eliminate the problem of obtaining data about competencies, for example, from all system personnel or every program area. The data gathering can

*For extended, complex, or multiple projects, it would probably be desirable to cast the planning activities in *PERT* form (see p. 229) for reasons of analysis, brevity, and as an indication of interactions among projects.

NEEDS/OBJECTIVES*
1-2

*Identify needs (issues, general goals, or problems); translate into specific objectives from the appropriate areas:***

1. **Substantive—curricular elements**
   - basic content, information to be learned
   - major themes, strands, structures
   - related skills, modes of investigation
   - evaluation measures and standards
2. **Staff competencies-skills re:**
   - instructional program, strategies
   - classroom, content-methods or management
   - interpersonal skills and relationships
   - professional roles
3. **Development and use of resources**
   - materials-media
   - facilities—school, community, university
   - access, acquisition, coordination
   - inter-agency participation
4. **Structure, school or system operations**
   - organization—management, roles, decision persons and points
   - processes, routines
   - time, schedules, operational sequences
   - staff utilization
5. **Attitudes**
   - feelings-self, peers, students, program
   - commitments, adaptability
   - value bases
   - readiness for change, openness
   - community expectations relations
6. **Needed information re:**
   - program rationale
   - research—needed or existing
   - content—classroom materials, media center
   - system, school, community, pupil data

TARGET(S)†
3

Determine specific target(s) appropriate to identified objectives:

1. **Outside influences**
   - general community and influentials
   - region-government, agencies, universities, business groups, media
2. **Total system**
   - all personnel
3. **Selected sub-systems:**
   - instructional personnel, consultants
   - administrators, supervisors
   - support and non professional
   - school levels—
     elementary
     middle, junior high
     secondary, senior high
     community college, adult
4. **System staff or committees**
   - organizations, e.g., teacher association
   - content, department, grade level
   - cross role, instructional council
   - student leadership, groups
5. **Program personnel**
   - leadership
   - staff members
   - support personnel
6. **Individual school(s)**
   - teaching staff
   - leadership, principal
   - parents, community
7. **Teaching teams**
   - department, grade level
   - peer groups
8. **Individual staff**
   - selected teachers, support personnel
   - student teachers
   - teacher aides
9. **Business/industry/labor**
   - agencies, organizations, service groups
   - establishments, plants
   - leadership

FIGURE 3.2 Design Agenda for Staff Development or Instructional Improvement.

*Collect baseline data (for panels 1 and 2).
**See Chapter 2 and Appendices A and B.

†For related discussion, see pp. 45-47.

SYSTEM MEANS 4	PROGRAM FORMATS 5
*Determine basic resources to be used with objectives and targets**	*Determine effective grouping, format for achieving objectives***
1. Media, materials, books, films, bulletins, modules, exhibits, artifacts 2. Organization/provess • central office committees • instructional council • university, SDE, publisher organization • school—LEA personnel/regular committees • outside agency • establish special system committee(s) 3. Information—substantive • inputs to target(s) • communication process and facilities 4. Resources—major facilities • TV, computer, EDP • building modifications or facilities • sharing resources with other school system, agency, or community site • lease arrangement • special budget provisions for time, materials, personnel, etc. 5. Personnel • existing staff • staff trained or obtained to achieve objectives • outside consultant—adhoc, continuing • designation of specific change agent(s)	1. General session lecture, presentation, demonstration, television, slides, film, recording, audio-slide, meeting, panel discussion, radio, exhibit 2. Workshop seminar, small group, discussion, group interview, dialogue, consultation, value clarification; brainstorming, micro-lab, microteaching, interaction analysis, field trip 3. Task force assigned target, action or experimental research and analysis, study and reporting responsibility, team approach; product production re: curricular program, curriculum guide, teaching units; testing, materials, selection; instructional council 4. Clinic sessions problem analysis and remediation, individual help, directed experience, visitation, simulation-practice and feedback situations, role playing, critiques, observed performance, confrontation or encounter group, training 5. Directed individual study credit course, learning packets, modules, cassettes, programmed instruction, selected readings, case studies, individual contracts, visitation, individual interview, observation, professional writing 6. Combination of above

FIGURE 3.2 Continued.

*For related explanation, see pp. 56–59.

**For related explanation, see pp. 17–19 and pp. 67–69.

SPECIFICATION 6	DEVELOPMENT* 7
Summarize and specify program plans for review and implementation	*Complete preparation activities as planned*
1. Analysis—selected program goals, objectives 2. Policy parameters (and relationship to other system operations) community, system, school, staff, resources; feasibility, validation, authorization check points and decision-makers 3. Relationship to other, ongoing programs 4. Specifications re: priority targets, selected means, program format and related costs; budget line or code, performance indicators 5. Alternative approaches or options re: time, credit, status, access, achievement 6. Structure • leadership, management process • change strategies • communication-dissemination • monitoring, research • evaluation—process, summative • logistics—schedule, budget 7. Role assignments and responsibilities 8. Strategy for staff development operation; PERT or flow chart 9. In-service training requirements 10. Support features—processes, facilities, personnel, instruments	1. Assign tasks for development or search re: specified program plans—time, place, sequence, leadership, acoountability 2. Develop materials to be used—objectives, media, facilities, content, instructional strategies, learner activities, evaluative measures; include alternative activity, access possibilities 3. Prepare program orientation materials and logistical information for appropriate target(s); disseminate 4. Consolidate information re: policy and process parameters—cost, priority, relationships 5. Continue monitoring, management activities including process evaluation 6. Develop support data, procedures, roles, policies, instruments

FIGURE 3.2 Continued.

*See Chapter 4.

IMPLEMENTATION* 8	EVALUATION 9-10
Perform tasks as specified and developed	*Conduct evaluative activities***
1. Conduct orientation of staff, learners, community; also orientation of support personnel	1. Review progress and determine objectives to be assessed
2. Hold meetings, institutes, clinics, workshops, classes; conduct training as specified and developed—for staff, support, community personnel	2. Design, search, prepare instruments, schedule for evaluation
3. Establish communication and feedback system	3. Conduct summative evaluation; consolidated with monitoring and process evaluation data
4. Utilize materials, resources, personnel means, instruments; install and implement as planned	4. Indicate discrepancies
5. Monitor, coordinate, manage	5. Relate to standards, make judgments, re: gain-loss, cost effectiveness
6. Modify schedules, plant-facilities, etc., as required	6. Feedback to appropriate targets
7. Conduct related research	7. Recycle, redesign or continue
8. Prepare process information for audit, evaluation, feedback, and dissemination	

FIGURE 3.2 Continued.

*See Chapters 5, 7, and 8, and Appendix D.

**See Chapter 6.

focus upon the targeted program area and personnel. Thus, a critical task and decision is the point at which standards (program objectives and achievement data) are applied. This preliminary analysis can occur at the initiation stage and/or in connection with any state prior to development and implementation.

Thus, each design element has a logical placement in the sequence, has related items to consider, and has basic tasks to be achieved. In every case, these are proposed in the Design Alternatives, see Figure 3.2, pp. 62–65, and in the related chapters that follow.

In addition to completeness, the major advantage of using such a design is that all persons who are involved can see at a glance the basic stages and dimensions to be accomplished. They will know:

1. The total scope of the task to be done.
2. The progress that is being made.
3. The next task or phase to be undertaken.
4. The awareness of progress by management personnel.
5. The points when defined jobs are accomplished and ready for review or implementation.

The following chapters discuss the various personnel and task elements to be considered, especially those concerned with designing, developing, implementing, and evaluating. The final chapters deal with the coordination and management of these program elements. The appendices include selected specific examples and study items.

PROGRAM PROFILES

The following patterns, Figures 3.3, 3.4, and 3.5, are illustrative of those that can be developed. As presented, the profiles include only points of emphasis, since a comprehensive plan will incorporate elements from every segment of the design agenda and others that are unique to loca-circumstances and are not listed here. In an actual situation, such simplified profiles would be useful for policy review or decision making, but would be incomplete as planning statements unless the objectives were of a very limited nature. Likewise, it is probable that each objective would require its own profile for planning and operation. More comprehensive planning is suggested in connection with the task analysis phase, pp. 72–79.

Possible inclusions in any one program pattern are almost as numerous as the problems to be solved. This selection process is valid whether the problem is focused on content substances, organization, or instruction. The profiles, as modeled, deal only with staff development aspects and not community understanding, modification of routines and schedules, use of multiple means, and other such system variables. Following chapters deal more extensively with development, implementation, evaluation, and management considerations.

General Goal: To Introduce Linguistics into the Language Arts Program.

NEEDS/ OBJECTIVES 1-2	TARGET(S) 3	SYSTEM MEANS 4	PROGRAM FORMAT 5
1. Substantive-curriculum 2. Competencies re program 3. 4. 5. 6.	1. 2. 3. 4. System staff-content, language arts 5. 6. 7. 8. 9.	1. 2. 3. 4. 5. Directed individual study	

FIGURE 3.3 Program Design Profile—Substantive Objective.

The proposition in Figure 3.3 is that specific objectives be developed to incorporate knowledge about linguistics (content) and instruction. By instruction is meant how it could be taught as a part of the ongoing instructional program of language arts—not as a single or special course. The target group is the language arts teachers at the elementary and secondary levels. Directed individual study (a course taught by qualified instruction from outside the system) places emphasis on competence in the information and the level of classroom instruction.

Follow-up, not specified here, could be done by other procedures included as individual study alternatives or by clinic sessions (not indicated here but included as format grouping 4 of Figure 3.2). Development, validation, implementation, and evaluation would require additional design specifications.

In Figure 3.4, specific objectives are proposed that would be developed to focus on the competencies required to utilize TV as a regular component of the instructional program. Target persons would be elementary school personnel/teachers, supervisors, and principals. The means suggested use television as an instructional tool to provide inputs as well as experience. The existing staff persons would provide the leadership and the format would be a clinic approach emphasizing directed experience with critiques—simulations of actual classroom situations with practice and feedback.

Additional design details would be necessary regarding the specification of times, circumstances, resources required, and other like data.

General Goal: To Increase the Utilization of Instructional Television in the Elementary Schools.

NEEDS/ OBJECTIVES 1–2	TARGET(S) 3	SYSTEM MEANS 4	PROGRAM FORMAT 5
1.	1.	1.	1.
2. Competencies re program	2.	2.	2.
3. Use of resources–media	3. Selected sub-system-elementary	3.	3.
4.	4.	4. Resources-TV	4. Clinic-directed experience
5.	5.	5. Personnel–existing staff	5.
6.	6.		
	7.		
	8.		
	9.		

FIGURE 3.4 Program Design Profile—Instructional Objective.

Validation and evaluation would include actual classroom use and an assessment of increased staff competencies, utilization, and learner gain.

In the next illustration, Figure 3.5, it is proposed that specific objectives would be developed regarding needed changes in the staff organization as it related to instruction. Since this is a comprehensive modification, research is required to relate the proposed organizational structure to necessary changes in the ongoing program. The ultimate target group would be all professional personnel, although the initial effort would be by the instructional council to research, recommend, and pilot a limited effort—the systems process or means. Thus, the format would be that of a task force, persons authorized to do the necessary research and experimentation. The end product would be a set of recommendations based on their study and experience.

A good design provides a framework for a scenario that is flexible, communicable, and generative. As an agenda for growth and progress, many criteria could be applied; examples follow:

- Accommodates different value positions.
- Provides access for multiple talents and roles.
- Generates both options and specifics.
- Provides opportunities for personal reconsideration and renewal.
- Facilitates research, experimentation, and review.
- Encourages new efforts, new responses, and new means.
- Considers the context, the environment.
- Simulates subsequent transactions and repercussions.

General Goal: To Study the Feasibility of Restructuring the Staff to Provide for Differentiated Roles and Team Teaching.

NEEDS/ OBJECTIVES 1-2	TARGET(S) 3	SYSTEM MEANS 4	PROGRAM FORMAT 5
1.	1.	1.	1.
2.	2. Total system–all personnel	2. Process–instructional council	2.
3.	3.	3.	3. Task force–research, pilot and recommend
4. Structure–operation, organization	4.	4.	4.
5.	5.	5.	5.
6. Needed research re rationale	6.		
	7.		
	8.		
	9.		

FIGURE 3.5 Program Design Profile—Organizational Objective.

- Provides inter- and inner-connections.
- Facilitates communication, decision making, and feedback.
- Provides a reality base and relates ongoing to new.
- Accommodates complexity and support components.
- Includes times and terminal points including abort possibilities.
- Incorporates ad hoc, emergent, and status leadership.
- Generates both process and product outcomes.
- Clarifies objectives, target groups, and relationships.
- Promotes for qualitative, competent, and accountable performance.
- Provides for change, modification, and continuity.

An Individualized Design

Program objectives arise from many sources—learner needs, program goals or inadequacies, and staff or community concerns. It is only in an unusual or idealized situation that these all flow together in such a way that a single design, however comprehensive, will be adequate. Major program efforts usually concentrate upon specified learners and staff. Even when a number of complex projects are underway, it is unlikely that all staff members can be adequately or meaningfully included. Therefore, other inputs are required to identify staff needs and other design techniques are necessary to develop comprehensive and relevant staff development programs.[27,28]

One viable procedure is to relate personal or competency needs to an individual professional growth plan. Such plans may be elaborate or simple; they may relate to the system effort; they may be combined for group projects or courses; or they may be individualized and relate primarily to the status, skills, and aspirations of each individual. All these possibilities are achieved by some school districts. A common procedure is to regard such agreements as a form of supplementary "contract," whereby each staff person submits individual plans that are delineated, supervised, and evaluated. The records regarding such activities become a source of useful data regarding growth and expertise.[29] They may also be used for evaluation purposes, in which case the utilization could be included as an alternative among those to be discussed in Chapter 6, Evaluating.

The design for such planning usually incorporates at least four elements: (1) the selection of individual objectives or targets for the year; (2) a standard or proficiency level; (3) the means to be used, i.e., individual reading, group activity, observations, research, or visitation; (4) a schedule for review or conferencing regarding progress; and (5) a plan or person for evaluating the outcomes achieved. Areas for activity may be suggested or designated. Figure 3.6 suggests one form. In this illustration, it will be noted that activity areas are suggested. This approach can also be used by those persons directly related to a major project. Whatever the procedure or form, each individual must be provided with the opportunity to declare his personalized objectives, his commitments to growth, his standards, and the outcomes for which he will agree to be accountable.[30-32]

Specific Objectives and Achievement Criteria

In the system design illustrations given, only general program objectives are indicated. In an actual staff development or instructional change situation, additional and more specific objectives would be essential for purposes of development, communication to participants, and assessment. Achievement criteria would also be essential, providing, if possible, for objective measures and, in any case, subjective measures such as ratings or opinions. The objectives would be stated in accordance with the program format and reflect the style and duration of the planned activities. They would be built into the work packages and task statements; they would be the basis for all activities, processes, and products to be developed.[33-35]

Participants would know what to expect and how to respond. A *clinic* group would be expected to resolve an issue or develop a skill; a *seminar* would be expected to share alternatives and arrive at advanced positions; and a *task force* would be expected to produce the material or give evidence of the "contracted" gain. The same holds true for *individualized* projects. The specificity of the objectives, or the "charge" to the group, would reflect the school system's operational

Objectives (Possible Areas)	*Proficiency-Standard*	*Review-Conference Dates*	*Means to Achieve Objectives*	*Evaluation*
1. Personal-professional (status, certification, degree) 2. Professional effectiveness (competency, skill, information gain) 3. Professional participation (councils, department, professional-content association, writing) 4. School-community service (PTA, agency, government, club)				

FIGURE 3.6 Professional Growth Target(s).

procedures. This is also true of the individual's participation in the activity as voluntary, "expected," as the logical outcome of a mutual criteria and process, or as a required assignment. Ideally, an instructional council or a representative professional group would have advanced the planning to this juncture and would continue with the work of task analysis.

TASK ANALYSIS

Task analysis is a strategic responsibility. It follows after needs have been identified, analyzed, and validated; and after program objectives have been delineated. Very often, task analysis will proceed concurrently with the development of specific instructional objectives, selection of target personnel, project means, and the format decisions. Task analysis defines the dimensions and constraints that must be incorporated into the project plan, and it explicates the arrangements for program development, individual responsibility, and subsequent operations. Task allocation is its climax and is the substantive base for those items included in any statement of *specifications.*

Task analysis defines the way in which program objectives are to be realized and results achieved. It establishes and clarifies the nature and degree of individual *professional growth possibility.* The responsibilities and outcomes that are listed can become the criteria used in the selection and assignment of personnel. The adequacy and completeness with which the task analysis is done is a determining factor in a qualitative program. Without such an analysis, those responsible for managing or coordinating the activities are in an untenable position relative to decision making, planned support activities, formative evaluation, or any form of monitoring.

The Task Dimension

Task development is the "programming" phases of a PPBES application; whereby responsibilities, roles, resources, and standards are considered for analysis, costing, and prioritizing. In any project (not necessarily PPBES), it is the delineation of design elements. For planning and programming purposes, tasks are best stated as *events,* e.g., work packages such as reports prepared, decisions made, instructions circulated, and studies completed. Task analysis precedes the finalization of any visual presentation or PERT diagram. Time lines or PERT constructions flow easily once the specifics, the work packages, are developed. Lacking such detail, a plan can only indicate processes or organizational efforts in a very general way. The following items are intended to show how design elements can facilitate a qualitative delineation and analysis of the necessary tasks.[36–38]

These items may not be appropriate for every project. However, the development and use of checklists, planning guides, and matrixes can be useful items in the planning process. Three "check out" items follow and are presented as illustrations of the many possible guides that might be developed to assist in completing the programming or task analysis phase:

1. A *planning worksheet* that relates sub-system components to program possibilities and requirements.
2. A list of the instructional system sub-elements or *components* that should receive consideration if the analysis is to be comprehensive in scope.
3. A *development sequence* based on the model in Chapter 2, which provides a structure for ordering events with or without a specific time frame.

Task Analysis—a Worksheet

In any planning situation, the conditions that determine the important limits must be considered. The following worksheet combines the basic *Component Elements* (listed on p. 75) along with *Program Possibilities and Requirements.* (These are sometimes called parameters and constraints.) The worksheet is presented as a matrix in which the program requirements and possibilities are viewed in relationship to the components listed. This matrix has headings and cells. The cells are potential agenda items and are numbered for the purpose of including an identification system that recognizes the junctures of components and possibilities.

Group A—State, Federal Guidelines and Requirements. In the left margin are listed program possibilities or requirements that should be considered. The first grouping (A) includes state and federal guidelines that have been suggested to assist in planning, or the requirements that must be met if the project is to be funded or evaluated adequately.

Group B—Standards. The next segment suggests considerations of the standards or quality measures that must be considered. These may be state standards, regional standards, or expectations (such as regional accrediting agencies or consortia). Planning personnel who are developing comprehensive plans also need to consider professional "standards," which are sometimes officially stated, such as the American Library Association standards, or those less explicitly stated but still important to a quality program in any area.

Group C—Local Needs and Requirements. These may be adequately considered in Groups A and B. However, local expectations and needs always are present to require special attention. These might include racial, historic, demographic, cost, time, socio-economic, community or

	School/System Components						
Program Possibilities–Requirements*	*I. Policy Decision Making*	*II. Project Leadership-Management*	*III. Staff*	*IV. Project Program*	*V. Program Materials*	*VI. Support Features*	*VII. Community Involvement*
A. State, Federal Guidelines and Requirements	1	5	9	13	17	21	25
B. Standards–State, Regional, Professional–National	2	6	10	14	18	22	26
C. Local Needs and Requirements	3	7	11	15	19	23	27
D. Exemplary Practices from Research and Professional Literature	4	8	12	16	20	24	28

*See Chapter 4.

FIGURE 3.7 Task Development-Analysis (Planning Worksheet).

facility considerations, which should be thoroughly addressed. The process elements proposed in the guidelines, pp. 79-82 and 121-122, are relevant to this category.

Group D—Exemplary Practices and Research. As in any undertaking, there are research findings, the experience of similar or exemplary school systems, and reports/articles discussed in the professional literature. These can suggest cautions, help provide a data base, or suggest alternatives. For long term, extensive, or expensive projects, such items can be examined as part of a feasibility study to assess the usefulness of various approaches or substantive elements concurrent with other planning activities.

Task Development Using Component Sub-Systems

In any comprehensive project, numerous elements are to be considered. It is often useful to construct a list of these elements or sub-systems for a constant reference as to incorporable dimensions as planning and decision making are performed. Therefore, the list that follows is only that—a list. It is to suggest possible items and configurations of items that might be useful to consider in regard to the planning sequences and planning levels as they relate to instructional planning. Where organizational changes or administrative concerns are involved, it would be necessary to add those areas.

Instructional Components to Consider

1. *POLICY-DECISION MAKING*
   - Local Education Agency (LEA)—Superintendent/Board of Education—Rationale, Priority Agreements
   - State Department of Education (SDE), University Relationships
   - Budgeting-Funding
     - Resources—Staff, Materials
     - Policy-Implementation
   - Community Role—Personnel, Sites, Involvement
   - Time Frame; Planned Interventions
     - Review-Decision Points, Procedures
   - Legal Considerations
2. *PROJECT LEADERSHIP*-MANAGEMENT
   - Regional Agency-Relationship
   - SDE; University Roles
   - LEA-Designated Roles
   - Communication-Feedback System
   - Advisory Committee—
     - System, Community, Region
   - Project Design, Task Delineation, Implementation
   - Monitoring, Evaluation, Coordination

3. *STAFF*
   Staffing-Acquisition, Selection, Deployment
   Staff Development, Training Program Regarding Needs, Competencies
   Specific Roles, Accountability Measures
   Orientation, Climate, Involvement-Process Elements
4. *PROJECT PROGRAM*
   Needs, Design, Development
   Objectives—Structure; Domains; Program Levels
     Departments; Grade-Instructional Levels
     Courses; Content, Skills, Attitudes
   Relationship to Ongoing Program, to Data about Learners
   Relationship to Regional, Professional Standards
5. *PROGRAM MATERIALS AND RESOURCES*
   Budgeting Implementation
   Acquisition and/or Development of Resources and Media
   Coordination and Utilization
   Curriculum Guides
6. *SUPPORT FEATURES*
   Testing Program, Counseling
   Staff, Learner Evaluation
   Marking Practices, Promotion
   Organizational Structure
   Scheduling-Logistics
   Special Facilities, Equipment
   Research
   Media, Renewal Center
7. *COMMUNITY INVOLVEMENT*
   Participation by Organization, Agencies, Business-Industry
   Experience Sites, Resources
   Personnel, Sites, Resources
   Orientation, Public Relations, Reporting, Media Utilization

Cell Development. The list of School System Components (I-VII) and the Program Possibilities and Requirements (A, B, C, D) intersect to provide cells or possible agenda items to be developed. When the tasks appropriate to each cell are stated, a comprehensive list then has been produced for tasks to be accomplished. Thus, cell number 1 calls for those tasks involving decisions and policies that would be needed in relationship to project guidelines and requirements. For example, if a school were moving towards a more flexible school year, representative tasks for cell 1 might be such items as:

1. Board of education approval of budget and personnel to devote time to this item, to visit, to research, to provide task forces for study, and so forth.
2. An assignment by the administration to an individual or group to proceed with the investigation.
3. A letter of intent from a local education agency to the state board of education.
4. A decision as to the degree and nature of community involvement (prior to

such involvement as suggested in cells 25–28).

5. Decisions regarding time frames, school(s) to be involved, budget, priority in regard to other programs, etc.
6. Others of similar nature.

Cell number 2 tasks would suggest a check of state standards regarding school year requirements and possible alternatives for staff deployment, student attendance, curriculum requirements, and the like.

Thus a series of tasks would be developed to consider systematically components of the system, program possibilities, and requirements. If the task statements were written on cards, notations could also be made as to the likely placement sequence and, in time, the expected production or activity time required to complete the task. Persons or organizational elements could also be suggested. By checking each relevant cell, it would be possible to make a preliminary decision as to the adequacy of the plans-tasks already delineated.

If an outline format was the most comfortable device, the use of the worksheet would result in something akin to the following, assuming each element is appropriate and used:

I. Policy—decision making
   A. State, federal guidelines and requirements (listing of policy tasks as developed)
   B. Standards—state, regional, professional, and national (listing of developed policy tasks)
   C. Local needs and requirements (listing of developed policy tasks)
   D. Exemplary practices from research and professional literature (listing of developed policy tasks)

II. Project leadership and management
   A. State, federal guidelines and requirements (listing of developed leadership and management tasks)
   B. Standards—state, regional, professional, and national (listing of developed leadership tasks to achieve standards)
   C. Local needs and requirements (listing of developed leadership tasks)
   D. Exemplary practices from research and professional literature (listing of developed leadership tasks to incorporate appropriate elements)

III–VII. E., F., . . (Developed and listed when relevant)

An Alternative Format Using Program Phases

An alternative form for task analysis and development is provided in Figure 3.8. In this illustration, a matrix is formed using component areas (left column) and staff development program phases (right column) as listed on the design agenda, pp. 62–65. Cells are numbered for purposes of reference and analysis. The same matrix could be developed using the instructional change elements developed in Chapter 2. Additional tasks would be suggested by using the list of components,

SCHOOL DISTRICT COMPONENTS	*PROGRAM PHASES*									
	Needs	*Objectives*	*Target*	*Means*	*Formats*	*Specifications*	*Development*	*Implementation*	*Evaluate*	*Feedback*
1. Policy-Administrative Decisions	1	8	15	22	29	36	43	50	57	64
2. Project Management	2	9	16	23	30	37	44	51	58	65
3. Staff	3	10	17	24	31	38	45	52	59	66
4. Project Program	4	11	18	25	32	39	46	53	60	67
5. Materials	5	12	19	26	33	40	47	54	61	68
6. Support Features	6	13	20	27	34	41	48	55	62	69
7. Community Involvement	7	14	21	28	35	42	49	56	63	70

FIGURE 3.8 TASK ANALYSIS (Staff Development: Who Does What?).

pp. 75-76 to propose alternatives or sub-tasks. Thus, a planning matrix that uses a more complete listing of relevant components could add significantly to the number of possibilities for consideration or development.

Task delineation is only one part of the total purpose. What has been described is the task dimension; specifically, the jobs to be done if the project is to eventuate successfully, if personnel, budget, and time are to be allocated realistically, and if planning is to anticipate and facilitate essential results.

THE HUMAN RELATIONS DIMENSION

An accompanying and equally critical dimension is the personal and professional growth of participating staff. The human dimension will also require strategy considerations. These factors and forces impinge upon the project in dynamic ways. Thus, it may be important that some tasks be spread over a longer period of time in order to accommodate attitudes, skill development, and consensus, or to establish constructive group processes. It is important that human relations purposes alter any "logical" program sequence or time frame.

Task analysis assumes more than the production of artifacts or the scheduling and management of events; it also requires attention to very personal transactions and process considerations. Staff competencies and relationships make any "imported" design or plan unrealistic in a particular situation, except as a guide or reference. These factors suggest that task analysis and development must be done by those sensitive to both process and product objectives, not by technicians. Task statements can be developed by individuals, by task forces, instructional councils, or other organizational elements. In any case, they must be done in concert with system leadership. Whether the process is highly participatory or limited is a school system decision, its philosophy and style are being represented.[39]

Task statements, however developed, also can include *process* dimensions. Interaction and participation can be built into the ongoing structure; its review is via monitoring, process, or formative evaluation procedures.[40]

Process Elements and Design

What follows is a restatement of many design, guideline, and process elements that have been included in the text. The intent of the listing here is to suggest their relationship to program phases for planning, managing, or evaluating. The following are a few such examples: Are these elements to be included in the *plans* that are made? Are they to be considered key items in the *management* of the change? Are they to be *reviewed* in regard to their adequacy and achievement in the monitoring procedures? In the formative or summative evaluation? To assist with the functional consideration of such questions, each of the following process suggestions includes a list of items representative of the concerns that need to be addressed.

1. *State clearly the nature of the desired program change*
   A. Information gain
   B. Skill-competency development
   C. Attitude, perceptual change, internalization
   D. Organizational, media modification
2. *Seek variety in the means that are used*
   A. Media, materials
   B. Organization-utilization, modification
   C. Information exchange
   D. Resources-facilities
   E. Personnel; differentiating individual and group tasks
   F. Process-oriented approaches
3. *Implement objectives at various program levels*
   A. Objectives at (1) program, (2) school, (3) individual levels and related activities—specify and utilize
   B. Rationale based on involvement and consensus; commitment, understanding
   C. Functional relationship between objectives and program levels, between system objectives and individual performance objectives
   D. Long range and short term objectives
4. *Clarify relationship of improvement project to ongoing programs and processes*
   A. Durability and continuity requiring integral, not "add-on," activities; need, not fad
   B. Stability—use of regular mechanisms and procedures for leadership, processes, change, gains
   C. Permeability—impact upon regular operation and activities as regular, not intermittent, force necessary for gain and influence; change in many elements, not just one
   D. Viability and realism regarding plan and desired outcome; individual and group readiness
5. *Actively-openly seek involvement and commitment*
   A. Continuous check-out of project objectives and personal objectives; morale, climate
   B. Established system organizations, processes, committees, procedures
   C. Multiple leadership, both emergent and status; competition and cooperation
   D. Forces that facilitate and those that restrict; alternatives
   E. Trust, openness; diversity of ideas, independence
   F. Opportunities for testing ideas, brainstorming, assessing status quo
   G. Degree of internalization, feeling, satisfaction, identification

6. *Build in relevant and possible incentives*
   - A. Time—to work, think, perform, visit
   - B. Money—stipend, salary, supplement
   - C. Status—leadership, recognition
   - D. Course credit—in-service, graduate, certification
   - E. Personal-professional gain, satisfaction, and motivation
   - F. Resources, facilities, aides, flexibility
   - G. Local "trade-off" possibilities
7. *Define the management elements that are involved*
   - A. Time frame—calendar time or phases
   - B. Landmarks and intermediate points
     - (1) tasks to be accomplished, outcomes
     - (2) events to be conducted, progress points
     - (3) materials to be produced, progress points
   - C. Organizational structure and decision making
     - (1) developed decision points, decision makers, processes
     - (2) accessible—how to relate, how to be involved
     - (3) known—communicated, understood by participants
   - D. A plan to follow through on objectives
   - E. Communication flow—information, inputs, feelings
   - F. Monitoring, in-process decision making, evaluation
   - G. Interagency (regional-university-schools) relationship
8. *Develop guidelines to clarify process dimensions*
   - A. System "style"—open, participatory; closed, directed
   - B. Nature of involvement by individuals and groups, planned interventions
   - C. Processes to be followed—discussion, consensus, degree of formality, records to be kept, roles and responsibilities
   - D. Relationship to individual, project evaluation
   - E. Basic approach—mandated, problem-solving, heuristic, developmental
9. *Proceed in accordance with the acknowledge support system*
   - A. System policy statements regarding intent, budget, time, personnel; importance of priority stance by Board and administration
   - B. Stated roles of leadership persons such as principals, regional personnel, consultants, curriculum directors, lead teachers, committee chairpersons
   - C. Clarification of relationship with existing routines such as scheduling, standardized testing use of counselors, time and personnel use, resources
   - D. Provision for time—time to think, work, practice, accommodate new ideas
   - E. Use of outside consultants—university, commercial, other school systems, regional, state department of education
   - F. Relationship of project objectives and activities to regular operations
   - G. Critical importance of facilities, resources, media center
10. *Use individual schools as a basic operational unit*
    - A. Leadership—principal and teacher cadre
    - B. Evaluation and accountability
    - C. Achievement—relationship to stated objectives
    - D. Implementation—utilization, contribution; local adaptations

- E. Activity—input, feedback, and participation
- F. Atmosphere, morale, relationships

11. *Include leadership training as an integral element*
    - A. Review of techniques, processes, roles, skills; importance of task achievement, not dependence upon charisma
    - B. Relation to project plan, management concerns; accountability, productivity, and flexibility
    - C. Involvement in evaluation—formative, summative, and process
    - D. Relation to levels of activity—central office, school, work groups, class-teacher performance
    - E. Development of maturity as individuals and groups; group decision making, not coercion: group development as well as production
12. *Clarify and delineate the role of evaluation and research*
    - A. Nature of monitoring—who, when, how
    - B. Relationship or project gains to individual evaluation, to program evaluation
    - C. Use of outside or inside evaluation procedures
    - D. Collection of data—times, purposes
    - E. Use of particular instruments, standards, check points
    - F. Use of guidelines, events, and outcomes as critical elements in evaluation
13. *Develop process for communicating with community*
    - A. Regular meetings, reports, and releases
    - B. Organizational or individual inputs
    - C. Appropriate review, discussion points, and involvement
    - D. Feedback procedures to minimize static and confusion
    - E. Consideration of power groups and influentials
14. *Provide continuous information and feedback to those who are concerned*
    - A. Leadership, participants, consumers
    - B. Establishment of mechanisms for getting and disseminating information and feedback
    - C. Feedback as routine, not crisis operation to establish support and credibility
    - D. Progress reports as substantive gain as well as procedural activity
15. *Build in appropriate standards and developments*
    - A. Relation to state, regional, professional standards, and criteria
    - B. Provision of information flow regarding new and related developments including research
    - C. Development of role expectations and performance criteria
    - D. Reconciliation of differences in expectations and standards from various groups, agencies, and individuals
    - E. Review of legal constraints; local expectations, realistic non-imposed limitations

In Figure 3.9, the guideline and process elements are positioned in relationship to the planning phases, which were proposed earlier in the chapter. The resultant figure provides a technique for developing and systematically reviewing process elements as well as task achievements.

*Representative Process Elements**	*Program Phases***									
	Needs	*Objectives*	*Target*	*Means*	*Formats*	*Specifications*	*Development*	*Implementation*	*Evaluation*	*Feedback*
1. Clarifying nature of desired change	1	16	31	46	61	76	91	106	121	136
2. Utilizing a variety of means	2	17	32	47	62	77	92	107	122	137
3. Implementing objectives at various levels	3	18	33	48	63	78	93	108	123	138
4. Relating project to ongoing programs	4	19	34	49	64	79	94	109	124	139
5. Seeking involvement and commitment	5	20	35	50	65	80	95	110	125	140
6. Incorporating incentives and motivation	6	21	36	51	66	81	96	111	126	141
7. Communicating management elements	7	22	37	52	67	82	97	112	127	142
8. Defining and utilizing process guidelines	8	23	38	53	68	83	98	113	128	143
9. Developing and using support features	9	24	39	54	69	84	99	114	129	144
10. Using individual schools as basic units	10	2[illegible]	40	55	70	85	100	115	130	145
11. Providing related leadership training	11	26	41	56	71	86	101	116	131	146
12. Using monitoring and formative data	12	27	42	57	72	87	102	117	132	147
13. Involving and communicating with community	13	28	43	58	73	88	103	118	133	148
14. Providing feedback and reinforcement	14	29	44	59	74	89	104	119	134	149
15. Relating to standards and developments	15	30	45	60	75	90	105	120	135	150

*Subordinate items for each of these process elements were given on pp. 79-82.
**Program phases are also described in this chapter.

FIGURE 3.9 Relating Process Elements to Program Phases (*Planning*, *Managing*, and *Evaluating*).

For example, process element no. 1, which indicates the concern for clarifying the nature of the desired change, also suggests the need to develop and subsequently check out the various objectives of the change at regular intervals—not just at the initiation or orientation stage. The matrix indicates various points at which individual or group understanding can be reviewed as the project matures. Process element no. 2, which proposes utilizing a variety of means, suggests that several different techniques be provided enroute, rather than a single approach.

Planners can decide the uses to be made of these processes and guidelines by:

1. Determining the importance and relevance of a particular item.
2. Building the process item into the plan (150 possible review points are suggested).
3. Managing the project in such a way that this concern is properly addressed.
4. Evaluating the occurrence and impact of each selected element.

These items also could be cast as program objectives with related means, criteria, and events (implementation). By both formal and informal procedures, individuals or groups can help ascertain utilization, progress, or feeling in regard to them. Obviously, the list is only suggestive. Not all cells can be used in a given project. More direct process objectives (such as improving human relations, providing opportunities for dialogue, increasing the degree of individualizing, and developing more confidence) could be more explicitly stated if they were important objectives of the program.

Likewise, while possible points of interaction and review are shown in a structure, the actual experiencing by participants need not be so structured, much less, be mechanical or pre-programmed. The nature of the desired experiences or encounters, as well as the instruments to be used, can be as formal or informal as desired.

Thus, individual ways of working, personal commitment, degrees of participation, and the like, need not be excluded from the ongoing and comprehensive program strategies. It is important that these considerations be made specific and integral and that process and human relations elements become an important aspect of task analysis, delineation, and evaluation.

SEQUENCING TASKS

Assuming that the list of tasks is adequately representative and comprehensive, the next job is to sequence the stated tasks. One recommended procedure is to categorize the tasks in a time or developmental sequence. A *time* sequence could be a simple calendar using weeks, months, or years—depending upon the extent and duration of the project—or a developmental order (perhaps combined with decisions as to time). The advantage of listing events in a *sequential-developmental* order before the time decisions are made is the greater flexibility that such a procedure provides. The time for the project can easily be expanded or contracted, depending upon budget, personnel, priorities, other ongoing programs, and unanticipated events (budget cuts, personnel changes, new mandates, etc.). Also, the developmental sequence, by definition, provides another look at the adequacy of each event and the flow of work over time. The following continuum based on the model in Chapter 2 is typical:

1. Initiate project or program; orient and involve appropriate staff (and/or students, parents, community, etc.).
2. Establish leadership or management responsibilities, including evaluation, coordination, and accountability measures.
3. Determine needs and collect baseline data.
4. Develop overall program objectives, basic strategy, and structure for continuity; determine target group.
5. Develop design for project, based on objectives; develop necessary and related materials and resources.
6. Validate developed program elements by research and pilot/feasibility study. Decide regarding specific implementation and support needs.
7. Implement program, including staff training, support features, installation procedures and responsibilities.
8. Evaluate achievement of objectives using formative, process data; provide feedback regarding discrepancies and suggested next steps.

Such ordering facilitates the development of a time line, PERT chart, outline, or a similar visualization and structure, which will be discussed in Chapter 8. Events will need to be shown as they relate to other events in the time sequence and in necessary preliminary products. It is likely that the work of sequencing events for purposes of decision making and planning will indicate gaps that need to be filled, tasks that need to be expanded or subdivided, and some items that can be eliminated as duplications or sub-items of more significant tasks.

Examples of Approaches

The design elements and procedures have been used with different groups, different processes, and purposes. The following three examples may be instructive:

1. A school system with a large central staff devoted a whole day to the generation of tasks. After an orientation to the planned work, the staff was divided into seven committees, each representing a school system component area, namely, Policy-Decision Making, Budget and Auditing, Curriculum and Instruction, Support, Community, and Leadership. Each group was given a set of 3 X 5 cards upon which to write the tasks appropriate to their area of responsibility.

After the tasks were written on the cards, each group taped their cards on a three year time line, which was put on a wall of the room. As a follow-up, a task force converted the tasks items into a PERT chart, showing the time and impact (interface) relationships. This was subsequently printed for board of education review and communication with other staff members and community persons.

2. A school system, using a modified Delphi technique, charged a series of committees (task forces) to develop a list of specific tasks and to recommend personnel and procedures for the achievement of each task. These "work packages" were duplicated and discussed further in subsequent staff meetings, and then, a basic plan was developed. Unlike situation no. 1, these separate committees did not share a common time or place until they met to reconcile tasks, time, and personnel. After the group discussion, a second iteration was made wherein the tasks and time elements were reconsidered in light of the group discussion. A working group comprised of chairpersons from the separate task forces did the final compilation for board review and decision making.[41,42]
3. A graduate class studying *supervision of instruction* was given the assignment to generate tasks, a time line, and convergence or dependency points. Elements from the work of various individuals were then used as a class project to develop a generalized plan.

Once experience and proficiency are achieved, such detailed explanations will not be needed. However, the worksheets, the list of components, the planning sequence, and the alternative formats will continue to be useful items that contribute to systematic and comprehensive planning for staff development and instructional improvement programs.

Task Analysis and Professional Competencies

In a particular program, one advantage of carefully defining work in relation to task and process elements is that the analysis lends itself to the development of a critical staff competencies list. These knowledge and skill elements cut across system roles and responsibilities and range from administrators and managers to instructional and support personnel. As different projects are undertaken, the identified competencies can be used to define and determine the tasks and skills most necessary to program success and to develop content for university or extension courses, plus assisting local staff development and curriculum improvement activities.[43]

Also, this information helps supervisors and teachers appraise their own adequacies and provides a base for supervisor–teacher conferences and assistance. Competencies in order of priority can be developed into modules for individual or group study, and for additional research, development, and renewal activities; these uses also lend themselves to university–school system projects and to preparation programs.[44–46]

Job specifications can then be recast on the basis of these experiences and decisions regarding objective/achieving competencies. As role analysis items, they indicate the achievements to be sought and the gains to be anticipated, rather than a general listing of activities in which personnel will engage. Role specifications developed in terms of desired outcomes can minimize such terms as consulting, coordinating, supervisory visiting, conducting meetings, attending conferences, and general leadership. Instead, job statements can be framed as targets to be achieved, change items to be accomplished, and objectives to be realized. Such specifications and role statements become functional monitoring and evaluation measures. Thus, supervisory and leadership reports can relate directly to the improvements for which their services were contracted, not to generalized activities. Such records make accountability and public stewardship an integral function and can minimize the doubts and suspicions with which leadership and supervisory personnel must now contend.[47]

Staff development needs and objectives can be approached using the same general procedure as that for designing programs for learner achievement.[48–51] Staff needs can also be identified as discrepancies between the program objectives and program achievements with special attention given to those skills, attitudes, and the competencies essential to make up the deficit. (Obviously, other system components will also require consideration—such as adequacy of curriculum plans, materials and resources, time allotments, and the like). If the discrepancy between objectives and achievement is too great, it may be necessary to revise objectives or to establish intermediate objectives for achievement within a reasonable time. Such realistic and thoughtful considerations are the hallmarks of good planning and appropriate program response.

One major difference between the planning for learner needs and for staff needs is the role of the participant. While learners should be included in considerations relative to their needs and objectives, no question arises as to the role of staff persons who, by virtue of maturity, preparation, and professional commitment, should be intimately and continuously involved in programs designed to improve their competencies. Without this involvement and participation, staff development projects become manipulative or superficial. Staff insights, knowledge, sensitivities, existing skill levels, and perceived relationships to the desired objectives are critical inputs and facilitating factors. Further, planners must be aware that the approach to adult learners must be different; they already have acquired a reservoir of information and a repetoire of skills. The in-service function, therefore, may well be to assist colleagues in reordering their priorities, refreshing their knowledge about concepts or knowledge, or adapting skills and competencies to the new approach/program. To deprive staff persons of the opportunity to share in this process is to delay or negate the likelihood of achieving the desired objectives.[52,53]

Decision Making and Task Allocation

Once the work packages, the task elements, and the process indicators are developed, analyzed, and sequenced, the plan is ready for decision making, personnel assignment, and resources/means allocation. This is a process of responsible and accountable "sub-contracting." Additional elements are developed in greater detail in Chapter 6. Budgets, personnel, priorities, timing, and total program considerations become important administrative and system decisions at this point.

The decision may be formal or informal. The nature of this step depends upon the status of the project and the planner, and the degree of formality required in a particular system. In many cases, no additional statement will be required. Whatever the policy stance, the decisions made at this point will determine the power, the nature, and the extent of development and implementation phases that follow. Before the time and expense of the development effort, commitment to the proposed treatment must be evident. Without such a commitment, it is useless to proceed; with such a commitment the developers can proceed with appropriate vigor or caution.

The task of *specification* is dependent upon the decision making apparatus of the system. For example, in PPBES applications all objectives including clerical and maintenance would need to be related to program goals and designated budget procedures and codes. This degree of specification is not yet common. However, good planning and design should be apparent whatever the situation.

Program development logically follows. The nature of the development effort has been determined. The work of detailing and developing the substantive elements is described in the next chapter.

ACTION GUIDELINES

Designing is a process of so structuring the elements and means that the stated objectives can be achieved. Standard or imported designs have utility, but they should be modified to fit the local situation. Varied, creative, and qualitative programs require the infusion of individual, school building, and system idiosyncrasies.

Developmental concepts are useful to the planner. These concerns reflect the sequencing of activities for individuals, groups, ideas, and resources in accordance with entry capabilities as well as for the desired outcomes. The flow and timing of these events should reflect a growth pattern appropriate to the target group(s). Stages and sequences are best viewed as flexible constructs that can be used and modified in accordance with the gains that are made. Alternative design features can provide for different rates of change, gain, or accommodation. Comprehensive plans will require the inclusion of individual elements as well as system or school components. Staff development requires modification in attitudes, competencies, and commitments if program elements or product outcomes are to be durable.

Staff development and instructional improvement efforts can be enhanced by process as well as product considerations. The means to be utilized, the nature of involvements and incentives, the conscious attention to personal, professional, and local concerns are among the critical elements to be addressed. Systematic planning results from attention to the many facets of the operation that can or should affect the outcome. A quantitative and accountable program requires a thorough task analysis, which includes the specification of outcomes, responsibilities, resources, and time requirements. The nature of the dialogue and decision making, the processes and procedures employed, and the utilization of human as well as material resources are important indicators of philosophy and style.

RELATED REFERENCES

1. Beauchamp, George, *Curriculum Theory.* 3rd ed., Wilmette, Illinois: Kagg Press, 1975.
2. Hosford, Philip L., *An Instructional Theory: A Beginning.* Englewood Cliffs, New Jersey: Prentice-Hall, 1973.
3. Gross, Neal, and Herriott, Robert, *Staff Leadership in Public Schools.* New York: John Wiley, 1965.
4. Havighurst, Robert J., "Educational Leadership for the Seventies." *Phi Delta Kappan,* 53:403 (1972).
5. Jacobs, James N., and Felix, Joseph L., "Developing Developers: The Race to Improve Education." *Theory into Practice,* 11:225 (1972).
6. Torrance, E. Paul, and Torrance, J. Pansy, *Is Creativity Teachable?* Bloomington, Indiana: Phi Delta Kappa Educational Foundation, 1973.
7. Barnes, Ron E., *Learning Systems for the Future.* Bloomington, Indiana: Phi Delta Kappa Educational Foundation, 1972.
8. Dale Edgar, *Audiovisual Methods in Teaching.* New York: Dryden Press, 1969.
9. Brown, James W., et al., *A-V Instruction: Technology, Media, and Methods.* 4th ed., New York: McGraw-Hill, 1973.
10. McLuhan, Marshall, *Understanding Media: The Extensions of Man.* New York: McGraw-Hill, 1964.
11. National Society for the Study of Education, *Media and Symbols: The Forms of Expression, Communication and Education.* Seventy-third Yearbook, Part I, Chicago: University of Chicago Press, 1974.
12. Wooten, Lutian R., "Media Center: Avenue to Personalized Learning." In *Improving Supervisory Competencies,* edited by Leslee J. Bishop. Georgia Association for Supervision and Curriculum Development and the Center for Curriculum Improvement and Staff Development. Athens, Georgia: The Center, Department of Curriculum and Supervision, University of Georgia, 1973.
13. Jackson, Shirley, "The Curriculum Council: New Hope, New Promise." *Educational Leadersnip,* 29:690 (1972).
14. Macagnoni, Virginia, "Aesthetic Management: Supervision and Democratic Planning Processes." In *Improving Supervisory Competencies,* edited by Leslee J. Bishop. Georgia Association for Supervision and Curriculum Development

and the Center for Curriculum Improvement and Staff Development. Athens, Georgia: The Center, Department of Curriculum and Supervision, University of Georgia, 1973.

15. Schwartz, Henrietta, "When University and Schools Relate." *Educational Leadership*, 30:397 (1973).
16. Tanner, Laurel N., "The School-University Program." *Educational Leadership*, 30:420 (1973).
17. Unruh, Glenys, "Staff Development in University City." *Theory into Practice*, 11:239 (1973).
18. Whatley, R. Steven, "Performing the Change Role Function—The Curriculum Council." In *Improving Supervisory Compentencies*, Supervision and Curriculum Development and the Center for Curriculum Improvement and Staff Development. Athens, Georgia: The Center, Department of Curriculum and Supervision, University of Georgia, 1973.
19. Owens, Robert G., *Organizational Behavior in Schools*. Englewood Cliffs, New Jersey: Prentice-Hall, 1970.
20. Ford, Richard W., "How to Use a Consultant." *Educational Leadership*, 30:116 (1972).
21. Loadman, William E., and Mahan, James M., "The External Consultant and Curriculum Change Strategies." *Theory into Practice*, 11:329 (1972).
22. Educational Technology Supplement, *Saturday Review: Education*. 1:4 (1973) p. 42.
23. Koerner, James, "Educational Technology: Does It Have a Future in the Classroom?" *Saturday Review: Education*. 1:4 (1973) p. 42.
24. Wurman, Richard S., ed., *Yellow Pages for Learning Resources*. Philadelphia: Group for Environmental Education, 1972.
25. McGuffey, Carroll W., *Systematic Planning for Educational Facilities*. Chicago: Simu-School, 1973.
26. Farguhar, Robin H., "New Developments in the Preparation of Educational Leaders." *Phi Delta Kappan*, 54:26 (1972).
27. Harris, Ben M., "Supervisor Effectiveness: A Research Resume." *Educational Leadership*, 30:73 (1972).
28. Berman, Louise M., and Usery, Mary Lou, *Personalized Supervision: Sources and Insights*. Washington, D.C.: Association for Supervision and Curriculum Development, 1966.
29. Perritt, Marshall C., "Professional Growth in the Shelby County Schools." *Theory into Practice*, 11:324 (1972).
30. Bishop, Lloyd K., *Individualizing Educational Systems*. Harper and Row, 1971.
31. Kopp, O. W., and Zufelt, David L., *Personalized Curriculum: Method and Design*. Columbus, Ohio: Charles E. Merrill, 1971.
32. Unruh, Adolph, and Turner, Harold, *Supervision for Change and Innovation*. New York: Houghton-Mifflin, 1970.
33. Jung, Charles, "Instructional Systems for Professional Development." *Theory into Practice*, 11:276 (1972).
34. Redfern, George B., *How to Appraise Teaching Performance*. Columbus, Ohio: School Management Institute, 1963.
35. Rogers, Carl, *Freedom to Learn*. Columbus, Ohio: Charles E. Merrill, 1969.

36. Cook, Desmond L., *PERT: Applications in Education.* Cooperative Research Monograph No. 17. Washington, D.C.: U.S. Government Printing Office, 1966.
37. Curtis, William H., *Educational Resources Management System.* Chicago: Association of School Business Officials, 1971.
38. Hartley, Harry J., *Educational Planning-Programming-Budgeting: A Systems Approach.* Englewood Cliffs, New Jersey: Prentice-Hall, 1968.
39. Feyereisen, Kathryn V., Fiorino, A. John, and Nowak, Arlene T., *Supervision and Curriculum Renewal: A Systems Approach.* New York: Appleton-Century-Crofts, 1970.
40. Sergiovanni, Thomas J., and Starratt, Robert J., *Emerging Patterns of Supervision: Human Perspectives.* New York: McGraw-Hill, 1971.
41. Sweigert, Ray L., "The Delphi Technique: How Well Does It Work in Setting Educational Goals." Paper presented at the annual meeting of the American Education Research Association, Chicago: April, 1974.
42. Weaver, W. Timothy, "The Delphi Forecasting Method." *Phi Delta Kappan,* 52:267 (1971).
43. Culbertson, Jack A., Henson, Curtis, and Morrison, Ruel, *Performance Objectives for School Principals: Concepts and Instruments.* Berkeley, California: McCutchan Publishing Corp., 1974.
44. Florida Department of Education, *Florida Modules on Staff Development.* Bureau of Teacher Education, Knott Building, Tallahassee, Florida 32304.
45. Neagley, Ross, and Evans, N. Dean, *Handbook for Effective Curriculum Development.* Englewood Cliffs, New Jersey: Prentice-Hall, 1967.
46. The School Personnel Utilization Project. Dr. Raymond G. Melton, Florida Department of Education, Tallahassee, Florida 32304.
47. National School Boards Association, *Job Descriptions in Education: Handbook for Developing Performance Job Descriptions.* Evanston, Illinois: author, 1973.
48. Benathy, Bela H., *Instructional Systems.* Belmont, California: Fearon Publishers, 1968.
49. Briggs, Leslie J., *Handbook of Procedures for the Design of Instruction.* Pittsburgh: American Institutes for Research, 1970.
50. Kemp, Jerrold E., *Instructional Design.* Belmont, California: Fearon Publishers, 1971.
51. Popham, W. James, and Baker, Eva L., *Systematic Instruction.* Englewood Cliffs, New Jersey: Prentice-Hall, 1970.
52. Congreve, William J., "Implementing and Evaluating the Use of Innovations." In *Innovation and Change in Reading Instruction,* Sixty-Seventh Yearbook of the National Society for the Study of Education. Chicago: University of Chicago Press, 1968.
53. "Sharing in Change." *Educational Leadership,* Entire issue. 27:326 (1970).

4

Developing

The development phase seeks the achievement of dimension and substance by fleshing out design elements and defined tasks. It is the development of specifics for the instructional plan, and the content and artifacts to be used in achieving the objectives of the curricular or staff development plan. It is the substantive elements to be taught, experienced, and learned—existing as a sub-system within the larger instructional change plan. It is the heart of the instructional effort, the detailing and completion of the task responsibilities—as learning gain for pupils or professional growth for staff.[1-3]

The Tasks

The emphasis in this segment is related to instructional improvement projects. The focus of the development work is the objectives that have been determined, and the necessary content, resources, experiences, standards, instructional strategy, and evaluative measures essential to a qualitative program. It is program delineation built upon the basic objectives, the target personnel, the system means, and the agreed to program formats and specifications. Concern for balance among the domains (cognitive, affective, and psychomotor) should be reflected in both the objectives that have been established and in the planned curricular elements, the activities, and the events that are to be achieved. The same is true for the taxonomic levels; learning objectives and concepts should exhibit an appropriate and qualitative range in the developed content and experience opportunities.

The necessary considerations include degree of learner or staff involvement via didactic or inquiry transactions, the nature and extent of materials, and the timing and use of evaluative measures. However, the work must go beyond generalized expectations; it must result in explication that will impact as implementation. Implementation can only be as good as the design, support, and substantive elements that have been produced.

The task of developing the necessary materials and program content will likely result in writing committees of teachers and/or supervisors. It may be done by consultation with university personnel who are to assist.[4]

Development activities will likely require a search among commercially prepared materials for resources and usable realia. Obviously, the personnel to be involved at this point and the materials to be selected for use depend largely upon the design elements—needs, targets, means, format, and specifications. The quality of the work, likewise, would be indicated by these decisions. This phase is concentrated very often in summer work or in connection with university courses.

A decade of curricular experimentation with hundreds of projects and plans provides one useful base for program guidelines and options.[5,6] The professional literature is full of creative ideas, program approaches, research data, and well developed proposals.[7-17] A consideration of these options can shorten design time. While modifications will be required, a study of the publicized objectives and "validated" innovative programs can provide a significant opportunity for the staff to achieve an overview of possibilities and a new look at the range of specific means. Such a review can assist in the task of providing new possibilities, new routes, new conceptualizations, and alternatives.

INSTRUCTIONAL IMPROVEMENT—ELEMENTS AND FORCES

Instructional improvement efforts, whatever their nature, have many common elements and forces. Teacher competencies, instructional materials for learners, and organizational or media changes all have substantive, process, and context elements that must be conceptualized, developed, and subsequently implemented.

A Model for Development

Most in-service and staff efforts have improvement of the instructional-learning situation as their objective. Therefore, the following model elements warrant examination as a checklist for making the plan for instructional improvement both comprehensive and qualitative. All of the identified elements are present to some degree in any curricular or instructional situation—for young or adult learners. The explication of these elements and the consideration of these forces will facilitate the likelihood that a significant change can be made and that it will endure.

The assumption exists that any significant modification must affect all of the elements given in Figure 4.1. Also, from among them will be certain selected *emphases*, depending upon such factors as staff competency, existing resources, and performance level of the target population. At least three purposes are envisioned for using this model:

1. To assist in analyzing any instructional situation or circumstances by identifying component parts and their interrelationships.
2. To assist in developing the substance of staff development activity, using these elements as the basis for systematic and comprehensive planning so that consideration is given to each element, whether or not it is chosen for development.
3. To assist in analyzing learner or staff needs, and in providing a focus for discussions and research as they relate to ongoing instructional and in-service programs.

The approach to improvement, for example, may center on content, media, instruction, or organization. It is important that the emphasis be clear. While a change in any one instructional element will affect the others to some degree, accuracy in such processes as monitoring, implementing, and evaluating will be greater if the expectations and limitations are clearly established. Clarifying the nature and extent of the staff development or change effort at any one time will provide a more realistic base upon which to build subsequent programs. To do otherwise is to risk professional credibility and staff morale.

Figure 4.1 illustrates the dynamic relationship existing among the various elements. Persons familiar with design will recognize them as standard items used in the study of curriculum and instruction. They are also used in the development of learning units and as the framework for developing curriculum guides.

For completeness and durability in implementation, some modification must be made in all elements, even though the activity may focus on one. *Completeness* requires that all the supporting elements both impact upon and be reflective of the desired change. *Durability* requires modification in all; otherwise, the unchanged items will soon absorb or abort the change. For example, it is useless to attempt to change the content of a course or its methodology without changing the materials of instruction, instructional strategies, and evaluative measures. Of note is the *centrality of objectives.*[18]

In the required examination of variables that affect curriculum and instruction, educational leaders are confronted with multiple, and at times, conflicting pressures. Comprehensive project planning and program development become significant and substantive responses to the problems and needs that must be met. A systematic approach requires a consideration, and at times, a reconciliation of constraints or resources as they infringe, impinge, or assist. What follows is not a complete list, rather, a suggested way of patterning representative items for planning purposes.

Each project situation, each school, and each program emphasis will encounter a different combination of elements, and a different weighing of the forces that facilitate or inhibit. It behooves leadership and management to consider, communicate, and contend with these

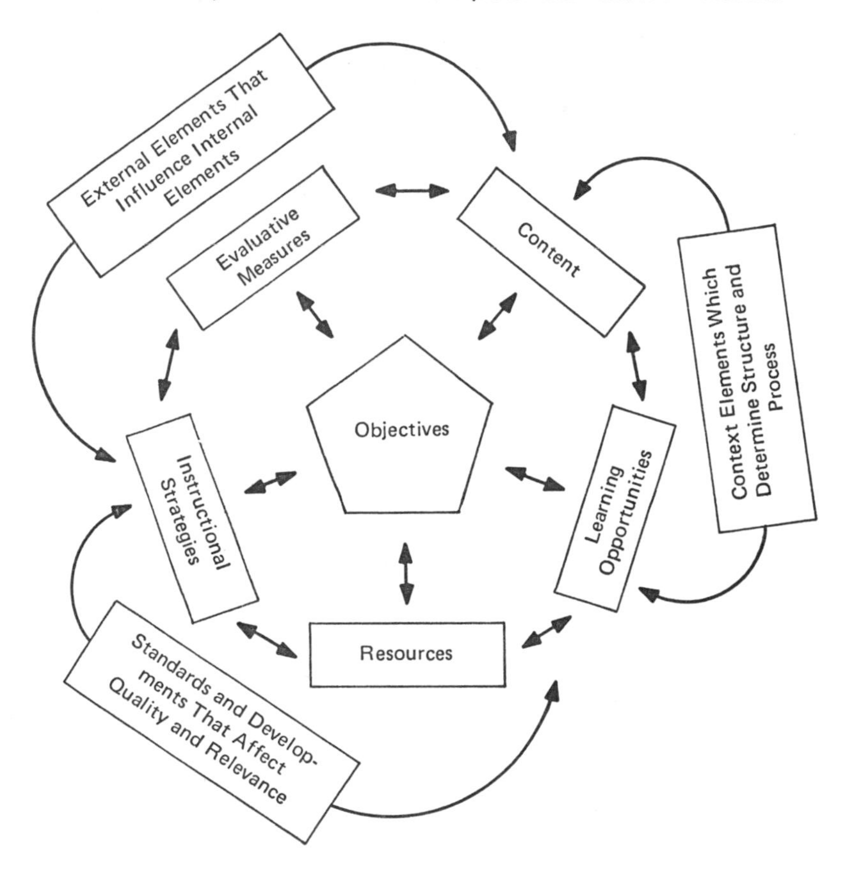

FIGURE 4.1 Program Development For Staff or Learners.

interacting elements. Also, leadership and management must proceed on the assumption that education and schooling are complex and require more adequate handling of complexity than has been true in the past. The failure rate for significant change is too high. Basic modifications are required, rather than tinkering, piecemealing, or instituting ad hoc activities.

Impact from External Elements

External elements consist of pressures from society and the immediate community, having both a direct and an indirect influence upon the priorities and processes that transpire within a school system or classroom.[19-25] An increasingly evident pressure is exerted by government, both state and federal. Guidelines, funding requirements, and legal concerns have a pervading influence upon the organizations of school districts, individual schools, and teachers. Necessary compliance as well as allocation of resources become essential considerations. Governments require that certain days be observed, that certain courses be taught, and that textbooks be from a particular list. They often specify attendance days and hours, graduation requirements, adequate record keeping, and accounting. Certain broad goals or values are assumed in the regulations, which become much more specific as they are tailored for a particular district or locality.[26-29]

Community agencies exert powerful influences through special pressure groups: religious, political, economic, civic, social, or parental. Individuals with status positions or power bases affect the nature of decisions as do the stance of organizations contributing to the shaping of public and private opinion; however, less discernible are value orientations that relate to economic and social aspirations, life-style considerations, and various "ethics"—work or play.[30-34]

Some would suggest that schools and teachers have reacted too timidly. This view holds that educators avoid the dynamics of survival and quality, that they too lightly dismiss the interplay of cultures and the realities of interdisciplinary existence, and that through the curriculum they have consigned reality to an abstraction that considers value confrontation an intrusion. Also, it is believed that the single textbook, isolated classrooms, and proprietary and specialized disciplines have combined with enervating rules and routines to draw the lines too tight about the instructional act and the curricular intent.[35-40] This view would also hold that learning requires sites other than just the school, personnel other than just teachers, and, that experience should be expanded by a reduction in legal and institutional requirements and include multi-age, community, commercial, industrial, agency, and service arenas.

These pressures for change, or for continuity, affect the nature of generalized aims and priorities, the impositions of constraints, and the allocation of resources. Such forces affect how curricular, staff, or instructional changes are generated and shaped, how the response is managed, and how the program content is named. They are reflected in broad concerns for strategy, priorities, consensus, public relations, and community involvement.[41-43] They surface as criticisms, as concerns for alternatives and accountability, as constraints regarding the use of funds and resources, and as requirements to add tests, norms, and participation. The intent here is not to exorcise them, but to propose that they be included as significant elements with which to work. The "target" discussion, Chapter 2 (Figure 2.5), provides one way of systematically visualizing various pressures and relationships.

Standards and Developments

Powerful influences also operate from professional groups, associations, commercial developments, foreign practices, and successful innovative or leadership institutions. Among the inclusions here would be regional accreditation standards, state standards, professional standards, and certification and staffing regulations. National and statewide testing has forced a new look at outcomes and learner achievement levels. Media and commercial interests present powerful and sometimes attractive "alternatives" that can quickly become requirements. Witness the use of computers, cassettes, programmed materials, audio-taped instructional kits, and electronic calculators—to name a few. National commissions propose problems, alternatives, and research requiring study and decision making.[44-55]

Research and development in the various subject fields, standards of scholarship, and concern for essentials, relevance, and improved methodology are constant pressures. In every discipline, organizational level, or mode of inquiry, reminders as to what constitutes quality expectations are offered by professional and popular literature. These criteria must be reconciled with existing local practices, competencies, and resource uses. In addition, new developments in science, space, ecology, energy, pollution, conservation, and world-wide power relationships add new content and require new procedures to meet changing conditions and expectations.[56,57]

Other pressures arise from staff members, parents, and learners as to what rules, competencies, outcomes, and standards should exist. Professional organizations, unions, and business interests demand an increasing involvement and particular adjustments. Student and ethnic rights groups are better organized and more articulate about their concerns. These values, perceptions, and resources are facilitating factors to be built upon; they are elements to be examined when concerns surface or when program improvements are needed to eliminate inadequacies in order to raise standards or to generate effective response.[58-60]

Contextual Elements

The organizational, process, or structural features that affect instructional or curricular design comprise the contextual elements. They exist as policies and practices to determine administrative procedures, physical facilities or arrangements, departmentalization, promotion, staff utilization, and staff and learner differentiation and grouping. These factors involve the nature of an access to media and other instructional materials as well as the relationships with community resources, sites, and personnel. They are reflected in the administrative style, the degree of trust, the nature and process of decision making, and the operative system of control, incentive, and reinforcement. These are value as well as process considerations.[61-66] Such viewpoints affect the kinds of problems that will be selected and the nature of the responses that are possible.

Many school district, personnel, and process dimensions are to be considered; for example, whether a school or district is centralized or decentralized in its structure and support features, whether it is open or closed in its philosophy, and whether it operates from a long range or crisis orientation. What exists concerning interdisciplinary approaches, flexibility in content, readiness for change, and the nature and impact of supervision? What is the impact of negotiations from the professional as well as from the school district organization? What are the competency levels of leadership, of staff, of learners, of support personnel; and how do these factors relate to concepts of adequacy and to the utilization of test or evaluation data? Can the planned project build upon previous successes or is it necessary to initiate new achievement patterns and processes? Are the budget, proposed time frame, and task allocations adequate to the expected researching, writing, and planning? Are the priorities and policies clear and explicit?

As indicated, the listing of items is suggestive, not complete; the intent is to propose representative influences and norms that contribute to the shaping of instructional plans—whether for learners or staff persons. Developing a design and its substance is not performed in a vacuum; rather, it requires a complex matrix that realistically examines, structures, and contends with the critical existing variables.

Internal Elements

Objectives are the goals to be achieved and the specific behaviors to be taught and learned. Ideally, they will reflect individual and substantive items in addition to social and institutional aspirations. The concern here is for performance outcomes, those central to the structuring of the other instructional elements. Developmental levels, learner needs, content areas, attitudes, skills, taxonomies, and domains offer structures from which to draw the specifics for students. Personal and professional aspirations, morale, institutional adequacy, self-awareness, improved learner relations, and resources and their use offer bases for staff objectives. See Figure 4.2; also, Chapter 2 and Appendix B discuss these items in greater depth.[67-69]

Content is a category for considering what particular information is to be studied or what skills or competencies are to be attained in order to meet the objectives. Content may be indicated as information, concepts, skills, modes of investigation, or instructional processes to be learned. The way in which content is organized will depend upon the nature of the objectives and the organization and philosophy of the system. "Content" represents the concern for the *substantive* elements of curriculum and instruction. The scope, breadth and depth, is an important consideration, as is sequencing—the order of items to be considered. The selection of the content to be investigated also depends upon developmental growth, placement of other and related content items, learner or staff achievement to date, expectations, relevance to the learner, and other factors discussed in connection with the various instructional elements and the target population.[70-75]

Content as determined for staff and/or learners should relate directly to the discrepancies identified in connection with the needs assessment, and, to the related competencies necessary to eliminate the deficiencies in meeting the determined goals and objectives. Substance or content includes more than "subject matter," which is usually per-

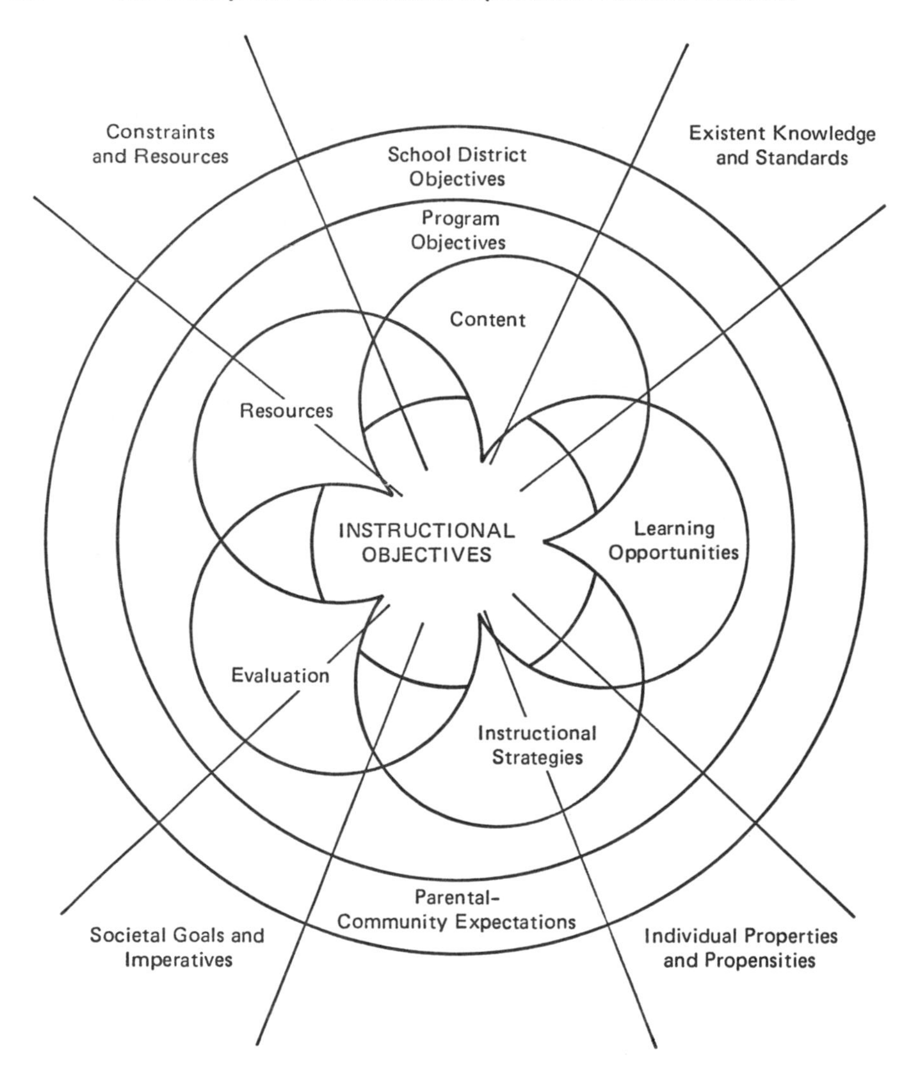

FIGURE 4.2 Objectives—Focal Point for Planning.

ceived as information or concepts from the discipline areas of English, social studies, mathematics, and so forth.[76-79] The content of a project for staff persons may consist of skills and knowledge about new media and how they can best be utilized; as well as the rationale relative to staff differentiation with the related research, interpersonal concerns, and necessary conditions. It also may relate to the experience and data base for instituting a four-quarter school year. Thus, "content" includes professional literature, research, skill acquisition, and the other necessary information and behaviors essential to the project(s) being undertaken. For example, accompanied by an understanding of the change process, of the program structure, and of the management and evaluation plans, content also becomes a concern for broader meaning and application as an integral feature of its substantive dimensions.

Resources are the media, materials, and realia to be used in connection with the selected objectives and content. School or community personnel and outside consultants belong in this category as surely as do the expected items: language or science laboratory, the library or media center, facilities for vocational, technical, or homemaking classes, specialized art, photography, television, and related resources and learning sites, classroom supplies, learning packets or A–V kits, and individualized cassettes or textbooks. All of these developments demonstrate that resource elements have become more central in planning and utilization. These were previously considered at length in Chapter 3—in connection with the *means* to be used.[80–86]

Learning Opportunities are the activities, the plans for what learners or staff persons do in connection with objectives, content, and resources. They are the counterpart of the instructional strategy. They reflect the orientation of the community and staff regarding the role of the learner from direct or contrived experiences to visual or verbal signals. Current examples include the use of communities in the Parkway Plan, the production of the *Foxfire* books, the development and use of learning centers, and the great variety of mediated, programmed, and computer applications. The school, staff, and community can preplan and provide opportunity, objectives, and resources; however, the quality of the educative experience is highly dependent upon the individuals who are involved and the nature of their involvement.[87–97]

Instructional strategies are the plans for managing the learning environment in order to provide learning opportunities and meet objectives. Whether the procedures are named modes, strategies, approaches, or whatever, they involve the methods used—lecture, demonstration, committee activity, tutoring, individual study, group discussion, laboratory work, case study, library use, trip, programmed instruction, community utilization, etc., along with similar concerns for motivating, sequencing, pacing, and grouping.[98–101] Research regarding teaching—learning styles, interaction analysis, and instructional gain—suggests the importance of a variety of approaches. Inquiry, gaming, simulation, discovery, problem solving, "hands on" activities, individualization, openness both for classroom and school, and media utilizations are among those high in current interest (see Appendix E). How much time to devote to a given topic, skill, or concept is an important question.[102–109]

Strategy is not value or content free;[110–112] the methods used reflect the attitude of the planners toward the learners and their roles, competencies, and participation—especially in such approaches as behavior modification or learner contracts. Thus, the instructional approach includes a substantive concern that affects the information or skills to be achieved. Seldom is information or inspiration enough; also required is real and simulated experiencing that will provide the confidence and practice necessary to deliver the desired objectives. The activities related to the development phase are designed to result in the implementation of the desired outcomes. Therefore, they represent a significant contribution toward these ends.

Evaluative measures reflect the concern for participant progress as well as facility and program adequacy. These are designed to assess utilization, feeling, and achievement at program, school, classroom, staff, or individual learner levels. Some measures will be for process determining or monitoring; others will be terminal, e.g., at the end of an activity, lesson, unit, or term. Instruments may range from formal tests to a variety of observational and self-assessment techniques. Evaluation is a process that seeks to identify and determine gains, the nature or extent of discrepancies among the objectives, the procedures, and the resources employed. It also should assist in the ordering and structuring of all other elements.[113-123] Evaluative measures provide critical feedback data for decision making and self-correcting processes; they are the major focus of Chapter 6. These dynamic elements interact in every instructional situation. Concerns for balance and adequacy are essential to a qualitative program for youth or adult learners and require systematic and continuous evaluative procedures.

The model just discussed presents, basically, a "check-out" rather than a "dynamic" plan or model—no sequential action being specified. Instead, the particulars to be developed are shown as they relate to each other. Their ordering and timing are important leadership and participant decisions.

A standard procedure is to use these elements and structures as the basis for building instructional units or learning packets and for writing course outlines, mini-courses, or curriculum guides. A sequence can be built into the materials as they are developed; one such format would be:

Unit (or project area)____________________

Specific unit (or project activity) title____________________

____

General objective____________________

____

Introduction (relationship to other units and objectives, or rationale)

____

Specific Objectives	*Content*	*Activities*	*Resources*	*Evaluation*

Another utilization of the model elements involves the development of learning packets or instructional modules for staff persons. These materials range from compilations of information to highly programmed and structured approaches to instruction. The organization is essentially the same, but the modules are likely to be more self-contained than are units or curriculum guides. For example, it is common practice to provide the following items:

- General or interim objectives that indicate the nature of the module and its relationship to other objectives or activities.
- Specific outcome or product objectives that specify the learnings to be achieved if the module and learner perform as indicated.
- Specified activities that may include reading, developing, generalizations based on the material, individual or group activity, worksheets, research, simulation, experimentation, or visitation.
- Achievement levels or learning routes that propose alternative activities as they relate to a particular mode of activity, or performance levels that range from knowing or repeating information through application and managing or directing such activities.
- Related and usually accompanying materials. These may be readings that are included, bibliographical references for further study, audio or video tapes, films, flip charts and film strips, or other media.
- Evaluative measures that may include pre- and post-tests, observer reports, logs, diaries, supervisor reports, or standard testing procedures. Some modules include an evaluation of both the module and also the achievement made by the individual engaged in its use. Whether these are self-testing or depend upon an external evaluator becomes an option in building or using the module.

Other refinements or utilizations may be included. The modules can be stored for personal use when desired, e.g., in professional library or school office. They may be required for a particular course, job, credential, or advancement. They may require group consideration and evaluation, or, may include the production of materials that are reviewed. Because of their flexibility, modules have become an integral part of many preparation programs, in-service or staff development projects, and as introductory or culminating items where combinations of individual and group activities are productive. New media possibilities have extended the range of possibilities for such utilizations, concerns for developed competencies have added impetus to their use, and the need for specification in objectives, activities, and outcomes has made module production a professional skill and has made module utilization an expected experience.

It is important that the persons responsible for the program elements, which are to be developed and used, be capable of discharging the related duties. This requires a melding of design features with staff competencies, a requirement that exists whether the proposed program elements are intended for learners or staff. It is in this connection that the following model (Figure 4.3) is presented for consideration and application.

INSTRUCTIONAL COMPONENTS	*INSTRUCTIONAL COMPETENCIES-DESCRIPTORS*							
	Know, Understand, Comprehend, Be Aware	*Respond, Relate, Assist, Communicate, Utilize*	*Implement, Facilitate, Coordinate, Consult*	*Initiate, Observe, Modify, Develop*	*Organize, Direct, Monitor*	*Analyze, Research, Evaluate*	*Structure, Conceptualize, Design*	*Manage, Decide, Administer*
External Elements 1. Social and Cultural	1	10	19	28	37	46	55	64
2. Context-Structure and Process	2	11	20	29	38	47	56	65
3. Standards and Development	3	12	21	30	39	48	57	66
Internal Elements 1. Objectives	4	13	22	31	40	49	58	67
2. Content	5	14	23	32	41	50	59	68
3. Resources	6	15	24	33	42	51	60	69
4. Learning Opportunities	7	16	25	34	43	52	61	70
5. Instructional Strategies	8	17	26	35	44	53	62	71
6. Evaluative Measures	9	18	27	36	45	54	63	72

FIGURE 4.3 **Instructional Components and Competencies.**

COMPETENCY AND ACCOUNTABILITY DIMENSIONS

Once the basic program structure and substance have been determined, many applications and possibilities then naturally flow. The instructional components previously introduced are listed in the following matrix with a rough taxonomy evident in the competency indicators. It is intended that the indicators suggest competencies increasing in complexity, power, responsibility, and accountability as they move from left to right. Clusters of words are given in each column to suggest roles and tasks; therefore, each column, rather than each word, should be used as the key to the suggested competency level. It should also be recognized that roles do not remain static; they depend upon the context and the level of responsibility within the school system, and with the phase of planning being considered—in this case, development. Items in the horizontal dimension (descriptors, competencies) or in the vertical dimension (instructional components) of the matrix should not be considered final as listed.

In connection with a project or program, one of the following may be needed to add as a third dimension to the model items (Figure 4.3). The list below provides additional ways to use the model ideas to generate other applications.

1. Develop statements of desired *competencies* for each cell that relates to leadership persons, instructional personnel, or others. Certain cells will likely be priorities in a given situation.
2. Determine basic *instructional elements* to be developed to achieve a given level of performance as a part of a university course, school workshop, or a particular curricular development or project.
3. Establish *accountability measures* (objectives, monitoring, intervention strategies) for those responsible for a particular development.
4. *Conduct research* via formal or informal procedures and/or instruments regarding the adequacy of existing operational or desired instructional elements.
5. Assign instructional *leadership roles* at various levels for particular cells, e.g.,
   a. System-wide
   b. Individual school
   c. Grade level or department
   d. Classroom or learning site.
6. Study the *past, present, and likely future* of a particular element or series of elements.
7. Develop the ingredients of individual cells for further intensive investigation or *as modules for individual study.*
8. Identify and analyze appropriate *process technologies or techniques* to assist with particular instructional elements, cells, or sequences (see Appendix E).
9. Produce *guidelines, process, or policy statements* regarding the stance of the school or district in regard to developing or implementing particular instructional elements.
10. Determine the *priority elements* and specify their performance or impact level in regard to a particular program.

11. Designate priority elements and competency levels for intensive *preservice, in-service, or clinic sessions* for target personnel.[124]

Thus, the intent of the matrix, including instructional components and competency descriptors, is to propose alternatives, possible combinations, and comprehensive review. Cells (or clusters) could be ordered in priority ranking or by weighing procedures for a particular project, for a role to be performed, or for a study program to be developed. It may be desirable to collapse the list of competencies into fewer clusters, thus limiting the cell areas to be considered and developed. The dialogue attendant to such considerations and decisions would be useful in building in the concerns and perceptions of many persons, and would create a base for the subsequent work to be done. It is unlikely that all the possible cells would represent priority matters. However, the development phase is crucial and can be useful in providing important opportunities for such interaction, decision regarding focus, and proprietorship by the involved personnel at this phase. Obviously, these further refinements of the development phase are similar to those proposed in the design phase (Chapter 3), where roles and design competencies were considered. They could also be scheduled as part of the pre-operation phase of implementation, to be discussed in the next chapter.

Program development is the process of writing or finding those content and skill elements, plus activities, strategies, and resources, which will achieve the objectives in an effective and efficient manner. It is "putting meat on the bones" of design; it is providing the plan and the *substance* that is called "curriculum" or program. Thus, development "implements" the objectives of the design (but not the program),[125-128] which requires installation and operation as discussed in Chapter 6.

It should be recognized that each instructional element (objectives, content, and so forth) also provides necessary clues as to what *support* efforts will be required to develop and sustain these elements. Thus, the items are not only useful in the development phase, but also, in the implementation and maintenance phases that follow. Each element requires leadership, data, and resources. Each is an area for staff development effort whenever evidence indicates that the persons charged with development responsibilities are not prepared to go ahead without training or assistance. Development activities represent unique researching, organizing, and language skills; these cannot be assumed.

The next task is to implement or institutionalize the developed program. Persons involved in the development phase will have furthered this process—as they functionally internalized the objectives, accepted and responded to the new content, and developed a commitment to the ideas. The tasks, roles, functions, and strategies for program implementation provide the subject matter of the next chapter.

ACTION GUIDELINES

The development phase involves the expansion and explication of objectives and design features. Those persons who will use and implement the developed materials should participate in this process and product. Participation is a crucial means to capture expertise as well as the experience and personal dimensions. Proprietorship and commitment are also critical ingredients of this phase; therefore, involvement is a necessity as well as a strategy.

Developing program ideas into products and activities requires a knowledge of the complex and powerful forces that impinge upon improvement efforts. Thus, conscious attention should be directed to the external and internal dynamics that will modify the substantive, procedural, and contextual elements. Similarly, comprehensive planning requires the knowledge and use of the various instructional ingredients. Objectives, instructional strategies, resources, evaluation, content, organization, learner experiences, and support are among the crucial areas to be addressed.

The development phases presents a functional opportunity for the assessment, development, and utilization of the competencies necessary to implement the project or program. Such activities both anticipate and enhance the implementation phase that is to follow. Leadership can often be diffused at this juncture as various persons assume responsibilities for the materials and plans for which they are to be responsible. Good data, adequate resources, quality criteria, and time for work are important leadership concerns.

RELATED REFERENCES

1. Bruner, Jerome S., *Toward a Theory of Instruction.* New York: W. W. Norton and Company, 1968.
2. yereisen, Kathryn, Fiorino, A. John, and Nowak, Arlene T., *Supervision and Curriculum Renewal: A Systems Approach.* New York: Appleton-Century-Crofts, 1970.
3. Hudgins, Bryce, *The Institutional Process.* Chicago: Rand McNally, 1971.
4. Zenger, Weldon F., and Zenger, Sharon K., *Writing and Evaluating Curriculum Guides.* Belmont, California: Fearon Publishers, 1973.
5. Halverson, Paul M., ed., *Curriculum Innovations 1966: Trends and Issues.* Syracuse, New York: Syracuse University Press, 1966.
6. Unruh, Glenys G., ed., *New Curriculum Developments.* Washington, D.C.: Association for Supervision and Curriculum Development, 1968.
7. Eisner, Elliot W., and Vallance, Elizabeth, eds., *Conflicting Conceptions of Curriculum.* Berkeley, California: McCutchan Publishing Corp., 1974.
8. Esbensen, Thorwald, *Working with Individualized Instruction: The Duluth Experience.* Palo Alto, California: Fearon Publishing, 1968.

9. Fantini, Mario, *Public Schools of Choice: A Plan for the Reform of American Education.* New York: Simon and Schuster, 1973.
10. Henrie, Samuel N., ed., *A Sourcebook of Elementary Curriculum Programs and Projects.* San Francisco: Far West Laboratory for Educational Research and Development, 1972.
11. Hillson, Maurie, and Bongo, Joseph, *Continuous-Progress Education: A Practical Approach.* Chicago: Science Research Associates, 1971.
12. Hyman, Ronald T., *Approaches in Curriculum.* Englewood Cliffs, New Jersey: Prentice-Hall, 1973.
13. Inlow, Gail, *The Emergent in Curriculum.* New York: John Wiley and Sons, 1965.
14. National Advisory Council on Supplementary Centers and Services, *Innovative Education Practices.* Washington, D.C.: George Washington University, October, 1973.
15. Reimer, Everett, *School Is Dead: Alternatives to Education.* New York: Doubleday, 1971.
16. Saxe, Richard W., ed., *Opening the Schools: Alternative Ways of Learning.* Berkeley, California: McCutchan Publishing Corp., 1972.
17. Weinstein, Gerald, and Fantini, Mario, eds., *Toward Humanistic Education: A Curriculum of Affect.* New York: Praeger Publishers, Inc., 1970.
18. Bishop, Leslee J., "The Centrality of Objectives." In *Improving Supervisory Competencies,* edited by Leslee J. Bishop. Georgia Association for Supervision and Curriculum Development and the Center for Curriculum Improvement and Staff Development and the Center for Curriculum Improvement and Staff Development. Athens, Georgia: The Center, Department of Curriculum and Supervision, University of Georgia, 1973.
19. Association for Supervision and Curriculum Development, *Curriculum Decisions and Social Realities.* Edited by Robert R. Leeper. Washington, D.C.: author, 1968.
20. Gwynn, J. Minor, and Chase, John B., *Curriculum Principles and Social Trends.* 4th ed. Toronto: Macmillan, 1969.
21. Hass, Glen, Wiles, Kimball, and Bondi, Joseph, eds., *Readings in Curriculum.* 2nd ed. Boston: Allyn and Bacon, 1970.
22. Illich, Ivan, *Deschooling Society.* New York: Harper and Row, 1971.
23. National Society for the Study of Education, *The Curriculum: Retrospect and Prospect.* Seventieth Yearbook, Part I. Chicago: University of Chicago Press, 1971.
24. Saylor, J. Galen, and Alexander, William, *Planning Curriculum for Schools.* Holt, Rinehart, and Winston, 1974.
25. Smith, B. Othanel, Stanley, William O., and Shores, J. Harlan, *Fundamentals of Curriculum Development.* (Rev. ed.) New York: Harcourt, Brace, and World, 1957.
26. Cay, Donald F., *Curriculum: Design for Learning.* New York: Bobbs-Merrill, 1966.
27. Morphet, Edgar L., Johns, Roe L., and Reller, Theodore L., *Educational Organization and Administration.* 2nd ed. Englewood Cliffs, New Jersey: Prentice-Hall, 1967.
28. Oliver, Albert I., *Curriculum Improvement.* New York: Dodd, Mead, and

Company, 1971.
29. Taba, Hilda, *Curriculum Development: Theory and Practice.* New York: Harcourt, Brace, and World, 1962.
30. Dodson, Donald, *Power Conflict and Community Organization.* New York: Council for American Unity, 1967.
31. Keniston, Kenneth, *The Uncommitted: Alienated Youth in American Society.* New York: Dell, 1965.
32. Kimbrough, Ralph B., *Political Power and Educational Decision Making.* Chicago: Rand McNally, 1964.
33. Pinar, William, ed., *Heightened Conscoiusness, Cultural Revolution.* Berkeley, California: McCutchan Publishing Corp., 1974.
34. Warren, Donald I., and Warren, Rachelle, "Six Kinds of Neighborhoods: Parochial, Diffuse, or Stepping-Stone?" *Psychology Today,* 9:1 (1975), p. 74.
35. Goodman, Paul, *Compulsory Mis-Education.* New York: Horizon Press, 1964.
36. Herndon, James, *The Way It Spozed to Be.* New York: Simon and Schuster, 1968.
37. Holt, John, *How Children Fail.* New York: Dell, 1964.
38. _______, *How Children Learn.* New York: Pitman Publishing Co., 1967.
39. Kozol, Jonathan, *Death at an Early Age.* Boston: Houghton Mifflin, 1967.
40. ___________, *Free Schools.* Boston: Houghton Mifflin, 1972.
41. Burns, Richard, and Brooks, Gary, eds., *Curriculum Design in a Changing Society.* Englewood Cliffs, New Jersey: Educational Technology Publications, 1972.
42. Campbell, Clyde M., "Coordinating Leadership in Resource Use." *Educational Leadership,* 30:110 (1972).
43. Downey, Lawrence, *The Secondary Phase of Education.* New York: Blaisdell Publishing Co., 1965.
44. American Association of School Librarians, *Media Programs: District and School.* Washington, D.C.: American Library Association, 1975.
45. American Library Association, Personnel Publications Committee, *Personnel Organization and Procedure.* 2nd ed. Chicago: author, 1968.
46. Georgia Department of Education, *Standards for Public Schools of Georgia 1974.* State Board of Education. Atlanta: author, 1974.
47. Weinstock, Ruth, *The Greening of the High School.* A report by Ruth Weinstock on a conference co-sponsored by Educational Facilities Laboratories, Inc., and Institute for Development of Educational Activities, Inc. New York: Educational Facilities Laboratories, Inc., 1973.
48. "Improvement in Secondary Education." In *Continuity and Discontinuity,* edited by the Carnegie Commission on Higher Education. New York: McGraw-Hill, 1973.
49. "Library Resource Centers in Schools, Colleges, and Institutions of Higher Education: A General Policy Statement." *Library Association Record,* 75:52 (1973).
50. Miller, Richard I., *Selecting New Aids to Teaching.* Washington, D.C.: Association for Supervision and Curriculum Development, 1971.
51. National Association of Secondary School Principals, *American Youth in the Mid-Seventies.* Conference Report of the National Committee on Secondary Education. Washington, D.C.: author, 1973.

52. *The Reform of Secondary Education.* National Commission on the Reform of Secondary Education, B. Frank Brown, Chairman. Washington, D.C.: McGraw-Hill, 1973.
53. Southern Association of Colleges and Schools, *Guide to the Evaluation and Accreditation of Secondary Schools.* Commission on Secondary Schools. Atlanta: author, 1973.
54. Southern Association of Colleges and Schools, *Principles and Standards of Membership.* Commission on Secondary Schools. Atlanta: author, 1973.
55. *Standards of Quality and Objectives for Public Schools in Virginia, 1974-76.* Richmond: Virginia Department of Education, 1976.
56. Bronwell, Alfred B., ed., *Science and Technology in the World of the Future.* New York: John Wiley and Sons, 1971.
57. Krug, Mark, *What Will be Taught—The Next Decade.* Itasca, Illinois: F. E. Peacock Publishers, 1972.
58. Banks, James A., "The Imperatives of Ethnic Minority Education." *Phi Delta Kappan,* 53:268 (1972).
59. Curriculum for Economic and Ethnic Diversity, *Educational Leadership.* Entire issue, 31:579 (1974).
60. "Student Unrest." Chapter 2 in *Crucial Issues in Contemporary Education,* edited by Theodore W. Hipple. Pacific Palisades, California: Goodyear Publishing Co., 1973.
61. Association for Supervision and Curriculum Development, *Freedom, Bureaucracy, and Schooling.* Yearbook. Washington, D.C.: author, 1971.
62. Gilchrist, Robert S., and Roberts, Bernice R., *Curriculum Development: A Humanized System.* Belmont, California: Fearon Publishers, 1974.
63. Goodlad, John I., *School, Curriculum, and the Individual.* Waltham, Massachusetts: Blaisdell Publishing Co., 1966.
64. Lawler, Marcella, ed., *Strategies for Planned Curricular Innovations.* New York: Teachers College Press, 1970.
65. Petrequin, Gaynor, *Individualizing Learning Through Modular-Flexible Programming.* New York: McGraw-Hill, 1968.
66. Rosenthal, Robert, and Jacobson, Lenore, *Pygmalion in the Classroom.* New York: Holt, Rinehart, and Winston, 1968.
67. Eiss, Albert F., and Harbeck, Mary, *Behavioral Objectives in the Affective Domain.* Washington, D.C.: National Science Supervisors Association, 1969.
68. Mager, Robert F., *Preparing Instructional Objectives.* Belmont, California: Fearon Publishing Co., 1962.
69. Tyler, Ralph W., *Basic Principles of Curriculum and Instruction.* Chicago: University of Chicago Press, 1950.
70. Berman, Louise, *New Priorities in the Curriculum.* Columbus, Ohio: Charles E. Merrill Publishing, 1968.
71. Firth, Gerald R., and Kimpston, Richard, *The Curriculum Continuum in Perspective.* Itasca, Illinois: F. E. Peacock, 1973.
72. Glass, Bentley, *The Timely and the Timeless: The Interrelationships of Science, Education, and Society.* New York: Basic Books, 1970.
73. National Education Association, *Rational Planning in Curriculum and Instruction.* Washington, D.C.: Center for the Study of Instruction, 1967.
74. Parker, J. Cecil, and Rubin, Louis J., *Process as Content.* Chicago: Rand McNally, 1966.

75. Van Til, William, ed., *Curriculum: Quest for Relevance.* 2nd ed. Boston: Houghton Mifflin, 1974.
76. Association for Supervision and Curriculum Development, *New Insights and the Curriculum.* Yearbook. Washington, D.C.: author, 1963.
77. Bruner, Jerome S., *The Process of Education.* Cambridge, Massachusetts: Harvard University Press, 1961.
78. Frazier, Alexander, ed., *A Curriculum for Children.* Washington, D.C.: Association for Supervision and Curriculum Development, 1969.
79. King, Arthur P., and Brownell, John A., *The Curriculum and the Disciplines of Knowledge.* New York: John Wiley and Sons, 1966.
80. Briggs, Leslie J., et al., *Instructional Media: A Procedure for the Design of Multi-Media Instruction.* Pittsburgh: American Institutes for Research, 1967.
81. Dale, Edgar, *Audiovisual Methods in Teaching.* New York: Dryden Press, 1969.
82. *Individually Prescribed Instruction (IPI).* Philadelphia: Research for Better Schools.
83. Knirk, F. G., and Childs, J. W., *Instructional Technology.* New York: Holt, Rinehart, and Winston, 1968.
84. *Learning Activity Package (LAP).* Fort Lauderdale: The Nova School.
85. *PLAN, A System for Individualized Instruction.* New York: Westinghouse Learning Corporation.
86. *UNIPACS.* Anaheim, California: IDEA Materials Centers.
87. Bhaerman, Steve, and Denker, Joel, *No Particular Place to Go: The Making of a Free High School.* New York: Simon and Schuster, 1972.
88. Bremer, John, and Von Moschzisker, Michael, *The School Without Walls: Philadelphia's Parkway Program.* New York: Holt, Rinehart, and Winston, 1971.
89. Evans, Thomas W., *The School in the Home.* New York: Harper and Row, 1973.
90. Featherstone, Joseph, *Schools Where Children Learn.* New York: Liveright, 1971.
91. Gagne, Robert M., *The Conditions of Learning.* 2nd ed. New York: Holt, Rinehart, and Winston, 1970.
92. Kohl, Herbert R., *The Open Classroom.* New York: Random House, 1969.
93. Kravas, Konstantinos, and Kravas, Constance, "Transactional Analysis for Classroom Management." *Phi Delta Kappan,* 56:194 (1974).
94. Neil, Alexander S., *Summerhill.* New York: Hart Publishing Co., 1960.
95. Rapport, Virginia, and Parker, Mary, *Learning Centers: Children on Their Own.* Washington, D.C.: Association for Childhood Education International, 1970.
96. Wigginton, Eliot, ed., *The Foxfire Book.* New York: Doubleday, 1972.
97. ————, ed., *Foxfire 2.* New York. Doubleday, 1973.
98. American Association of School Administrators, *New Forms for Community Education.* Arlington, Virginia: author.
99. Aronstein, Laurence W., and Olsen, Edward G., *Action Learning: Student Community Service Projects.* Washington, D.C.: Association for Supervision and Curriculum Development, 1974.
100. Skinner, B. F., *The Technology of Teaching.* New York: Appleton-Century-Crofts, 1968.

101. Travers, Robert, *Man's Information System.* Scranton, Pennsylvania: Chandler Publishing, 1970.
102. Ashton-Warner, Sylvia, *Spearpoint: Teacher in America.* New York: Alfred A. Knopf, 1972.
103. Borton, Terry, *Reach, Touch, and Teach.* New York: McGraw-Hill, 1970.
104. Hyman, Ronald T., ed., *Teaching: Vantage Points for Study.* 2nd ed. Philadelphia: J. B. Lippincott Co., 1974.
105. Hyman, Ronald T., *Ways of Teaching.* Philadelphia: J. B. Lippincott Co., 1970.
106. Nagel, Thomas, and Richman, Paul, *Competency-Based Instruction: A Strategy to Eliminate Failure.* Columbus, Ohio: Charles E. Merrill Publishing, 1972.
107. Raths, Louis, et al., *Teaching for Thinking: Theory and Application.* Columbus, Ohio: Charles E. Merrill Publishing, 1967.
108. Sanders, Norris M., *Classroom Questions. What Kinds?* New York: Harper and Row, 1966.
109. Wilson, L. Craig, *The Open Access Curriculum.* Boston, Allyn and Bacon, 1971.
110. Overly, Norman V., ed., *The Unstudied Curriculum: Its Impact on Children.* Washington, D.C.: Association for Supervision and Curriculum Development, 1970.
111. Postman, Neil, and Weingartner, Charles, *Teaching as a Subversive Activity.* New York: Delacorte Press, 1969.
112. Raths, Louis, Harmin, Merrill, and Simon, Sidney, *Values and Teaching: Working with Values in the Classroom.* Columbus, Ohio: Charles E. Merrill Publishing, 1966.
113. Ahmann, J. Stanley, and Glock, Marvin D., *Measuring and Evaluating Educational Achievement.* Boston: Allyn and Bacon, Inc., 1971.
114. Association for Supervision and Curriculum Development, *Evaluation as Feedback and Guide.* Yearbook. Washington, D.C.: author, 1967.
115. Bloom, Benjamin S., Hastings, J. Thomas, and Madaus, George F., *Handbook on Formative and Summative Evaluation of Student Learning.* New York: McGraw-Hill, 1971.
116. Eiss, Albert P., *Evaluation of Instructional Systems.* New York: Garden and Breach Publishers, Inc., 1972.
117. Glaser, Robert, "Objectives and Evaluation. An Individualized System." In *Contemporary Thought on Public School Curriculum,* edited by Edmund C. Short and George D. Marconnit. Dubuque, Iowa: William C. Brown Publishers, 1968.
118. Grobman, Hulda, *Developmental Curriculum Projects: Decision Points and Processes.* Itasca, Illinois: F. E. Peacock Publishers, 1972.
119. Gronlund, Norman E., *Measurement and Evaluation in Teaching.* New York: Macmillan, 1965.
120. ——————, *Preparing Criterion-Referenced Tests for Classroom Instruction.* New York: Macmillan, 1970.
121. Provus, Malcolm, *Discrepancy Evaluation.* Berkeley, California: McCutchan Publishing Corp., 1971.
122. Walberg, Herbert A., *Evaluating Educational Performance.* Berkeley, California: McCutchan Publishing Corp., 1974.

123. Wittrock, Merlin C., and Wiley, David E., *The Evaluation of Instruction.* New York: Holt, Rinehart, and Winston, 1970.
124. Cyphert, Frederick R., and Gant, Walter L., "The Delphi Technique Technique: A Case Study." *Phi Delta Kappan,* 52: 272 (1971).
125. Anderson, Vernon E., *Principles and Procedures of Curriculum Improvement.* New York: Ronald Press, 1965.
126. Macdonald, James B., Anderson, Dan W., and May, Frank B., *Strategies of Curriculum Development: Selected Writings of the Late Virgil E. Herrick.* Columbus, Ohio: Charles E. Merrill Books, 1965.
127. Tanner, Daniel, and Tanner, Laurel, *Curriculum Development: Theory into Practice.* New York: Macmillan, 1975.
128. Caswell, Hollis L., and Campbell, Doak S., *Curriculum Development.* New York: American Book Co., 1935.

5

Implementing

Implementation is the critical phase of any instructional or staff development project. This is where and when "it happens." This is when the project is conducted, when the instructional plan is effected, and when the objectives impact upon persons and program to bring about the planned change. Because each situation is unique, most staff development or change models do not attempt to develop an installation scheme except to indicate processes, tasks, or guidelines.[1]

If the plans are to eventuate, the "lesson plans" for this phase of the operation should be as clear and defined as they are expected to be for any classroom operation, or, for that matter, any physical plant construction. Failure to delineate at this point is a major reason for failure of plans, for having the project slip "between the cracks" between planning and operation. Very likely, the new idea may be aborted by other activities—unprepared for the new events, the new skills, the new materials, or the new methods. The lesson of post-Sputnik curriculum developments is that implementation is tough, that it too seldom lives up to the promise of the planning, and that without involvement, commitment, and training, any significant modification will be rejected as soon as the pressure is diminished or as personnel are reassigned.[2,3]

Professionals need to understand and to *participate;* products and processes need to be modified to provide support. Support features, a reinforcement system for the change, must be as deeply imbedded in the new operation as is the ongoing program. Implementation is installation and operation, not discussion or "dissemination" of information.[4-6]

Implementation is a complex series of transactions that includes all the previous phases and all the other processes. Therefore, in this segment, a number of options and considerations are proposed. The overall pattern of the school district is reviewed to emphasize the need for comprehensiveness. Two models are given, the first is based on task assignments rather than events or generalized roles; the second is an alternative strategy that uses a force-field approach, rather than highlighting particular events or tasks. These items anticipate structural elements that are consolidated for evaluation purposes in Chapter 6. Subsequent chapters incorporate operational suggestions as they relate to managing and organizing. Early or late in the process of change, early or late in the presentation of planning notions, the program elements must all come together at this point if the implementation phase is to achieve the desired objectives.

Implementation and Structure

Implementation requires a restructuring and replacement. In existence are established personal habits and emphases, organizational elements, routines, and ongoing programs that were once priority items. These in-place operations are difficult to change in an institutionalized setting. Hopefully, the early beginnings related to needs assessment; and if so, the simulated modifications accompanying design and development work will have created an enthusiasm and impetus that will continue. But such continuity for the change cannot be assumed when the time comes for installing the revised, adapted, or imported instructional effort. Power alone can only create a token or temporary realignment. How smoothly and durably the implementation activities occur depends upon the thoroughness of the planning and the commitment of those who are involved.

Implementation cannot occur apart from other functions and programs. It must be finely tuned to the system elements and program operations critical to the change. Not to be overlooked is the continuing maintenance of the desired program. Any significant modification requires the realignment of the existing situations, and an orchestration of the intents, persons, and plans for the new. To do this requires a comprehensive view.[7-9]

BASIC SYSTEMS AND SUBSYSTEMS

Figure 5.1 summarizes many of the basic elements with which the program manager (administrator, supervisor, or director) must contend, and within which this person must work if the implementation effort is to succeed. In the analysis that follows, a number of assumptions have been made to summarize the basic system components. Each element is numbered and described briefly for analysis and subsequent discussion. They are delineated in relation to implementation efforts regarding instruction and staff development, not as an administrative structure *per se.*

1. Schools have been established by society as an agency providing for cultural continuity and improvement. These responsbilities are framed as general goals

and priorities, then redefined as specific objectives to be achieved by the school system. One basic problem is to keep the specific instructional objectives congruent with the nebulous and often contradictory larger social goals; another is to bring about needed changes and at the same time maintain stability and continuity.[10,11]

2. The achievement of these goals and objectives is reflected in student behaviors, understandings, and products. Products are often viewed as achievement data, skills demonstrated via art exhibits, musical concerts, industrial arts exhibits, honors received, athletic prowess, competencies demonstrated on the job, college success, general citizenship behaviors, etc. These items constantly recycle into number one (1), as inputs, concerns, and mandates.[12,13]

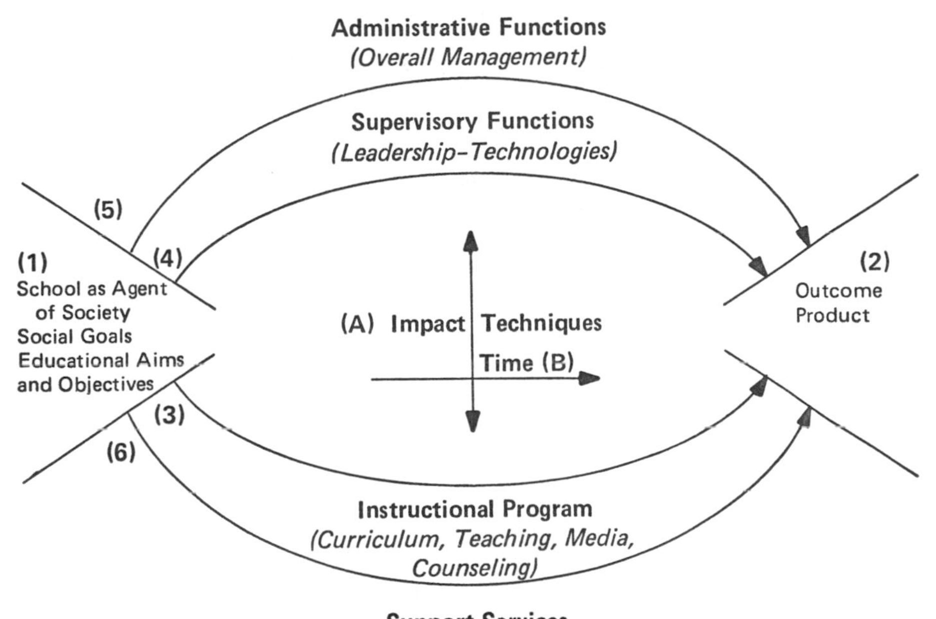

FIGURE 5.1 Instructional Systems and Subsystems.

3. The basic purpose of the school system must be contained in the instructional program, which is composed of such items as the curriculum (the basic plans), instruction (essentially the responsibility of teachers), and related media, resources, and procedures.[14]
4. The supervisory sub-system (principals, supervisors, and curriculum leaders) is designed to impact upon the teacher-learner subsystem, which provides program continuity and improvement. The supervisory and leadership responsibilities are incorporated into a number of functions, determined and structured by each school and school system. This leadership (combined with classroom instruction and related resources) comprises the basic instructional system.[15-25]
   a. Leadership functions are achieved through *impact* processes and means.

These reflect the choices and competencies of the leadership persons as well as the philosophy and resources of the school district.

b. Likewise, the supervisory and leadership functions are performed over *time* periods; these are related (but not necessarily identical) with the other time elements of the instructional program.

5. The task of managing the overall functions of the school system is assigned to the administration. It is administration's responsibility to translate policies into program and operation—to organize and administer. One problem is to realize that the basic *responsibility* to manage not the same as the basic *purpose*, which is to facilitate instruction, learning, and staff renewal.[26–29]
6. Many supportive services also are provided by the school district. Most of these are not directly related to the instructional leaders' role—such as maintenance, transportation, food services, business, personnel, and the like.[30,31]

It is assumed that the school district is an open system, responsive to and contributing within the social and political matrix. For purposes of closure, definition, and analysis, the school operation has certain elements of independence and separateness; however, it is construed to be a subsystem of society. Within this context, the teacher leadership and supervisory/administrative functions contribute to a continuing flow of inputs, influences, and impacts.

In regard to the elements delineated in Figure 5.1, an improvement in any of the operations can and should better the instructional program and learner achievement. The instructional supervisor and project director usually has more contact with items 1-4 on the model and may select activities from any of these components. Implementation requires a modification in all of these areas, the nature and degree of which depends upon the extensiveness of the desired change.

With learner gain as the central purpose, the leadership personnel in the system can select the appropriate targets for implementation activity; likewise, these persons can analyze their own functioning and work for improvement in the needed impact strategies and techniques. Hence, staff development must also include supervisors and administrators. Balance among the various alternatives is more likely to achieve a maximum and durable impact. Any single technique or improvement scheme requires the coordination and reinforcement of the other elements in the total operation.

A few significant relationships are not indicated. For example, there must be close coordination with the central administration; this is not shown. It is necessary to relate to the outside and community forces that impinge upon educational objectives, resources use, and curricular emphasis; this is not indicated. An awareness of the relationship to the various non-instructional support elements (for these affect schedules, conveniences, and facilities) are only suggested in this analysis. Also, other omitted functions might include personnel, research, budgeting, public relations, and record keeping.[32]

Thus, this analysis centers upon the project or program leader as a functioning agent who is concerned with self-adequacy, supervisory *impact*, instruction-program improvement, staff development, and learner gain. These are assumed to be the priorities addressed by the text.[33]

Basic Responsibilities of Leadership

Simplifying the model still further, one might posit leadership persons as being primarily concerned with three major elements:

1. The identification and explication of objectives for learners, programs, professionals, and other staff.
2. The design and utilization of means to facilitate the achievement of these objectives.
3. The review of products and outcomes to assess their fit with the objectives and means, and the efficiency and effectiveness of the measures taken to achieve the objectives.

1	*2*	*3*
OBJECTIVES	*MEANS UTILIZED*	*PRODUCTS AND OUTCOMES*
	Functions	
Learners	Resources	Learner Gain
⟶	⟶	⟶
Programs	Processes	Program Improvement
Professionals	(Impact techniques)	Staff Development

FIGURE 5.2 Objectives, Means, and Outcomes.

Leadership and management competencies exist for each segment; these can be improved. Program elements for learners can be improved in regard to each element. In-service and staff development activities can be developed to improve the leadership and instruction—teaching and resources—that are critical to the "delivery" of the desired objectives and outcomes. These can be piece-meal or system design projects.

Implementation is the culminating activity in a sustained series of developments. Operationally, the implementation stage begins once the decision has been made to institute a particular program effort. Technically, it begins when the planned change is developed and ready for installation. The duration of these intervals depends upon the nature of the planning, the complexity of the project, and the strategy as envisioned by leadership.

In some instances, the pilot testing of units or program elements is viewed as a validating process for the developmental phase. It is a time when trial efforts identify problems and strong and weak points that will need to be reviewed as a part of the feedback. The feedback is incident to developing the major elements that are to be implemented. In this case, revisions in content, instructional strategy, materials, or organization will be made prior to any large-scale or officially sanctioned implementation.

These same activities, along with staff training and community awareness/involvement can be viewed as first stages in the implementation scheme. This more or less assumes that the product-program, as designed, is adequate to the objectives that have been determined. In this case, the selection of personnel, schools, materials, and preliminary testing, and the collection of monitoring data and the administrative restructuring and logistical arrangements all comprise explicit pre-implementation preparation that will result in general or large-scale involvement with no significant reconsideration of the project objectives or program.

The distinction is important primarily to management decision-makers and to evaluators, and, only to these persons or agencies when they are charged with determining speed, direction, and adequacy of this phase of the program effort. Also, it may be that at this stage the focus for responsibility changes from the central office to the schools, and from selected individuals to large numbers of staff persons or learners.

The strategy to be employed in these high risk and complex activities should model the desired outcomes and methodologies. A change in organization can be mandated, but the effectiveness and feelings relative to the change cannot. A new technological device may be installed with minor modifications; however, its utilization and integration into instructional approaches may cause problems. An open education plan will require modification in all component areas—use of resources, staff attitudes and competencies, building modifications, community understandings and cooperation, testing, grouping, and instructional procedures—to list a few. Open schools, individualizing instruction, and career education—as comprehensive objectives these are instances where long range planning and comprehensive staff education, involvement, and competencies are essential. If the design for implementation does not include help with the necessary behaviors and attitudes, then token compliance and minimal change can be expected. New attitudes, competencies, and approaches are learned by practicing and experiencing. They are not the product of inspirational talks, consultant demonstrations, organizational restructuring, or pressure.[34-37]

Thus, the important determiners of the necessary strategy for implementation are those that should have permeated the change effort from its inception. And, there is the need to reconsider such basic questions as:

1. Is the organization for implementation adequate to the need?
2. Can roles, responsibilities, and tasks be delineated?
3. What new requirements (information, skills) are essential features of the curriculum or staff change to be instituted?

4. What are existing competencies of the instructional staff who will be expected to implement the new ideas?
5. How reasonable is the time frame? Are funds available?
6. What modifications will be required in staffing patterns, in organizational realignments, in selection and recruitment, in pupil scheduling?
7. What support features and facilities require immediate change; which will need long range modification?
8. How adequate, how communicable is the plan?
9. Who needs to be involved and informed?
10. What is the climate, the readiness, and the attitude toward the desired changes?

Many such questions are inherent; their consideration should be explicit and comprehensive. The following material is directly related to these representative concerns.

Design and development efforts are evident in every planning phase. They recycle and reconstruct the basic purposes, products, and outcomes. Initially developed to provide the dimensions, targets, and means, the objectives need to be supplemented by processes that capture the operational intentions, and how persons are to be involved. As will be shown in Chapter 6, guidelines also have utility as process elements in formative and summative evaluation; this use reinforces their importance and creates a cumulative impact regarding the system style, that is, as it relates to relationships and accountability criteria for each change phase. Guidelines can also assist by providing directions for such items as communications, policy support, personal and organizational involvement, leadership, planning, and similar matters. Implementation, as with other segments of the change process, should proceed in accordance with the desired and determined emphases. The following listing is comparable to that given in Chapter 3, p. 80. It proposes a similar set of concerns.

Since each situation is different, no one prescription will suffice in all cases. The following criteria, however, can be useful as a basis for plan appraisal and as a discussion device for getting at specifics and completeness during any or all change phases, including implementation.

1. *Administration and board policy support must be evident;* the task to be undertaken must be clearly a priority. The power and project personnel must assist in the development of a climate and a commitment if the task is to be accomplished.
2. *The rationale and objectives must be clear;* there must be an obvious relationship between what presently exists and what is to transpire. The change must be superior to the present program.
3. *Professional staff members must know how to participate and relate to the program.* A participatory—peer power, developmental approach is recommended. Multiple modes for involvement to accommodate different styles and different stages of development, different entry points, and varying achievement opportunities should be provided.
4. *There must be adequacy, quality, and coordination in the materials to be used.* This is part of a support system that maximizes understanding, that minimizes

personal risk. Progress regarding support features, such as equipment or building modifications, should be explicit.

5. *Relevance and realism for professionals (as well as for learners) is necessary.* This relates to certification, status, attention, time, income, and especially to the ongoing tasks for which the staff member is accountable—content gain, skill acquisition, quality of work, professional role, and expertise.
6. *A reasonable plan for the achievement of the desired objectives is essential.* It must include short and long range goals, time frames, management expectations and interventions, and processes for modification. Back-up support (such as help from consultants or clinic sessions) and/or alternative routes are helpful.
7. *Leadership and role responsibilities (performance expectations) for all staff members should be defined.* Leadership should be determined on the basis of competency and accountability, rather than status per se; all segments of the system should contribute appropriately.
8. *Communication flow and feedback must be a part of the process and program.* Lack of feedback regarding performance, gain, or modification causes turbulence and reversion; this may affect learners and the community as well as the staff members who are involved. Communication is more difficult, but also more essential when interaction involves non-school agencies, businesses, or institutions.
9. *Time is essential for change—time for development and accommodation, time within the priority hours for activity.* If the program is an add-on, if it occurs only during "off" hours or days, all of the above elements, including support and commitment, are negated. Those involved must have the opportunity to reconcile project objectives with individual commitments.
10. *Support and modification must be observable in all components of the system.* A single change or thrust will be rejected or isolated by the routine, ongoing practices and procedures. Instructional change and personalized staff development programs must be systemic as well as systematic.

Guidelines are necessary; they are useful but seldom enough. Therefore, the following approaches propose ways by which guideline concerns and program implementation can be structured for purposes of communicating, understanding, accounting, evaluating, and decision making.

Two Phases of Implementation

For purposes of planning and analysis, two implementation phases can be identified, namely, pre-operation and operation. *Pre-operation* activities precede the actual implantation or execution of the plan. As implementation, this phase utilizes the development activities where materials are searched or developed, as teachers and others become directly involved and develop enthusiasm, skills, and commitment to the ideas. Orientation to the implementation phase is continued as reports of the work in progress are discussed. The validation activity extends this orientation and training for those involved in researching, observing, simulating, or piloting. Pilot efforts can do more than try out or validate; they provide the opportunity to enlarge the implementation on a gradual basis, moving in accordance with commitments, skills, and timing as required. A program that requires a redirection in objectives, a new configuration of teaching skills, or a significant modification of organizational features needs time and success experiences. In addition to substantive program materials, training sessions are needed for those who will be responsible for implementing, i.e., principals, counselors, teachers, supervisors, community personnel, and others. Finally, in this pre-operation phase of implementation, preparations are made for installation relating to organizational realignment, student and staff selection, schedules, facilities and materials preparation, policy and budget preparations, public relations efforts, and arrangements for researching, monitoring, evaluating, reporting, and similar activities.

The *operational* phase occurs when planning becomes action, when the design becomes the structure, when the instructional or in-service project directly impacts as intended. Planning, developing, and implementing are greatly facilitated by using the individual school with its functional units of leadership, instructional personnel, learners, parents, and community. These learning centers present uniqueness in organization, competencies, socio-economic characteristics, and context. Thus, general plans can move through specific environments. As with other difficult tasks, absorption is not an adequate means for implementation; therefore, a more direct and organized effort is necessary.

IMPLEMENTATION—A TASK ORIENTED MODEL

The following model was developed and used in a large urban situation; it also served in a number of regional situations where different rural school systems were involved. It may be more complex than will be desired for many projects, but simplification can be done by consolidating the listed tasks, functions, and processes. The scheme has greatest usefulness where tasks and responsibilities need clarification as a resource from which to develop specification statements regarding roles or functions, or in connection with monitoring or accountability. With the addition of a needs analysis phase, this design has also been used as a complete change model; in this application, the various developmental phases such as initiation, design, development, etc., were compressed into the two segments listed here as pre-operation and operation.

The model emphasizes individual roles and responsibilities rather than structure, organization, or events. However, it should not be viewed singly from the task perspective. The collaborative effort required to deal with the various tasks, functions, and processes provides a functional learning opportunity. The persons engaged quickly enter into personal and role negotiations that give insights into perceptions as to existing competencies and potentials. Procedural and philosophic differences quickly emerge. The analysis and alignment of personnel and responsibilities require a reconciliation of individual needs and organizational objectives. Consensus, group commitment, group problem solving, and open decision making are essential. Thus, the planning-deciding-assigning responsibility provides a simulation of the system's operations, and of the problems, personalities, and pitfalls likely to be encountered in the implementation effort. It provides an opportunity for issues to be confronted and resolved prior to the full scale impact.

The generalized role or task approach was especially appropriate to the regional-rural situation, for which task assignments have been indicated on the model. Final implementation efforts occurred in different school districts and each made appropriate modifications. Such constraints are important in studying the given task recommendations. Experience with the model indicates that specific functions, involvements, and processes are quite different when the model is used with a single school or school district than when it is used for a large urban center. In this regard, and characteristic of the implementation design when used in large urban school systems, many of the recommendations reflected more hierarchial concerns, more delegation of authority, less utilization of persons outside the system; and, more responsibility—for the central office in planning, for department chairpersons in the high schools, and for principals in the elementary schools. Also, still required and not indicated, is a work plan such as a flow chart, time line, or PERT, which would provide for the specific events, the time frame, and the unique conditions in a given locale (see Chapters 7 and 8). Thus, the intent here has been to present an overall scheme for planning, researching, and accounting; this is not to suggest that the task indicators are appropriate to another context or that the proposed plan meets the criteria for every comprehensive educational change.

The model makes the following assumptions:

1. The instructional or staff development area to be changed has already been identified, diagnosed, developed, and validated; also, some plan has been developed for its evaluation.
2. The visual model would operate as a work sheet to gain agreement on a two phase implementation plan—(1) pre-operation and (2) operation.
3. Once explicated, this model would operate as general guidelines and task assignments for the implementation of a particular program.

Implicit in this approach is the desirability of wide participation and accountability. By acknowledging the tasks, functions, and processes to be performed by each person in the process, the implementation can be expected to occur with minimum errors and maximum responsibleness. Also, it should be possible to evaluate the effectiveness of the implementation process itself.

It will be noted that the model shows a separation of personnel. Those on the left are *outside* the involved system, e.g., state department, regional education resources, university consultants, or other non-system personnel, plus external evaluators, program auditors, re-

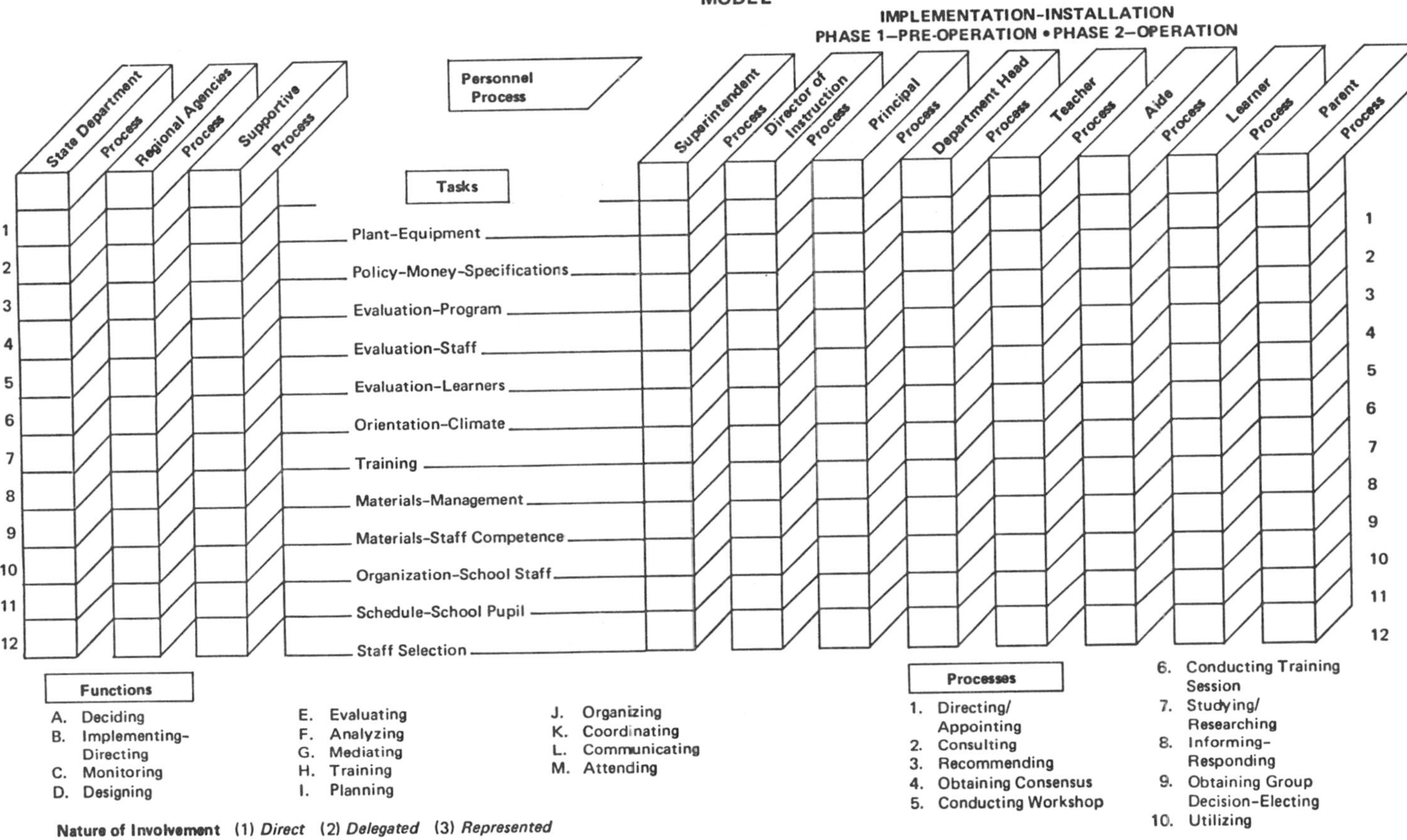

FIGURE 5.3 Role Analysis and Accountability.

searchers, or agencies. Those on the right of the task listing are *within* the system. Only individual roles are shown, but groups, teams, or committees could be indicated, in addition to other individuals such as counselors, media, or support persons.

The design for implementation can be used for both pre-operation and operation planning; this would suggest the completion of the model *twice*, once for each phase, since many roles change in the two phases. Some persons, e.g., subject area consultants, may be active in the pre-operation design phase but less active in operation. Administrative personnel, on the other hand, tend to be consultants in the pre-operation but implementors during the operation phase.

Implementation Tasks*

1. Plant-equipment—acquiring, building, or obtaining rights to large equipment, e.g., TV installations and computers, or significant building modifications; making necessary changes, maintenance.
2. Policy—specifications regarding program needs and objectives, designation of budget requirements, high level procedures to insure progress and implementation; support of implementation procedures.
3. Evaluation-program—evaluation of overall program, concern for balance instrumentation procedures; utilizing standards and procedures, providing feedback.
4. Evaluation-staff—determining personnel competencies to effect particular curricular changes; ongoing evaluation.
5. Evaluation-learners—determining personnel competencies to effect particular curricular changes; ongoing evaluation.
6. Orientation-climate—establishing tone or climate for change; maintaining a high level of understanding and commitment.
7. Training—involving participants in specific tasks necessary for achieving a particular outcome; maintaining and improving competencies.
8. Materials-management—selecting, procuring, and distributing instructional materials; maintaining flow and coordination.
9. Materials-staff competencies—determining the performance levels of personnel for utilization of instructional materials; and continuous evaluation of effectiveness of materials and use.
10. Organization-school-staff—determining criteria, patterns, and organizing staff to implement curriculum; making necessary staff adjustments.
11. Schedule-school, pupil—developing or overseeing student schedules; making necessary changes and assignments to program areas.
12. Staff selection—selecting staff for specific assignments; making necessary adjustments.

*In regard to the following tasks, some items on the list are separated by semicolons, the punctuation separates those aspects of implementation that are pre-operation from those that are operation responsibilities.

Other task areas may be added. In this connection a review of possible components, pp. 75-76, may be useful to recheck adequacy in regard to a particular project. Similarly, the task delineating phase (pp. 73-75 and 103-106) may also suggest additions or necessary changes in task or focus.

Implementation Functions

A. *Deciding*—making the critical judgment with respect to what is to be done in a particular situation or course of action.
B. *Implementing-Directing*—effecting previously determined decisions, policies, or procedures.
C. *Monitoring*—active surveillance or supervision with authority to intervene.
D. *Designing*—preparing plans that serve as guidelines for subsequent developments or actions.
E. *Evaluating*—determining the value or worth; making an appraisal in order to find strengths and weaknesses.
F. *Analyzing*—gathering evidence of and examining factors or parts in terms of the total.
G. *Mediating*—working with contending parties in order to bring about a settlement or compromise.
H. *Training*—helping others to become skillful or proficient in a particular task or process.
I. *Planning*—forming a plan (scheme or method) for doing something specific.
J. *Organizing*—making systematic or orderly arrangements for a program or activity.
K. *Coordinating*—performing integrating tasks or processes.
L. *Communicating*—relaying or conveying information.
M. *Attending*—being informed with interest or commitment.

Implementation Processes

1. *Directing-appointing*—taking action or putting a decision into effect.
2. *Consulting*—judgments usually sought as to the most beneficial or worthy action, may propose alternatives.
3. *Recommending*—being definitely involved but not the decision-maker.
4. *Obtaining consensus*—obtaining general agreement or collective opinion.
5. *Conducting workshop*—involving participants in activities designed for staff development.
6. *Conducting training session*—a limited involvement of participants designed to achieve specific objectives or skills.

7. *Studying-researching*—careful or disciplined inquiry directed toward the data collection, clarification, analysis, and/or recommendations for the resolution of a problem or for development.
8. *Informing-responding*—relaying or conveying information, limited response to a particular communication or situation.
9. *Obtaining group decision-electing*—formal determination or selection of alternatives.
10. *Utilizing*—using or implementing as previously determined.

As indicated, the purpose of the design is to suggest a possible structure for planning, research, and accountability that is related to the implementation phase. In operation, a task force composed of teachers, local school, and central office supervisors would be established to recommend a function, process, and level of responsibility for each of the personnel listed. Once completed, the proposals for pre-operation and operation tasks then become the basis for policy, decision making, and assignment. Obviously, many different styles are appropriate as to how these functions are analyzed and delegated.

Beside each task (listed in the center of Figure 5.3) is a series of three personnel related cells containing the policy determined responsibilities (e.g., first task—acquiring, building, or obtaining rights to large equipment or significant physical plant modifications, and so forth). In this illustration, the superintendent's *function* is listed as A, Deciding; the proposed *involvement level* is given as Direct (1); and the *process* is indicated in the diagonal cell as Directing and Appointing, 1.

In Figure 5.4, two cell clusters are shown, those for Task 1 and also Task 11. (establishing schedules for schools and pupils).

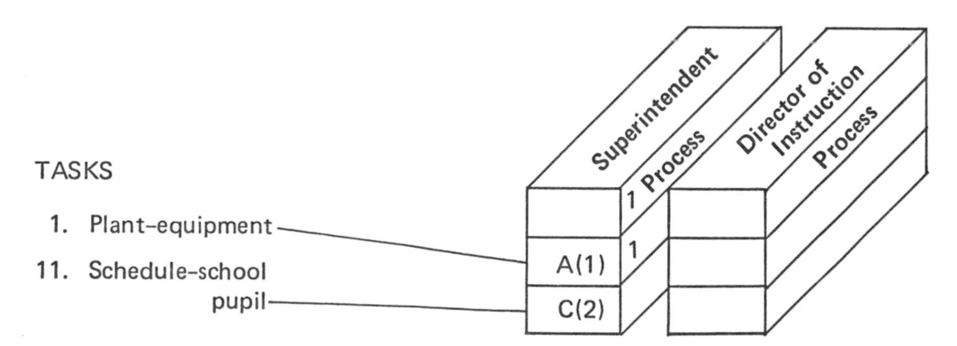

FIGURE 5.4 Superintendent Implementation Tasks.

Since Task 11. (school and student scheduling) is to be delegated, it is proposed that the superintendent assign this task to the school principal, as shown in Figure 5.5. However, the superintendent would be expected to monitor this responsibility. The principal, while responsible for the decision making (Function A), would be expected to delegate, (2), the actual work through the process of appointment. In this example, the profile for the principal reflects these decisions.

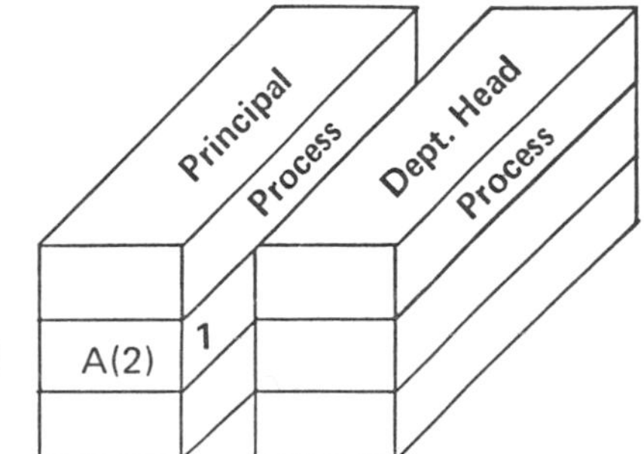

10. Organization–school staff
11. Schedule–school pupil

FIGURE 5.5 Principal Implementation Tasks.

In making recommendations and decisions regarding the critical tasks, it is important that all major tasks be assigned. The specifics for this work was the subject of Chapter 3, Designing.

To show these relationships, Figures 5.6 and 5.7, which follow, extend the model still further to illustrate pre-operation and operation responsibilities for the superintendent, director of instruction, principal, and lead teacher or department chairperson. The purpose of the model and its utilization is to provide a setting wherein task and policy parameters can be ironed out and wherein basic responsibilities can be determined—not to freeze any functionary into a task, role, or process. Changes would occur as events transpired or as unanticipated changes arose. To be complete, the model decisions should be combined with management phases (Chapter 7) and should be visualized by the use of a time line, flowchart, or PERT (Chapter 8). Finally, with objectives and roles defined, provisions for monitoring (see pp. 216-222, and Appendix C) and evaluating (see Chapter 6) can readily be made.

For a significant instructional change, the pre-implementation effort of determining role profiles has multiple benefits. Each professional knows the tasks, roles, and processes to be involved; each can see these roles in relationship to others. Responsibility and accountability are clear-cut. The operational philosophy of the system is also delineated. Persons inside and outside the system know to whom to go for what level of action. The data can be communicated by publishing the completed models or by summarizing role responsibilities in job description form. For purposes of analysis, comparison, or utilization, a completed model is given in Appendix D.

Large school systems would likely have specialized personnel to assist with many of these tasks; for example, persons assigned to research, evaluation, systems analysis, or computer programming. Also, people are usually available and especially skilled to perform particular instructional or training functions, e.g., diagnosticians and human relations or community education consultants. Obviously, these individuals or roles could be included in the list of critical personnel to be listed on the model. In such instances, assigned responsibilities could be delineated for them in connection with a specific educational improvement project to be undertaken.[38]

Tasks	Superintendent	Process	Director of Instruction	Process	Principal	Process	Department Chairperson	Process	
1 Plant-Equipment	A(1)	1	B(1)	1	B(1)	1	D(1)	3	1
2 Policy-Money-Specifications	A(1)	1	B(1)	1	B(1)	1	I(1)	3	2
3 Evaluation-Program	A(2)	1	B(1)	1	B(1)	1	D(1)	7	3
4 Evaluation-Staff	A(2)	1	B(1)	1	A(1)	1	B(1)	3	4
5 Evaluation-Learners	D(2)	2	A(1)	1	D(1)	1	D(1)	3	5
6 Orientation-Climate	A(1)	1	B(1)	1	A(1)	1	F(1)	3	6
7 Training	A(2)	1	H(1)	1	K(2)	8	D(1)	3	7
8 Materials-Management	A(2)	1	A(1)	1	K(2)	8	B(1)	3	8
9 Materials-Staff competence	A(2)	1	A(1)	1	B(2)	2	D(1)	3	9
10 Organization-School staff	A(2)	1	D(1)	1	A(1)	1	I(1)	2	10
11 Schedule-School pupil	C(2)	1	D(1)	1	A(2)	1	I(3)	2	11
12 Staff selection	A(1)	1	A(1)	3	A(1)	3	D(1)	3	12

Personnel, Process

FIGURE 5.6 Implementation-Installation Phase 1—Pre-Operation.

Tasks	Superintendent	Process	Director of Instruction	Process	Principal	Process	Department Chairperson	Process
1 Plant–Equipment	$E^{(1)}$	10	$C^{(1)}$	3	$C^{(1)}$	1	$F^{(1)}$	3
2 Policy–Money–Specifications	$F^{(1)}$	10	$B^{(1)}$	1	$C^{(1)}$	1	$K^{(1)}$	10
3 Evaluation–Program	$C^{(2)}$	4	$A^{(1)}$	1	$C^{(1)}$	1	$C^{(1)}$	3
4 Evaluation–Staff	$K^{(2)}$	3	$C^{(2)}$	2	$A^{(1)}$	1	$B^{(1)}$	3
5 Evaluation–Learners	$K^{(2)}$	4	$F^{(1)}$	3	$C^{(1)}$	1	$B^{(2)}$	3
6 Orientation–Climate	$L^{(1)}$	8	$B^{(1)}$	1	$A^{(1)}$	1	$C^{(2)}$	3
7 Training	$E^{(1)}$	3	$A^{(1)}$	1	$A^{(2)}$	8	$B^{(1)}$	3
8 Materials–Management	$F^{(2)}$	3	$C^{(2)}$	2	$K^{(2)}$	8	$B^{(1)}$	1
9 Materials–Staff competence	$F^{(1)}$	3	$F^{(1)}$	2	$D^{(2)}$	2	$B^{(1)}$	3
10 Organization–School staff	$F^{(2)}$	4	$F^{(1)}$	2	$A^{(1)}$	1	$B^{(1)}$	3
11 Schedule–School pupil	$F^{(2)}$	3	$F^{(2)}$	3	$A^{(2)}$	1	$C^{(1)}$	3
12 Staff selection	$A^{(1)}$	3	$F^{(2)}$	3	$A^{(1)}$	3	$E^{(1)}$	3

Personnel, Process

FIGURE 5.7 Implementation-Installation Phase 2—Operation.

The model as presented is not an "all or nothing at all" proposition; the following list offers some possible alternatives:

1. More tasks could be added, or the existing ones could be combined or dropped.
2. More personnel (positions) could be added, or those not essential to the particular implementation could be dropped.
3. The level of involvement could be expanded to include more options, or the segment could be eliminated, allowing the same options for process and functions.

The design could be used as a suggested checklist for determining tasks, functions, and processes. Then, a PERT chart could be developed directly instead of going through the procedure of completing an assignment for all persons involved—as was done in the illustration. Time frames or specific dates could be assigned, and one of the two phases (pre-operation or operation) could be eliminated. Individuals could utilize the ideas to develop role specification statements that could be reviewed for synthesis and decision making. A research, monitoring, evaluation, or accountability design could be instituted that would determine levels of proficiency or indicators of achievement for each task. Then, efficiency, impact, and effectiveness could be assessed. Competency modules could be produced for each role, task, process, or function; and these could be studied. The intent of the model and its presentation, therefore, is to present structural and procedural options.

To review, *pre-implementation* activities will likely emphasize planning, course work, program development, orientation, recruitment, feasibility studies, school visitation, and training. The critical events of this period will be the pilot or simulation efforts. These generally involve those willing and prepared to participate. Pilot or preparation activities should provide opportunities for others to observe, for problems to be examined, for materials to be tried, and for success experiences to be maximized.

During the *operation* phase, events are more likely to be characterized by clinic sessions, personal interventions, consultations, monitoring, decision making and modification, feedback, and process and formative evaluation. Of course, the most important activities during this period are the actual classroom or project transactions, which represent the culmination of all the efforts prior to this time. A single pilot attempt followed by total implementation is seldom advisable. It is far better to provide a realistic base of experience, to involve and train local leadership, and to proceed in accordance with the evidence, administrative support, and participant commitment by those crucial to the success of the planned objectives. These include the procedures and processes indicated by the developed guidelines.

As proposed here, implementation efforts are as carefully constructed as any of the other change phases or operations. It cannot be assumed that a staff renewal project or the installation of an instructional change will occur as a "logical consequence," or because information has been exchanged. The factors of personal or professional risk, new methodologies or technologies, and new materials or concepts all represent significant changes. However, if preparation has been cumulative and developmental, if time and involvement have been sufficient, if the activity has been researched and validated, and if installation responsibilities have been defined and authorized, then, the likelihood of success is greater.

Considerable time may have elapsed since the initial determination of needs and the statements of objectives. These, along with the design, development, and rationale need to be re-emphasized and renewed. Local schools, as well as individuals, need to have their responsibilities and roles clearly outlined. As part of the implementation task, teachers and supervisors must be aware of the district's commitment, the importance to learners, and the support elements that are "in place."[39,40]

In large systems, a major strategy change is essential. The locus will have changed from the planning phase to the operational phase, perhaps from a planning center to the local schools and personnel. If the proposed interim steps have been followed, this is a natural, not dramatic, shift; preparations will have been made in connection with all the various stages. A consequential change cannot be "plugged in"; it must be phased in.[41, 42]

Those most intimately concerned with the planning and trial stages initially can now operate as systems and building leadership persons. Their familiarity with the whole operation, their skill, and their commitment should assist with the initial efforts as well as in full scale installation. Local and on-site support is critical. So is the availability of the required supplies and equipment. Implementation is a very personal as well as a professional enterprise. The failures of an era of innovation and experience provide essential data as to the critical and difficult nature of the implementation process. The problems need to be resolved before, not after, the fact—that is the point of design, involvement, and preparation.

AN ALTERNATIVE STRATEGY

The previous model assumes the efficacy of a *role* or task approach to implementation. There are alternatives. One example is the force field analysis, which can be utilized in many situations where a psychologically oriented strategy is more compatible with the situation, or with the leadership and its style.[43-46] Were this technique to be used, it is likely that the project design suggestions made in Chapters 2 and 3 would also be considerably different from what was proposed.

Considering implementation as a tension or force field presents the opportunity to use this technique as a problem-solving device. Thus, it could be used as an overall design or as the approach at some particular juncture in the program development where problems had arisen. The following suggestions assume that problems or needs have been previously determined, or hopefully, that they have been translated into program objectives having some definition and dimension.

As with other approaches, this analysis and reinforcement plan should be augmented by a high level of participation. If the basic problems are to be dealt with honestly and fully, they must be encouraged to surface. In this way, the approach is realistic and recognizes basic value orientations and feelings, going beyond information transmittal. This is necessary if the plan is to become translated into personal-action strategies that provide an opportunity for changes in thinking as well as knowing, and for changes in commitments and behaviors. Therefore, while the emphasis appears to be on selected elements or forces, the design should be considered a process that results in a composite restructuring rather than a piece-mealing of the desired changes. Acceptance is a basic requirement for any change or implementation plan. This approach assumes both individual acceptance and group acceptance. Likewise, it assumes a desire on the part of leadership to effect a fundamental change, not merely to achieve passive or mandated compliance. Thus, action and change, not analysis, become the basic purpose. Finally, the use of force field analysis as a basic strategy would require

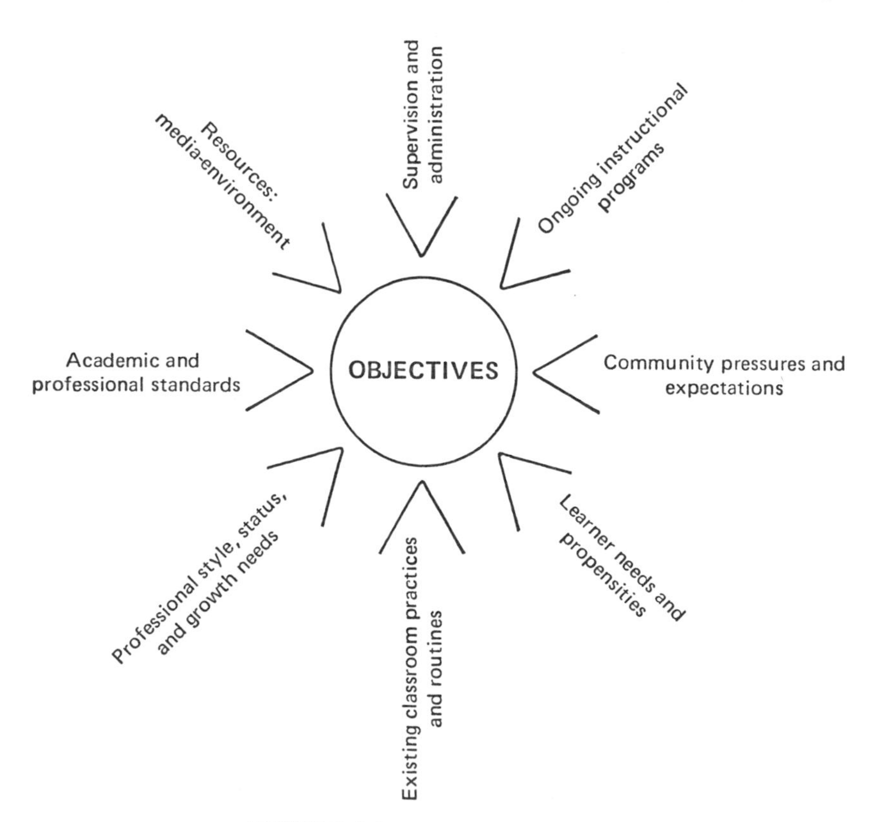

FIGURE 5.8 The Force Field.

that the analysis process be continuous. It could utilize many of the planning stages proposed in the text as renewal or review points for further design efforts.

Analyzing the Field

Any proposed staff development or program objective has a number of factors and forces impinging upon it. These pressures can be identified and acted upon directly, or they can be incorporated into the plan and approach indirectly. Realistically, any plan and its execution require an accommodation or modification of these tensions. Each factor exerts positive and negative pressures; the task of leadership is to enable the affirmative forces to prevail. It should be recognized, however, that *if the goal is professional growth, the original objective itself may be the element in need of change.* It is possible to have meetings and activities without such considerations, but it is unlikely that change or growth will occur.

In such an analysis, the recommended procedure is to identify the critical elements that are impacting upon the desired change, and then, systematically reinforce those forces that are supportive of the desired change (facilitation factors) and weaken those elements that are negatively influencing (restraining forces) the desired ends.

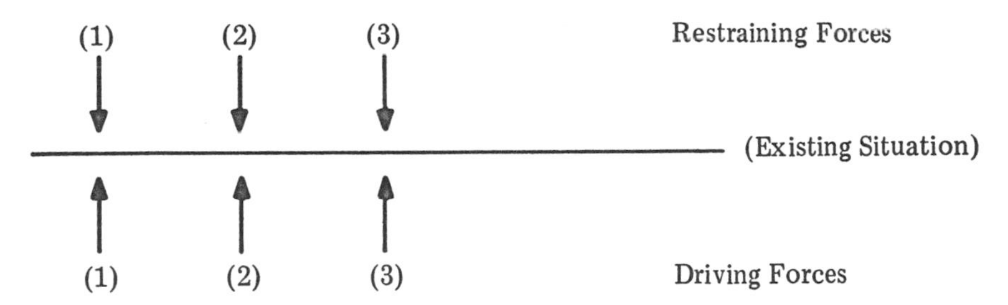

The analysis requires that the various impacting forces be viewed in realistic and operational terms. For example, if there is teacher opposition, this negative force should be translated into manageable items: (1) Teachers are fearful of the change because it requires skills they do not possess, or they do not feel adequate to perform in the classroom setting. (2) They are unaware of the existing resources in the school or community that could assist them. (3) They have not had experience in this type of instructional strategy.

The analysis should include favorable (driving) forces, also stated in operational terms. For example, it may be known that: (1) Parents are in favor of the change because they have heard or read of its success elsewhere. (2) They believe the proposed change would enable their child to be more competent in that skill area. (3) Parents expect the school to move in the direction of the proposed change. The process, then, is to describe the driving and restraining forces as completely and as objectively as possible.

At this point it would be appropriate to determine which elements are immediately amenable to change—how to strengthen the supportive forces and to reduce the impact of the negative forces. For example, the negative forces just described might be reduced by enabling teachers to observe a successful program in another school, by providing training in the appropriate skills essential to delivering the desired change, or by identifying the existing or potential resources that could be used. Likewise, the supportive forces can be reinforced by giving them attention, status, and publicity. Long-range concerns can be similarly approached.

Usually, more information about the objective and its likely consequences contributes to greater acceptance by those who are merely unfamiliar with the idea. However, those who feel threatened will need assurances, evidences of trust, involvement in the actions taken, and participation in the critical processes—from planning through implementation and evaluation. Thus, the initial analysis of the objectives desired and their personal and/or program impact are crucial decisions, as are involvement, flexibility, and compatibility with personal and program goals.

These actions represent basic elements to be incorporated into the plan. They can be identified, discussed, sequenced, and implemented; they signal the basic tasks to be achieved and the major activities and events to be scheduled and supported. Related management tasks are to continue to reinforce the affirmative actions and developments, and to be sure they are built into the ongoing program by support features (budget, staff assignments, policies, routines, and the like). Evaluation of the transactions and feedback to the participants are critical elements in the process.[47,48]

This strategy is relatively simple (in plan, not in execution) because most persons are familiar with the technique of deciding the pros and cons of any action. The difference is: that the relevant factors are considered thoroughly, that they are addressed systematically, that known and observable action is taken, and that the process is culminated in evaluation and feedback, with the achievements being built into the ongoing program and support elements. Many more refinements are possible for this approach than have been sketched briefly here.

Decision making includes a realistic consideration of the "field"—the arena within which changes are to occur. Too many times the vision is constricted so that the context in which the tasks are to be achieved is not broad enough. The result is hidden agendas, unrealistic expectations, and unanticipated conflicts. By now it should be evident that leadership cannot bypass the aspirations and demands of the professional staff or of the parents and community at large. For example, parents exhibit apathy or antagonism when they are uninformed and uninvolved. Teachers are concerned about the nature and application of standards as they relate to their work and their future. This involves the ingredients of teacher education programs, in-service and staff development activities, and admission to the profession (licensing, certification) and to decisions as to its direction. The consumer movement, the new legal suits, and political action groups are further evidences.

In any project, both leadership persons and participants can be expected to need help in *process* skills. Analyzing the progress being made and the difficulties being encountered makes it possible to meet with individuals or groups to deal with process as well as substance.[49-51] Non-project or outside personnel or resources may be used to facilitate movement past policy or procedural barriers that tend to defeat working committees. Therefore, design check points (see pp. 60, 212, and 224) should be viewed as opportunities for constructive assists, not as negative interventions. For those who supervise or monitor project activity, the previously discussed agenda elements (pp. 62–65) can be used as the basis for questioning/reviewing the rationale or the data base for the selected program alternatives. Such review should facilitate quality, structure, accountability, and variety.[52,53]

Process assistance also can include regional resources or a university related approach. Universities can be called upon for a course approach or for a "clinic" series that is designed especially for the local situation. These may focus on standards, research, models, or on options. The options may be based on successful practices existing in the area or detailed in professional literature. Other school systems can be surveyed to find visitation sites or persons who can act in an advisory role, including teachers. In many cases, this can result in a sharing or pooling of personnel and competencies. Consortia efforts among school districts are a largely untapped resevoir of help.[54]

For example, schools attempting to develop or implement an individualized education program would profit from a visit to a site where it was already in operation. This could be followed by inviting to their district a team of teachers and supervisors from that site who were familiar with the problems and advantages of this approach. Through released time procedures, depth discussions between the visiting team and local personnel could be held. Similarly, the host district could reciprocate and provide a comparable service to the other district by sharing ideas and personnel in regard to some project with which they were having success. Very little expense would be involved, and considerable gain in knowledge and feelings could be achieved. In some cases, regional agency or university persons could also participate by contributing information and insight.

This could be followed by feasibility studies, related course work at a university, or local study groups. Such activity fits into the proposed planning schedules. The program phases, discussed in Chapter 3, could be used as agenda items to get at specific or recommended courses of action. Confidence, competence, and commitment flow naturally from such exchanges and opportunities for leadership and planning.

WHEN DOES CHANGE REALLY HAPPEN?

Where curricular or instructional change occurs is seldom universally perceived. Perceptions tend to relate closely to the role persons play in the hierarchy, personal involvement, and decision making relative to the modification in question. The following is an over-generalized account. The intention of this description is to indicate the inadequacies of planning and decision making that too often occur regarding new applications, procedures, or products.[55-57]

Superintendents are often involved heavily at the initiation stage. They are made aware of deficiencies by parental criticism, mass media, research regarding learner achievement, or by curriculum councils or school district committees. If persuaded by the arguments or data, the superintendent becomes involved in policy decisions, budget and personnel agreements, and policy determinations. Administrative regulations become operational. At this point, many are inclined to assume a closure; that is, assume that implementation will occur as a consequence of the decisions, personnel, budget, and procedures underway. Thus, in regard to a particular innovation or change, once it is in the flow of activities in the district, the superintendent is prone to say, "We have *it* in our system."

Central office persons become involved early, perhaps in initiating or shaping the desired change. They organize committees, plan activities, conduct meetings, and provide resources and leadership. They are aware of the power of policy decision making and of the expectations. Once designed and underway, the new proposals will be built into the meetings and work flow of the organization. They are responsible for curriculum guides, the acquisition and development of instructional resources, and the in-service presentations and plans. Once committed to the change and involved in its implementation, they are inclined to believe that the modification really exists when the design phase and the program development phase occur. These stages are their major responsibilities. The new idea has shape and the procedure is defined; by and large "all is well."

School principals become aware of the impending idea. Perhaps they shared in its initiation or in the policy determination relative to the design, time, and personnel allocations. They likely have introduced the ideas to their staff in meetings, and have indicated their support by assigning staff responsibilities that include time and school resources and that inform parents. Groups are at work, schedules have been modified, and materials are being studied or used; the new idea is "underway," and they *have it in their school.*

Teachers and support personnel have heard the ideas and have been introduced to the policy, the program design, and the materials or process to be implemented. They have attended meetings, know of the pressures to institute the change, and feel the need to perform accordingly. Their commitment depends upon their initial acceptance of the idea, the compatibility of the proposal to their working style, and their agreement as to its efficiency in their classroom situation. Their response is compliance or endorsement depending upon their agreement and competence to achieve the desired outcomes. Thus, the project is being implemented on a range of possibilities from the token gestures to enthusiastic participation. Assuming preparation, training, involvement, and compatibility, the plan is now operational and the change is in effect—almost.

Usually the last persons to know are the learners, and in too many cases, their parents. Students study new course materials, do assignments that are different from those done by their peers the year before, follow new procedures, take tests with new items or a changed emphasis, use new materials in the classroom and media center, and different equipment in the laboratory. New building modifications may affect their activities. If pupils perform as required, new behaviors are exhibited and different skills and learnings are evident. (Many in-service or staff development projects have the teachers in the position described above for learners.)

Comprehensive and systematic change procedures should significantly modify this account. The time from initiation to implementation is too hierarchial and too linear in sequence. Involvement, commitment, and competency development need to occur sooner for those who must implement. In the situation just described, it is understandable and likely that short of full-scale implementation, school district leadership will have been caught up in other needs, other concerns, and other goals; and, therefore, the continuing impetus and support is not provided. Implementation must begin with initiation and it must be sustained through design and development stages if it is to impact effectively at the point of installation and operation.

Most changes cannot be decreed; they must be facilitated and processed in accordance with the multiple and professional roles of all the participants. Token involvement begets token commitment; token commitment usually results in minimal response.

Similarly, accountability and evaluation measures should include leadership, impact strategies, and the various sub-systems that contribute to the success or failure of a project. Those who wait until a program reaches the teacher-classroom-student levels are unrealistic and counterproductive. Such measures will be resisted. The use of resources, adequacy in planning, communication, involvement, training, and other system or school level responsibilities also need reviewing. The same holds for community responsibilities, which must be evident in policy determination, the provision of resources, and other support measures. Implementation is actualizing the intent. To be realized, this phase must be well planned, well timed, and well executed.

In some respects, it is strange that we acknowledge the need for great specificity in construction work for schools, houses, bridges, or roads. In these areas, highly detailed plans are developed that incorporate all the elements of time, cost, design, materials, and conditions. Roles and responsibilities are delineated in contract provisions. Monitoring inspections and supervision are explicit. Whether or not educational planning can or should assume such precise dimensions may be a moot question. Without doubt, however, is the evident need to plan, specify, and deliver educational plans with more attention to the dynamics and structure of the operation than we have heretofore achieved. A strategic element in this regard is the nature and role of evaluation, which is the subject of the next chapter.

ACTION GUIDELINES

Implementation is the culmination of a series of activities and events that began with diagnosis and proceeded through the planning stages of defining objectives, structuring and designing, developing, and validating. The implementation phase is where procedures, plans, and product impact to achieve the desired objectives. Implementation requires a change in attitudes as well as program modification or organizational restructuring. Thus, process and style continue to be critical elements.

The delineation of roles and tasks should clarify responsibilities. Such a procedure provides functional mechanisms for coordinating, monitoring, decision making, and evaluating. The strategies necessary to implement a program also should be as carefully considered as the program elements to be instituted. A visual model may be useful for this purpose.

Implementing a comprehensive program requires a modification in the various components or sub-systems. These administrative, leadership, staff, context, program, resources, support, and community elements must be in harmony if the phasing-in effort is to succeed, and if the new program or procedures are to be durable.

Accountability and credibility require sustained and systematic efforts. Parents, patrons, and critics view the outcomes and products as the key elements. The task of educational planning, therefore, does not terminate with the initiation, design, and development stages.

RELATED REFERENCES

1. Miles, Matthew B., ed., *Innovations in Education.* New York: Bureau of Publications, Teachers College, Columbia University, 1964.
2. Association for Supervision and Curriculum Development, *Freedom, Bureaucracy, and Schooling.* Yearbook. Washington, D.C.: author, 1971.
3. Goodlad, John I., and Klein, M. Frances, et al., *Behind the Classroom Door.* Worthington, Ohio: Charles A. James Publishing, 1970.
4. Carver, Fred D., and Sergiovanni, Thomas J., *Organizations and Human Behavior: Focus on Schools.* New York: McGraw-Hill, 1969.
5. Tannenbaum, Arnold S., "Control in Organizations: Individual Adjustment and Organizational Performance." In *Readings in Organizational Behavior and Human Performance,* edited by L. L. Cummings and W. E. Scott. Homewood, Illinois: Richard D. Irwin, Inc. and The Dorsey Press, 1969.
6. Kaufman, Roger A., *Educational Systems Planning.* Englewood Cliffs, New Jersey: Prentice-Hall, 1972.

7. Beckhard, Richard, *Organization Development: Strategies and Models.* Reading, Massachusetts: Addison-Wesley, 1969.
8. Cartwright Dorwin, "Achieving Change in People: Some Applications in Group Dynamics Theory." In *Readings in Organizational Behavior and Human Performance,* edited by L. L. Cummings and W. E. Scott. Homewood, Illinois: Richard D. Irwin, Inc. and The Dorsey Press, 1969.
9. Schmuck, Richard A., Runkel, Philip J., Saturen, Steven L., Martell, R. T., and Derr, O. B., *Handbook of Organization Development in Schools.* Palo Alto, California: National Press Books, 1972.
10. Raths, James, and Leeper, Robert, eds., *The Supervisor: Agent for Change in Teaching.* Washington, D.C.: Association for Supervision and Curriculum Development, 1966.
11. "The Shifting Sands of Educational Purpose." Chapter 1 in *Crucial Issues in Contemporary Education,* edited by Theodore W. Hipple. Pacific Palisades, California: Goodyear Publishing Co., 1973.
12. Caswell, Hollis L., *Curriculum Improvement in Public School Systems.* New York: Bureau of Publications, Teachers College, Columbia University, 1950.
13. Walberg, Herbert A., ed., *Evaluating Educational Performance.* Berkeley, California: McCutchan Publishing Corp., 1974.
14. Taba, Hilda, *Curriculum Development: Theory and Practice.* New York: Harcourt, Brace, and World, 1962.
15. Alfonso, Robert J., Firth, Gerald R., and Neville, Richard F., *Instructional Supervision: A Behavior System.* Boston: Allyn and Bacon, 1975.
16. Association for Supervision and Curriculum Development, *Role of Supervisor and Curriculum Director in a Climate of Change.* Yearbook. Washington, D.C.: author, 1967.
17. Feyercisen, Kathryn V., Fiorino, A. John, and Nowak, Arlene T., *Supervision and Curriculum Renewal: A Systems Approach.* New York: Appleton-Century-Crofts, 1970.
18. Gross, Neal, and Herriott, Robert E., *Staff Leadership in Public Schools.* New York: John Wiley and Sons, 1965.
19. Gwynn, J. Minor, *Theory and Practice of Supervision.* New York: Dodd, Mead, and Company, 1961.
20. Lucio, William, ed., *Supervision: Perspectives and Propositions.* Washington, D.C.: Association for Supervision and Curriculum Development, 1967.
21. Lucio, William H., and McNeil, John D., *Supervision: A Synthesis of Thought and Action.* 2nd ed. New York: McGraw-Hill, 1969.
22. Mosher, Ralph L., and Purpel, David E., *Supervision: The Reluctant Profession.* Boston: Houghton Mifflin, 1971.
23. Sergiovanni, Thomas J., ed., *Professional Supervision for Professional Teachers.* Washington, D.C.: Association for Supervision and Curriculum Development, 1975.
24. Sergiovanni, Thomas J., and Starratt, Robert J., *Emerging Patterns of Supervision: Human Perspectives.* New York: McGraw-Hill, 1971.
25. Tye, Kenneth, "The School Principal: Key Man in Educational Change." *National Association of Secondary School Principals Bulletin,* 56:364 (1972), p. 77.
26. Cook, Desmond L., *PERT: Applications in Education.* Cooperative Research Monograph No. 17. Washington, D.C.: Government Printing Office, 1966.

27. Cunningham, L. L., "Effecting Change Through Leadership." *Educational Leadership*, 21:75 (1963).
28. Getzels, Jacob W., Lipham, James M., and Campbell, Ronald F., *Educational Administration, A Social Process: Theory, Research, Practice.* New York: Harper and Row, 1968.
29. Milstein, Mike M., and Belasco, James A., *Educational Administration and the Behavioral Sciences.* Boston: Allyn and Bacon, Inc., 1973.
30. Council of Educational Facility Planners, *What Went Wrong, Maintenance and Operation Errors to Avoid in Educational Facility Planners.* Columbus, Ohio: author, 1968.
31. Neagley, Ross, Evans, N. Dean, and Lynn, Clarence, *The School Administrator and Learning Resources: A Handbook for Effective Action.* Englewood Cliffs, New Jersey: Prentice-Hall, 1969.
32. Knezevich, Stephan J., *Administration of Public Education.* 2nd ed. New York: Harper and Row, 1969.
33. Macy, Daniel J., "The Role of Process Evaluation in Program Development and Implementation." *Educational Technology*, 15:4 (1975), p. 42.
34. Education for Career Development, *Educational Leadership.* Entire issue. 30:201 (1972).
35. Goldhammer, Keith, and Taylor, Robert E., eds., *Career Education.* Columbus, Ohio: Charles E. Merrill Publishing, 1972.
36. Marland, Sidney P., *Career Education: A Proposal for Reform.* New York: McGraw-Hill, 1975.
37. Miel, Alice, and Lewis, Arthur J., "Toward an Open School." Part 2 in *Supervision for Improved Instruction*, Belmont, California: Wadsworth Publishing Co., 1972.
38. Burton, William H., and Brueckner, Leo J., *Supervision: A Social Process.* New York: Appleton-Century-Crofts, 1955.
39. Raths, James, and Leeper, Robert, eds., *The Supervisor: Agent for Change in Teaching. op. cit.*
40. Rubin, Louis J., ed., *Frontiers in School Leadership.* Chicago: Rand McNally, 1970.
41. Bennis, Warren G., Benne, Kenneth D., and Chin, Robert, eds., *The Planning of Change.* 2nd ed. New York: Holt, Rinehart, and Winston, 1969.
42. Brickell, Henry M., *Organizing New York State for Educational Change.* Albany, New York: State Education Department, 1961.
43. Eye, Glen G., and Netzer, Lanore A., *Supervision of Instruction: A Phase of Administration.* New York: Harper and Row, 1965.
44. "Force Field Analysis." *Journal and Handbook of Staff Development*, Washington, D.C.: National Education Association, March, 1965.
45. Deutsch, Morton, and Krauss, Robert M., *Theories in Social Psychology.* New York: Basic Books, 1965.
46. Lewin, Kurt, *Field Theory in Social Science.* New York: Harper and Brothers, 1951.
47. Association for Supervision and Curriculum Development, *Evaluation as Feedback and Guide.* Yearbook. Washington, D.C.: 1967.
48. Beatty, Walcott H., ed., *Improving Educational Assessment and an Inventory of Measures of Affective Behavior.* Washington, D.C.: Association for Supervision and Curriculum Development, 1969.

49. Bonner, H., *Group Dynamics: Principles and Application.* New York: Ronald Press, 1959.
50. Cartwright, Dorwin, and Zander, A., eds., *Group Dynamics: Research and Theory.* 2nd ed. Evanston, Illinois: Row, Peterson, and Company, 1960.
51. Watson, Goodwin, *Social Psychology: Issues and Insights.* Philadelphia: J. C. Lippincott, 1966.
52. Argyris, Chris, *Intervention Theory and Method.* Reading, Massachusetts: Addison-Wesley, 1970.
53. McGregor, Douglas, *The Human Side of Enterprise.* New York: McGraw-Hill, 1960.
54. Goodlad, John I., "Staff Development: The League Model." *Theory Into Practice.* 11:207 (1972).
55. Halverson, Paul M., "A Model for the Assessment of Readiness for Change in Curriculum and Instruction." In *Improving Supervisory Competencies,* edited by Leslee J. Bishop. Georgia Association of Supervision and Curriculum Development and the Center for Curriculum Improvement and Staff Development. Athens, Georgia: The Center, Department of Curriculum and Supervision, University of Georgia, 1973.
56. Innovation: Purpose and Effect, *Educational Leadership,* entire issue. 25:281 (1968).
57. Leeper, Robert, ed., *Strategy for Curriculum Change.* Washington, D.C.: Association for Supervision and Curriculum Development, 1965.

6

Evaluating

Evaluation is not research, testing, measurement, or statistics, although these will all probably be involved. Evaluation should contribute to decision making and in-process corrections; to program improvement, reporting, and feedback; to creativity and variety in the in-service efforts; and to improved staff renewal programs and related staff-learner gain. Evaluation and evaluative measures are integral to the educative process and the related management of that process. These valuing processes and instruments are essential in order to determine the efficiency and effectiveness of the programs in operation—the degree to which the means, design, development, coordination, and implementation meet the objectives.[1-3]

Some form of evaluation begins as soon as a program or project has identity, that is, as soon as it has been decided upon as an organized activity. Evaluation that is functional is also continuous and proceeds in accordance with the determined personal processes, change phases, objectives at various program levels, task and product decisions, and management structures (organization, time frames, use of personnel, facilities, and so forth). Data, outcomes, and artifacts produced by these elements should be amenable to evaluative review. Evaluative standards are used whether they are recognized as such and whether or not the evaluation is instrumented or officially done. Therefore, the task of management is to identify and make visible the various program elements for review and utilization. Qualitative planning consciously builds evaluation into the work flow and work structure.[4-6]

Many concepts of evaluation are possible. The intent of the text is not to explore them here, but rather, to summarize one stance: Evaluation of process as it transpires, or of product as it eventuates, should serve the objectives of the project rather than the demands of the evaluator or the instrumentation.

Evaluation has multiple uses and intents. To reiterate, the check-out of progress regarding the basic objectives, whether they are program, staff or student related, is needed continuously and for the following purposes: (1) To ascertain the extent of gain, not only in selected segments but also in regard to balance between special efforts and the total ongoing program. (2) To provide diagnostic and interim data for feedback, reporting, program modification, and decision making. (3) To continuously assess strengths and weaknesses of leadership as well as the performance of those for whom the objectives and program have been designed. (4) To assist in the development of growth in evaluative skills and in the production of appropriate instruments at all levels. (5) To acknowledge evaluation as an expected professional obligation. Such purposes can be approached by including evaluation as an integral functioning, rather than merely a pre-post test or a review conducted apart from the regular program activities.[7-10]

Thus, research and evaluation cannot exist apart from the leadership and process efforts. An accounting must be made for the means and measures employed in addition to the outcomes achieved. Interim measures require delineations and decisions based on the structures and processes utilized. The subsequent proposals deal less with specific evaluative procedures, instruments, and techniques than with the planning elements that facilitate and incorporate such utilizations. Hopefully, in this context many of the text suggestions mean more than mere management niceties.

BASIC CONSIDERATIONS

Basic considerations in evaluation are usually held to be the following:

1. Objectives—What was the intent of the project or activity?
2. Environment—What facilities, what processes, what inputs (time, money, staff, etc.) were used? What were the circumstances that preceded and followed the activity? What were the limitations, the constraints, the context?
3. What actions were taken? What were the transactions? What elements and inputs were modified or impacted in order to achieve the objectives?
4. What happened? Where was change or modification evident—in what regard, at what point, how much? To what extent did a direct result occur? To what extent was a side effect or indirect result obtained?
5. How close to the objective did the activity come? What were the merits, the shortcomings? Against what base line or standard can the progress or discrepancy be viewed? What unexpected or fortuitous results can be identified?
6. "So what?" How should subsequent planning, circumstances, and activities be modified? What alternatives should be attempted, what recommendations made; what should be recycled, what valued as satisfactory and worthy of reinforcement? Who should do these things and under what changed circumstances?

These *feedback* items are not evaluation *per se*, but are considered a basic reason for the evaluation to be made, often accompanying the interpretation of the data collected.

Figure 6.1 illustrates the text evaluation process. This process becomes functional once the program elements are delineated; with minor modifications, it operates at all program levels—from system-wide objectives and activities to classroom operations. Many competencies are required to complete the various phases and transactions in evaluation. These constitute professional skills that can properly be the content for staff development work.

Definition and Elements

A few brief definitions of terms as they are used in text may be a useful preliminary to the other design suggestions that follow. *Evaluative measures* are the techniques or instruments used to collect and ascertain the extent or nature of change that has occurred. *Evaluation* is the process and standard used to assign worth or value to the evidence that has been collected.

Many techniques are possible for gathering data; some are overused, others are seldom employed. Extensive programs will likely require formalized and instrumented procedures. Such measures are useful as records of particular events, simulation responses, performance records, targeted interviews, observer reports, tests, questionnaires, checklists, case studies, critical incident reports, activity logs, and ratings. Projects smaller in duration or scope may use informal measures such as audiotape interviews, check sheets, narrative data, opinionnaires, field notes, video tapes, or photographic evidence and anecdotes.[11-13]

In practice, most of these techniques are suitable for either short or long range operations, the nature of the measures and their use being the determining factors. Measures may be used by participants or observers depending upon the way in which the data are to be standardized and used. However developed or used, staff members must know the type of evaluative measures to be employed and the relationship between these data and the overall program, as well as their relationship to the evaluation of the staff person as a professional.

Discrepancy is a useful concept employed to indicate the difference between the objective or expected outcome and the measured achievement of that objective, that is, the fit between objectives and critical variables. This approach is viable regarding in-service and staff development activities as well as for the ongoing instructional program. They should be closely related. Discrepancies at the various program or instructional levels are useful data in determining staff and program needs, whether for all personnel or for limited numbers.[14] Too often, the data relating to learners are used to assign marks instead of establishing needs for instructional improvement or staff development activity. The proponents of *criterion-based evaluation* (advancement or achievement determined by meeting the stated objective, rather than

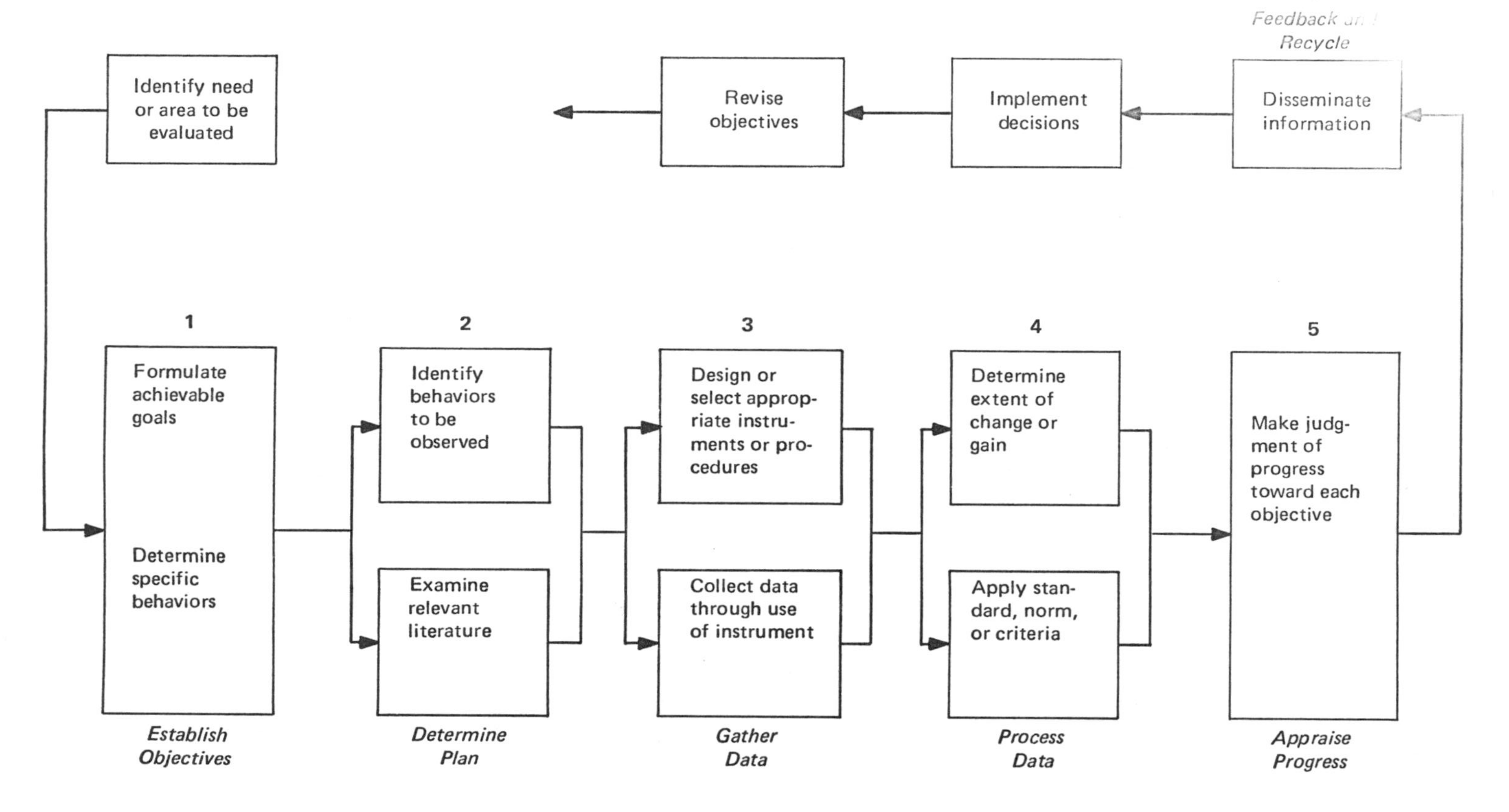

FIGURE 6.1 The Process of Evaluation.

falling within a norm) see this type of evaluation as particularly appropriate to staff development and any individualized project. Closely related is the use of *domain-referenced testing*, a process that systematically selects from the range of knowledge and skills those which are representative and predictive of the total field.[15-23]

Time frames contribute to a decision as to whether the evaluation shall be formative or summative. *Formative evaluation* was already suggested to be an increasingly significant utilization. It provides the en-route assessments that are made prior to the terminal point. Its uses include a review of the ongoing procedures and their effectiveness, areas of weakness, strength, cost in regard to efficiency, and effectiveness. It also shows the diagnosis and determination of emergent needs for leadership training or staff development, the adequacy of particular materials and processes, and the decisions regarding the impact of the design elements as they occur at various levels and with different persons—staff and students. *Summative evaluation* occurs at the termination of a project or program. It provides evidences as to overall effectiveness and offers a review of the total operation in terms of its design and implementation. These data are useful for predicting the utility of a plan and sequence. They provide baseline data for subsequent program planning and perhaps norms useful for innovative, interim, and individualized efforts. The results are obtained in pre-post testing, longitudinal research, and experimental designs; they also include consequences extending beyond, and perhaps unanticipated or not evident, in, the ongoing review process. As new evaluative techniques are developed, experimental and summative measures promise to become more realistic and more operational. In any case, they can exist as both longer term appraisal points and as the valuing of cumulative data.[24,25]

Other elements are critical to the process. *Baseline data* are those usually collected at the initiation (needs analysis or design) stage of a project or at the termination of a total program. *Process data* are interim checks that consider the adequacy of the procedures in achieving the desired objectives. Information may relate to such items as staff morale, communication flow, extent and nature of involvement (see pp. 80-82), and related products developed to date. *Monitoring* is a process usually related to formative and process evaluations by which management obtains necessary information as to what is happening—target achievement, utilization, and feeling. These data are for both review and prediction. In some cases, such data contribute to a decision, i.e., change plans, modify strategies or institute special interventions and planned assists. *Auditing* is a process instituted by the concern for accountability; that is, data collection to provide information as to adequacy and appropriateness of the evaluative measures and their results at given intervals. It is usually done by qualified persons outside the system. *Context* is the circumstances that surround the project activity—organizational climate, pressures, processes, and resources; it defines the parameters or limits within which the project activity occurs. The analysis of the results, or of alternative approaches as they relate to resources employed or planned, may be called *cost effectiveness;* value considerations also are inherent.[26-32]

IMPLEMENTING A NEW ROLE FOR EVALUATION

School programs do not stand still; they modify as they move, rather than wait for designated terminal points. Teachers change roles, students leave, conditions/requirements are modified. Therefore, a belief is developing that interim measures such as monitoring and formative evaluation are most useful and realistic to the practitioner. This requires taking a series of "snap-shots" for purposes of analysis and decision making, knowing full well that the dimensions will change even as they are being analyzed. As indicated, evaluation in this situation becomes a tool for decision making and process modification, not a grand summation of progress.[33,34]

This realistic view is changing the perception of evaluation and the evaluative process; it also is changing the instruments and the designs. This role for evaluation involves the necessity for systematically considering what has taken place and assessing the degree to which the project is achieving its stated objectives. If each design phase has been purposively followed, then data will exist for appraisal. For example, input decisions are made in connection with the needs analysis and objectives, and in target and means determination. Each of these stages and decisions requires and generates data for review. Likewise, as program elements are structured and delineated in the design, development, and specification phases, a relationship should be identifiable between the initial objectives or their subsequent culmination (outcome), even at the interim-program development stage. The processes employed to achieve this result generate context data and decisions that can be reviewed as to direction and effectiveness. These efforts were referred to as process evaluation. They would be achieved by recording and analyzing the processes underway and by assessing at that moment what had transpired, and with what impact. The judgments made about those efforts and data would be the evaluation.

Thus, research and evaluation cannot exist apart from the processes and plans made to achieve program goals. In any comprehensive project, evaluation that includes only learner impact data is both incomplete and unwise, however well-intentioned. Learner achievement is the heart of the school enterprise, but not the totality of it. Nor is it the only outcome for which leaders have responsibility and for which they will be held accountable. Within the context of school, many kinds of operations need to be reviewed and determined, using standards and using data. Schools, programs, courses, materials, processes, roles, and competencies—these and other elements may be contextural insofar as student learning is concerned. At the same time, they represent goals, costs, commitments, roles, and resources also to be examined . . . examined for their standards, their contributions, their adequacy, and their impact. Instruments and measures cannot ascertain these things from learner data alone—at least not yet. One evidence is the lack of "significant differences" that exist when some of these variables are modified. As indicated, the growing requirement for evaluation is that, whatever the target group, it also helps improve the quality of resource utilization, decision making, and program planning. This requirement must find expression in the instruments used, the standards employed, and the data reviewed and reported. Evaluation, therefore, becomes a continuous adjunct to program execution and staff functioning, not simply a terminal judgment.[35,36]

This development is evident because new needs are becoming a part of the leadership responsibility, for example:

- Cost (cost effectiveness measures/product effectiveness data)
- Program structure (PPBES, PERT and Systems Analysis, MBO)
- Design (systems approach, process evaluation, auditing, structure, and alternatives)
- Specification (program objectives, program delineation, and task standards)
- Outcome (professional competency, learner gain, program improvement, and credibility)
- Participation and decision making (feedback, process data, and reporting)
- Control (management, design, monitoring, evaluation, and decision making)

In these and other concerns, evaluation plays a strategic role that goes beyond scanning for management intervention, appraising, and decision-making. "Black box" measures or standard and hidden processes are inadequate for these requirements.

Within this context, the program being evaluated constitutes the decision framework. A unit for learners can have initial objectives, transactional variables, and a culmination. The same is true of a project emphasizing staff gains or curricular change. The important consideration is that these be viewed as important entities . . . but entities that exist within larger goals, objectives, and desired outcomes. The related function for planners and planning is to identify and delineate the basic elements of any instructional endeavor in order to research and assess their adequacy and impact. Selection becomes critical, since only representative segments can be examined in depth. Decision-makers must determine which program purposes and outcomes are crucial or useful, and, what the requirements of the school system are in addition to the requirements of a particular enterprise. In many situations, political and policy questions may overshadow the instructional issues that are involved. National, statewide, and standardized testing reflect these concerns. Credibility, accountability, and progress require that programs be scrutinized fully and realistically. Since the major purpose of program development for staff or learners is continuous gain and improvement, whether the evaluation is "formative" or "summative" is largely a matter of definition dependent on the perspective and time frame of the definer and decision-maker. The measures used, the judgments made, and the use of the data will reflect these decisions.[37,38]

The ideas of the following section illustrate these considerations, focusing upon program elements rather than on an individual teacher, learner, or program objective.

Work Flow and Evaluation

As a consequence of the various program elements being implemented, there is a constant flow of activities, events, and the production of artifacts. Also, stated and unstated objectives move through the time frame, so that:

- Changes are made in the sub-systems (schools system components and planning levels).
- Organizational processes operate (involvement, impact strategies, and decision making).
- Inputs are made and recorded (time, money, resources, and energy).
- Events are planned and executed regarding program objectives (workshops, research, and reports).
- Process objectives are implemented (guidelines and relationships).
- Learner and staff behavior are changed.
- Problems are encountered and resolved, and modifications made.

As these objective generated activities move through time, they intersect with the structural elements of the program. These elements are composed of the following items:

- Designated time intervals (weeks, months, or years).
- Planning or management phases (needs analysis, design, development, and implementation).
- Program limitations (time, cost, personnel, emergencies, and conflicts with other ongoing programs).
- Planned interventions (process check points, consultant use, and formative evaluation procedures).

These intersections of activity flow and organizational structure provide many alternatives for decision and review. The task of the planner is to decide which of these flows need to be reviewed, at what points, for what purpose, and with what means.

What follows is a list of possible concerns, some of which are typical in any program and some of which are unique or specialized. Listed in the past tense here, they could be restated as formative or summative evaluation items. From these and other concerns, it should be possible to select appropriate evaluation junctures and emphases.

Representative Evaluation Possibilities

1. Which program objectives have been implemented as planned, and with what result?

2. What new objectives became operational, at what points, under what circumstances, and for what reasons?
3. What specific skills or instructional competencies were sought? What changes or gains were evident and to what extent?
4. What learner behaviors were changed? By what means? With what outcome?
5. How were concerns for validity and reliability built into the processes and instruments that were used?
6. What data were most productive for decision making, for assessing quality, and for reordering or recycling?
7. What materials or program resources were most productive and most often used? By whom? Under what circumstances? With what results?
8. Which procedures or routines were most useful? Why? For what purpose?
9. What incentives seemed most powerful, with which personnel, and at what points?
10. What data were reported (feedback) to participants, auditors, learners, school board, community, system personnel, and committees?
11. What limitations, concerns, or unexpected successes were evident?
12. Which events were most successful? Which artifacts were most useful?
13. What quantifications were possible and by what means?
14. Which processes (guidelines and activities) were implemented? Which were reviewed? Which caused improved morale? Which remained unfulfilled or disappointing?
15. What program or process alternatives were needed or used? What new cost or time factors arose? How were they managed?
16. What persons or processes failed? At what points were there unexplained, unplanned, and undesirable delays or problems? Which constraints were most causal or limiting?
17. Where did special or personal prerogatives result in needed facilitation or in negative intervention?
18. Which sub-systems, or program components exceeded expectations? Which faltered or did not develop as planned?
19. What happened to the design elements or phases; were they implemented or modified? Who participated in the decisions to alter?
20. Which instruments or formulae were most useful in the assessment task? Which provided unnecessary, conflicting, or unused data? Which became onerous because of time consumed, unexpected sensitivity, or lack of consensus regarding outcome?
21. When and under what circumstances were parents involved and with what result? When were other community personnel or resources utilized?
22. How did the involved personnel participate in data gathering, assessing, and reporting?
23. At what points was staff, learner, or community consensus and commitment most evident? How was it secured, with what consequences?
24. What support elements were most useful? Which support features were missing or should be emphasized in another similar effort?
25. At which points was the ongoing program changed? For what reasons, to what extent, and in what ways was it most evident?
26. Where were outside agencies or consultants most needed, most productive, or least useful?

Work Flow	*Collection of Results/Data*	*Analysis and Interpretation*	*Evaluation*
Achievement of stated objectives (program, staff, and learners)			
Developments within system component areas and program levels			
Completion of events and personal responsibilities (project tasks)			
Implementations of planned time intervals and/or management phases			
Developments and achievements regarding guidelines and organizational processes.			

FIGURE 6.2 Work Flow and Evaluation.

27. What new leadership involvements, alignments, or organizational elements emerged? With what impact, with what continuing implications?
28. At what points were pre-post or longitudinal data most useful?

Obviously, the list of possible items could be as extensive as the project demanded, or as ingenious as the imagination of the planners and participants. The structuring and use of such concerns are important design and management responsibilities; the items in Figure 6.2 are interdependent, illustrating possible emphases and implications taken from the above list.

The segment that follows lists a number of ways whereby these elements of structure and work flow can be organized for evaluative purposes. A number of the matrices used earlier have been repeated to show the direct relationship between the planning and structuring devices and the tasks of evaluation.

In most of the following illustrations, only two dimensions have been indicated although additional ones should be considered. The reasons are that more than two dimensions cause a problem of visualization on the flat plane of the page, and that the additional dimensions usually include so many options that even the briefest listing overloads the figure. In what follows, the first, left column, dimension usually includes the elements, components, or sub-system considerations. The second, or right hand side, lists the change phases and stages—usually some way of depicting time and its use. The third dimension, which would be at the conjunction of the other two and indicated by the cells, would represent *treatment;* namely, the quantifications, standards, or criteria that would be applied, and the subsequent decision making or valuing of the data under consideration.

How data are to be collected, analyzed, and judged lies beyond the scope of this "guide." That does not minimize their importance; rather, it admits the difficulty of trying to deal in a single text with all the research methodologies, statistical measures, formulae, treatments, and quantifications that are possible in a qualitative evaluation program. Also, these uses depend upon such diverse factors as purpose, research sophistication, personnel, instruments, access to computers, data processing equipment, and operational style.

Another characteristic to be noted is that the suggested approaches to evaluation tend to be system (macro) oriented rather than focused on the individual (micro), which was the emphasis in Chapter 4. The system view involves both the total organism of the school and district and a systematic research effort that includes the program design and implementation. This does not exclude the individual; it, instead, incorporates learner data within the context and conditions that have existed during the learning intervals. Such considerations assume that, in most instances, the data emerge from natural rather than contrived situations. More gross data are, therefore, likely to be used for certain aspects of the evaluation. This will be discomforting to some; it will admittedly call for new measures of analysis, new skills by the evaluator (more likely requiring a team effort), new instruments, and standards.

However, the yield should be more realistic in terms of what actually transpired and more useful to subsequent research and evaluation schemes. This approach should help close the gap between research and practice, and, thereby, should provide missing longitudinal data regarding design, program operation, and impact procedures.

EVALUATION APPROACHES AND ELEMENTS

Purpose, then, determines the time, the instruments, the judgments, and the utilization of the consequent data. Likewise, the structure of the project, the processes used, and the outcomes, all present useful handles for assisting in the review purpose. A number of approaches are suggested below; they are compatible and show possible emphases, they are not mutually exclusive.

Approach When Objectives Have Been Determined (Fig. 6.3)

Because of their specificity, objectives are a major device for ascertaining and reviewing outcomes as well as for determining intent. Those statements of objectives that contain conditions, treatment, criteria, and standard are also likely to be measurable, and thus, amenable to review. Very often, resources are allocated and time frames determined in relationship to the objectives. As a project unfolds, objectives are met, achieved in part, or bypassed. Therefore, at any given time, it is possible to check out the outcomes and progress that have been made and to review the products and artifacts that have been produced. This information may exist as a result of the monitoring and information flow processes; if so, it is available for evaluation and decision making without needing additional measures (pp. 216-222).

Objectives are the organizing elements for such approaches as those discussed in Appendix D, such as: management by objectives, planning, programming, budgeting and evaluating system, organization development, facilitating practices such as clinical supervision, and regional accrediting agencies—to name a few.

An important consideration in these schemes, in addition to specificity, is the program level. As indicated in Chapter 2, objectives can be framed at program levels where the general performance or outcome and broad responsibility have been indicated. They may be regarded as interim objectives where observable results are evident and where responsibility and resources have been indicated, although the outcome may be achieved by a variety of inputs. And most importantly, they also may be viewed as instructional objectives where clear statements exist as to performance, outcomes, conditions—including time, and criteria.[39]

In some organizational arrangements, PPBES being one example, objectives reflect the structure of the plan and the substance of the

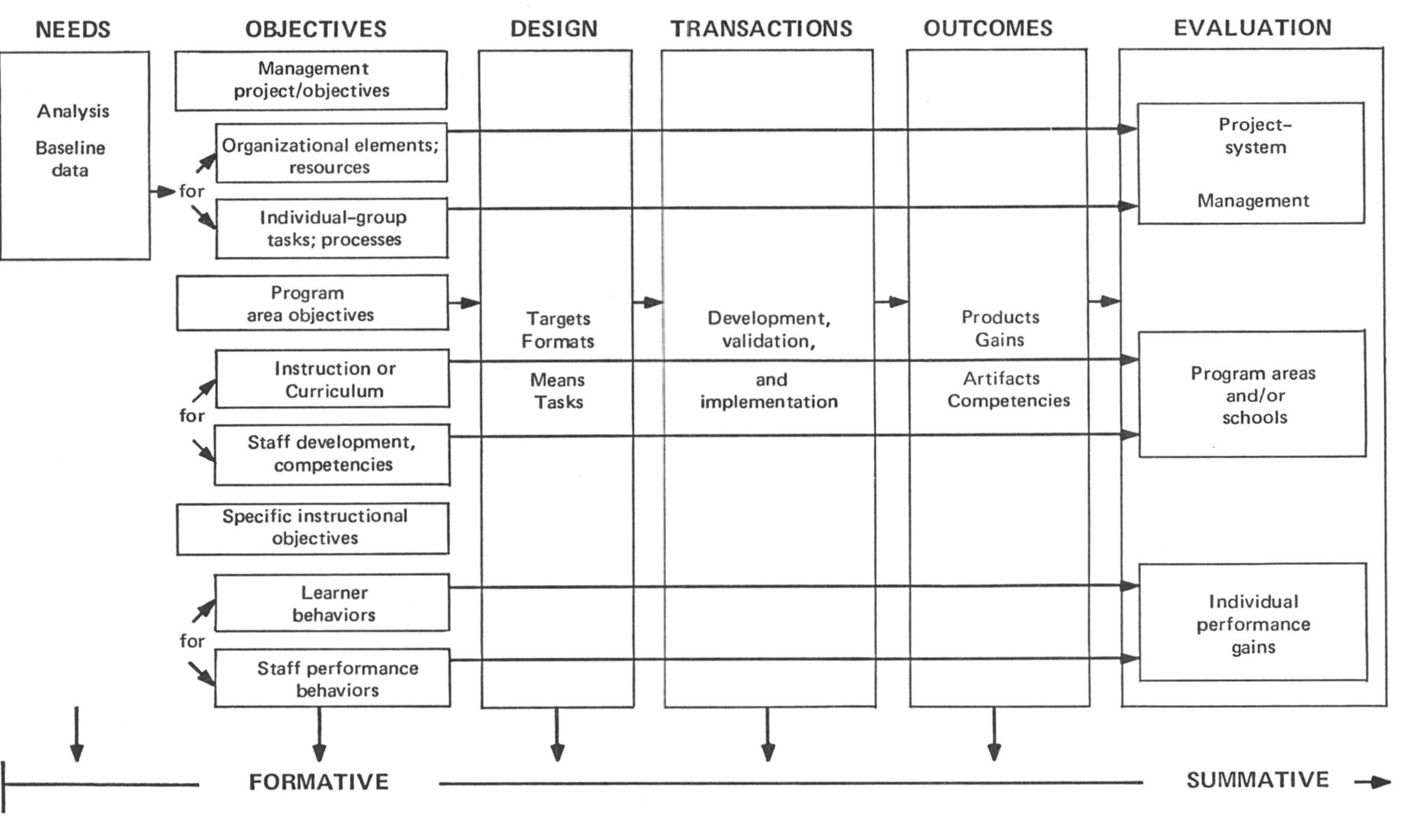

FIGURE 6.3 Follow-Through on Objectives: Design Elements and Levels.

program. Therefore, each program level is a potential source of review since each has its own structure, rationale, roles, and operational modes. As objectives are achieved at the various levels, often in relationship to planned sequences, functional intersections exist for evaluative measures and purposes. Figure 6.3 illustrates these occurrences. In this situation, the provision exists to check out macrodistrict data (project level) where evaluative inquiries would indicate the overall changes and discrepancies, in other words, the effectiveness of management to move the program along.

These changes and data would also exist in relationship to the subject area (content or program), or, depending upon project definitions, they could also be at the school level. Such data would indicate program and staff progress within that designated arena. For a limited project, this could constitute a grade or course level as well.

Finally, these objectives and their outcomes would be related to performance objectives at the micro (learner or instructional) level. For students, this would be a check of impact and gain regarding a particular lesson; for staff, perhaps a particular teaching skill. It is at this point in development that test items are written, such as those on a standardized test. These may be either criterion or norm based questions. Such tests have wide use, but few of them involve motor or application skills. Evaluation of the effectiveness of a systemwide or school program then becomes a mix of judgments regarding project activity, program or school areas, individual learner progress, staff-instructional competencies, and program improvement. The literature regarding performance level objectives and outcomes is so extensive that subsequent examples will focus on ways to review developments at program or management levels.[40]

Approach When a Monitoring Scheme Has Been Used

By its nature, monitoring is an evaluative activity. The data assembled, interpreted, and reviewed, relate very closely to those required in formative evaluation. In this case, it is likely that the data will be more instrumented and more quantified, thus subject to a more critical scrutiny. Since decisions and modifications will have been made, the collected data become available for use in the summative evaluation; the decisions will indicate the modifications that have to be considered in the terminal review. Further amplifications of this approach can be reviewed in connection with the discussion on monitoring, see pp. 216–222. Monitoring data are especially useful at the management level if they are combined with program phases or with event analysis. In addition to the suggestions given above, many of the "critical questions" contained in Chapter 7 on management can also be structured to provide monitoring or formative evaluation possibilities.

An obvious problem here is the possibility of confusion between the needs of the planner or decision-maker and the needs of the evaluator. Both need data, both must analyze and interpret. However, the follow-up responsibility for management is to make decisions—to restructure, to recycle, or to proceed. The responsibility of the evaluator is to assess progress in terms of criteria, to determine discrepancy or congruence between objectives and outcomes, and, perhaps, to recommend action based on the analyzed data.

Approach When a Program Design Has Been Followed

If the design recommendations suggested in Chapters 1 and 3 were followed, each panel or phase would represent a logical place for an evaluative review. In this connection, Figure 6.4 demonstrates one way whereby each program development segment can be evaluated in terms of the concepts given in the CIPP Model (by Stufflebeam), except for the positioning of the input segment.[41]

Operationally, when the planner and the project move from one program phase to the next, an implicit (if not explicit) evaluation and decision has been made. For example, a judgment must be made that the needs as determined (Panel 1, p. 62) are adequate and valid. The same judgments exist for the other phases, such as stating objectives, determining target population, deciding about means, and so forth. The judgment made is that the processes and products relative to the design task are adequate or that the activity proceeds or recycles until adequacy is achieved.

In regard to planning, the most critical evaluative point is at the development stage. This is the culmination of the design work, when decisions regarding objectives, targets, and means are built into materials, environment, competencies, and processes. These will impact upon learners, staff, and community and result in resource use, cost, time, commitment, and concern for the outcome.[42]

Program adequacy and effectiveness, on the other hand, are determined at the implementation stage. This is the operational test of both planning and executing. Evaluation may suggest the need to rewrite, recycle, and in any case provide extensive feedback. In project efforts where the design stages were short-circuited by adapting or adopting programs developed elsewhere, the responsibility still remains to generate evaluative data indicating that the adopted plan is working in this situation and with this particular group of learners or professionals.

If desired, these review points can be formalized. Perhaps, some stages will be more carefully scrutinized than others; or some combination of steps will constitute the review segment, depending upon the emphasis and the design. Examples are given subsequently in relationship to managing, see p. 201, coordinating, p. 212, and monitoring, pp. 216–222. Any decision point, in fact, represents a logical place for an evaluative review. Data collection and review at these junctures also can provide useful baseline data (as well as progress data) for further evaluation or for similar program efforts. The same holds for process evaluation, which may be separate or combined review. Some process items were proposed in Chapter 3 and are the focus of Figure 6.5.

		1	2	3	4	5	6	7	8	9	
		Needs	*Objectives*	*Target*	*Means*	*Format*	*Specifications*	*Development*	*Implement*	*Evaluate*	
INPUTS	Context	1.1	2.1	3.1	4.1	5.1	6.1	7.1	8.1	9.1	*Comprehensive–Summative Evaluation*
	Process–procedures	1.2	2.2	3.2	4.2	5.2	6.2	7.2	8.2	9.2	
	Outcome–product	1.3	2.3	3.3	4.3	5.3	6.3	7.3	8.3	9.3	

NOTE: Rows indicate cumulative and summative evaluation.
Columns are formative, in-process evaluation.

FIGURE 6.4 Evaluation–Decision Points Based on Design Agenda (pp. 62–65).

Approach When Process Guidelines and Elements Are Identified

Process items usually involve participation and involvement and often have less discernable results than are present with product and artifact related outcomes. Intervention strategies, organization development, and similar approaches make more use of psychological or personal development junctures than of arbitrary time, change design, or event related sequences. In any case, the function is to determine the impact, that is, the net result from the work to date, and to proceed in accordance with that analysis. While these may call for different structural intervals, the personal and process items given in Chapter 3 can be reviewed in much the same manner as that suggested for other schemes.

Figure 6.5 is a repeat of that given in Chapter 3. It lists various intersections that can be determined as review points in connection with staff development program phases. A similar listing was called "guidelines," see pp. 79–82. Chapter 7, Managing, proposes an evaluation-feedback check as a functional responsibility in connection with each management phase, see p. 201. The responsibility to check is also appropriate at points designated for coordination or decision making, see p. 212.

The degree to which these progress stages and process gains are formalized, monitored, instrumented, and assessed depends upon the resources, requirements, and management style to be used.

The processes and products of evaluative efforts constitute a powerful lever that should be considered a strategy for change, in addition to a source of useful data. This impact affects the nature and quality of the program and the persons included in the evaluation. Such information and its valuing become incentive factors for involved staff persons who have pride in their achievements as well as concern for their effectiveness. While evaluation can constitute a threat, the proper use of resulting data should be supportive. Evaluative measures provide additional opportunities for staff to contribute knowingly to record keeping, decision making, and the documentation of gain. In the process, project leadership can contribute to the provision of linkage between the production of new knowledge (research) and the utilization of that knowledge (practice).[43,44]

Approach When a PERT Figure Has Been Developed

Since PERTed events, see p. 236, have a profile representing an artifact, a decision, or landmark; each event is a potential source for evaluative treatment. Obviously, some are more appropriate and others are more critical or strategic, but the decision making opportunity exists. Also, the activities (lines between events) lend themselves to a review of the processes that have been employed. In this connection, see the previous approach; also, evaluation suggestions are given re PERT in Chapter 8.

PERT networks present other possibilities. As indicated on p. 235, it would be desirable to check out critical sequences—as time sequences,

REPRESENTATIVE PROCESS ELEMENTS	*PROGRAM PHASES*									
	Needs	*Objectives*	*Target*	*Means*	*Formats*	*Specifications*	*Development*	*Implementation*	*Evaluation*	*Feedback*
1. Clarifying nature of desired change	1	16	31	46	61	76	91	106	121	136
2. Utilizing a variety of means	2	17	32	47	62	77	92	107	122	137
3. Implementing objectives at various levels	3	18	33	48	63	78	93	108	123	138
4. Relating project to ongoing programs	4	19	34	49	64	79	94	109	124	139
5. Seeking involvement and commitment	5	20	35	50	65	80	95	110	125	140
6. Incorporating incentives and motivation	6	21	36	51	66	81	96	111	126	141
7. Communicating management elements	7	22	37	52	67	82	97	112	127	142
8. Defining and utilizing process guidelines	8	23	38	53	68	83	98	113	128	143
9. Developing and using support features	9	24	39	54	69	84	99	114	129	144
10. Using individual schools as basic units	10	25	40	55	70	85	100	115	130	145
11. Providing related leadership training	11	26	41	56	71	86	101	116	131	146
12. Using monitoring and formative data	12	27	42	57	72	87	102	117	132	147
13. Involving and communicating with community	13	28	43	58	73	88	103	118	133	148
14. Proving feedback and reinforcement	14	29	44	59	74	89	104	119	134	149
15. Relating to standards and developments	15	30	45	60	75	90	105	120	135	150

FIGURE 6.5 Relating Process Elements to Program Phases (Planning, Managing, and *Evaluating*).

component developments, or program achievements. If desired, a time frame could be imposed upon a PERT diagram, e.g. vertical lines, with formative evaluation occurring at significant or defined time intervals. If the network had been developed as suggested, see p. 231 (Fig. 8.9) and p. 236 (Fig. 8.16), using component (input) considerations, then these event-activity lines would also represent appropriate evaluative possibilities.

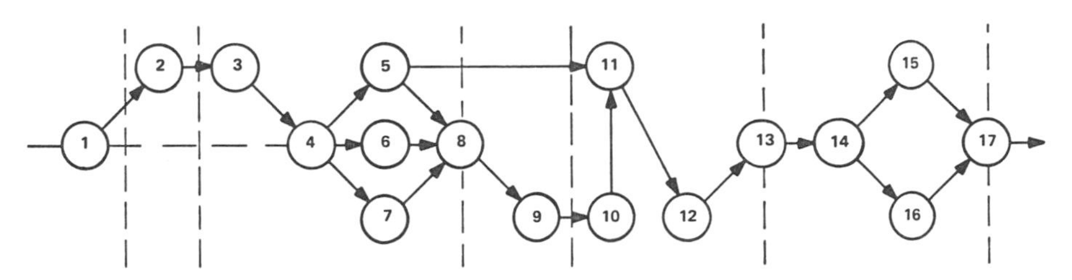

FIGURE 6.6 PERT (Events and Activities—Time Frames).

Approach When Related System Components Are Critical to Program Success

For large scale or system wide projects, one major concern should be the development of the related sub-systems or instructional components. They include those items discussed in connection with designing, see pp. 75–76, such as policy and decision making, project leadership or management, staff-personnel, project program, program materials and resources, support features, and community involvement.[45] While this is not a complete list of any school district's basic sub-systems, they are emphasized here because of their direct relationship to the instructional program, especially to staff members and learners. These are critical input items that can lead to the development of alternative designs or procedures. Schools cannot depend upon research and development centers, universities, or individual scholars to provide essential and continuing data. A distant agency or institution can hardly research the developments, products, unique gains, and problems that relate to a particular school district and its many internal systems and sub-systems. Program development and implementation require realignment of all the related components. They are context and environment items, too often minimized and the elements possibly most in need of change or revision rather than the program itself.[46]

Thus, as a program plan becomes operational, it is necessary to review progress taking place in these component areas. This is crucial to the development of the support features that must reinforce the project effort. Similarly, any comprehensive plan will include events and activities in these related sub-systems (see regarding PERT, p. 229). Each sub-system should demonstrate growth, for example, materials and resources. In this instance, materials should be purchased or developed in accordance with the implementation schedule. They should be evaluated as products that meet instructional specifications and should show

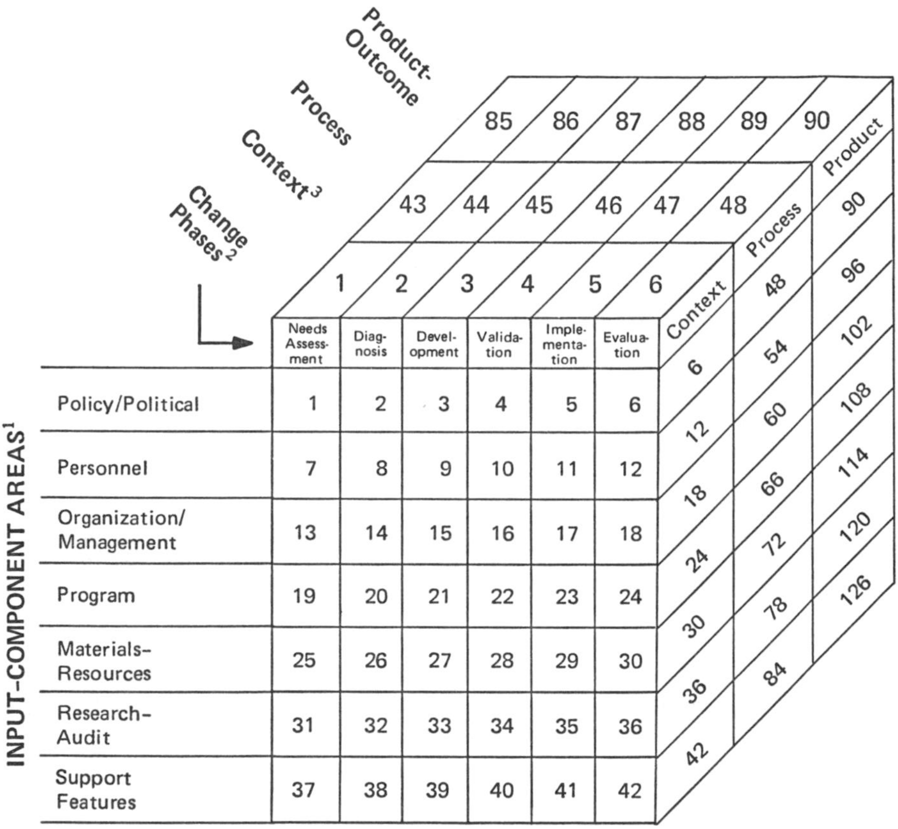

Product-Outcome
Process
Context[3]
Change Phases[2]

85 86 87 88 89 90
43 44 45 46 47 48
1 2 3 4 5 6

Product: 90 96 102 108 114 120 126
Process: 48 54 60 66 72 78 84
Context: 6 12 18 24 30 36 42

INPUT-COMPONENT AREAS[1]	Needs Assessment	Diagnosis	Development	Validation	Implementation	Evaluation
Policy/Political	1	2	3	4	5	6
Personnel	7	8	9	10	11	12
Organization/ Management	13	14	15	16	17	18
Program	19	20	21	22	23	24
Materials-Resources	25	26	27	28	29	30
Research-Audit	31	32	33	34	35	36
Support Features	37	38	39	40	41	42

(1) See p. 75-76 and 225-226
(2) See p. 5
(3) See p. 149

FIGURE 6.7 Functional Segments for Evaluation—Change Phases and Component Areas.

coordination in acquisition and utilization. They should indicate effectiveness regarding learner or staff gain, they should be adequately housed for retrieval and storage, and they should relate directly to the systems goals and objectives. Finally, they should be within the established cost parameters. Developers of major curriculum packages regard these considerations as critical in terms of particular situations and learner outcomes. They should also be critical considerations in any school district program.

Once defined and related to the project effort, these sub-systems represent significant items for review and evaluation. To disregard them is to court disaster and miss important data in regard to the total operation and its impact on the targeted objectives and personnel. Figure 6.7 illustrates one approach, in this case using CIPP items and the instructional change model from Chapter 2. The left column lists component elements. The change phases are given across the top of the illustration. The third dimension includes standard elements usually considered in *evaluative measures*—context, process, and product-outcomes. Thus, 126 cells are developed for consideration in this figure.

A simplified plan would be to use the surface cells (1-42) and incorporate the three dimensions of process, context, and outcome within each cell. Ways for managing this function can be found in the reference section. The cell divisions also present a way of making decisions about *points* for evaluation and what *elements* to incorporate. For example, different elements could be emphasized at strategic points—to review process at one point, and at another, to review product. It is highly unlikely that any project would need the number of decision-evaluation points suggested here as possibilities. However, the point of the expanded model is to present options that make many combinations or configurations visible and viable.

One growing concern closely related to component operation and effectiveness is cost. What segments of the school district are affecting outcomes within reasonable cost parameters? Which are not? In a sense, each school district sub-system is itself a project; thus, each could be researched and evaluated as an entity directly related to program objectives and operation. Within these components, which change phases are most successful and at what point is there a diminishing impact? Are related component areas operating in accordance with the process guidelines, the philosophical orientation, and the planning increments regarding time and product development? New policy, planning, and budgeting procedures are requiring different instruments and analysis to determine answers to such questions. Figure 6.7 shows *program* as a central component, but it does not, nor can not, operate without effective interchange with the other elements.

Approach Where Role or Task Definitions Are Specified

Style elements as reflected by individuals, schools, or school systems are critical determiners of what ideas are to be emphasized, what structure is most appropriate, and what decisions should be supported by evaluative review. A program structured on the basis of roles or tasks provides one example. Such an approach was utilized in Chapter 5, Implementing; it was also shown in its relationship to Designing, Chapter 3; and Managing, Chapter 7, among others.

Figure 6.8 is the same as that in Chapter 3 (Figure 3.8). However, at this point, the emphasis would not be on the explication of task statements, which was proposed earlier, but rather on the review of the task *achievements* that had been delineated according to the development design. Thus, a program that incorporated task statements as a structural feature could review (1) the adequacy of the task statements, (2) the effectiveness of the related personnel in achieving the specified

School District Components	*Program Phases*									
	Needs	*Objectives*	*Target*	*Means*	*Formats*	*Specifications*	*Development*	*Implementation*	*Evaluate*	*Feedback*
1. Policy-Administrative Decisions	1	8	15	22	29	36	43	50	57	64
2. Project Management	2	9	16	23	30	37	44	51	58	65
3. Staff	3	10	17	24	31	38	45	52	59	66
4. Project Program	4	11	18	25	32	39	46	53	60	67
5. Materials	5	12	19	26	33	40	47	54	61	68
6. Support Features	6	13	20	27	34	41	48	55	62	69
7. Community Involvement	7	14	21	28	35	42	49	56	63	70

FIGURE 6.8 Task Achievement—Assessed at Selected Program Phases.

task assignments, and (3) the project outcomes as reflected in products, events, or learner and staff progress. These could be assessed at each program juncture (determining needs, writing objectives, and so forth) as part of the summative evaluation, or both.

Such an approach obviously places more emphasis on personal–role achievements than some of the other evaluative schemes proposed. This tends to be more threatening to individuals since it utilizes an individual accountability design. As with other measures and approaches suggested, it is better utilized in concert with other measures.

Reconsidering Options for Monitoring, or Formative and Summative Evaluation

The following visuals, Figures 6.9 and 6.10, are included to provide an opportunity to reconsider some of the proposed alternatives. They are presented in a visual and composite form. Since each option includes slightly different design elements, each would yield different data; these nuances of process and data may be important to the decision makers and evaluators.

When clear objectives have been stated for the program mission, many viable options become available for evaluative treatment. Their achievement is enhanced by the existence of sequential or developmental growth stages. The existence of objectives for the project are indicated by the numbers listed on the left column. Mission statements could be stated as: developing a curriculum for the four quarter plan, instituting an open education program in the middle school, and developing learning centers for the elementary science classes. It would be most useful to have the objectives phrased as enabling statements so that they would provide an indication of focus and related activities.

Across the top are suggested program phases that could be operational stages or discrete time indicators. Those given are: initiation, needs/objectives, design (structuring), development, and implementation. Formative evaluation could be considered an aspect of each phase; summative evaluation could represent an additional phase, if desired.

These two elements of design, objective and phases, converge and form cells; they are numbered for purposes of identification and decision making. The figure thus developed provides a macro-framework that now will be considered in more detail by Figure 6.10. The framework is one way of envisioning the domain of the project. The selection of representative and critical cells in that domain constitutes a significant decision by leadership persons. Only cell 1.1 will be considered at this point, although each cell could be given the same treatment. Cell 1.1 represents *objective 1* at the *initiation* stage of project development.

One way of examing cell 1.1 would be to use the techniques associated with the *CIPP* model (*c*ontext, *i*nput, *p*rocess, *p*roduct). While these procedures have multiple uses, they are proposed here as especially appropriate where the decision has been made to assess the basic elements of the project or program. They may also be used when

Program Mission Statements	*Project Development Phases*				
	Initiation	*Needs/ Objectives*	*Design*	*Development*	*Implementation*
Objective 1	1.1	1.2	1.3	1.4	1.5
Objective 2	2.1	2.2	2.3	2.4	2.5
Objective 3	3.1	3.2	3.3	3.4	3.5
Objective 4	4.1	4.2	4.3	4.4	4.5

FIGURE 6.9 Options for Monitoring, Formative and/or Summative Evaluation.

a complex or extensive project is being undertaken with the need to review such items as: the environment that obtains while the project moves along (context); the measures taken to provide plans, personnel, and resources (input); the procedures, activities, and personal growth elements (process); and the yield of events (products). These evaluation units are indicated by the letter "A."

A second possible approach for examining cell 1.1 is suggested by "B." Here the emphasis is upon *learning domains*, which have great utility when assessing individual learners—students or staff. Cognitive, affective, and psychomotor are the basic categories. Considerable literature has been developed relative to their examination in regard to objectives, test items, programmed instruction, and questionnaires, plus other evaluative inquires and instruments. Each of these domains can be further subdivided into decision elements by using such taxonomies as Bloom's *cognitive:* (1) knowledge, (2) comprehension, (3) application, (4) analysis, (5) synthesis, and (6) evaluation; and Krathwohl's (et al.) *affective:* (1) receiving, (2) responding, (3) valuing, (4) conceptualization, and (5) organization and characterization. Various taxonomies exist for the *Psychomotor*, e.g., by Harrow. They often relate to training functions and have not yet achieved acceptance to the same degree as the other two.[47–49]

A third series of indicators is proposed by "C." They are called *system components* and have been expanded for visual purposes in the lower left corner of Figure 6.10. The school district sub-systems could be reviewed as total entities, or they could be further subdivided. Ways of subdividing these categories could be: (1) by school *district levels:* early childhood, primary, upper elementary, middle school, high school, post high school and adult; or (2) by *organizational divisions:* central office, area offices, individual school, department, subject area, grade level, course, learning-instructional unit, and individual; or (3) by the specific personnel assignments as proposed in Chapter 5—where they were related to particular tasks and functions. Another reason for listing these operational elements and approaches of a school or district is to emphasize the importance of evaluating multiple rather than single segments of the related and support features.

As suggested, the intent of this segment has been to suggest possible approaches and elements for review, not to propose that all approaches or all sub-elements should be investigated. However, by referring to the various objectives and development stages (see Figure 6.9) and then considering how each could be broken out into approaches and sub-units of manageable or viable proportion, planners and evaluators will be able to identify the priority cells, approaches, and sub-sets that can be evaluated productively to serve the purpose of the project.

Many decisions would need to be made. Do specific data need to be collected? Is a particular instrument required? What are the evaluation resources or capabilities of the staff? Which approaches would be most useful; which configuration of elements would best capture the intent of the project? How comprehensive or thorough will be the evaluation effort?

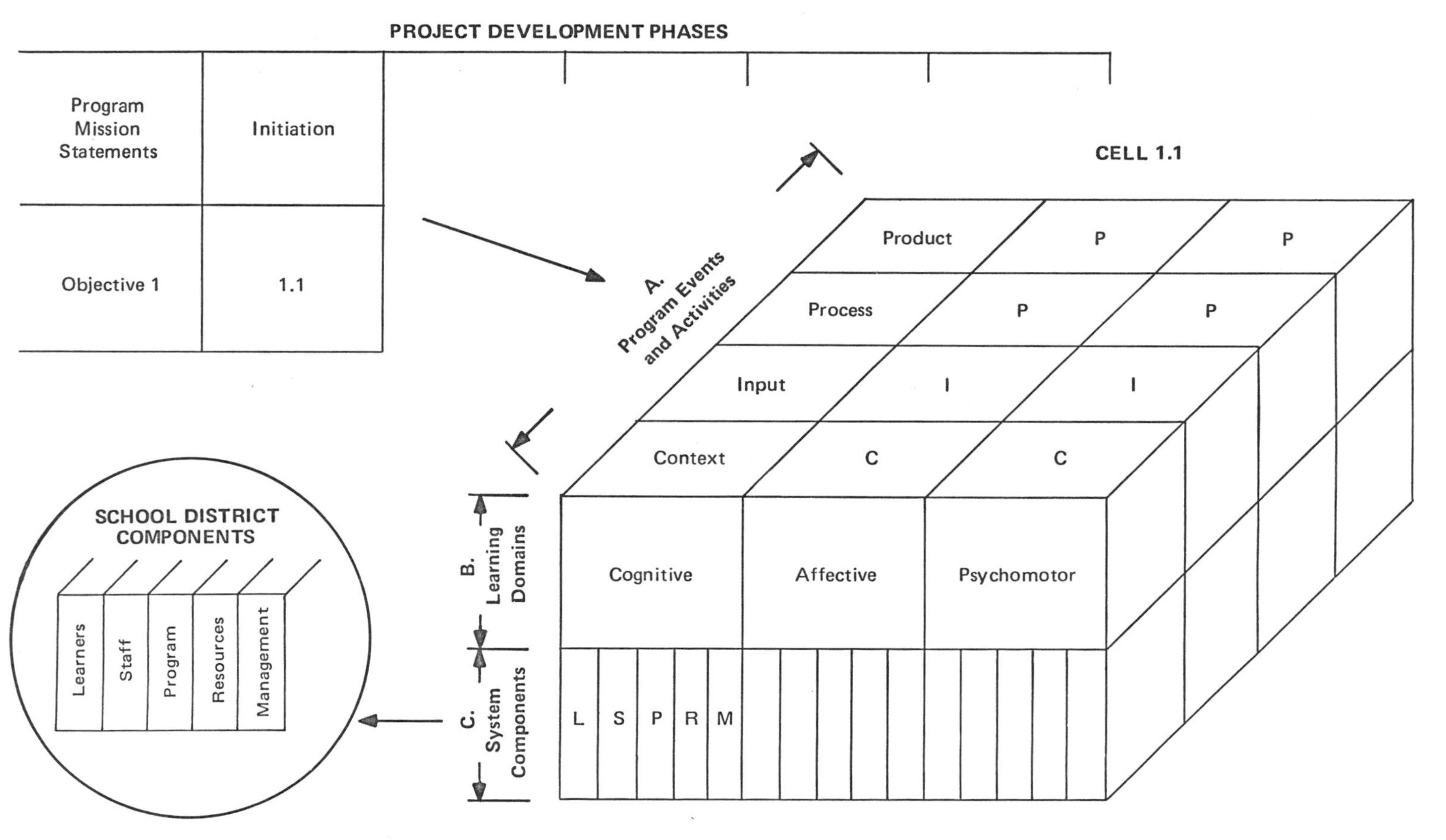

FIGURE 6.10 Examining One Cell for Monitoring, Formative or Summative Evaluation.

The areas proposed for evaluative treatment are broad and complex. However, school districts are faced with the necessity for policy, learner outcome, and resource decisions. Spearheaded by systematic planning, comprehensive research can provide the necessary support data as a function of related processes such as monitoring and managing. Similarly, purpose and form contribute categories useful for the production of review data, since such assessments are directly related to the ongoing developmental activities and the necessary decisions and changes that must be made. Summative and program impact evaluation can incorporate these interim assessments within their purview, whether this function is performed by persons inside or outside the district.

These possibilities only begin to suggest the utilizations that potentiate both formative and summative evaluation. The philosophy of the school system, the necessary degree of accounting, and the resources and sophistication of the research capability will determine the number of approaches, the phases to be examined, and the formality of the instrumentation. The important thing to note is that they can exist operationally and without consternation if they are built into the design. Their purpose and dimension must be the result of a developmental effort rather than a superimposed intervention. In any case, multiple and continuing measures are usually the recommended approach.

Figure 6.11 summarizes many of the concepts that have been discussed as useful to the planner. Whether planned in relationship to program, staff, or student learners, evaluation procedures and techniques are similar in structure. Staff development activities should exhibit the same concern for sharpened objectives and particularized program responses, which include evaluation, as that usually reserved for students. Evaluative measures are essential if feedback is to include answers regarding the effectiveness and efficiency necessary for staff growth and program planning.

One unique evaluation problem is the difficulty of remaining close enough to the operation to know its features and context, yet removed enough to be "uncontaminated" by proprietorship, i.e., to be objective in observation and appraisal. A related consideration is the capacity to provide in-process information that can contribute to redirection and modification as necessary. Yet, it must also maintain continuing parameters that make a summative evaluation relevant to the whole operation rather than to just a terminal point. For some, these problems suggest the need for maintaining different research and evaluation sub-systems for auditing and in-process concerns than exist for summative evaluation.

At various points, the text proposes the importance of a team approach utilizing various types of abilities and different instructional levels. Evaluation is one area where a need exists to provide more persons with the opportunity to participate in data gathering, analyzing, and valuing. However these problems are resolved operationally, there is no question about the need for more precise information, more use of such data for change and improvement uses, and more rigorous

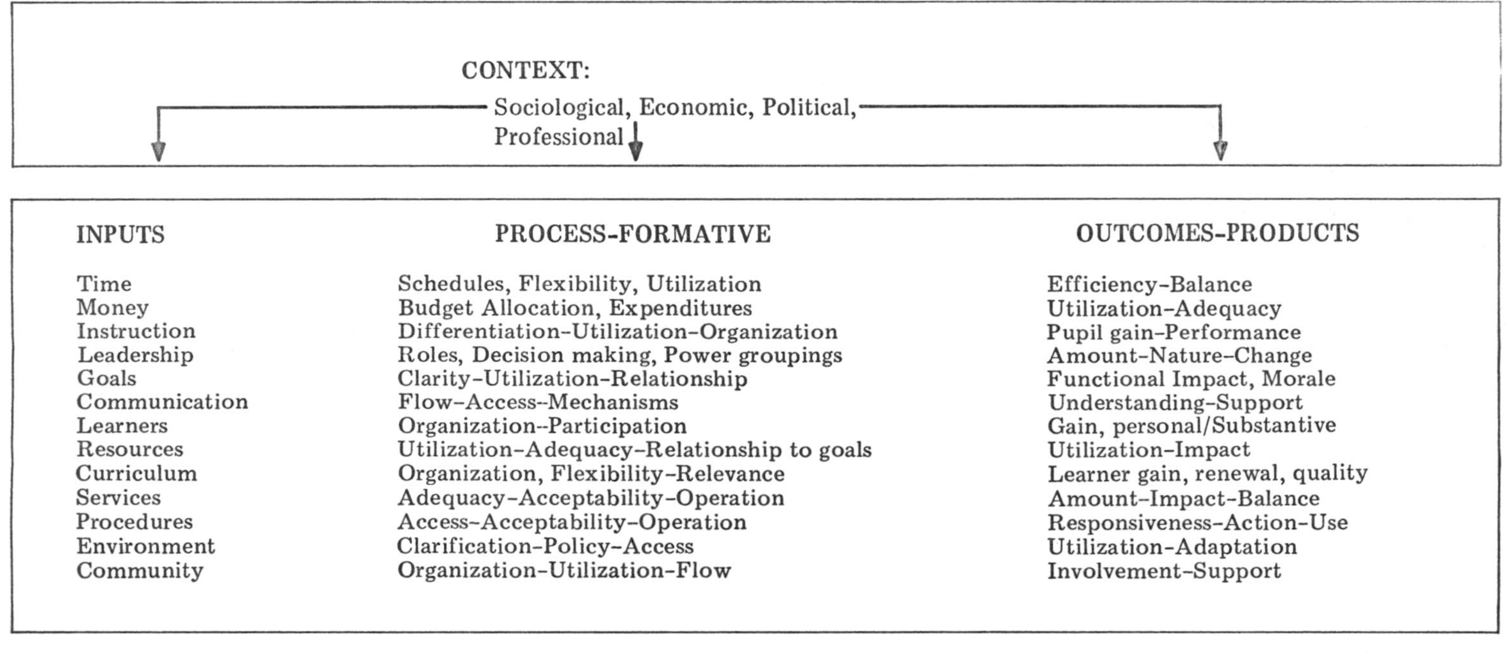

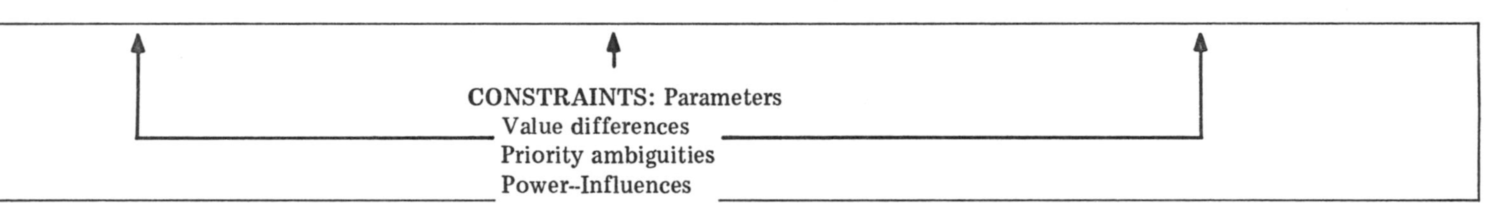

FIGURE 6.11 Factors in Evaluation.

examination of programs of curricular change and staff development.[50-52]

While the evaluator strives for objectivity, for instruments, and data that possess reliability and validity, it is interesting that a large input of philosophy exists at the point of valuing—that is, making decisions about the adequacy, utility and worth of the findings. Here is found a return to understandings about goals and purposes and to larger concepts and beliefs than may be included in the instruments and their yield. The evaluator, in the search for objectivity and "hard" data, may try to ignore or deny the implications of his work. This is no more possible than a scientist who attempts to ignore the many political and ethical ramifications of work with genetic, chemical, or biological mediations, with personality modification, conditioning, or nuclear experimentation.

Similarly, the problem of control is always present in schools, i.e., of getting all the participants to perform in the prescribed way for the determined time. At that point, the larger question of professional judgment becomes complicated. At what point with learners do you continue a practice for the sake of research and design, when your experience and insight convinces you that another alternative, or significant modifications, could effect greater gain?

Continuing credibility and relevance require a more comprehensive view that includes the clients, the consumers, and the implementors of the educative effort. Without this larger look, fragmentation of results occurs because the response appears only piecemeal; also, there is lack of support because basic questions and purposes do not appear to have been addressed. The final result is often failure to incorporate the new findings into the bloodstream of the continuing program.

Such a view also requires a Janus look back to the genesis of the endeavor, to the needs and the consequent objectives. Also, a look ahead is needed for the utilization of the findings and to the subsequent prediction and planning that will be required as to decisions regarding continuity, funding, or replications.

Obviously, elements of program structure have great utility in regard to evaluation. They are the purposes, processes, and products that can be held up for review. However, structure must yield to purpose if education is to be a humane enterprise, if it is to perform its "people purpose." To maintain the structure of a school or a society requires a plan; it is important for continuity, even change. But the structural elements in the final analysis must be subsumed at the point of valuing. This has not always been the case as bureaucracies, institutions, and functionaries strive for durability.

It is the author's intention to show the integral relationship of staff involvement and planning to the possibilities and requirements of a comprehensive, valid, objective, and functional evaluative program. A major reason for developing and drawing upon explicated structural and systematic design elements is to facilitate the evaluative process and related gains in the quality of staff development, curriculum improvement programs, and decision making. Evaluation is not only a process and product; it is also a professional attitude. A clear relationship must exist between the program design and the pay-off, the outcome. This necessitates commitment to change and to evidences of change; it requires evidences that are real and related, not extraneous and intrusive.

Attitude and commitment cannot be concomitants. They are a product of the plans and processes that are employed. For this reason, the following chapters are critical. They suggest procedures and concerns that include formal and informal approaches. Their skillful use can develop staff competencies and commitment, or they can alienate and polarize. Thus, the impact technologies have importance beyond structuring and managing. They are the means for growth, involvement, understanding, and achievement, but only when used as tools, not ends in themselves. Involvement of the instructional staff in these undertakings should contribute to major gains toward such improvement.

ACTION GUIDELINES

Evaluation is a process designed to assist in decision making, in assessing learner gain or program efficiency and effectiveness. It usually involves the application of standards to data produced routinely or to instrumented data designed specifically as evaluative measures. Thus, there are both process and product elements.

Evaluation should determine whether or not a learner or program is meeting, or has met, the desired objectives. This requires a criteria or standard. The discrepancy between the standard and actual gain provides a basis for planning and decision making. Thus, data, standards, judgments, and decisions are involved. These elements posit the need for valid and reliable measures. Like other planning processes, evaluation should be continuous and integral to the context structure, procedures, events, and outcomes of the program being examined. Evaluation is facilitated by conscious attention to these on-going elements. Critical program junctures, program outcomes, and defined process elements provide functional evaluation points.

Multiple measures that capture critical gains are more useful than single or simple means. Decision making and reporting out are enhanced by formative and monitoring data that are generated for evaluative purposes. Summative data provide a base for other or similar programs, as well as for the learner, program, or process under investigation. Evaluative processes provide a means for participants to share in the generation of data, the application of standards, and the modification of program efforts. This process should contribute to the related staff development competencies and program improvement efforts, that is, to a more effective diagnosis of individuals and program elements, and to an improved credibility and accountability.

RELATED REFERENCES

1. Association for Supervision and Curriculum Development, *Evaluation as Feedback and Guide.* Yearbook. Washington, D.C.: author, 1967.
2. Stake, Robert, "The Countenance of Educational Evaluation." *Teachers College Record,* 68:523 (1967).
3. Wick, John W., and Beggs, Donald L., *Evaluation for Decision Making in the Schools.* Boston: Houghton Mifflin, 1971.
4. Alkin, Marvin C., "Towards an Evaluation Model: A Systems Approach." In *Readings in Curriculum Evaluation,* edited by Peter A. Talor and Doris M. Cowley. Dubuque, Iowa: William C. Brown Co., 1972.
5. Payne, David A., *Curriculum Evaluation: Commentaries on Purpose, Process, Product.* Lexington, Massachusetts: D. C. Heath, 1974.
6. Tyler, Ralph, ed., *Educational Evaluation: New Roles, New Means.* Part II, sixty-eighth yearbook of the National Society for the Study of Education. Chicago: University of Chicago Press, 1969.
7. Beatty, Walcott H., ed., *Improving Educational Assessment and An Inventory of Measures of Affective Behavior.* Washington, D.C.: Association for Supervision and Curriculum Development, 1967.
8. Cronback, Lee J., "Course Improvement through Evaluation." *Teachers College Record,* 64:672 (1963).
9. Tyler, Ralph W., *Basic Principles of Curriculum and Instruction.* Chicago: University of Chicago Press, 1950.
10. Wittrock, Merlin D., and Wiley, David E., *The Evaluation of Instruction: Issuses and Problems.* New York: Holt, Rinehart, and Winston, 1970.
11. Aldrich, Ruth Anne, "Innovative Evaluation of Education." *Theory into Practice,* 13:1 (1974).
12. Buros, Oscar K., ed., *The Seventh Mental Measurements Yearbook.* Highland Park, New Jersey: Gryphon Press, 1972.
13. Jung, S. M., "Evaluative Uses of Unconventional Measurement Techniques." *California Educational Research Journal,* 22:48 (1971).
14. Provus, Malcolm, *Discrepancy Evaluation.* Berkeley, California: McCutchan Publishing Corp., 1971.
15. Baker, Eva L., "Beyond Objectives: Domain-Referenced Tests for Evaluation and Instructional Improvement." *Educational Technology,* 14:6 (1974), p. 10.
16. David, Frederick B., *Criterion-Referrenced Measurement.* Princeton: ERIC Clearinghouse on Tests, Measurement and Evaluation (Educational Testing Service), 1972.
17. Deming, Basil S., and Phillips, James A., "Systematic Curriculum Evaluation: A Means and Methodology." *Theory into Practice,* 13:41 (1974).
18. Hively, Wells, "Introduction to Domain-Referenced Testing." *Educational Technology,* 14:6 (1974), p. 5.
19. Housden, Jack L., and LeGear, Lonnie, "An Emerging Model: Criterion-Referenced Evaluation." *Thrust for Education Leadership,* 2:5 (1973), p. 41.
20. Jackson, Rex, *Developing Criterion-Referenced Tests.* Princeton: Educational Testing Service, 1971.
21. Johnston, Thomas J., "Program and Product Evaluation from a Domain-Referenced Viewpoint." *Educational Technology,* 14:6 (1974), p. 43.

22. Nitko, Anthony J., and Hsu, Tse-Chi, "Using Domain-Referenced Tests for Student Placement, Diagnosis and Attainment in a System of Adaptive Individualized Instruction." *Educational Technology*, 14:6 (1974), p. 48.
23. Popham, W. James, "Teacher Evaluation and Domain-Referenced Measurement." *Educational Technology*, 14:6 (1974), p. 35.
24. Bloom, Benjamin, Hastings, Thomas, and Maddaus, George, *Handbook on Formative and Summative Evaluation of Student Learning.* New York: McGraw-Hill, 1971.
25. Scriven, Michael S., "The Methodology of Evaluation." In *Readings in Curriculum Evaluation*, edited by Peter A. Taylor and Doris M. Cowley. Dubuque, Iowa: William C. Brown Co., 1972.
26. Airasian, Peter, Madaus, George, and Rakow, Ernest, "An Instructional Evaluation Monitoring System." In *Curriculum Evaluation: Potentiality and Reality*, edited by Joel Weiss, pp. 74-95. Ontario: The Ontario Institute for Studies in Education, 1972.
27. Alkin, Marvin C., "Evaluating the Cost-Effectiveness of Instructional Programs." In *Readings in Curriculum Evaluation*, edited by Peter A. Taylor and Doris M. Cowley. Dubuque, Iowa: William C. Brown Co., 1972.
28. Cook, Desmond L., "Have You Been Audited Lately." *Theory into Practice*, 13:31 (1974).
29. DeNovellis, Richard, and Lewis, Authur J., *Schools Become Accountable: A PACT Approach.* Washington, D.C.: Association for Supervision and Curriculum Development, 1974.
30. Eiss, Albert P., *Evaluation of Instructional Systems.* New York: Gordon and Breach Publishers, 1972.
31. Stufflebeam, Daniel L., et al., *Educational Evaluation and Decision Making.* Phi Delta Kappa National Study Committee on Evaluation. Itasco, Illinois: F. E. Peacock Publishers, 1971.
32. Welty, Gordon, "Evaluation Research and Research Designs." In *Readings in Curriculum Evaluation*, edited by Peter A. Taylor and Doris M. Cowley. Dubuque, Iowa: William C. Brown Co., 1972.
33. Dyer, Henry S., "The Role of Evaluation." In *Proceedings of the Conference on Educational Accountability*, William Turnball, Chairman. Conference sponsored by Educational Testing Service. Princeton: Educational Testing Service, June 1971, p. 42.
34. Stufflebeam, Daniel L., "Evaluation as Enlightenment for Decision Making." In *Improving Educational Assessment and an Inventory of Measures of Affective Behavior*, edited by Walcott H. Beatty. *op. cit.*
35. Knox, Alan B., "Continuous Program Evaluation." In *Readings in Curriculum Evaluation*, edited by Peter A. Taylor and Doris M. Cowley. Dubuque, Iowa: William C. Brown Co., 1972.
36. Stufflebeam, Daniel L., "Toward a Science of Educational Evaluation." *Educational Technology.* 8:14 (1968), p. 5.
37. Averch, Harvey, et al., *How Effective Is Schooling? A Critical Review and Synthesis of Research Findings.* Santa Monica, California: The Rand Corp., 1971.
38. Tyler, Ralph, Gagne, Robert, and Scriven, Michael, *Perspectives of Curriculum Evaluation.* Chicago: Rand McNally, 1967.

39. Eisner, Elliot, "Educational Objectives: Help or Hindrance." In *Readings in Curriculum Evaluation*, edited by Peter A. Taylor and Doris M. Cowley. Dubuque, Iowa: William C. Brown Company, 1972.
40. Tyler, Ralph W., and Wolf, Richard M., ed., *Crucial Issues in Testing*. Berkeley, California: McCutchan Publishing Corporation, 1974.
41. Stufflebeam, Daniel, et al., *Educational Evaluation and Decision Making. op. cit.*
42. House, Ernst R., *School Evaluation: The Politics and the Process*. Berkeley, California: McCutchan Publishing Corporation, 1973.
43. Grobman, Hulda, *Development Curriculum Projects: Decision Points and Processes*. Itasca, Illinois: F. E. Peacock Publishers, 1970.
44. Welty, Gordon, "Evaluation and Planning in Education: A Community Concern." In *Readings in Curriculum Evaluation*, edited by Peter A. Taylor and Doris M. Cowley. Dubuque, Iowa: William C. Brown Company Publishers, 1972.
45. Grobman, Hulda, *Evaluation Activities of Curriculum Products*. Curriculum Evaluation Monograph No. 2, American Educational Research Association Series. Chicago: Rand McNally, 1968.
46. Flanagan, John C., *A Critique of the Measurement and Instrumentation Aspects of Educational Evaluation and Decision Making*. Palo Alto, California: American Institutes for Research in the Behavioral Sciences, 1971.
47. Bloom, Benjamin, et. al., *Taxonomy of Educational Objectives. Handbook I: Cognitive Domain*. New York: McKay, 1956.
48. Harrow, Anita, *A Taxonomy of the Psychomotor Domain*. New York: McKay, 1972.
49. Krathwohl, David R., Bloom, Benjamin, and Masia, Bertram, *A Taxonomy of Educational Objectives, Handbook II: Affective Domain*. New York: McKay, 1964.
50. Dempsey, Richard A., and Breyer, N. L., *Staff Development and Evaluation*. Santa Monica, California: Appleton-Century-Crofts, 1971.
51. National Society for the Study of Education, *Educational Evaluation: New Roles, New Means, Part II*. Sixty-eighth Yearbook. Chicago: University of Chicago, 1969.
52. Stufflebeam, Daniel, et. al., *Educational Evaluation and Decision Making. op. cit.*

7

Managing

The responsibility for work accomplishment is called directing or managing. It may be performed by an administrator with a status role, by a consultant with prestige but limited power, by a project director who has designated status and considerable influence in a restricted area, or by a group so-charged. Management has mixed meanings in education because the *process* is not usually separated from a designated position, hence a labor-management inference often is made. Also, some views of management make it synonymous with manipulation rather than leadership or facilitation. It is the intention of this segment to deal with management as leading, decision making, directing, and influencing; and as a responsible and responsive functioning, however vested or organized. Management is "seeing" as well as "seeing to it"; for above all, the manager should be able to comprehend the whole panorama and to visualize the configuration of elements and forces and the way they relate and interrelate. Such envisioning and sensing are more than mere "keeping track," or more than intervening upon occasion.[1-4]

"Making a difference" has long been an injunction to administrators and supervisors. This phrase highlights the need to help people change, to improve programs and resources, and to influence constructively the instructional situation for learners. Since many supervisors and other leadership persons are not usually in a position to affect learner gain directly, their impact must be made through the means they employ, the functions they perform, and the processes they use. Results are best achieved through a combination of data, power, competence, and participation, all of which are necessary to achieve the desired ends.[5-8] Among the critical processes needed are the following:

- *Coordinating*—the skills of informing and communicating, and the knowledge of who needs to know; the skills in providing, assisting, and facilitating, of integrating tasks and responsibilities.

- *Planning*—the skills of envisioning, ascertaining, validating, and prioritizing goals and objectives; developing data bases and rationale as to why action is necessary, of conceptualizing and developing specific plans, workflow, and structures essential to implementing the plans.
- *Organizing*—the skills of involving appropriate persons with defined tasks, of helping determine who will participate and in what organizational apparatus and what ways (means), of developing, coordinating, and delegating the necessary responsibilities, and of establishing relationships.
- *Directing*—the skills of decision making, leading, and initiating, of assigning and delegating particular responsibilities, and of determining strategies, timing, scheduling, and logistics.
- *Controlling*—the skills of regulating and redirecting on the basis of instruments, data, and observations; of judging performance relative to objectives, roles, and standards; and of monitoring and intervening as necessary.

These are not fixed processes. They vary on the basis of perceptions, roles, persons, and context. However definitive or accurate the list, the important factor is that leadership persons must engage in these functions, singly and in concert with others. Impact and outcome depend upon the competencies that are brought to bear upon the problems and the tasks that need to be done. For, plan without power is inert, and power without substance is turbulence. Work flow without standards and direction is aimless, and a change without rewards and support has no durability.

Management, as envisioned here, is seeing that the needed tasks are identified, explicated, organized, implemented, and evaluated. In keeping with other sections of the text, this assumes that management is a professional process that includes product and task achievement, as well as that which evinces concern for growth and involvement by the participants and consumers. Obviously, a humane mix is desirable in this product and process orientation. Rather than dealing with leadership and management as tasks, processes, or roles, these elements have been organized into a plan for change; i.e., an agenda for achievement that incorporates management ideas into a sequence and that illustrates the functioning as it would likely occur in a realistic setting.

A MANAGEMENT PLAN

Many techniques, processes, and organizational-managerial plans can be employed to enhance the likelihood that objectives will become outcomes.[9-15] Some impact technologies have a people or human relations orientation; others have a task or organization orientation. These designations (people or task) are not fixed, since it is possible to make a human relations technique very rigid and product-oriented; but it is also possible to make a task-oriented procedure very personal and interactive.[16-18] It is sometimes difficult for the "managers" to keep their role in perspective—realizing that it is the means to an end, not the end to be achieved.

The operational structure described in Figure 7.1 is based on the instructional change model proposed in Chapter 1; thus, it includes essentially the same phases and sequence. These have been modified to emphasize the responsibility of management to achieve certain landmarks rather than the change elements as such. The plan presents an alternative and dynamic planning design; and, as such, it is a *dynamic* plan: each phase is dependent upon previous efforts and is modified by subsequent activities. Thus, task analysis cannot occur until needs and objectives have been determined; operation cannot occur without program specification, and so on. However, it also should be noted that each phase (shown on the visual as horizontal elements) can be used to note and assess progress to date, to anticipate the next phases, and to consolidate gains achieved. Each vertical listing can be used as a criterion to check out the work of individuals or groups, program quality, and comprehensiveness; as well as to review progress via such measures as monitoring, auditing, process, and formative evaluation.

The management plan was generated by a number of situations and has been utilized in a number of ways. These may suggest a variety of uses, for example: (1) by persons with a regional service role, charged with the responsibility for coordinating a number of instructional projects, or central consultants who operate in a staff relationship to local school personnel; (2) as a basic study document for new superintendents to propose ways by which their instructional tasks could be structured and integrated into other system operations; (3) as a staff development document for urban principals who were concerned about improving their effectiveness as instructional leaders; and (4) as a reference item for a curriculum council in a large school system where it was used as an agenda to relate council recommendations and activities to the necessary administrative decisions and tasks. In this connection, it served the useful purpose of sorting out the council responsibilities for data, work, and support from the administrative actions to which these were allied. It helped delineate the relationship between recommendations and research, which were their function, and the necessary administrative policies and procedures, which were not their function. The *critical* questions varied considerably from group to group.

As an agenda, the plan does not require a particular process or style. Neither does it prescribe by whom the tasks will be achieved, nor the time frame. Its usefulness is most evident in long term or developmental projects rather than for routine or emergency procedures. However, it should be noted that a skilled and experienced leader will use the ideas and sequences, however abbreviated or selectively omitted in a particular situation. This is because the plan is essentially a problem-solving approach.

The intent, then, is to display a total operational process that encompasses a systematic, long range, and systemwide effort to achieve significant instructional objectives.[19-22] In developing the plan, an effort was made to eliminate all but the most critical steps and activities; it is not intended to indicate all the roles and responsibilities required to perform the total leadership functions of any given individual. *To be complete in a specific situation, the plan would need to be augmented by those particulars essential to the local leader or management group and the target population.* Although many school systems operate without a developed operational strategy, the evidence is clear that requirements at both state and federal levels, as well as mandates by local boards of education, are forcing some variation of the management by objectives approach. Likewise, issues such as accountability, professional negotiations, and community involvement add further pressures for specification.[23-27]

Figure 7.1 visualizes the overall plan. Here are the six *management phases* arranged sequentially:

I. Identify Goals and Needs.
II. Develop Program Objectives.
III. Perform Task Analysis.
IV. Allocate Tasks.
V. Operate Program.
VI. Conduct Summative Evaluation.

In an actual operation, it is unlikely that these phases will exist as discrete segments; rather, they will be fused and in some cases run concurrently. However, they still exist as developmental stages having unique elements that can be identified and used as suggested.

Below the management phases, three other elements are represented: (1) Management Tasks and (2) Input and Support Activities. These element-phases, management tasks, and input/support are shown as they impact upon (3) Program Operation—the transactions, developments, and essential implementation activities. Later in the chapter, another item is added, Critical Questions, which are listed as they relate to the phases, tasks, input, and support functions. As a matter of fact, the model could be restructured as a series of questions building upon the representative items that have been listed.

Thus, as presented here, management tasks, input/support items, and critical questions all constitute a single item. While they were separated in this analysis, in a given situation they would be interrelated considerations. Similarly, the items in any particular management phase would not necessarily be sequenced, as they are on this model, for every project or activity. Essentially, the numbered (arabic) items would operate as a checklist for consideration; and as organizational categories for products, memos, forms, and policy statements; and for purposes of discussing, filing, and accounting, and for sharing efforts.

Uses of the Model

It can be observed that listings are given of priority tasks and suggested input and support activities for each management phase and related

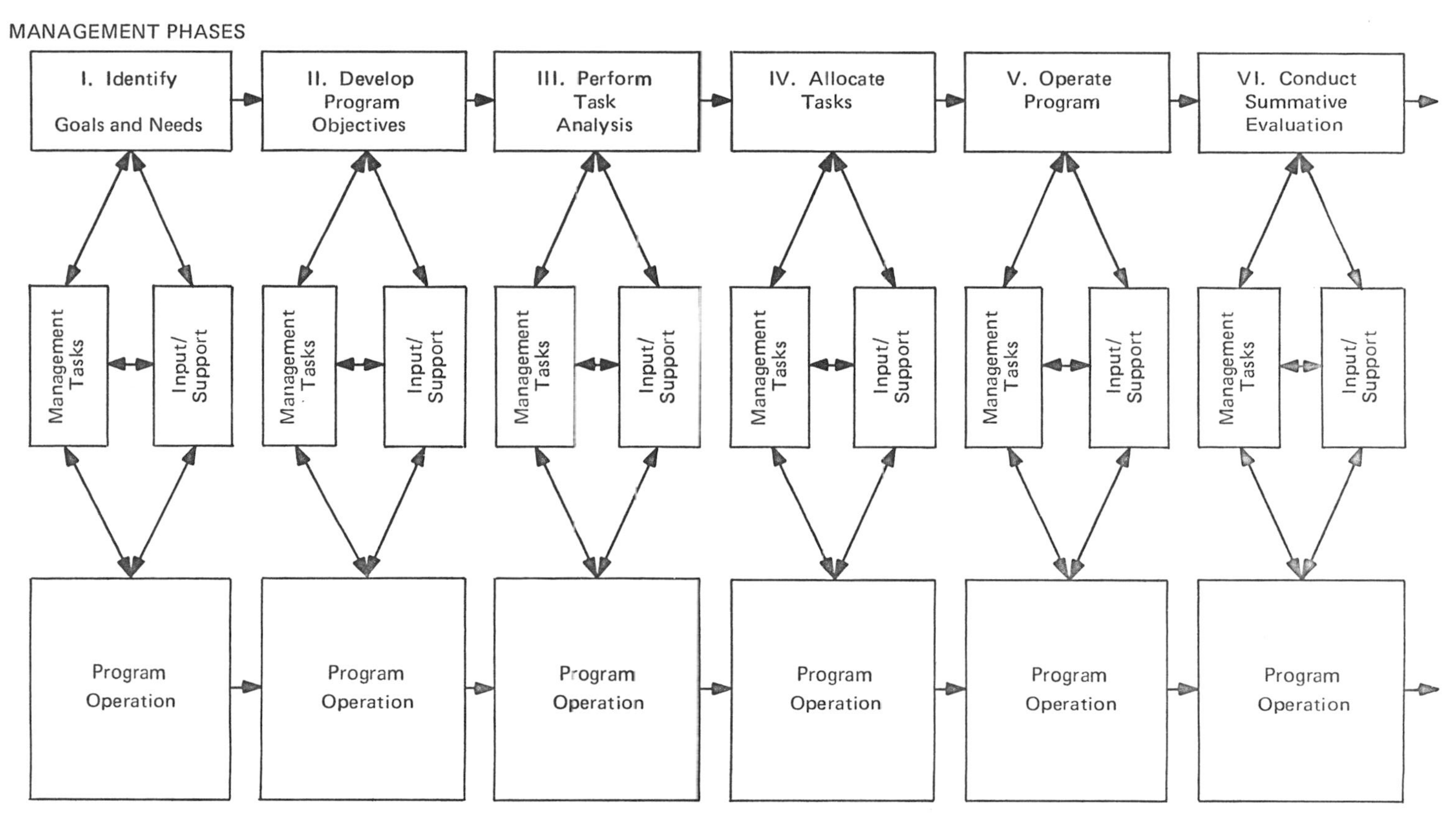

FIGURE 7.1 Operational Plan.

I. IDENTIFY GOALS AND NEEDS

Management Responsibilities	*Input/Support*	*Critical Questions*
1.1 Identify issues or needs based on staff information, student data, community-state-LEA priorities. Authorize further investigation.	1.1 Collect existing evidence of problem, issue, etc.	1.1 • What are the basic concerns? Are the present goals being met? Are present goals adequate to meet new needs? What is the situation now? • What is the ideal situation? What changes are necessary? What are the sources of the concerns expressed?
1.2 Review identified needs regarding preliminary or existing program–process implications.	1.2 Develop or find appropriate instruments or processes for identifying necessary additional information.	1.2 • What changes are implied by needs expressed? • What is the relationship of the needs to the ongoing program? • What information and processes are required to obtain direction from the needs expressed?
1.3 Conduct needs assessment, validate.	1.3 Investigate need areas including such things as: a. *student* data—SES, achievement, interests, concerns b. *staff* data—personal, competency, professional advancement c. *context* data—school system, organization, climate, community d. *other*—research, newspaper, media, professional.	1.3 • What information assists us in determining where we need to go? • What does research say about the concerns we have identified? • What information already exists concerning: -student achievement, activities, desires, needs . . . -teacher abilities, desires, expectations

Management Responsibilities	*Input/Support*	*Critical Questions*
		-community resources, needs, elements . . . -support for the concerns expressed? • What instruments and processes are required for obtaining necessary data?
1.4 Review data in order to determine (1) nature and extent of needs and (2) areas of proposed activity.	1.4 Develop recommendations for action based on data and discrepancies.	1.4 • What are the implications of the needs expressed? • What are the limitations of reality? • What can reasonably be done with regard to resources, reality, etc.? • What are the possible areas of difficulty? • What system or community priorities represent factors to be considered?

II. DEVELOP PROGRAM OBJECTIVES

Management Responsibilities	*Input/Support*	*Critical Questions*
2.1 Translate identified and validated needs into general program	2.1 Develop specific statements for planning and decision making.	2.1 • What objectives are implied by needs identified? • Are all groups served by the school represented in the planning and decision making process? • What performance criteria will

Management Responsibilities	Input/Support	Critical Questions
		satisfy the requirements of the needs identified? • Are the process goals clear and acceptable?
2.2 Determine priorities among objectives. Consider ongoing programs, staff competencies, problems, etc.	2.2 Develop recommendations that show the relationship of proposed objectives to local or regional programs.	2.2 • We can not do everything—what can we do? • What rationale do we have for selecting priorities? • What information is required to make the priority decisions? • How do the objectives selected relate to ongoing programs? • Why is a change really necessary?
2.3 Frame and authorize rationale for decision making by board of education and involved schools and persons.	2.3 Prepare required statements; circulate proposal to critical personnel for study and review.	2.3 • What do the rationale and the related objectives mean to various groups within the school community? • Do the objectives convey the meaning intended? • Are the objectives attainable?
2.4 Schedule and present rationale to administration, board, and advisory committee.	2.4 Prepare schedules and logistical arrangements. Review support elements that need to be "in place"—routines, testing programs, supervisory assistance, materials, etc.	2.4 • Who makes the decisions? • What information is required to make the decision? • What are the consequences of the decision?

Management Responsibilities	Input/Support	Critical Questions
		• What happens if the decision is *no*? • What alternatives or contingencies have been considered?
2.5 Develop representative enabling and performance objectives to clarify focus and program emphasis.	2.5 Arrange for workshops or task forces to prepare the necessary materials.	2.5 • What consensus presently exists among staff and community? • What skills exist or are necessary to develop in order to produce the necessary materials?

III. PERFORM TASK ANALYSIS

Management Responsibilities	Input/Support	Critical Questions
3.1 Define specific objectives or tasks to be accomplished by: 1. Board of education 2. Regional agencies 3. LEA-leadership 4. Individual schools 5. Teachers 6. Learners.	3.1 Write detailed task statements based on objectives developed in phase II. Consider alternative means to achieve objectives.	3.1 • Who is involved? What are their functions? • What courses of action are effective in accomplishing the objective? • What is the most efficient course of action? • Who makes the decisions? • Does each objective have viable criteria?
3.2 Determine policies, conditions (time, cost), personnel; consider constraints, community-patron involvement (target personnel), information, facilities, compatibility.	3.2 Collect baseline data using preliminary and supplementary data and instrument. Include competency levels of consultants as well as targeted personnel.	3.2 • In what sort of environment will the groups function? • In what way can the tasks be facilitated? • Who can help the program? Who can hurt it?

Management Responsibilities	*Input/Support*	*Critical Questions*
		• What resources do we have? How will they be used? Are they adequate? • What will receive less attention because of the program? • What is the rationale for the specific resources identified? Are the means efficient and effective? • What are the consequences of the limiting factors? • What baseline data do we already have? • What additional data do we need?
3.3 Establish performance standards (specifications) to be achieved by groups (see item 3.1).	3.3 Develop recommendations for management review relating desired outcomes to existing and proposed conditions, including criterion measures.	3.3 • Are the standards realistic? • Will the program outcomes satisfy the standards desired? • How will changes be measured? Are there process as well as product criteria?
3.4 Determine monitoring, process--formative evaluation procedures. Determine plan for summative evaluation.	3.4 Prepare instruments, schedules, processes, and personnel. Develop visualized PERT or flowchart to communicate plans, stages, and responsibilities.	3.4. • What monitoring techniques will be employed? • Who will do it? Who will receive a report? • How will recommendations coming from formative process be handled, changes made?

Management Responsibilities	*Input/Support*	*Critical Questions*
		• How will the related personnel be affected by the decisions and changes? • Who needs to examine and decide regarding the visual plan and format?

IV. ALLOCATE TASKS

Management Responsibilities	*Input/Support*	*Critical Questions*
4.1 Assign specific responsibilities for determined objectives and tasks, including contingency plans.	4.1 Develop specific plans, procedures, logistics, cost, credit provisions, release of teachers, etc. Consider existing skills and competencies that will be utilized.	4.1 • Who will share in decisions regarding tasks? • What are the expectations in terms of personnel, cost, time, and support? • Do tasks meet abilities and expectations of personnel involved? Are roles clear? • What are program and process needs? How will they be satisfied?
4.2 Begin formative evaluation procedures.	4.2 Utilize instrument and processes as determined. Collect data for review for duration of project. Feedback and communicate progress (or problem) data.	4.2 • Who will make the evaluation? What processes will be employed? • What information is required to effectively monitor the program? • What are the decision making and change structures and processes?

Management Responsibilities	Input/Support	Critical Questions
4.3 Authorize dissemination of specific plans to interested and affected personnel and agencies.	4.3 Prepare and disseminate as necessary to schools, teachers, media, etc.	4.3 • Who will contact various groups involved? • What do tasks mean to various groups concerned? • Have all involved personnel shared adequately in the development of specific plans?
4.4 Review progress, inform board of education, instructional staff, and community. Make necessary changes and decisions regarding contingencies.	4.4 Develop documentation of progress to date, including data regarding project.	4.4 • Who will receive the information? • Who will make decisions based on information obtained? • How will recommendations be handled? • How are ongoing routines and programs being affected? • Are leadership and related personnel in need of new skills to be trained, or is help required from consultants?

V. OPERATE PROGRAM

Management Responsibilities	Input/Support	Critical Questions
5.1 Continue monitoring, evaluation, and review–staff reporting regarding project operations.	5.1 Maintain records regarding activities and gain. Recommend changes based on monitoring and feedback data.	5.1 • Are the performance criteria being met? • What impact is the program having? • What new concerns are surfacing as a result of the program implementation?

Management Responsibilities	*Input/Support*	*Critical Questions*
		• Are we doing what we want to do? • What other instruments and processes are needed to provide feedback for monitoring or process evaluation?
5.2 Support program effort with policy, resources, and consultant help at all program and school levels.	5.2 Provide feedback to persons in schools and community regarding progress and problems. Modify logistics as needed, provide personnel with data regarding changes.	5.2 • Is management responding adequately to new data? • What outside groups are interested in the program? Are they involved? • Is a modification in the policies delineated desirable? • Are means and measures adequate and functioning?
5.3 Facilitate ongoing implementation, supply needed equipment and resources.	5.3 Develop necessary plans, materials, etc. Implement, coordinate proposed activities, and check out forces, relationships, and local leadership.	5.3 • Any breakdowns in schedules or plans? • What provision is made for suggestions? • How are staff needs handled? • What resources are required? • Are resources and data adequate? On schedule? • Are there new constraints that need treatment?
5.4 Provide continuing information regarding desired staff development activities, instructional materials,	5.4 Develop appropriate recommendations based on experience with the program operation.	5.4 • What issues or needs have arisen? • What staff competencies, logistics, instructional materials, facilities,

Management Responsibilities	Input/Support	Critical Questions
professional-community climate, etc.	Meet with appropriate agencies, committees, and groups. Prepare releases, data, reports, and new agenda.	time, or cost factors need change or adjustment? • Are new indexes needed regarding adequacy or progress? • Are channels of communication open and accessible? Are they functioning? • What changes are evident in both ongoing and project activities? • Are school system and community groups involved in the recommendations and evaluations?

VI. CONDUCT SUMMATIVE EVALUATION

Management Responsibilities	Input/Support	Critical Questions
6.1 Review process–formative data available for study.	6.1 Prepare formative data for management review.	6.1 • How does formative data facilitate the summative evaluation process? • What components do we want to examine more closely? • Was formative evaluation effective? • What appears to have higher priority?
6.2 Make final decisions regarding objectives, instruments, and data requirements—inputs, product, context, and process. Consider	6.2 Develop or find instruments and processes based on determined objectives, formative data, and changes that have been made.	6.2 • What information will best indicate relationship between objectives proposed and standards realized? • What alternatives do we have?

Management Responsibilities	*Input/Support*	*Critical Questions*
changes that have occurred as project has matured.		• How will changes affect final review?
6.3 Assign evaluation responsibilities, schedule.	6.3 Administer evaluation instruments, collect data.	6.3 • Who will conduct evaluation? How will it be done? • When and where will it take place? • Any special conditions to be considered?
6.4 Review summative data for gain-effectiveness, efficiency, and relationship of summative data to initial and baseline information and objectives.	6.4 Analyze data for review, make recommendations regarding program activities, design, and relationship to ongoing program.	6.4 • Have the standards been met? • What are the shortcomings of the program? • What additional data are required? • What is the rationale for the outcomes that were realized? • What recommendations are implied by the summative evaluation?
6.5 Determine strategy—recycle, abort, terminate, and disseminate.	6.5 Prepare statements for management use (recommendations, releases). Use summative data to prepare new baseline data, and new need statements for ongoing or new program efforts.	6.5 • What information is required to make a decision? • Was the program worth the effort? • What modifications are necessary? • Should we continue, terminate, modify, or start again? • What impact will decision have on various groups? • Who should be involved and informed? What should their role be in the final decisions and reports?

sub-structure. Tasks and activities are clustered for purposes of study and selection. As a project or program develops, it should be possible to take the stylized model and: (1) select those items to be implemented; (2) convert the general language of the model to the specific terminology of the proposed project (along with the designation of personnel time, resources, and conditions); (3) communicate the tasks, personnel, impact methods, and points to those who make decisions (board of education, administration) and who will be involved (principals, teachers, and others); (4) monitor, review, and support the implementation of the activity; and (5) evaluate, feedback, and modify as needed.

Thus, each continuing activity or project can be visualized and communicated before significant allocations are made. They can be reviewed and reinforced as the plan becomes operational, and can be improved upon as experience, results, and competencies develop.

The *style* of operation is not indicated on the design. The style can be highly developmental and participatory; or it can be predetermined and centrally run, that is, a system or leadership decision. It is assumed that interim decisions, meetings, training sessions, and crises are surmounted as the project moves along. What is indicated is *what needs to be done if gains are to be achieved*, not the techniques, methods, or procedures employed. As operational procedures are determined, it will be logical to develop research instruments and data for particular items, to develop competency objectives for consultants and staff, and to relate the desired competencies against the required outcomes. It will also be possible to communicate the program "track record" with some credibility and specificity and to justify costs in terms of program effort and learner outcome.

Management Patterns for Staff Development and Instructional Change

The difference between a staff development and an instructional improvement program is basically one of emphasis. In both instances, objectives and provisions are provided for improved staff functioning and for better experiencing and learners programs. While the fundamental goal may be the same, procedures, impact points, and, especially, the nature of the subordinate tasks are different. Thus, in each case, while the overall design may be similar, the elements that are used and the data that are generated by the application of the plan will demonstrate major differences.

Staff development projects tend to focus upon the needs and competencies of the instructional personnel—administrators, supervisors, teachers, and support persons. They include such items as more effective leadership procedures, improved planning or management approaches, instructional skills related to particular content and program areas, diagnostic and interpretive procedures, utilization or production of media and materials, and content acquisition and curricular application. Staff development projects also tend to emphasize target personnel and assume that the activities will result in improved understandings, competencies, and professional gain, which will also contribute to learner achievement.[28-32]

Instructional improvement projects, on the other hand, tend to focus upon substantive or curricular areas; these are instructional methodologies as they impact upon the learner, and organizational-contextual modifications that will improve the resources and conditions for learning.[33-36] One major difference is that curriculum improvement projects often use a representative sampling of personnel to pilot the project and to develop the materials/examine the problem. It is usually assumed that a ripple effect will improve the situation for all. This assumption cannot be made in staff development efforts because a staff development approach cannot exclude personnel who are essential to the achievement of the desired objective.

The key to differences between staff development efforts and instructional improvement projects, then, lies not so much in the design as in the particulars developed—in the objectives, data, and program elements that are generated and implemented. For example, a learner need, to improve in language competency, could be cast as an objective that proposes the development of a sequential skills program to be installed in all content areas and all grade levels. As such, the existing and necessary curricular items could be identified and structured. The result would be new instructional objectives, materials and resources, new classroom activities, new evaluative measures, and a rewritten curriculum guide. An accompanying program would be needed to enable staff members to review the new sequences and materials and to implement them in the classroom. The emphasis, however, would be on program elements.

The same need could be translated into a staff development project that would focus upon the existing and needed skills of the instructional staff, i.e., on the attitudes, knowledges, skills, and support processes essential to the *delivery* of an improved language experience for learners. In this case, the concern for the discrepancy between the existing program and the desired outcome would result in a program to improve the ability of the staft members to manage and instruct. The evaluative measures would emphasize the adequacy and delivery capabilities of the staff to implement the program rather than the program elements and materials, although these items should be included as vital context data. In both cases, the desired objective would be learner achievement; however, the emphasis and means would show important differences.[37-39]

Leadership and management plans must explicate these contracts in focus, whatever the program design. Major differences will be evident in the proportion of time, in the nature and the sub-tasks required, in the program elements developed, and in the emphasis to be checked out by evaluative measures. The key is the focus and whether the objectives and program stress program adequacy and its related impact on learners, or whether the stress is for staff adequacy and the compe-

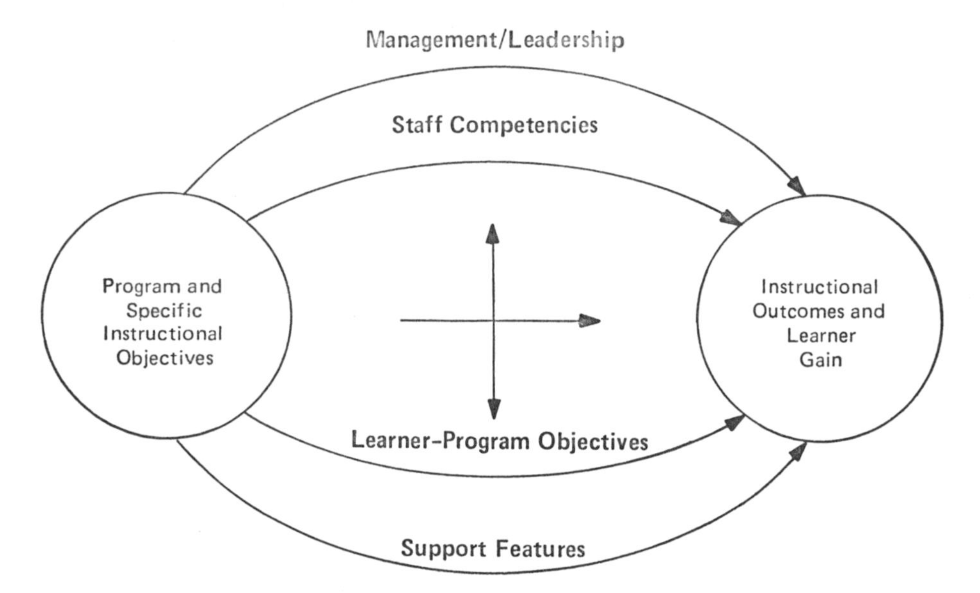

FIGURE 7.2 Basic Elements in an Instructional Improvement-Staff Development Plan.

tencies that result in learner achievement. Woven together, the strands of program adequacy and staff competency become a powerful fabric that enhances the likelihood of a successful change and improved experiences for both learners and staff (see Figure 7.2).

Management Considerations in the Larger Perspective

Leadership persons who are responsible for directing and coordinating must maintain perspective relative to the larger dimensions and impact of the project, as well as to check to see that the specific tasks are achieved. Figure 7.3 shows one way of describing this mix of developments and concerns.

Item number 1 (*Management Tasks*) refers to the major responsibilities that must be met; these are shown sequentially as the left column.

Item number 2 (*Instructional Change Program Requirements*) refers to the sequential phases through which the project will move; i.e., the center horizontal line. Arrows have been drawn to relate management responsibilities to program development items.

Item number 3 (*Component-Impact Areas*) suggests system elements that need to be considered in relationship to each change phase and management task. These are listed at the top of the page; they are not sequential.

Item number 4 (*Logistics*) at the far right is a reminder that each phase and each responsibility requires arrangements as to personnel, place, the development of schedules, correspondence, records, and other necessary artifacts and plans.

This visual could be used as the basis for asking critical questions, as an accountability check, and as a reference guide for decision making, information flow, evaluation, and monitoring purposes. In addition, the sequential listing of the *Management Tasks* and *Program Requirements* indicates the necessary next tasks to be undertaken: What has been done? Where are we now? What is the next logical move?

It is not expected that each school system or each project will involve all of these elements or have items necessarily identical to those listed. However, by starting with these suggestions, it should be possible to determine more easily the variables that are to be reconciled into the appropriate configuration, and to combine the appropriate elements so that they operate as criteria in the development of programs that emphasize either staff development or instructional change.

The following displays expand this hypothesis. They are the same in both uses except for item number 2. Figure 7.3 includes *Instructional Change Program Requirements* and lists the design phases that have been used throughout the "guide." They are shown as the horizontal-top items on the visual.

1. Needs—awareness, data, and mandate.
2. Analysis-Diagnosis—objectives, resources, and specifications.
3. Development—design, products, and strategy.
4. Validation—research, pilot, and feasibility.
5. Implementation—train, install, and support.
6. Evaluation—objectives, standards, and feedback.

The *management* tasks are those developed earlier in this chapter—summarized in Figure 7.1. Certain tasks are especially related to program elements; accomplishing these tasks would result in the generation of a program for instructional change. The program should include concerns for component-impact areas (item number 3) and particular arrangements relative to personnel, schedule, and other operational requirements (item number 4).

Management considerations in designing and operating a *staff development* program are shown as Figure 7.4. This time, element number 2 is changed to indicate an emphasis on Staff Development Program Requirements. As in the previous figure, management and impact items remain the same. It should be obvious that the data generated by the design alternatives would be quite different. The design items are those summarized in Figure 3.2 and discussed in Chapters 3–6.

1. Needs.
2. Objectives.
3. Target.
4. Means.
5. Format.
6. Specifications.
7. Development.
8. Implementation.
9. Evaluation.
10. Feedback.

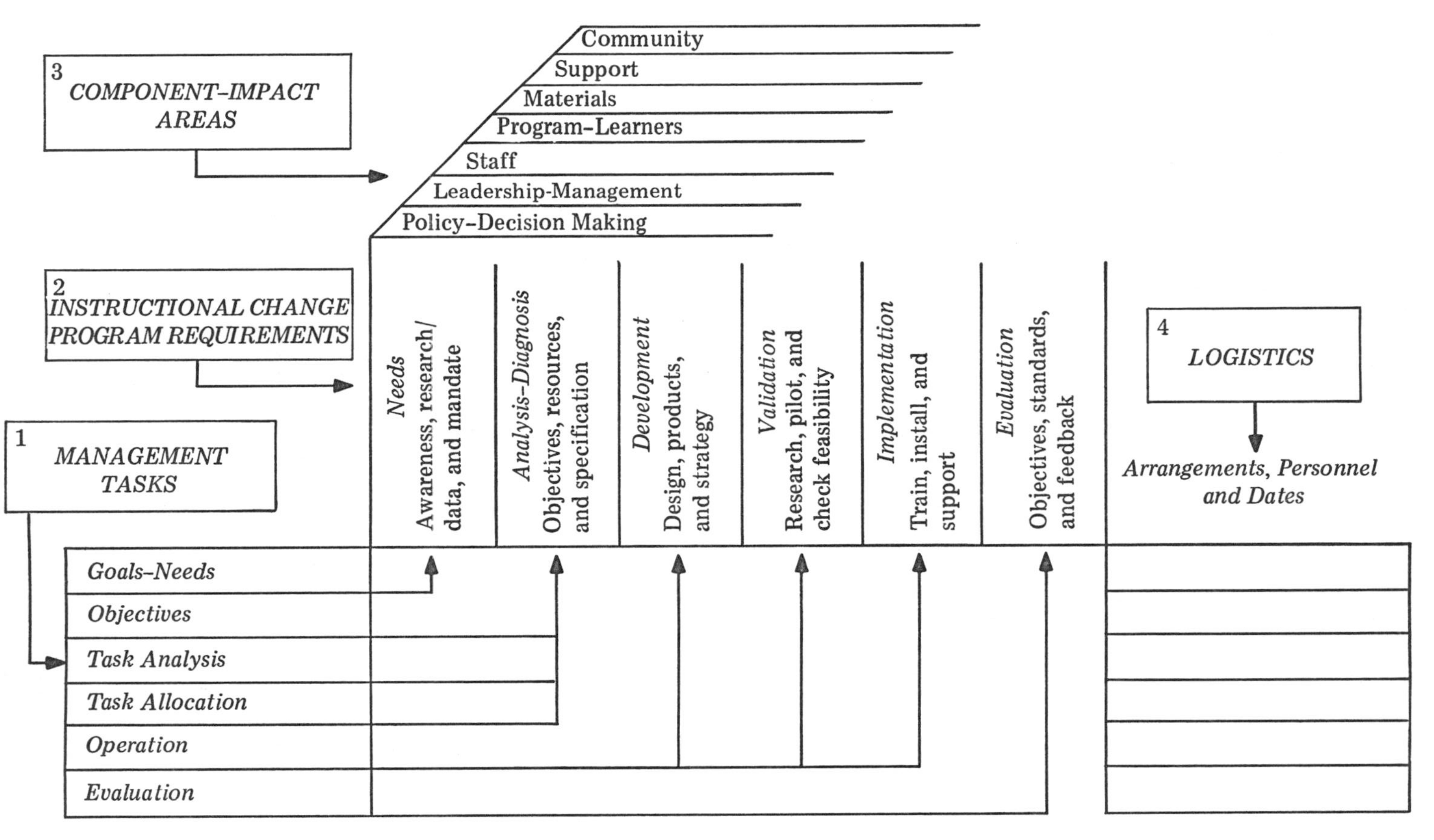

FIGURE 7.3 Management Considerations in Designing and Operating an *Instructional Change* Program.

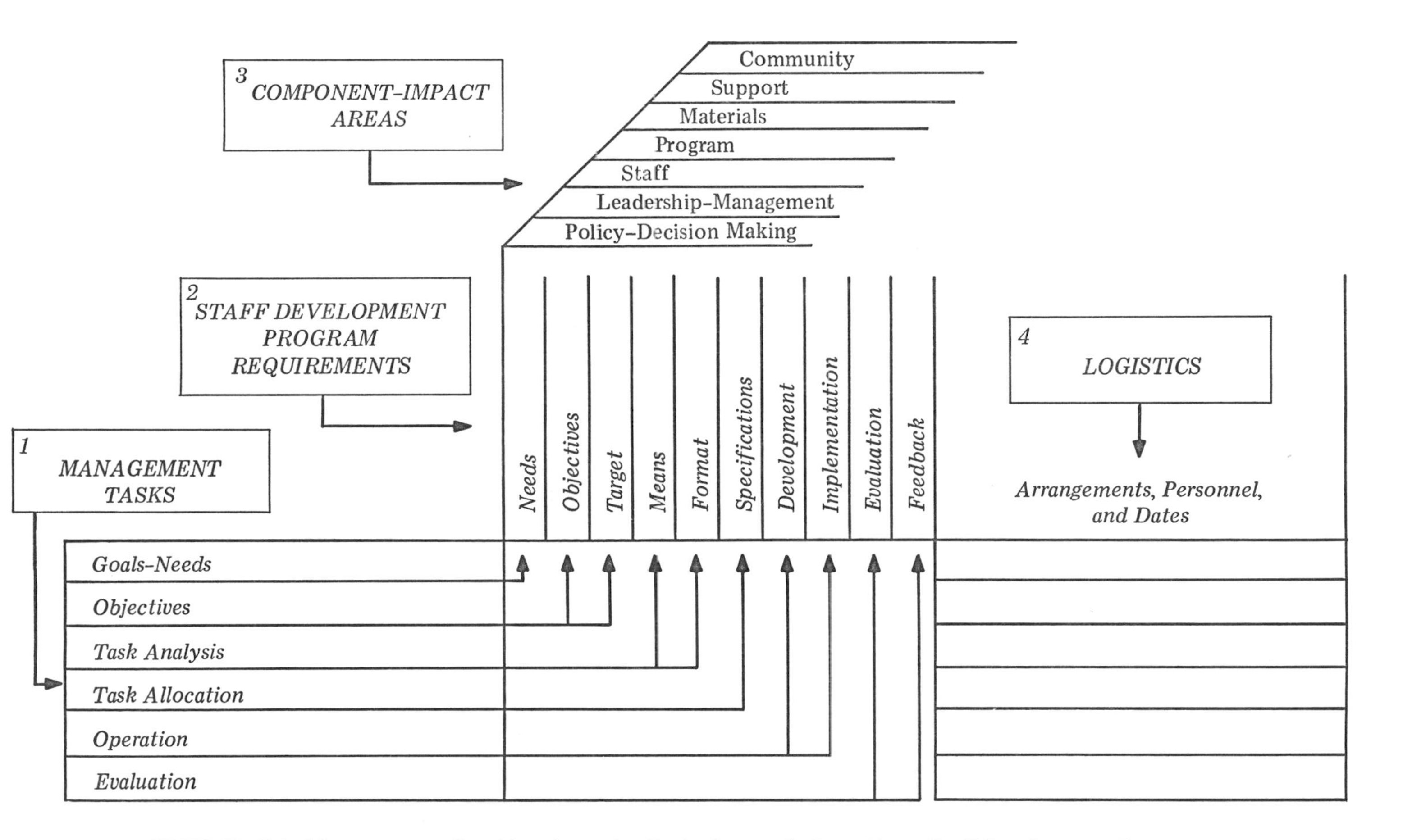

FIGURE 7.4 Management Considerations in Designing and Operating a *Staff Development* Program.

Again, the same management phases and tasks are listed on the left column (item number 1); the same impact considerations and components are given (item number 3); and the same reference shows the logistics and arrangements (item number 4). Lines and arrows indicate the relationship between management phases and the staff development program requirements. Thus, those persons responsible for program design and operation would have a guide as to how the management responsibilities delineated in the model (Figure 7.4) would be employed to produce the desired program. After a number of staff development or instructional plans are written, the personnel in a school system will have identified their own sub-system elements, requirements, standards, decision points, management, and planning patterns.

CONCEPTUAL PLANNING LEVELS AND COMMITMENT

Planning levels as used here indicate a progression from broad goals to specific program details. They are related to program levels (p. 36), but they are not the same items. The conceptual level designations are useful in determining design, cost, and degree of specification. Thus, when the operational model is used for a series of projects, each project heading or title is at level 0; the title in this case would also indicate the "mission" of the project. The next level, 1, designated here as Management Phases, often includes what are called "major work units," and so on, as indicated below. The vocabulary may not be important for isolated projects; but once a number of projects are underway and a number of visualizations depict the process and substance of the efforts, it then becomes useful to have a standard reference system for the various planning levels. This will avoid confusion and assist in the development of plans and decisions relative to them.

In Figure 7.5, the basic management model has been recast to indicate these work levels as conceptual considerations. The following five levels are indicated:

Level 1—Planning or management *phases* (I, II, etc.).
Level 2—Management tasks (decisions, authorizations, etc.).
Level 3—Work packages (designated as input/support).
Level 4—Specific arrangements made, artifacts produced, etc. (indicated on Figure 7.1 as Program Operation).
Level 5—Implementation/transactions.

Conceptual work levels are important in determining who will perform the tasks and the degree of task specification. As these levels are explicated, it will be observed that more detail and logistical data are included. In developing plans or project visualizations—flow charts or PERT—this fact will explain why task statements or work packages increase in specificity as they move from level 1. This should be anticipated. In many cases, levels 4 and 5 are not included on the major

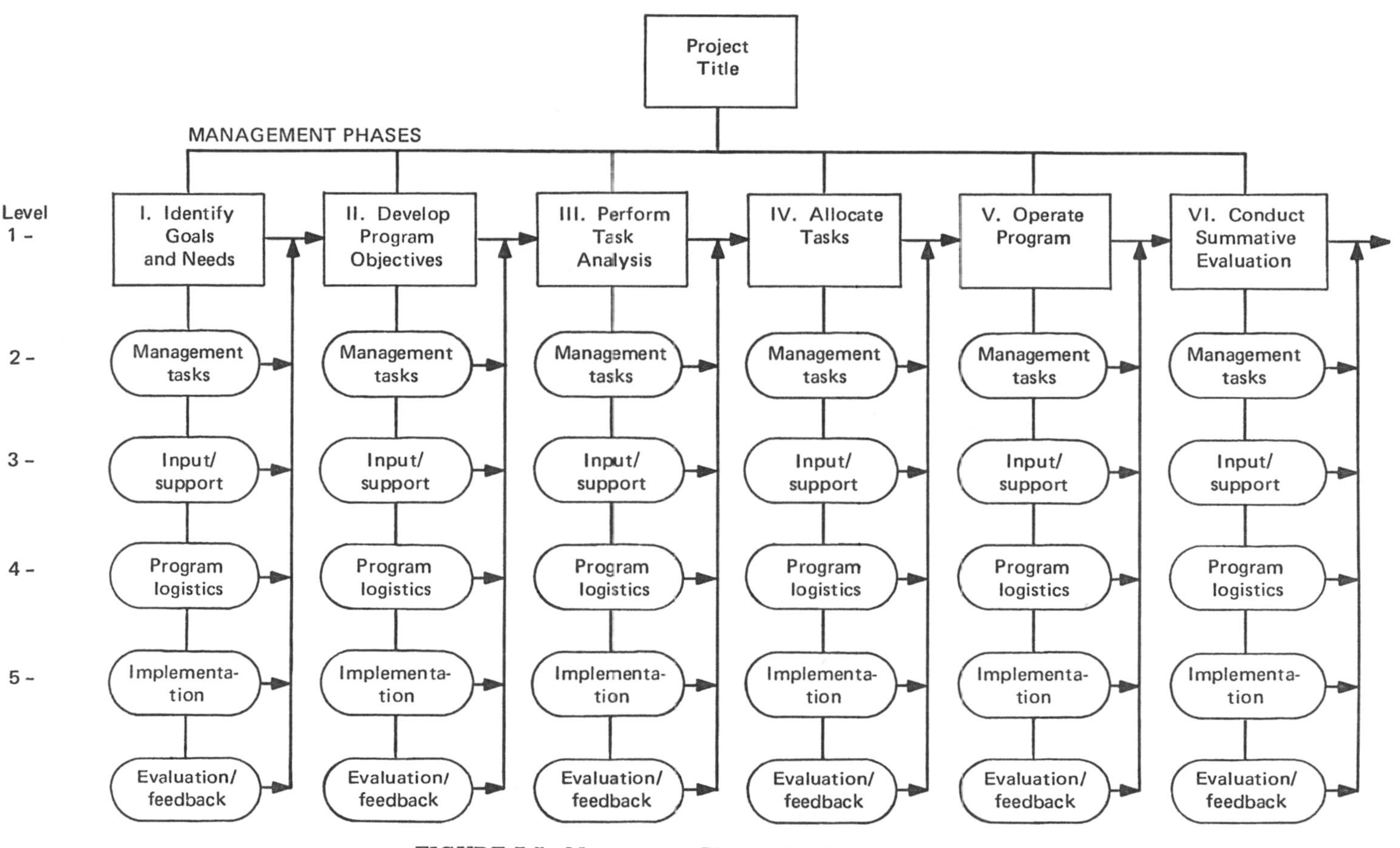

FIGURE 7.5 Management Phases, Levels, and Tasks.

display but become subordinate PERT or supplementary documents, which are to be developed and consulted as necessary. This eliminates what might otherwise be an overloaded visualization of the basic plan.

One significant item (evaluation and feedback) appears as the final element within each phase. As each task segment is achieved and new objectives are approached, the perceptions and commitments of involved personnel should be checked: How do they *now* relate to the new plateau, the new progress stage in goal achievement? The significance of this effort is evident in the research, experimentation, and experience of those working in organization development, intervention strategies, clinical supervision, management by objectives, and other developed approaches (see Appendix E). The perceptions and internalizations of participants become critical data that leadership must consider. It is at this point that systematic reference to the developed *guidelines* can reinforce their importance and facilitate the desired review. Thus, recycling occurs not only within each management phase as it relates to task achievement but also in terms of the relationships, feelings, competencies, and commitments of all participants.

The more complex the operation (the number of persons, variables, and related program) is, the more important this evaluation–feedback step becomes in the management process. This evaluation–feedback function is not only important in assessing the current status and performing necessary changes or corrections, it is also predictive in the sense that the manager can intervene for purposes of modifying subsequent activities and events (feed forward) on the basis of this information.[40] As indicated, this status-determining, correcting, and role changing has both personal and product dimensions. It is most functional when it becomes an anticipated event by the participants and an assigned responsibility for the manager. This responsibility is indicated on the display of the management model (Figure 7.5), where it is shown as the last element in the vertical listing of each phase. There it is given as an *evaluation* (in this case, essentially process) and *feedback indicator*. This is not a "level" per se, but it is a necessary function relative to morale and commitment. In no case can such a designated review point take the place of informal sensors and sensitive antennae.

An increasing and related problem is the need in each school district to analyze the relationship between *ad hoc* (temporary) status roles and those assigned continuing or ongoing responsibilities. With more decisions to institute high priority but short duration projects, this problem will increase. This situation centers on a mix-in function and impact; it contributes to the need for specifying roles and objectives more precisely (if conflict is to be avoided). Even with greater role delineation, an over-arching policy is essential to provide a framework within which to work so that functionaries are not obliged to battle for position, budget, or attention. Some pressure can be removed by the use of task forces, curriculum, or instructional councils; and by differentiated staff arrangements that make it possible for persons to move in and out of leadership roles without permanent reassignment, personal disappointment, or peer conflicts. The same should be true of major program efforts.[41–43]

The mobility of professionals adds another impetus to a need for established procedures of structure and policy delineation. Change and renewal efforts have historically been negatively affected by the loss of strategic leadership personnel, who take with them the expertise to manage change. Some of this is inevitable in a human setting. However, role, plan, and process clarity can make program continuity more likely; and also, these make criteria for the selection of new personnel more realistic. The development and use of organizational assists such as instructional councils are also relevant in this regard. Accountability, program approaches, and public data will require leadership and community support in addition to the maintenance of classroom and instructional quality. Thus, program durability in change posits the need for systematic planning and a related support system that pervades the total school district and its processes, as well as the internal instructional program elements.[44,45]

Finally, continuing concerns for competency and pressure for accountability and credibility require that leadership determine the points and processes by which they can make a more significant *impact.*[46–48] Many techniques, well enough described in professional literature, offer promising and viable alternatives. Many of these are included as Appendix E. Critical instructional needs also must be addressed if staff members are to exhibit competencies and if learners are to demonstrate the expected outcomes in substantive gain, ego enhancement, cultural awareness, and fundamental skills.

Planning and managing are multi-dimensional tasks. One dimension always involves at least one of the system component areas (or sub-systems) that are involved (for example, one of those listed on pp. 75–76). The focus may be on student or staff personnel, on the decisions and logistics necessary for managing the progress and its forward motion, or on program elements involving the search for/development of the necessary materials and resources. While the attention at the moment is on one particular aspect, others have to be kept in mind—related objectives and levels of operation that need attention and other or similar projects that interact or infringe upon either staff personnel or learners.

A second dimension is the developmental stage, whether it is identified as a particular phase or is functionally underway. The recognition of the progress or product stage is important for decision making relative to that point, or to subsequent changes or activities; for monitoring or formative evaluation; and for consciously considering the impact of the current activities upon both predecessor and subsequent stages. This involves a concern for sequence, for productivity and progress, for meeting commitments as planned, for converging with other projects and routine sequences, and for keeping pace with the schedules and time frames. Explicit in well-planned programs is a regard for the continuing quality of the process and product as the project moves along, and the effectiveness of interventions and leadership.

A third dimension involves the impact technology—the processes, involvements, and feelings of the participants. Each style or strategy has different modes to achieve the desired results. Each has a philosophical orientation as to the importance and nature of participation, the roles, and perceptions of the participants, and the affect upon morale, trust, and commitment. How each phase is negotiated or transacted, the degree to which process guidelines are observed, and the continued growth in appropriate expertise round out this dimension. These represent critical areas for data collection, decision making, anaylsis, and personal regard.

Leadership or Lament

Problems that educational planners need to solve are not easily amenable to solution. Most of them are, at best, only somewhat resolvable. This is because important educational issues are value-laden; they are compounded by pluralistic aims and tacit assumptions. Consensus can sometimes be achieved at the goal level, less often at the operational or methodological level. The political "load" of important issues makes even the processes appear self-serving or displeasing to some persons, whether such processes are the humane engagement type or rational, task oriented approaches.[49]

In contending with multiple and complex issues, educational leaders become prone to engage in a rhetoric of response rather than to attack systematically the basic causes. Each element from goal statement to impact technique requires some form of negotiation. Lesser problems or symptoms seem to be more easily managed, even though stop-gap solutions often cause other problems to surface in another form or in another arena. Inadequacies are evident in the diagnosis as well as the implementation stage; and "best" solutions often yield to manageable pieces and token efforts. Thus, the total issue too often is never confronted or resolved.

Success can lead to new expectations rather than to satisfaction with the gains achieved. Outcomes become new inputs as the program spirals through time and context. The openness required for realism and consensus appears to conflict with the needs for control or closure, which are essential for consolidation. Competition for attention arises from professional as well as lay sources. Results become diffused, continuity becomes contaminated by new priorities, and optimism is defeated by new orderings of resources.

These are the realities of leadership in an era of change, in a pluralistic culture, in a high-risk, priority enterprise such as education. Comprehensive, systematic, and adaptive approaches, however difficult to conceive and mount, offer one kind of hope. So do operations that exhibit a strong sense of purpose, a will to contend, and a concern for in-process achievement for a final/total product somewhere down the line in time. Trust and credibility can be the yield of healthy and optimistic efforts, whose priorities and problems are openly shared.

Leadership can seek for credibility by searching for priorities, by developing criteria, by planning in accordance with resources, by providing operational handles to facilitate engagement, and by presenting personal growth opportunities that consolidate gains at the individual as well as at the institutional level.[50,51]

Continuous sensitivity and action combined with a vision of the whole enterprise are requirements if both the human and product dimensions of the project are to be successful.[52-54] Operationally, these operate within a field of complex interactions, within a matrix of variables. The next chapter deals with suggestions for achieving such an overview—for organizing purposes and plans so that the leadership can transform what *is* to what *can be*.

ACTION GUIDELINES

Management is a combination of leadership functions designed to achieve particular objectives. High priority functions include planning, coordinating, organizing, directing, and controlling. Whether such functions are vested in particular roles or diffused is a style matter determined by each school system or agency. Management functions occur at all levels in the organizational structure; what varies are the decisions, tasks, arenas, and consequences of the results achieved.

Managers, whether they are classroom teachers, school administrators, or system-wide supervisors must "see to it" (achieve certain tasks). They must also "see" (comprehend) the relationships between their specific area of responsibility and the total system operation. These achieving and envisioning competencies are critical if the desired results are to occur; if the managers, whatever they are called, are to "make a difference" happen.

An important assist to managers, at whatever levels, is a plan—a framework for activities and events. This plan can be the basis for decision making, programming, implementing, monitoring, and evaluating. The plan can also represent a mechanism for capturing the contributions of many persons, as well as communicating the necessary objectives and means.

Thus, process considerations are crucial; staff development and program improvement programs have personal and professional, as well as organizational and task, dimensions. Management is the art of fusing these elements into a viable set of activities and outcomes to which participants have commitments. Results, then, are achieved by a composite of both individual and organizational responsibilities.

RELATED REFERENCES

1. Doll, Ronald C., *Leadership to Improve Schools.* Worthington, Ohio: Charles A. Jones Publishing, 1972.

2. Haissain, Khateeb M., *Development of Information Systems for Education.* Englewood Cliffs, New Jersey: Prentice-Hall, 1973.
3. Kravetz, Nathan, ed., *Management and Decision Making in Educational Planning.* Paris, France: International Institute for Educational Planning, United Nations Educational, Scientific, and Cultural Organization, 1970.
4. Saunders, Robert L., Phillips, Roy C., and Johnson, Harold T., *A Theory of Educational Leadership.* Columbus, Ohio: Charles E. Merrill, 1966.
5. Association for Supervision and Curriculum Development, *Supervision: Emerging Profession,* edited by Robert R. Leeper. Washington, D.C.: author, 1969.
6. Association for Supervision and Curriculum Development, *The Supervisor: New Demands, New Dimensions,* edited by William H. Lucio. Washington, D.C.: author, 1969.
7. Granger, Robert L., *Educational Leadership: An Interdisciplinary Perspective.* Scranton: Intext Educational Publishers, 1971.
8. Williams, Stanley W., *New Dimensions in Supervision.* Scranton, Pennsylvania: Intext Educational Publishers, 1972.
9. Callahan, Raymond E., *Education and the Cult of Efficiency.* Chicago: University of Chicago Press, 1962.
10. Hartley, Harry J., *Educational Planning-Programming-Budgeting: A Systems Approach.* Englewood Cliffs, New Jersey: Prentice-Hall, 1968.
11. Immegart, Glenn, and Pilecki, Francis J., *An Introduction to Systems for the Educational Administrator.* Reading, Massachusetts: Addison-Wesley, 1973.
12. Knezevich, Stephen J., *Program Budgeting (PPBS): A Resource Allocation Decision System for Education.* Berkeley, California: McCutchan Publishing Corp., 1973.
13. Odiorne, George S., *Management by Objectives: A System of Managerial Leadership.* New York: Pitman Publishing Corp., 1965.
14. Morrisey, George L., *Management by Objectives and Results.* Reading, Massachusetts: Addison-Wesley, 1970.
15. Whitner, John A., and Antin, Arthur P., *Program Planning—Using MBO in School Administration.* Englewood Cliffs, New Jersey: Prentice-Hall, 1972.
16. Likert, Rensis, *New Patterns of Management.* New York: McGraw-Hill, 1961.
17. Schmuck, Richard A., and Miles, Matthew B., eds., *Organization Development in Schools.* Palo Alto, California: National Press Books, 1971.
18. Sergiovanni, Thomas J., and Starratt, Robert, *Emerging Patterns of Supervision: Human Perspectives.* New York: McGraw-Hill, 1971.
19. Banghart, Frank W., and Trull, Albert, *Educational Planning.* New York: Macmillan, 1972.
20. Kaufman, Roger A., *Educational Systems Planning.* Englewood Cliffs, New Jersey: Prentice-Hall, 1972.
21. Romiszowski, A. J., eds., *A Systems Approach to Education.* London: Kogan Page, 1970.
22. Thompson, Robert B., *A Systems Approach to Instruction.* Hamden, Connecticut: Shoe String Press, 1971.
23. Bell, Terrel H., *A Performance Accountability System for School Administrators.* West Nyack, New York: Parker Publishing Co., 1974.
24. Browder, Lesley, Jr., ed., *Emerging Patterns of Administrative Accountability.* Berkeley, California: McCutchan Publishing Corp., 1971.

25. Combs, Arthur, *Educational Accountability: Beyond Behavioral Objectives.* Washington, D.C.: Association for Supervision and Curriculum Development, 1972.
26. Lessinger, Leon M., and Tyler, Ralph W., eds., *Accountability in Education.* Worthington, Ohio: Charles A. Jones Publishing, 1971.
27. Redfern, George G., "Negotiations Change Principal-Teacher Relationships." *The National Elementary Principal.* 47:5 (1968), p. 25.
28. Edney, Philip J., *A Systems Analysis of Training.* New York: Pitman Publishing Corp., 1972.
29. Harris, Ben M., Bessent, Wailand, and McIntyre, Kenneth, *In-Service Education: A Guide to Better Practice.* Englewood Cliffs, New Jersey: Prentice-Hall, 1969.
30. Models of Staff Development I, *Theory Into Practice.* Entire issue, 11:205 (1972).
31. Models of Staff Development II, *Theory Into Practice.* Entire issue, 11:273 (1972).
32. Rubin, Louis J., ed., *Improving In-Service Education.* Boston: Allyn and Bacon, 1971.
33. Eisner, Elliot W., ed., *Confronting Curriculum Reform.* Boston: Little, Brown, and Company, 1971.
34. Frymier, Jack R., and Hawn, Horace C., *Curriculum Improvement for Better Schools.* Worthington, Ohio: Charles A. Jones Publishing, 1970.
35. Lawler, Marcella, ed., *Strategies for Planned Curricular Innovation.* New York: Teachers College Press, 1970.
36. Rodgers, Frederick A., *Curriculum and Instruction in the Elementary School.* New York: Macmillan, 1975.
37. Baker, Robert L., and Schutz, Richard E., eds., *Instructional Product Development.* New York: Van Nostrand Reinhold Company, 1971.
38. Banathy, Bela, *Instructional Systems.* Belmont, California: Fearon Publishers, 1968.
39. Briggs, Leslie J., *Handbook of Procedures for the Design of Instruction.* Pittsburgh: American Institutes for Research, 1970.
40. Provus, Malcolm M., "The Discrepancy Evaluation Model." In *Readings in Curriculum Evaluation,* edited by Peter A. Taylor and Doris M. Cowley. Dubuque, Iowa: William C. Brown Co., 1972.
41. Jackson, Shirley, "The Curriculum Council: New Hope, New Promise." *Educational Leadership,* 29:690 (1972).
42. Miel, Alice, and Lewis, Arthur J., *Supervision for Improved Instruction.* Belmont, California: Wadsworth Publishing Co., 1972.
43. Trusty, Francis M., ed., *Administering Human Resources.* Berkeley, California: McCutchan Publishing Corp., 1971.
44. Blumenberg, Eleanor, "The School-Community Advisory Council: For Better or for Worse." *Journal of Secondary Education,* 46:2 (1971), p. 60.
45. Estes, Nolan, "Operation 'Citizen Involvement' Spells Help for School Challenges." *Educational Leadership,* 31:365 (1974).
46. Competency/Performance-Based Teacher Education. *Phi Delta Kappan,* Entire issue, 55:289 (1974).
47. Lessinger, Leon M., *Every Kid a Winner: Accountability in Education.* New York: Simon and Schuster, 1970.

48. Shearron, Gilbert F., "Inservice-Needs Assessment-Competency-Based Teacher Education." In *Competency Assessment, Research, and Evaluation*, Syracuse, New York: National Dissemination Center for Performance Based Education, 1974.
49. Nunnery, Michael, and Kimbrough, Ralph B., *Politics, Power, Polls, and School Elections*. Berkeley, California: McCutchan Publishing Corp., 1971.
50. Milstein, Mike M., and Belasco, James A., *Educational Administration and the Behavioral Sciences*. Boston: Allyn and Bacon, 1973.
51. Schmuck, Richard A., Runkel, Philip, Saturen, Steven L., Martell, R. J., and Derr, O. B., *Handbook of Organization Development in Schools*. Palo Alto, California: National Press Books, 1972.
52. Ends, A. Walden, "Organization Development: An Alternative for Achieving Planned Change in Contemporary School Systems." In *Improving Supervisory Competencies*, edited by Leslee J. Bishop. Georgia Association for Supervision and Curriculum Development and The Center for Curriculum Improvement and Staff Development. Athens, Georgia: The Center, Department of Curriculum and Supervision, University of Georgia, 1973.
53. Kast, Fremont E., and Rosenzweig, James E., *Organization and Management: A Systems Approach*. McGraw-Hill, 1974.
54. Lawrence, P. R., and Lorsch, J. W., *Developing Organizations: Diagnosis and Action*. Reading, Massachusetts: Addison-Wesley, 1969.

8

Organizing

In one sense, all the materials in the "guide" are directed toward organizing the necessary ideas, means, and personnel in order that the desired objectives be achieved. The suggestions in this chapter relate directly to basic program efforts rather than schemes that organize a particular school or school district. The proposals are drawn from the wide repetoire of available procedures. Since many have been alluded to in previous chapters, what follows constitutes sub-elements of the various coordinating and organizing techniques that appear to warrant further examination or expansion.

Organizing and coordinating procedures are the ways by which leadership distributes and assigns tasks; how such moves are assembled and structured in order to mesh the various elements into a purposeful configuration. They are contingent upon system style and upon previous decisions that have provided intention and direction.

Organizing is also a way of facilitating the involvement and contribution of many persons to achieve power and purpose. By and large, the ideas are built upon a synergetic principle—that the whole is more than the sum of its parts, and that the competencies of various staff persons produce a product and process superior to that of any single agent, agency, or status role.[1,2]

Collaborative and cooperative action requires many considerations. For example, team efforts can be achieved by using such groups as the curriculum council, the building cadre, or the administrative team. These collegial approaches are consistent with the needs for a variety of impacts, a range of expertise, and a humanistic approach that values the contributions of many staff persons, whatever their role. The membership of such groups depends upon the general purposes and focus of the intended program; and typically, it will be drawn from administrative, supervisory, instructional, and support personnel. In many cases, students and community persons are also represented. Such a grouping of talent provides for balance in concerns, includes various levels of responsibility, and utilizes a range of competencies. This grouping also should constitute a "critical mass" of commitment and experience. The desired procedures are those that facilitate trust, power sharing, and also access to direction setting and program structuring. Thus, each staff person is enabled to participate or to have peer representation. One major advantage is that, in addition to providing a functional growth process that encourages the development of perspective and expertise, staff persons have opportunities for significant involvements not requiring the restructuring of the leadership apparatus.[3-8]

BALANCE IN PLANNING AND RESPONSE

Principals, supervisors, and curriculum workers who are responsible for instructional improvement and staff development projects too often are defeated by an "undeclared conspiracy" to keep them immersed in routine and immediate tasks. The result is a lack of balance between activities that are fragmentary and reactive and those that deal with basic long range and program development needs. Consequently, the systematic long-range projects are pushed aside. They suffer because of the persisting style of crisis orientation. It takes courage to say "no" to a specific request for help even when other more fundamental problems exist. However, it should not be a matter of courage, but of priority, determined and supported by policy, which permits the supervisor to place such requests in perspective and to respond in accordance with developed policy, process, and program agreements.[9,10]

The following simple design is offered to assist the leadership person in analyzing and systematizing the work. This becomes a form of log or record of requests and responses.

1. Make a list of activities engaged in over a period of time (or those objectives for which help is requested or noted).
2. Tally where these activities fall on the diagram.
3. Analyze the pattern in terms of policies, priorities, and desired roles.
4. Decide whether the pattern is satisfactory or whether changes should be made in planning the activities and responses being given.

It should be stressed that the question is not whether one should respond or not respond to requests for help, but whether one will exert a constructive and continuing leadership function. Involvement is not the same as entrapment. Conceptualizing, planning, and structuring are as much leadership tasks as are mediation and rescue. In fact, with effective planning and structuring, assistance will be more readily available on a continuing basis. When analyzed and categorized, some solutions can more easily be identified as common to the basic problems that are creating the needs; and when these are identified as such, the

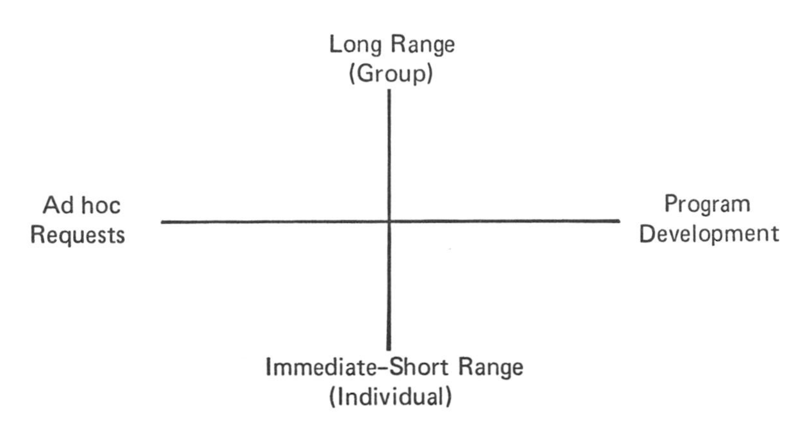

FIGURE 8.1 Patterning the Response.

help will be wider in scope and longer in duration. Immediate or problem situations do develop patterns that can be determined and then addressed systematically, based on the issues that have been noted.

Keeping Track of Developments

Every supervisor or principal has a number of projects underway. One problem is to keep track of these undertakings, particularly where others (teachers, consultants, etc.) have major responsibilities for moving the project along. If the sequence that is proposed here (or one like it) could be adopted, it would be possible to record, manage, and communicate the coordinating and accountability functions.

Somewhere on a wall or bulletin board, a stylized sequence such as the following could be posted. (This is really a modification of the standard "activities schedule.") As projects move through the various stages, progress could be indicated by notations, check marks, or dates "achieved" on the "activities record," e.g., Project 1. If designated review or check points are needed or desired, a second line could be added to each project line as indicated below by A, B, C, e.g., Project 2. This could also be done with the expectation that the project leader or program committee would provide a communication when the specified progress point was reached.

If desired, further detail can be handled by having folders for specified program phases, events, or activities. Over a period of time, these items become very useful to administrators, supervisors, and those vested with project responsibilities. Minutes, notices, data, and other artifacts can be placed in these folders along with questionnaires that have been developed, policy statements that affect a particular phase of the operation, procedural suggestions, or examples of courses or programs. The intention of this record keeping is not to formalize or overstructure but to systematize and facilitate. A comprehensive under-

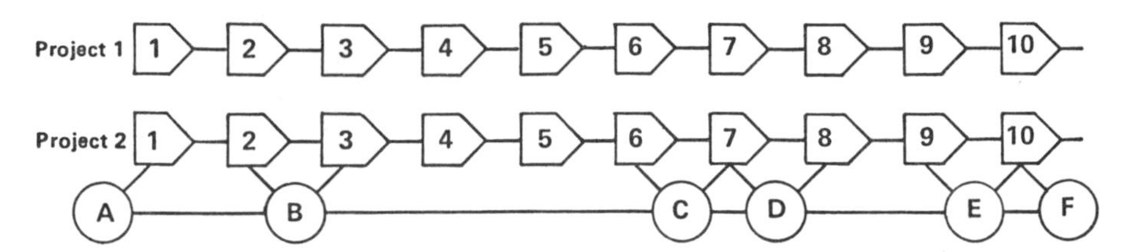

FIGURE 8.2 Design for Coordinating and Communicating.*

*The numbers used in the figure are consistent with others used throughout the text. Thus, number 1 refers to needs analysis; no. 2, to determination of objectives; and so forth. Also, these are the same numbers used on the flow charts, see p. 60, and on the Design Agenda, pp. 62-65.

taking necessitates an orderly and acceptable organizational scheme if continuous progress is to be ensured.

Program records become particularly useful in a school or system where a number of projects are underway and where different persons have responsibility for the activities. Since the illustration is essentially a developmental framework, dates or time intervals could easily be added; or the program phases could be spaced within the desired time frames. Color coding could be used to indicate whether or not a project was on schedule; to designate different types of activities such as research, adoption, adaptation, experimentation, and media utilization; or to specify which were federal, state or local, or similar variations. In using this communication system, it becomes a relatively easy matter to give feedback to teacher groups, parents, board of education members, instructional councils, and others concerning what developmental projects are operating and the progress each has made.

Feedback

Feedback, as currently viewed, involves certain principles of cybernetics, i.e., information flow used to regulate an operation or system. Such a process requires a variety of sensors to detect the nature and existence of critical information, an evaluation of the data to ascertain the relationship to standards or quality, and the subsequent action or input into the system to correct or redirect the process. In this context, feedback is not only data related to specifications, but it is also the instrumentation and process for gathering data and for providing self-correcting measures. Auditing may be part of the process; monitoring, with the capacity to intervene, is definitely related. The information sensing, evaluating, disseminating, and decision making loop is a critical functioning of those charged with management or project leadership. The use of such a process requires basic structural elements within which to operate; namely, plans, events, phases, and in-process evaluation data.

These elements and processes can be realistically understood and developed when the school district and the project management are operated as an "open system," influencing and being influenced by the context within which it exists. This open system requires strategic process that provide for exchanges of inputs and outcomes, that seek a balance between internal and external elements, that make decisions and modifications based on these components and subsystems, and that manage to maintain the status and integrity of the entities or agencies that are involved.[11,12]

Feedback is essential to progress and to the feeling of progress. It is not just the data being collected; rather, *feedback is the data plus the process for constructive reshaping.* It is a critical assist in the process of determining more adequately the current situation and what still remains to be done. Feedback does not wait for the implementation or evaluation phases, but must exist continuously in connection with all phases and processes. Pilot testing, field testing, and simulations are important; but too often they tend to be one-time adjustments, occurring too late to change significantly the materials, the format, or the instructional strategies. Feedback can take many forms: memos to individuals or groups, conversations and dialogue, newspaper accounts, research data, bulletins, audio tape responses, pictures, reports in meetings, telephone messages, and bulletin board exhibits. Feedback should include communication with concerned individuals, community elements, and feeder institutions. The various checklists, models, and structural ideas included in the "guide" are all designed to contribute to this critical process and information flow.[13-16]

Some insights and techniques can be adopted from other fields. The use of public opinion polls that seek specific responses from carefully sampled audiences is one example of both input and feedback related to evaluation, policy formulation, and operational decision making. Athletics and sports provide another example. Performance ratings are used by experts who know the intricacies of the art to be executed. For example, in the Olympic games, gymnasts, divers, and skaters perform certain skills and are judged by a panel of judges. Both the skill of the performers and the ratings of the judges are viewed by millions of persons. Video tapes are used to validate the total performance as well as the reliability of a particular judge in regard to various performers. More absolute judgments are possible in those sports where speed, score, time, or distance provide outcome data. Process elements exist as the athletes perform within certain rules and boundaries. These evidences, too, are captured by the recorded scores, by the accumulated data, and by video or film. The instant replay in most professional sports has become a standard expectation, providing review, analysis, and evaluation.

The sports field provides other suggestions. Computer studies have been developed to indicate relationships between conditions and outcomes. In football, for example, studies are made of momentum, location on the field, time and timing factors, turnovers, and the like. In baseball, such items as weather, speed, right-handedness or left-handedness, performance under specified pressure conditions, or time in the season are studied. In golf, it is the lie, the club, and the swing. These examples illustrate situations where objectives, conditions, performance criteria, and treatment are increasingly subject to analysis and prediction. Likewise, in these situations, data offer an improved understanding regarding probability, the fortuitous (luck), and the human factors that can challenge the reliability of the "baseline" data at any given time. Significantly, such visual and performance data are used as training aids, both to improve performance and to analyze competitors and their styles.

Admittedly, these are gross performance areas of a more obvious nature than, for example, symbolic management in reading, perceptual bases in language, or attitudinal concepts in social science. Nevertheless, the proposition exists that—by determining objectives and conditions and by gaining insights from multiple sources and instruments, participant inventories, observer reports, ratings, and test scores—useful data can be produced and used to make decisions regarding individual and group effectiveness, style, and achievement and to assist with subsequent improvement.

Renewing and Restructuring Program Objectives

A related problem of a maturing project is the need to recycle and reconsider the objectives as they are being built into the program. Agreed upon initially and validated by staff processes and consensus, program objectives have a way of becoming redefined, sometimes in wording, sometimes in the perceptions and intentions of those who are doing the planning. Redefining is easily and sometimes unconsciously done by those responsible for the project as they extend and organize the structure of the program. Redefining also may come from those who are participating as they internalize and implement the original objectives. This process of renewing or revising need not result in a problem; as a matter of fact, it should be anticipated as a natural development.[17]

Any differences in perception or interpretation can be minimized by interactive procedures that bring together those who are involved in the planning, structuring, and developing. Communication should result in agreements as to changes, and these can then be consolidated into the design and development activities. Such an effort will stabilize the objectives, both as statements and as personal and structural agreements. Since each objective should be built into the program operation (or be changed or eliminated), there should be a continuing dialogue to maintain congruence, to develop functional process data, and to permit mutual changes throughout the duration of the project.[18-20] This is especially true in the initial structuring efforts. As indicated by Figure 8.3, once objectives are incorporated into program elements (design,

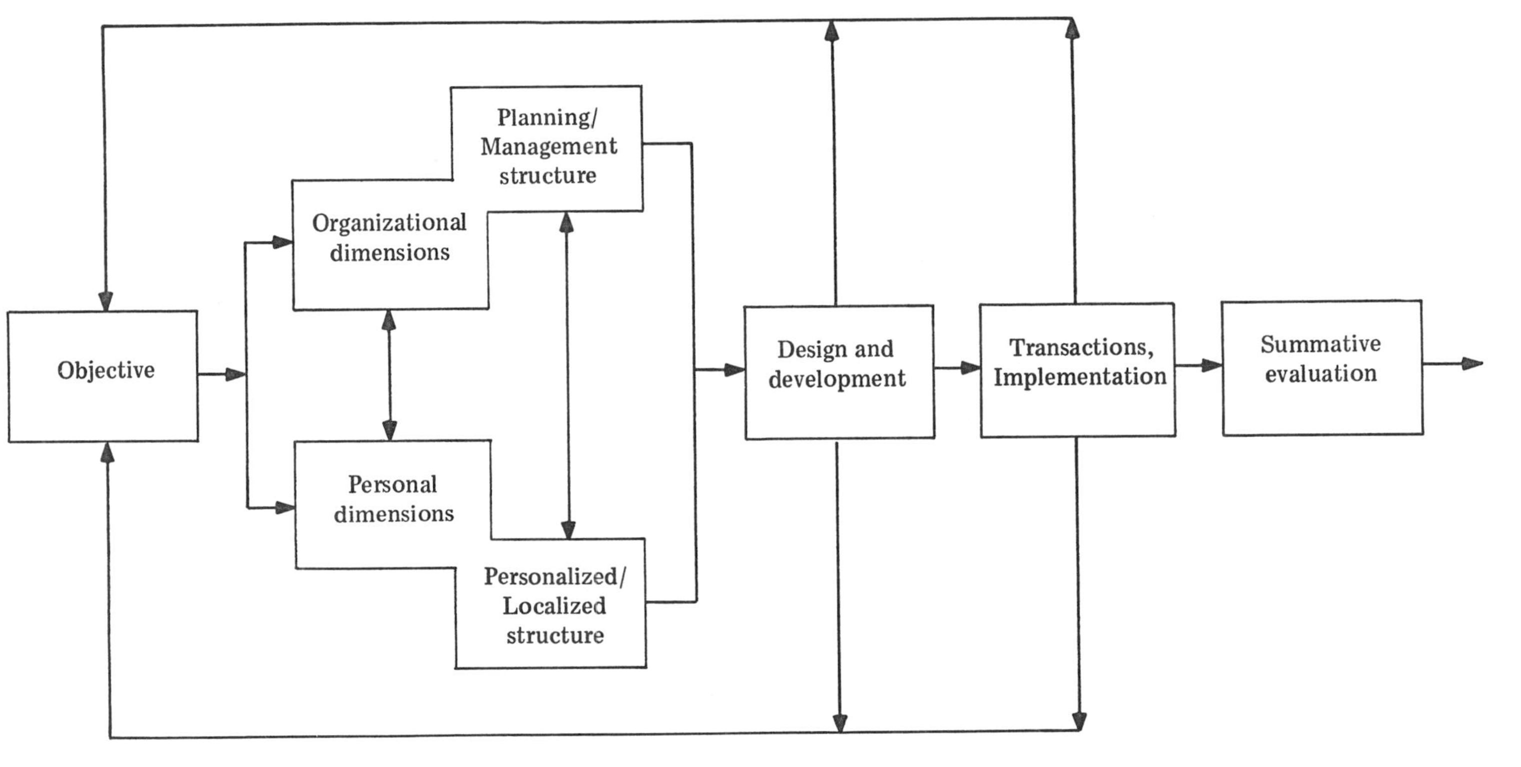

FIGURE 8.3 Renewing and Restructuring Objectives.

development, and implementation), any differences tend to be operationally resolved. This process of clarification and renewal of objectives can be functionally included in formative evaluation, in the development and use of performance criteria, and in the review of outcomes and process elements. These cyclic modifications of objectives and related changes are a critical management responsibility. They are detailed in the technologies of such procedures as *management by objectives*, *management by exception*, *clinical supervision*, *organization development*, *intervention strategy*, and other communications-oriented approaches.

MONITORING

Monitoring is a procedure for "overviewing" the processes and products of a particular program. As used here, this review process includes the responsibility to intervene when necessary with changes and corrections. This is a stronger definition of monitoring than occurs in data processing, instrument monitoring (in medicine, for example), or many business operations where the function is limited to information gathering and recording. As defined here, it is a response to the need for more effective techniques for ascertaining and recording such critical elements as the nature and degree of student learning, the program efforts to improve educative conditions, the competencies of the staff to facilitate and deliver the desired objectives, and the adequacy of organizational functioning.[21,22]

Monitoring is more effective when it operates within the same boundaries that have been established for the program effort (see Appendix C). That is, it should be in harmony with the design, the organization, and the operational context. Thus, the processes that are used should be compatible, not contradictory, to the determined human relations guidelines and procedures. The data generated and used should be explicitly related to that necessary for program information and decision making. Feelings—identification, satisfaction, and commitment—are also important elements to be ascertained and considered. The time frames and interventions should coincide with the agreed-upon developmental phases or schedules. In this way, monitoring becomes integral to the other program elements. As such, it can be anticipated by the participants as a regularized function in connection with the planned inputs, evaluative measures, communication points, events, decisions, and changes. Monitoring can exist as an external process and as a different style; but, as such, it will likely be considered as an interruption in the work flow and have a negative rather than an affirmative impact.

Concerns of the monitor in many procedures deal with efficiency and effectiveness as determined by instruments that indicate process and product outcomes. Such a review is enhanced by developed and communicated structural elements and is closely allied with process and formative evaluation, although it may be a separate responsibility. How closely monitoring is identified with ongoing evaluation is a result of both management decision making and design. A highly developed task analysis with specified events and performance standards is both informative and evaluative. The uses of such data and their incorporation into the functioning of leadership personnel thus determine whether the monitoring function is identical, complementary, or separate from other operations.

Using Design Elements and Data Inputs for Monitoring

Monitoring involves the collection and utilization of data. These inputs are necessary to ascertain the situation, to provide dimensions as to progress and problems, and to facilitate the decision making and action that are to follow. The matrix shown as Figure 8.4 is intended to suggest how particular organizational or style elements can be viewed in relationship to information and feedback data. Thc style elements or program approaches are labeled design elements and are listed as the left column. The second series of items are labeled "Sources of Input and Feedback Data." The matrix so formed does not constitute a monitoring device per se, rather it suggests basic elements that can be developed into a plan uniquely appropriate to a particular situation or system. Design elements are as follows:

1. *Program objectives*—those projects or programs that have developed objectives, the completion of which represents the major tasks to be accomplished, e.g., *management by objectives.*
2. *Roles/Tasks*—a program structure based on defined job descriptions that include the responsibilities delineated in operational terms. When these roles are being performed as specified, the desired tasks are being achieved.
3. *Phases/Events*—those program efforts defined by PERT charts or stated landmarks. As these occur, they generate data and outcomes that can be reviewed.
4. *Procedures or processes*—such approaches as *organization development, clinical supervision,* and other participatory approaches that have significant procedural and personal growth outcomes.
5. *Organization/Work flow*—an emphasis upon standard operations not particularly defined by any of the previous categories. As persons engage in their expected capacities and as committees and organizational elements, they produce evidence in minutes, reports, and time use.
6. *Time Frames/Schedules*—the operations that stress time elements as the basic review structure, where work flow and outcomes are organized into time segments or routine schedules that incorporate the desired outcomes. In this utilization, review periods are determined primarily by time periods, i.e., months, marking periods, quarters, semesters, and so forth.

None of the above are exclusive; the intent of the listing is to identify the style or emphasis, not to suggest that only one of the approaches is utilized. However, by noting the emphasis or a functional combination thereof, it will be possible to anticipate and plan for the

DESIGN ELEMENTS	SOURCES OF INPUT AND FEEDBACK DATA				
	Official Data—decisions, policies, votes, regulations, resolutions, and allocations	*Routine Data*—reports, logs, letters, cases, records, minutes, and recommendations	*Instrumented Data*—surveys, tests, studies, evaluative measures, questionnaires, external audit, and ratings	*Interaction Data*—interviews, observations, consultation, discussion, VTR, and audio tape	*Informal Data*—behaviors, utilization, parent inquiries, newspaper articles, and photographs
1. Program Objectives	1	7	13	19	25
2. Roles/Tasks	2	8	14	20	26
3. Phases/Events	3	9	15	21	27
4. Procedures/Processes	4	10	16	22	28
5. Organization/Work Flow	5	11	17	23	29
6. Time Frames/Schedule	6	12	18	24	30

FIGURE 8.4 Elements in Formative Evaluation and Monitoring.

type of data and the nature of the reporting that will occur, or that is to be recommended.

"Sources of Input and Feedback Data" constitute the right column. There, categories of data sources are organized into useful, non-discrete combinations, which can be reorganized for a particular school system or project. Words are clustered to suggest a classification, rather than to fix a particular input item. These general categories are self explanatory.

The two columns produce cells that are numbered for purposes of identification or decision making. Most monitoring utilizations would include a combination of cells, although a particular datum or instrument could be assigned to a single cell on the basis of its emphasis or intent. The cells are intended to be generative. That is, their purpose is to suggest possibilities or limitations, not to propose that all could or should be used. Thus, it might be desirable at a particular planned juncture: (1) to develop and treat data from a single cell area, (2) to fuse deliberately a combination of cells, or (3) to select a range of cell utilizations for purposes of variety and coverage. This would apply to one particular development phase or for many. Variety is encouraged because, for example, to use only tests or questionnaires as project monitors would likely be repetitious and boring to participants. To never use instrumented data of some sort could result in the use of the only "soft" or indirect data for decision making and program management. This could also pose a problem of reliability.

The third dimension for each cell would be the *treatment* given to the information or the identified outcome. Obviously, data created expressly for review purposes are more easily utilized than those that were produced for other, perhaps incidental or unrelated purposes. In cases of the latter, it would be necessary to extract needed information by research methodologies in order to assess progress or make decisions. The extent and requirements of the program, combined with the demands of the monitoring or evaluating function, would determine the criteria for the desired data—such as matters of time, cost, amount, nature of reported detail, degree of quantification, instrumentation, and the like.

The matrix, therefore, suggests items for use in developing a monitoring or evaluating scheme. For example, in standard utilizations, persons in leadership roles are expected to provide minutes of meetings and reports of work to their supervisors (cells 8 or 11). Also common, many teachers are expected to file final examinations, scores, and grades with a particular office (cell 14) and at a specified time (cells 14 and 18). Progress reports are expected of all functionaries, and these items can be built into the desired monitoring program. In regard to design element number 1, "Program Objectives," a simple continuum can be used in connection with objectives: At a regular interval the program director would review the progress of each program objective as (1) not applicable, (2) being planned, (3) being implemented, or (4) completed. The required supporting data would be produced by items in row 1–25, depending upon the nature of the project activities and events (see Appendix C). In long-range or complex projects, sub-objectives likely would be present that could be listed and reviewed. A more complicated form could be developed using Figure 8.5.

The requirements for the data so generated would depend upon whether it was to be used for formative evaluation, for monitoring, or for both. Formative evaluation would likely utilize cells 13–18 more frequently than others because of the need for more formalized, quantifiable, and objective data. Monitoring could include this information, but that function would be facilitated by the use of data from a greater variety and range. In either monitoring or formative evaluation uses, it would be necessary to have further treatment of the developed information. This treatment could include such factors as:

- The application of standards or criteria and a check of the discrepancy between intended achievement and progress to date.
- The development of recommendations as to desirable interventions or changes.
- The decision that the program operation should continue as it is.
- Extending a proposed deadline to provide more time to prepare for a scheduled event.
- The recommendation that progress or problems should be reported to participants and interested publics (feedback).
- Filing of the data pending further information, or as part of the summative evaluation data.
- An action terminating the program.

Such decision making assumes that the person or group performing the monitoring function has the power to intervene. If such is not the case, the analysis then would be formulated into a recommendation to the appropriate decision-maker(s) for action.

Other utilizations of the ideas presented in Figure 8.4 are possible. For example, intersection points (cells) could be used as agenda items for the following:

1. Develop additional program objectives, some of which may relate to procedures as well as product or event outcomes.
2. Consider new or desirable organizational elements—a committee, a policy statement, a role description, a budget item, and a needed resource or facility.
3. Conduct empirical research to obtain better baseline data regarding process, performance, or achievement standards.
4. Develop or use evaluative measures to determine efficiency, impact, feeling, and criticality.
5. Produce data banks relative to a developmental or program phase. Develop storage and retrieval facilities to more adequately house the evidences of change, gain, discrepancy, or congruity.

The use of many input and data sources admits both the inadequacy of any one item and the desirability of more complete information obtained from multiple sources. Changes wrought in any program effort are not likely to be identified with single measures. Also, the purpose of obtaining data at many outcome points is to provide a more longitudinal review rather than depend upon a single or one-time instrument or measure. After a series of programs have been documented and reviewed, it would be expected that leadership could determine the most useful input items and procedures and the most critical points, and their relationship to style or process elements. Within this context, individual performances could be sampled by interviews, observation reports, logs, or self inventories; however, the design is to suggest possible ways to ascertain program progress and related changes, not evaluate individuals.

Monitoring, auditing, and formative evaluation can be based on relatively simple procedures or be more complex. As indicated, the degree of completeness depends upon the number of projects underway, the formality of procedures, "accountability" measures, and preferences regarding roles and data requirements. The following items are among those commonly used for reporting purposes where *objec-*

Schedule for Initiation, Analysis and Design								*Schedule for Implementation and Evaluation*						
1	*2*	*3*	*4*	*5*	*6*	*7*	*8*	*9*	*10*	*11*	*12*	*13*	*14*	*15*
Objective—the task and objective, conditions	Target—impact group, person(s), agency	Initiation—who authorizes process, develops charge	Responsibility—who performs specified task	Baseline Data—pre-conditions, available data	Instrument—specific technique, criteria	Report Date—for completed analysis, preparation	Monitor—who reviews progress, authorizes to proceed	Responsibility—who inputs, presents	Target—audience, agency, persons	Procedure—method, program elements, format, logistics	Date—transaction performed, presented, installed	Response—quality measures, data	Review—quality check, assessment	Management—who authorizes completion, file, feedback, recycle

FIGURE 8.5 Elements for Constructing a Form for Monitoring, Auditing, or Formative Evaluation.

tives constitute the focus. Codes, numbers or abbreviations, can be used to minimize space and writing requirements.

Checklist for Monitoring and Decision Making

In project development, agenda building, and monitoring, a checklist is often useful for discussion and decision making. The following items are suggestive of those needing policy review and decision. The school system and administrative-supervisory leadership must be clear about such factors as:

- Policy statement and budgetary support.
- Personnel role specification and responsibility.
- Materials adequacy, availability, quality, and selection process.
- Evaluative measures to be used regarding program, leadership, and staff.
- Monitoring, scheduling, and implementing plan.
- Relationships between ongoing instructional efforts and the proposed concepts and staff activities.
- Community support as reflected in policy, personnel, organization, learning sites, and agency participation.
- Leadership roles and accountability measures.
- Communication flow, feedback system, and coordination of efforts.
- Strategies for building in the new content or instructional procedures.
- Support and management system—procedures, organization, instruments, and logistics.
- Individual and group involvement, clear relationship to decision making.
- Client and participant feelings—satisfaction, identification, input opportunities, and subsequent consideration of data.
- Nature of teacher, learner, parent, and patron involvement.
- Instructional competencies essential to the delivery of the particular educational methods and use of materials and substantive information.
- Outcome specifications as they relate to students.

No list can be adequate; conditions differ so markedly from time-to-time and situation-to-situation. What needs to be "checked out" depends upon the nature of leadership style, the system climate, the competencies of personnel, and outside pressures. In a highly human relations orientation, it is likely that sensitivity to persons and their needs for autonomy are operating; therefore, the important reminders may be for structure, organization, and adequacy of resources and materials. In a task or product oriented environment, the need may be to become more alert to personal expectations, commitment, and dialogue. Organizing and coordinating have both personal and task dimensions. The perceptive and effective leader recognizes the necessity and power of each; for neither inspiration alone nor techniques alone can achieve the desired changes and improvements in a complex, human setting.

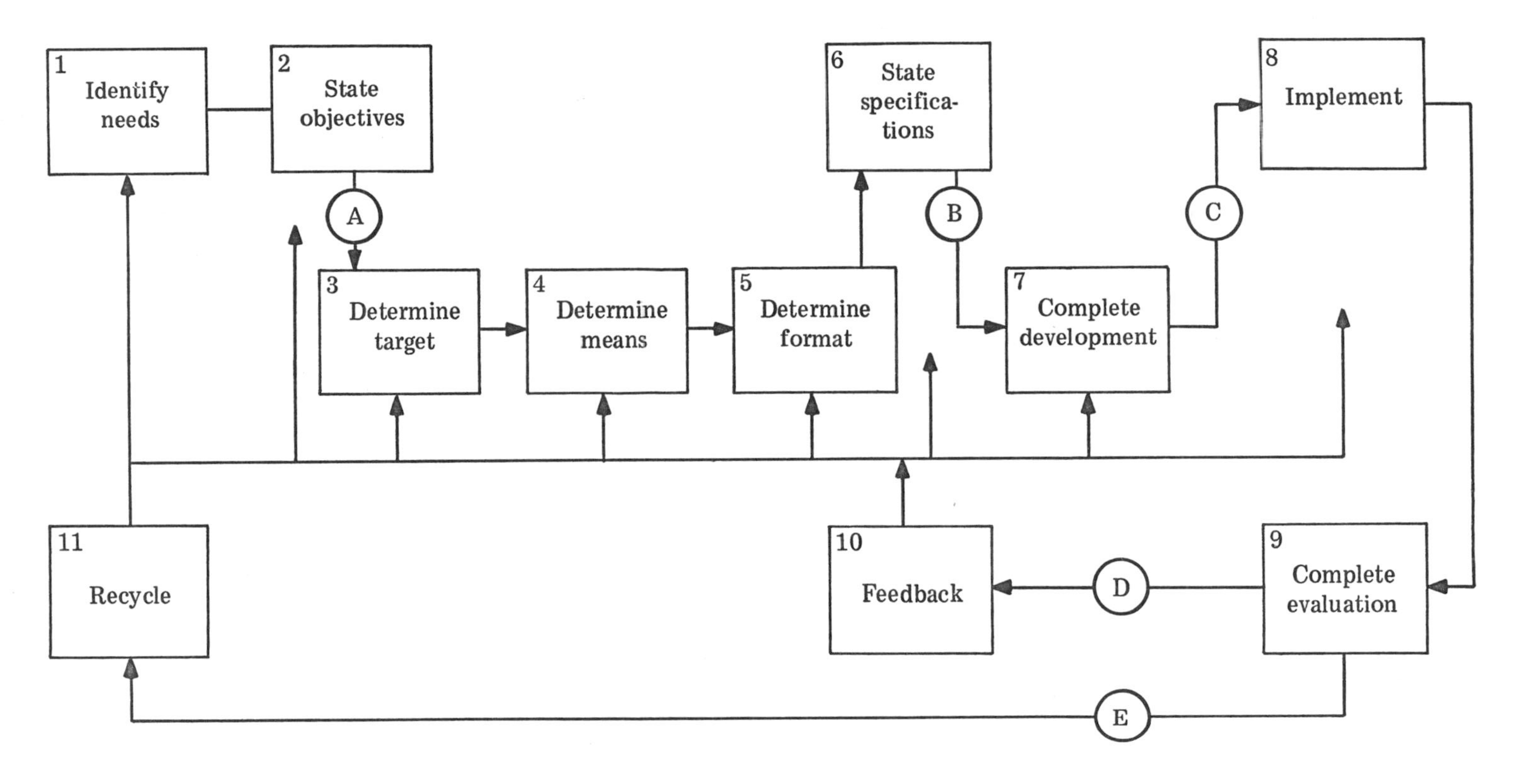

FIGURE 8.6 Flowchart Indicating Communication or Decision Points.

DEVELOPING A PLANNING NETWORK

For long-range or complex projects, the development of a system for analyzing and coordinating the proposed events and sequences likely will be necessary. One such device is the *flow chart*, of which Figure 3.1 and Figure 8.6 (previous page) are representative, both using the same elements.

Basically, a flow diagram is a way of visualizing major steps, decision-points, or stages of a plan (or process). This technique visualizes the sequence, parallel flow, intersection, or linking of these points as they move from objectives to solutions.[23]

Usually, ideas are shown as square or rectangle boxes. If desired, different shapes can be used to convey different meaning, e.g., diamond shape for decisions, square for events, rectangle for information, and the like. Lines and arrows can be used to indicate the direction of activity, the dependencies, and the convergence points.

The flow chart is a way of visualizing the order of a planned series of events that need to be studied, communicated, and implemented. One advantage of this technique is the manner in which cycles and the recycling of events can be depicted easily. The flow diagram is an especially useful device when the data needs are not too demanding, that the critical elements to be examined can be shown on a reasonably sized (for handling) display.

In addition to indicating the flow of activities, Figure 8.6 also suggests key points—shown by capital letters A, B, etc.—for monitoring, decision making, or formative evaluation. The number of such intervention points could obviously be increased or reduced. By specifying them on the flow chart, all participants are made aware of their placement and intent. (See also Figures 8.2 and 8.16 for comparable utilizations.)

A Decision Making Design

The following flow chart, Figure 8.7, is based on a computer model. It demonstrates a decision making and work flow scheme. It was developed from a need to provide a statement of agreement that was built upon group consensus; also, it was needed as a technique for communicating procedures.* As with many such devices, the preliminary plans and staff discussions that preceded the formulation of the design were the most productive results, since many persons participated in the decisions that were summarized in the final draft of the flow chart. Thus, the production of the model provided a learning situation as well as an operational plan.

In an actual utilization, names and dates are added to the particular decision points; these are shown in relationship to the developmental

*This was primarily the work of Dr. James Eisele, a colleague in the Curriculum and Supervision Department, University of Georgia, Athens, Georgia.

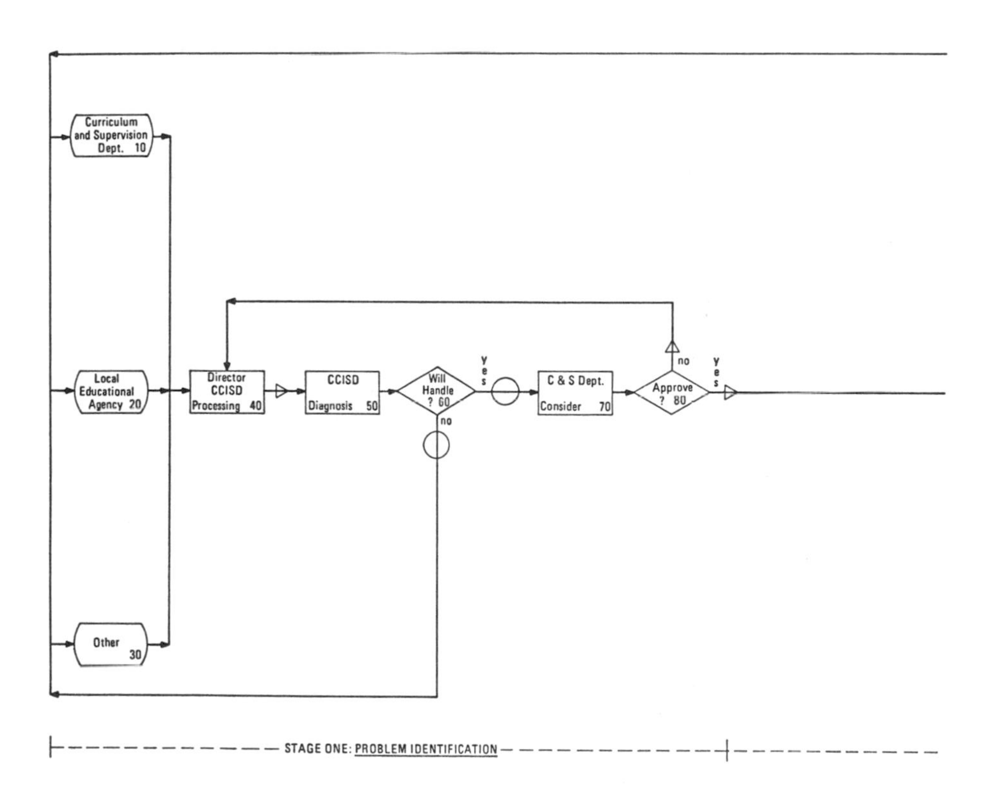

FIGURE 8.7 Decision Making Flowchart.

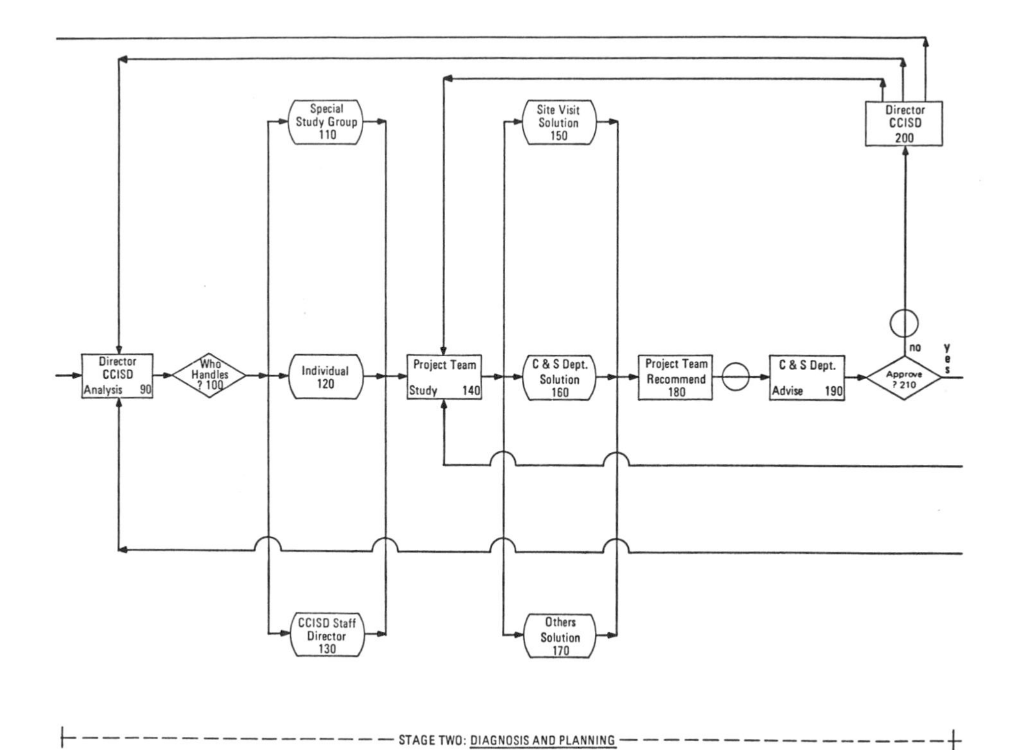

FIGURE 8.7 Continued.

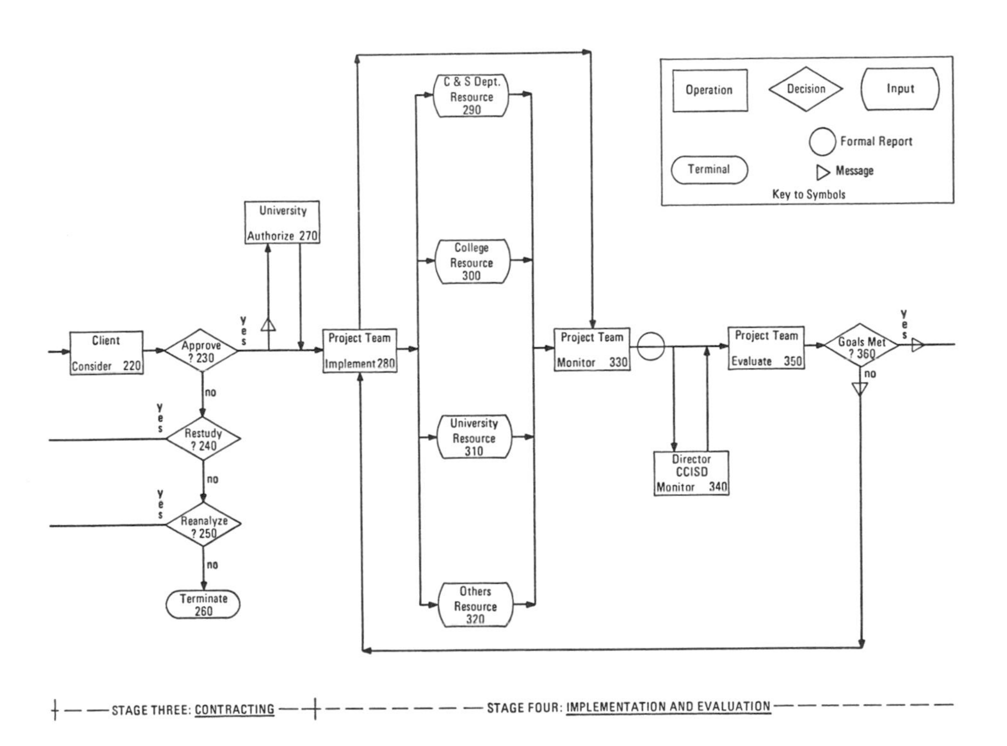

FIGURE 8.7 Continued.

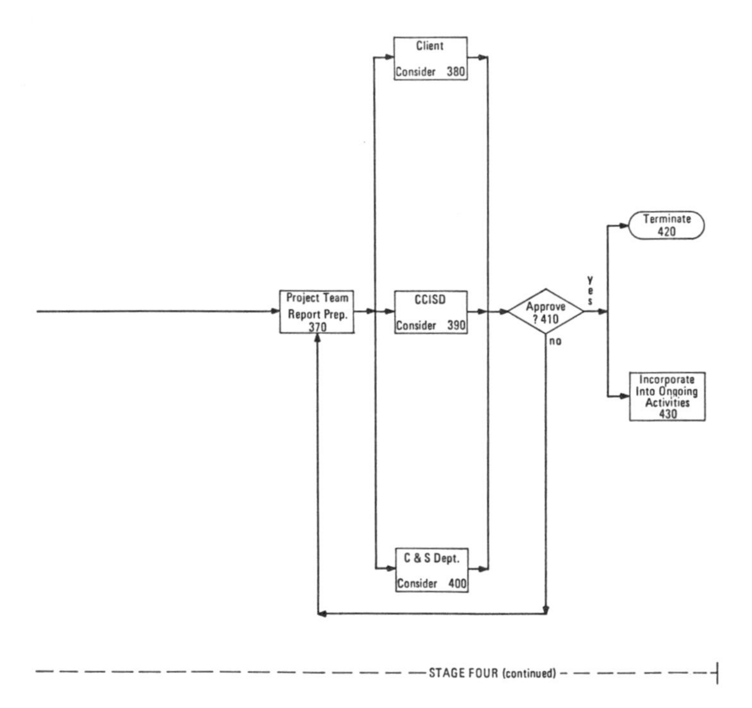

Figure 8.7 Continued.

sequence placed at the bottom of the chart. Modifications are made as needed in connection with specific projects: Who makes decisions? And/or what points? What the consequences are of certain decisions, and where and with whom certain processes take place, all become important elements in a cooperative plan.

Another commonly used device is the time line or Gantt chart. For this visualization, events are indicated in regard to their timing and duration. It is particularly useful where beginning or terminal points are not critical, but where it is helpful to indicate generalized events and activities. See Figure 8.8.

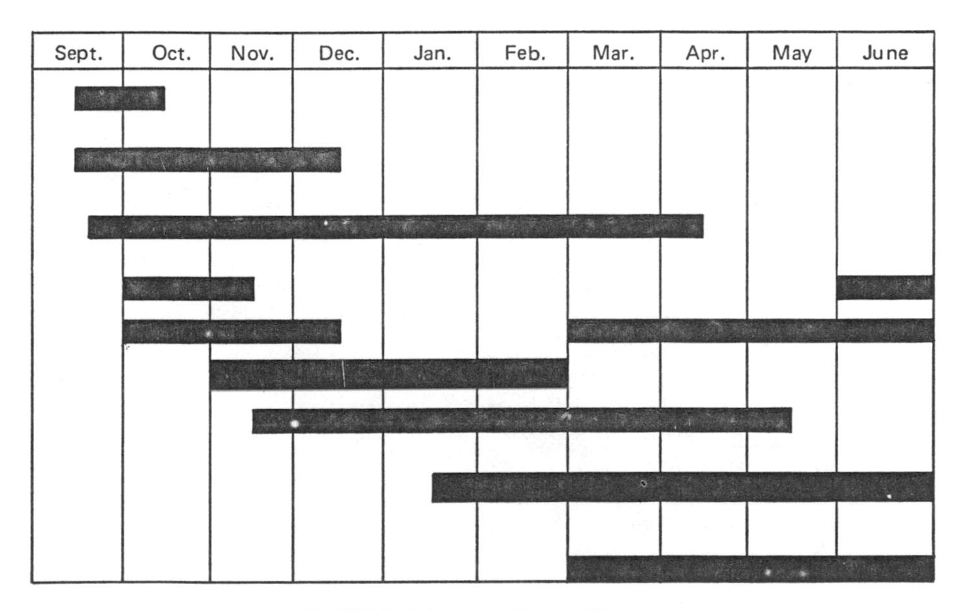

FIGURE 8.8 The Gantt Chart.

On such a visual format, it would be necessary to specify the particular activities indicated by the lines above. This would be done by a listing on the left of the page, by a list with a key number to indicate the nature of each line, or by including the description within the rectangle formed by the "bar graphs" shown here. Key events or impact points can be indicated by circles, rectangles, or other marks placed at appropriate points on the task lines.

The Gantt Chart is similar in purpose to the "Time Line," with which most professionals are familiar. When it becomes necessary or desirable to show an interrelationship or dependency among the work lines, then a visual system more amenable to these indications should be used. One procedure is the use of the PERT chart, which is explained briefly on the following pages.

PERT

Assuming the need for a complex planning scheme, consider a PERT (*P*rogram *E*valuation and *R*eview *T*echnique) chart.[24] PERT is a device for facilitating the planning process and the project design (see Appendix E). As with other management techniques, it requires first that objectives be determined, that these objectives then be translated into manageable program elements, and that these elements be subdivided into work areas and work packages. Once accomplished, it is then possible to construct a graphic portrayal of these tasks into a related and interdependent network of planned activities and events. As such, the explicated program—this was discussed in Chapter 3 as work packages or tasks—represents an interpretation of the previously made decisions and becomes a guide to the actions necessary to implement the plans and decisions. It is only a guide, however, and variations and exceptions become the continuing in-process responsibility (managing and monitoring) of those directing the program (See Figure 8.16).

As a delineation of decisions, plans, criteria, and needed resources, the PERT chart should also represent contributions from those who are to implement the program. In addition to goal clarification and consensus, participants can contribute ideas and alternatives from their experience and expertise; these may include what needs to be done to achieve the objectives, how these tasks can be organized and sequenced, and what time and competency factors are required to complete them well and on schedule. PERT is most useful for "one time" projects, innovations, and large scale efforts; it is not recommended for routine or recurring operations where a flow chart is more feasible. It is a good way to lay open the events (what needs to be done) for participation, for examination and review, and for operation.

In this approach, it is helpful to follow a few guidelines in conceptualizing and charting the work to be done. (1) Decide upon a goal, e.g., the installation of a new program in environmental science. (2) Decide that it shall be operational on a given time in the future. (3) Then, with that goal and time in mind, plan the strategy for resource allocation to reach the goal. The gap between the present situation and the conditions necessary by the due date gives a "time frame" and a context that must be purposefully managed. For this purpose, a planning form is proposed by Figure 8.9. Listed on the left margin are representative components, see pp. 62–65 and 236, the work areas to be considered. These work areas are listed on the planning form but need not be included on the network as finally visualized. In most situations, each of the listed areas (or similar sub-systems) would need to be considered, with activities and events developed for each to some extent depending upon the focus of the project.

Some suggested components to assist with the initial sketching are listed as follows:

1. *Policy/Political.* This involves school system policies and community priorities. Both administrative policy and community support are essential if the necessary

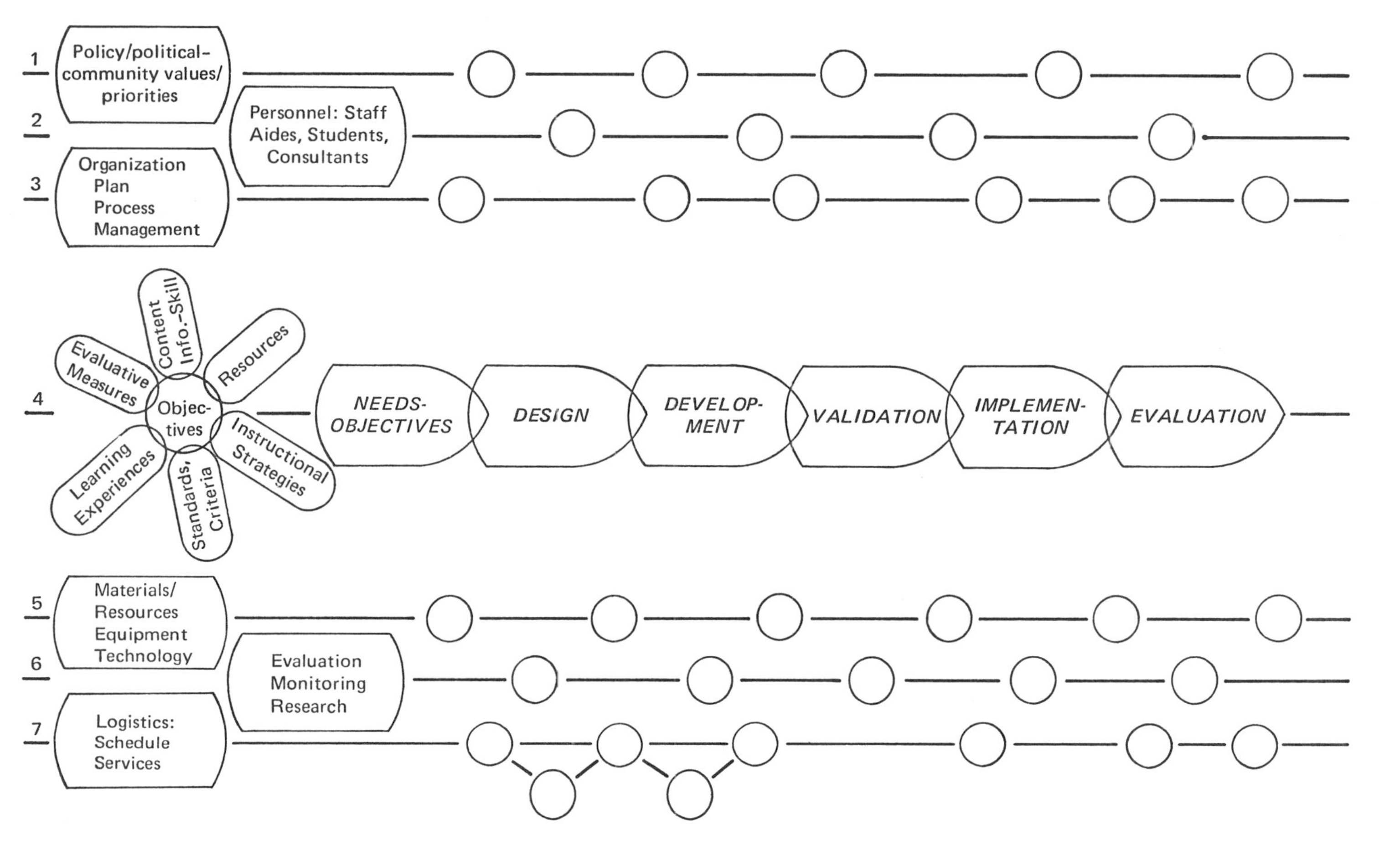

FIGURE 8.9 Instructional Improvement Program and Support Elements.

priority and reinforcement are to be assured. Public relations and any activity, including use of community sites or agencies, would be included here.

2. *Personnel.* To be considered here are all persons who are to be involved, their acquisition, selection, training, and involvement. Leadership is a critical element of this component, as are outside consultant help or liaison with a university for assistance or course credit (for the activity).
3. *Organization and Management.* This involves the determination of how the activity is to be organized, managed, and monitored. A major part of this component is the plan—the project design—and its relationship to the ongoing operation and administration of the school system.
4. *Program Thrust.* Both the instructional elements to be developed and implemented and the phases of the change can be delineated here. This is the heart of the plan and planning. As indicated, each instructional emphasis will have its own requirements as the project moves through the change stages. (For an extended explanation of the program particulars, see Development Phase, Chapter 4.
5. *Materials and Resources.* In any project, however modest, books, media, equipment, and other instructional resources will need to be secured for use and coordinated.
6. *Evaluation, Auditing, Research.* These are shown as separate from management activities. They are often separate functions in large projects. If the in-service efforts are to receive continued support, evidence must be obtained that has substance and credibility. In less ambitious projects, these operations could be a functional part of the management activity, especially process evaluation. This work would include finding or developing processes and instruments for evaluation (formative and summative), conducting the accompanying research effort, and auditing progress as the project matures.
7. *Support Features.* Essential to any project, however simple, are necessary changes in procedures and ongoing programs; the specifics to logistics and scheduling; and the detailing, support, and response related to uses of time, facilities, routines, personnel, and other necessary arrangements.

To be determined are the events and sequence for each work area component and the points at which these events impact, intersect, or are dependent upon previous or concurrent developments. In the initial sketching, it is best to use a chalkboard, since many changes will likely be required. The initial planning for the network should place circles (events) in a rough time line to show time of impact, sequence, and points where events will likely converge. Keeping in mind these general characteristics, consider the PERT design and nomenclature items that follow.

Events are defined as reports submitted, meetings held, studies completed, decisions made, documents produced—work packages that are identifiable, and achievable "landmarks." Each circle (event) can be assigned a number; these need not be in exact sequence since they will be difficult to assign. It may be desirable to number by two's or five's to facilitate the insertion of additional events without having to redo the plan.

Activities such as the work of committees, report preparation, and so forth are not shown in circles but are indicated by lines between the circles. Dotted arrow lines are sometimes referred to as "dummy" lines; they indicate sequence and work flow but no activity or time requirement between events. Activities are the time-consuming work that involves organizing, preparing, searching, planning, and consulting.

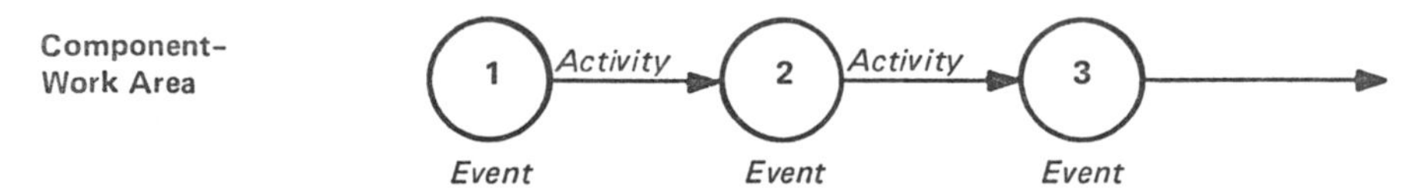

FIGURE 8.10 PERT: Series and Events.

As indicated by the Figure 8.10 series, lines indicate the activity and time that precede the event. Lines drawn between the events with arrows indicate work flow or dependency. When a *critical path method* (CPM) is to be used, these time considerations become the basis for sequencing and placement on the network. If desired, probable *time requirements* can be indicated by notations on the arrow lines. (A fraction of a week is a common practice.) Such notations assist in showing which events are too time-consuming and need to be broken into lesser tasks. The notations would provide a basis for determining which events need to be reassigned more personnel, reconsidered as single events, or given a different placement on the network.

Task sheets can be developed for the events and activities. The events are identified by numbers—1, 2, 3, etc., and the activities by combinations of numbers—1-2 or 3-4, etc. Thus, planning, monitoring, or communicating can be done with very specific reference points. Worksheets can indicate such items as objectives to be achieved, leadership or responsibility, performance requirements, means to be used (method, time, cost), and related sub-tasks. (See the section on monitoring, p. 216, for a more complete listing; also task analysis, p. 77-79.)

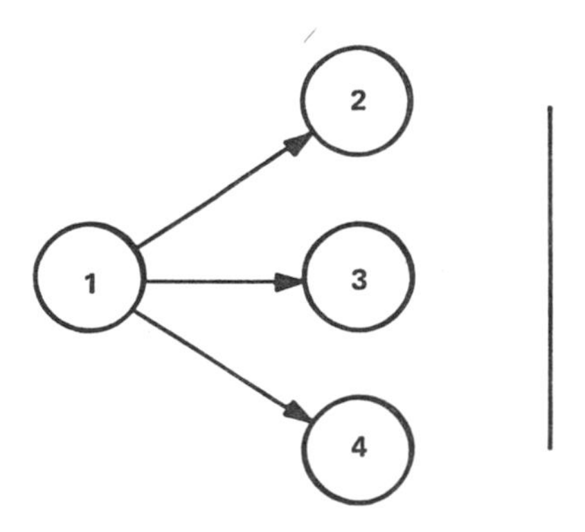

FIGURE 8.11 Burst Construction.

An analysis of activities and events permits decision making regarding costs, alternatives, resource, and personnel uses. These are important in project planning or in PPBES applications.

Many constructions are possible, but only a few will be illustrated here. For example, to indicate a work expansion a *burst* configuration may be used as shown in Figure 8.11.

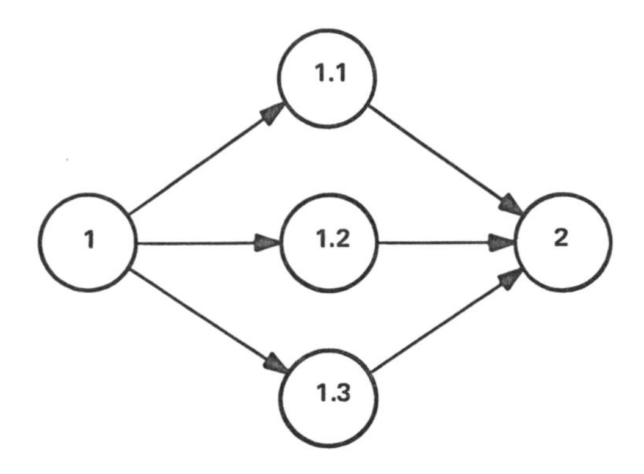

FIGURE 8.12 Subordinate Tasks.

Sub-tasks (sometimes referred to as second or third level work packages) can be shown in Figure 8.12.

Likewise, subordinate PERTs can be developed to indicate the task necessary to move from one event to the next. The subordinate PERTs are especially useful in situations where the PERT incorporates only major events and it is necessary to explicate some steps with greater detail. Where the events and activities *merge* is shown in Figure 8.13.

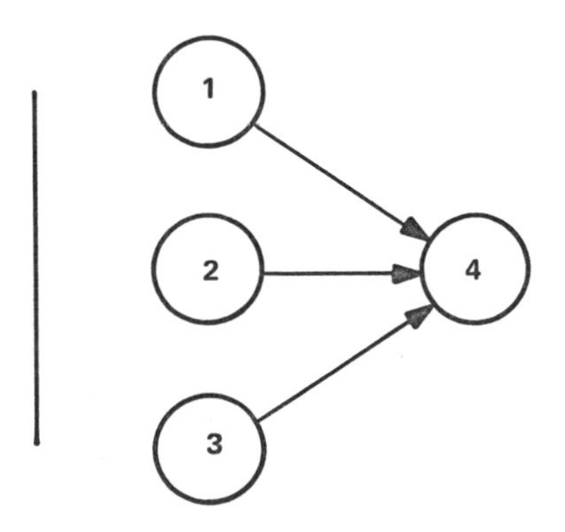

FIGURE 8.13 Merge Construction.

(These are only examples of possible visualizations since no event begins or ends by itself. Except for *start*, each develops from previous events; and except for project *end*, each continues into subsequent events.)

If an activity cannot start before a preceding event is finished, it may be desirable to show *start* and *complete* events, see Figure 8.14.

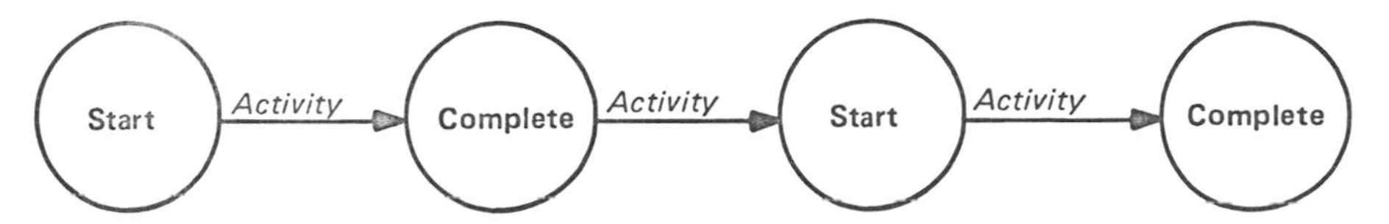

FIGURE 8.14 Start-Complete Construction.

Construction becomes more complicated at *intersection* points. These are the places where work lines converge (or interface), see Figure 8.15.

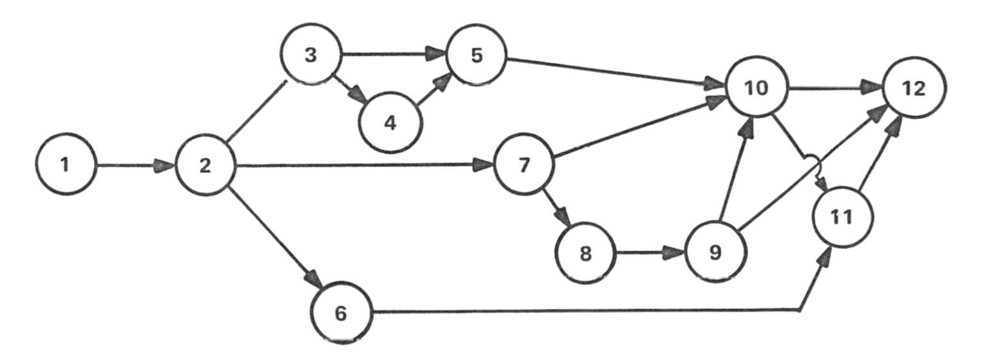

FIGURE 8.15 Intersection Points: the Network.

Using Figure 8.15, it is also possible to refer to work flow, e.g., 1-2-3-5-10-12 or to 1-2-6-11-12, etc. This is useful in reviewing larger sequences, time allocations, personnel, or component responsibilities.

The following visual, Figure 8.16, uses PERT techniques to indicate the nature and flow of a typical program development scheme. It shows the possible relationship of events in time and dependency. This generalized form could be used with minor modifications for many instructional projects and purposes.

Various component elements (program, leadership, policies, resources, etc.) have been built into the three lines. The top line indicates policy making and public relations. It could also have included more emphasis on management functions. The center line is basically program, indicating major activities that will involve the instructional staff and other targeted personnel who will be developing and implementing the program objectives. Such objectives could have been specified to indicate major emphasis on staff development (and teacher competencies), curriculum (program development and learner gain), or organizational change. The lower line represents research and evaluation and suggests the timing and nature of events in these areas.

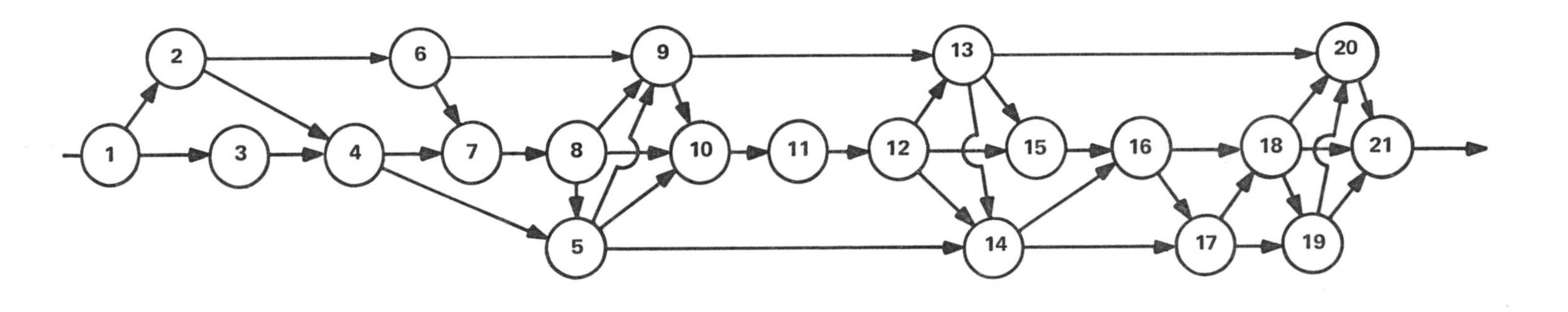

1—Begin, needs identified, rationale developed.

2—Priority-policy statement, monitoring underway.

3—Statement of validated objectives.

4—Targets determined.

5—Baseline data collected, evaluation procedures determined.

6—Project leadership assigned and operational.

7—Means and parameters determined, resources allocated.

8—Preliminary decisions re program design-format.

9—Review of progress and process data.

10—Complete statement of specifications and strategy.

11—Decisions re program alternatives—cost, time, personnel, facilities.

12—Program details and arrangements completed.

13—Policy decision to modify or continue.

14—Complete evaluation instruments and policy re use.

15—Pre-implementation arrangements in operation.

16—Review re program validation and feasibility.

17—Process evaluation and feedback data.

18—Transaction-program implementation.

19—Complete summative evaluation.

20—Policy decision to recycle or continue.

21—Complete. Tie in with ongoing program.

FIGURE 8.16 Representative PERT Events.

Other items could easily be built into this generalized plan. Numbered intervals of two or five, for example, could facilitate the later insertion of sub- or additional tasks without changing the basic configuration. Another modification would be to show "beginning" and "complete" points; only terminal points have been indicated. Vertical lines could be drawn to include time periods through which the program was moving, or times could have been indicated in connection with the stated events. Additions could be made to each event, delineating who was responsible, the charge or objectives for each, and the standard or evaluative criterion for each. Authorization, required data, and logistics could be indicated if the project was being monitored and/or audited. Of the three lines, the center one is obviously the critical path, since the time consuming activities, skill developments, and basic program responsibilities are contained within that flow of work.

The following plan is one that was developed and used by a large urban school system. It includes the basic events that preceded an ambitious summer workshop involving over 400 persons. The visualization, Figure 8.17, demonstrates a number of design features.

1. Component lines are used to clarify responsibilities in those areas. For example, the top line includes leadership persons—coordinators and a teacher cadre. The second line includes the basic program areas to be addressed; namely, curriculum improvement, organizing for instruction, professional responsibilities, and community relations and resources. The third line deals with media and dissemination; the fourth line, with resources and materials.
2. A modified "begin-complete" pattern is used. This pattern is demonstrated by paired events.
3. The format visually illustrates a developmental plan showing the relationship between events. Rough time lines could be inserted vertically. These are not shown, but the PERT plan covers a period of 12 weeks.
4. The visualization was distributed to all personnel as a communication and planning schedule. It was also used by a leadership person to monitor the events as planned and to make appropriate changes as needed.

These preliminary events culminated in a workshop; the schedule for the workshop inputs and activities is another artifact but is not shown here. Both of these planned sequences resulted in plans being written and implemented by the personnel and leadership in the separate schools of the district.

PERT-Type Plan: Preparation for Summer Workshop

1. Begin: develop preliminary plans for Summer Workshop.
2. Develop preliminary plans for *curriculum improvement component.*
3. Develop preliminary plans for *organization for instruction component.*
4. Develop plan for document re *community relations and resources component.*
5. Complete and distribute document summarizing *individual school improvement program areas.*

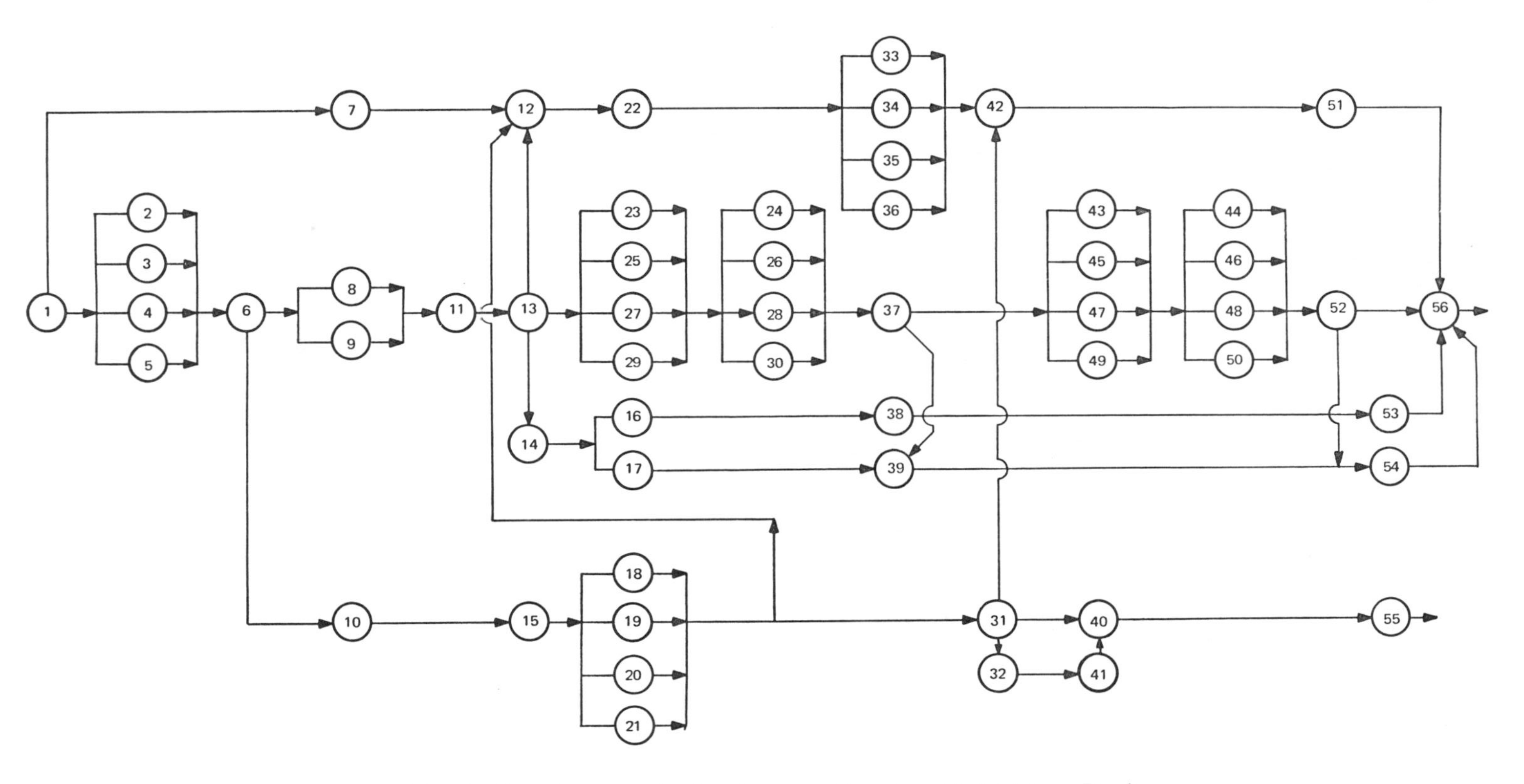

FIGURE 8.17 Preparing for the Summer Workshop (PERT Type Plan).

6. Complete and distribute document summarizing *individual school improvement program plan.*
7. Select *project director.*
8. Select *leadership teams* for each school.
9. Complete *administration and analysis of school improvement planning questionnaire* for all schools.
10. Begin development of *resource banks* for each component area.
11. Conduct *orientation session for school leadership teams.*
12. Complete *staff assignments and responsibilities for Summer Program.*
13. Conduct *program planning session for summer in-service activities.*
14. Begin *dissemination program* regarding data and plans.
15. Determine *criteria for resource bank* materials.
16. Provide first *news release to mass media* (TV stations, radio, and newspapers).
17. Disseminate first *report to professional staff* regarding *progress and plans.*
18. Develop plan for *staffing and responsibilities for resource bank* for *curriculum improvement component.*
19. Produce statement of *staffing* and *responsibilities for resource bank* for *organization for instruction component.*
20. Produce statement of *staffing and responsibilities for resource bank* for *professional resources component.*
21. Produce statement of *staffing and responsibilities for resource bank* for *community resources component.*
22. Develop *plan for two-day leadership training* for school leadership personnel.
23. Preliminary *planning session for curriculum improvement component.*
24. Complete *staffing for summer program curriculum improvement.*
25. Preliminary *program planning* session for *organization for instruction component.*
26. Complete *staffing for summer program* for *organization for instruction component.*
27. Preliminary *planning* session for *community relations and resources component.*
28. Complete *staffing for summer program professional responsibilities.*
29. Preliminary *planning* session for *community relations and resources component.*
30. Complete *staffing for summer program community relations and resources component.*
31. Develop *plan for organization and retrieval systems for resource bank.*
32. Begin *purchasing for resource bank* materials.
33. Select *coordinator for curriculum improvement component.*
34. Select *coordinator for organization for instruction component.*
35. Select *coordinator for professional responsibilities component.*
36. Select *coordinator for community relations and resources component.*
37. Complete *summer schedule of events.*
38. Disseminate second *news release to media.*
39. Disseminate second *report to professional staff.*
40. Complete preliminary purchasing for *resource banks.*
41. Catalogue *resource bank* materials.
42. Complete *planning* for two-day *training program* for coordinators and leadership cadre.
43. Complete *plan for monitoring and evaluation design* regarding *curriculum improvement activities.*
44. Complete *budget for monitoring and evaluation design for curriculum improvement activities.*
45. Complete *plan for monitoring and evaluation design* for *organization for instruction activities.*
46. Complete *budget for monitoring and evaluation design* for *organization for instruction activities.*
47. Complete *plan for monitoring and evaluation design* for *professional responsibilities activities.*
48. Complete *budget for monitoring*

and evaluation design for *professional responsibilities activities.*

49. Complete *plan for monitoring and evaluation design* for *community relations and resources activities.*
50. Complete *budget for monitoring and evaluation design* for *community relations and resources activities.*
51. Conduct two-day *leadership training program.*
52. Complete *design* for all *monitoring and evaluation.*
53. Disseminate third *news release to media.*
54. Conduct third *report to professional staff* re progress and summer plans.
55. Continue to *add to resource banks upon request.*
56. Complete and disseminate *plan for summer program.*

The combinations and possible variations are limitless, depending upon the imagination of the planners and the complexity of the design. Once a figure has been drawn that delineates the events, activities, sequences, and dependencies, a crude PERT chart will have been developed. This network can be used for purposes of analysis, decision making, communicating, and further planning. Those interested in a more sophisticated design should consult the Related References section of the text, or similar materials.

In retrospect, it is important to reiterate the premise that these techniques are means, not ends. They are ways by which the desired personal and program objectives can be incorporated into the task and procedural dimensions. By clarifying the program structure and purpose, it becomes easier to subsume the operational schemes rather than make them determining factors; for without such clarification, activities and events tend to become overloaded by the need to establish purpose and "charge." Likewise, the proper use of such notation techniques provides a mechanism by which the results of dialogue and interaction among leadership persons and participants can be captured and communicated for purposes of further decision making and implementing.[25-28]

In the view of the writer, one justifiable criticism of a systematic approach is that it appears to emphasize the task dimension, the structural features, and the product requirements. This concern is valid when the approach and its elements become ends rather than means. Therefore, the intents need constant reiteration—program improvement, learner gain, staff development, and improved conditions for learning. It is toward these larger goals that some of these techniques and procedures can be employed as appropriate vehicles for change.

Designing is often considered rational and "cool." The subsequent transactions, however, are human and "hot." Participation, communication, and decision making present ways to share and capture both the total vision and the tools to be employed. Ideally, the relationship is reciprocal, as planning provides a mechanism for reconciling reality with resources and human dimensions.

"Style" is a demonstration of numerous factors such as the nature of the dialogue, the regard and trust that have been developed, the procedures for decision making, and the particular techniques by which these multiple elements are arranged and utilized.[29,30] Thus, style tends to be a range of leadership behaviors rather than a single or polarized stance. This view is both productive and realistic. It is productive for recognizing that the necessary tasks that need to be achieved and the personal elements that need to be developed require different means. It is realistic because in practical situations the developmental activities may be open and participatory, while such tasks as evaluation may be more closed and more constrained. Finally, style emerges as a unifying force as participants share in the planning and detailing activities and as understandings and commitments flow from mutual sharing.

Classrooms, schools, and communities represent vast reservoirs of talent that are minimized or untapped.[31,32] The conceptual model is often that of a honeycomb with isolated cells, rather than that of a river with watersheds, tributaries, and flood plains. However, it is useful for research and analysis purposes to establish cells or stations as an ecologist might do to study rainfall, plant growth, and change. Ultimately, the studied cell is most realistically perceived as a representative segment within a larger arena of activity and purpose. Humane, significant, and institutional change are evolutionary, not a point or placement, since they represent a series of interactions and events.

A good design is not a blueprint to be rigidly followed. It is a conceptualization that considers people, purposes, plans, and resources and requires constant modification as gains are achieved or as the environment changes. A good plan is a focal point for decisions and transactions with functional utility. It is a roadmap with routes and intentions, not a programmed journey; it is a framework, not a rule.

Planning is a form of predicting. It is, in part, an attempt to translate needs into program objectives and program objectives into possibilities. To select from viable options those with the greatest potential, to align resources and realities, and to simulate via rational and human processes the most productive course to follow comprise its purpose. Both planning and predicting are precarious, but they represent responsible efforts to anticipate developments and consequences. Since choices will be made, educators are among those charged with the task of mapping events as well as reacting to them. Self renewal is each individual's responsibility, as is the improvement of instruction for learners. To forward these ends, the marshalling of ideas and resources at all levels is a central responsibility of leadership.[33,34]

ACTION GUIDELINES

Organizing is a leadership and process function. It comprises the ways by which tasks are delineated, assembled, distributed, and assigned. The deluge of ad hoc requirements can stifle work on long range goals and activities. Educational leaders can respond by analyzing and systematizing their responsibilities in order to exert a constructive and continuous assist. Leaders should strive for collaborative and cooperative action as a necessary ingredient of the organizing effort. The collegial, team approach makes available a range of competencies, values, and experiences. Staff development and instructional change efforts should model the desired processes as well as contribute to the desired product.

Monitoring procedures provide a functional flow of data about the progress or problems of individuals and program elements. Such data can assist decision making, changing, and facilitating. Monitoring can provide data for formative evaluation and reporting. Monitoring and sensing should be integral to the ongoing activities and should provide a basis for feedback and recognition.

Complex plans or projects are facilitated by planning schemes that provide an index for planned activities and events. The choice as to the most appropriate design is dependent upon the nature of the proposed events, the style of the operation, and the competencies of the participants. Such plans should represent participant deliberations and agreements, yet, should be flexible and amenable to change. Similarly, they should not propose arbitrary decisions, unrealistic time frames, or unachievable objectives.

RELATED REFERENCES

1. Miel, Alice, and Lewis, Arthur J., *Supervision for Improved Instruction.* Belmont, California: Wadsworth Publishing Co., 1972.
2. Owens, Robert G., *Organizational Behavior in Schools.* Englewood Cliffs, New Jersey: Prentice-Hall, 1970.
3. Avila, Donald L., Combs, Arthur W., and Purkey, William W., *The Helping Relationship Sourcebook.* Boston: Allyn and Bacon, 1972.
4. Franseth, Jane, *Supervision as Leadership.* Evanston, Illinois: Row, Peterson Co., 1961.
5. Lippitt, Ronald, Watson, Jeanne, and Westley, Bruce. *The Dynamics of Planned Change.* New York: Harcourt, Brace, and World, 1958.
6. Napier, Rodney W., and Gershenfeld, Mattick, *Groups: Theory and Experience.* Boston: Houghton Mifflin, 1973.
7. Roberts, Thomas B., "Transpersonal: The New Educational Psychology." *Phi Delta Kappan,* 56:191 (1974).
8. Schmuck, Richard A., and Runkel, Philip J., *Organizational Training for a School Faculty.* Eugene, Oregon: University of Oregon Press, 1970.
9. Harris, Ben M., *Supervisory Behavior in Education.* 3rd ed. Englewood Cliffs, New Jersey: Prentice-Hall, 1975.
10. Lucio, William H., and McNeil, John D., *Supervision: A Synthesis of Thought and Action.* New York: McGraw-Hill, 1969.
11. Alioto, Robert F., *Operational PPBS for Education: A Practical Approach to Effective Decision Making.* New York: Harper and Row, 1971.
12. Von Bertalanffy, Ludwig, "General System Theory—A Critical Review." In *Modern Systems,* edited by Walter D. Buckley. Chicago: Aldine Publishing Co., 1968.

13. Buckley, Walter, *Sociology and Modern Systems Theory.* Englewood Cliffs, New Jersey: Prentice-Hall, 1966.
14. Pask, G., *An Approach to Cybernetics.* New York: Harper and Row, 1961.
15. Provus, Malcolm, *Discrepancy Evaluation.* Berkeley, California: McCutchan Publishing Corp., 1971.
16. Wiener, Norbert, *Cybernetics.* 2nd ed. Boston: Massachusetts Institute of Technology, 1962.
17. Knox, Alan B., "Continuous Program Evaluation." In *Readings in Curriculum Evaluation,* edited by Peter A. Taylor and Doris M. Cowley. Dubuque, Iowa: William C. Brown Publishers, 1972.
18. Argyris, Chris, *Integrating the Individual in the Organization.* New York: John Wiley and Sons, 1964.
19. Miles, Matthew B., ed., *Innovation in Education.* New York: Bureau of Publications, Teachers College, Columbia University, 1964.
20. Palmatier, Larry L., "How Teachers Can Innovate and Still Keep Their Jobs." *Journal of Teacher Education,* 26:1 (1975), pp. 60–62.
21. DeNovellis, Richard, and Lewis, Arthur J., *Schools Become Accountable: A PACT Approach.* Washington, D.C.: Association for Supervision and Curriculum Development, 1974.
22. Thompson, James D., *Organizations in Action.* New York: McGraw-Hill, 1967.
23. Farino, Mario V., *Flow Charting.* Englewood Cliffs, New Jersey: Prentice-Hall, 1970.
24. Cook, Desmond L., *PERT: Applications in Education.* Cooperative Research Monograph No. 17. Washington, D.C.: U.S. Government Printing Office, 1966.
25. Argyris, Chris, *Personality and Organization.* New York: Harper and Brothers, 1957.
26. Bennis, Warren G., *Changing Organizations.* New York: McGraw-Hill, 1966.
27. Gibson, James L., Ivancevich, John M., and Donnelly, James H., *Organizations: Structure, Process, Behavior.* Dallas: Business Publications, 1973.
28. Likert, Rensis, *The Human Organization: Its Management and Value.* New York: McGraw-Hill, 1967.
29. Pfeiffer, J. William, and Jones, John E., *1974 Annual Handbook for Group Facilitators.* San Diego, California: University Associates, 1974.
30. Savage, William W., *Interpersonal and Group Relations in Educational Administrations.* Glenview, Illinois: Scott Foresman, 1968.
31. House, Ernest R., *The Politics of Educational Innovation.* Berkeley, California: McCutchan Publishing Corp., 1974.
32. Jacobs, James, "A Model for Program Development and Evaluation." *Theory into Practice,* 13:15 (1974).
33. Carlson, Richard O., *Adoption of Educational Innovations.* Eugene, Oregon: Center for the Advanced Study of Educational Administration, University of Oregon, 1965.
34. Helping Professionals to Grow, *Educational Leadership.* Entire issue, 31:483 (1974).

APPENDIXES

APPENDIX A

A Preliminary Needs Identification Questionnaire

What follows as Appendix A is one technique for identifying general areas of need or concern. In addition to establishing a list of interests or problems that need attention, the approach initiates a number of critical processes: (1) the opportunity to participate in the improvement plan from the beginning, (2) the involvement of participants in decision making and valuing, and (3) the clarification of items that will need to be researched, particularized, and diagnosed as discussed in Chapter 2. Displayed here in questionnaire form, the various sections and subsections can be refashioned in many ways to suit the conditions and resources of the local situation.

This particular format was developed by a large school system in connection with an extensive district-wide improvement project, in which there were to be system-wide, local school, and individual programs. The five categories were generated as the result of a series of open-ended meetings with teachers, counselors, principals, and central office staff. The proposed items were clustered into five headings and a second "pass" was made using this instrument. After the data from this effort were compiled, interviews with a representative sampling of each group added the necessary sub-elements, or dimensions, to each of the high priority items that had been indicated. Plans for school-based instructional improvement were then built using the more detailed concerns.

Utilizations with other school districts followed the development of the instrument and served the following functions:

1. As an initial survey to determine areas of staff interest prior to the development of a series of in-service opportunities.
2. As a statement of identified areas, which were further refined using standardized tests and inventories.
3. As a follow-up of various activities to ascertain the degree to which certain areas represented continuing concern and needed further attention.

4. As a supplement to other needs assessment approaches, in this case attempting to validate and quantify preliminary staff choices.
5. As a means to check with particular target groups (teachers, supervisors, parents, and students) and obtain their input.

The nature of the use would also determine the related instructions. For example, items could be ranked; such ranking would yield a different type of data than that shown. The number of choices to be checked per section could be limited to two or three. Priority indications could be on the basis of all items, not those in one section. Subsections could be added to expand the possibilities within a given subsection (language arts, for example). Instead of eliciting concerns, the instructions can ask respondents to indicate degrees of familiarity with the research, developments, or professional literature of the various items. In some cases, sections could be eliminated if they were not relevant to the search. Thus, the instructions would tend to open or close the number and range of possibilities. In any case, the nature of the local requirements would be built into the procedures for responding.

A section could be added to include particular methodologies such as: inductive teaching, questioning techniques, gaming, student contracts, open classroom approaches, and pupil-teacher planning techniques; and the development of particular resources or approaches such as LAPS, PLAN, IPI, MACOS, ISCS, and the like. In some cases, it has been found useful to scramble a selected group of items rather than list them in categories as shown here. The utility of any such listing is that it proposes a place to begin.

IMPROVEMENT AREAS AND PRIORITIES

I. CURRICULUM IMPROVEMENT	Needed for Students	Needed for Teachers	Priority
1. New curricular developments			
a. English-language arts			
b. Mathematics			
c. Science			
d. Social Studies			
e. Health and P. E.			
f. Arts--music, art, dance, etc.			
g. Humanities			
h. Ecology—environmental education			
i. Career Education			
j. Vocational-industrial Arts			
k. Others (please specify)			
2. Resources for instruction			
a. Multi-media facilities			
b. Computer use programs			
c. Programmed instruction			
d. ITV, films, audio, VTR			
e. Textbook selection and use			
f. Supplementary materials			
g. Curriculum guide			
h. Expendable supplies			
i. Teacher aides			
j. Others (please specify)			
3. Flexible courses			
a. Semester			
b. Mini-courses			
c. Year-round school			
d. Quarter system			
e. Others (please specify)			
4. Special programs			
a. For slow			
b. For gifted			
c. Vocational			
d. Handicapped (specify)			
e. Action—learning			
f. Community-based instruction			
g. Student tutors			
h. Alternative education			
i. Others (please specify)			
5. Reading skills			
6. Extra and co-curricular programs			

IMPROVEMENT AREAS AND PRIORITIES	Needed for Students	Needed for Teachers	Priority
7. Sharpening the instructional focus			
a. Performance objectives			
b. Language use			
c. Relevancy			
d. Values			
e. Inter-race communication			
f. Materials utilization			
g. Evaluative measures/testing			
h. Utilizing the taxonomies			
i. Achieving balance among the domains (cognitive, affective, and psychomotor)			
j. Others (please specify)			
II. ORGANIZING FOR INSTRUCTION			
1. Staff utilization			
a. Team teaching			
b. Differentiated staffing			
c. Aides			
d. Flexible scheduling			
e. Others (please specify)			
2. Vertical organization			
a. Nongraded			
b. Continuous progress			
c. Graded			
d. Instructional Levels			
e. Multi-age groupings			
f. Others (please specify)			
3. Horizonal organization			
a. Self-contained			
b. Semi-departmentalized			
c. Departmentalized			
d. Open classrooms			
e. Others (please specify)			
4. Classroom operation and teaching			
a. Micro-teaching			
b. Interaction analysis			
c. Student motivation			
d. Control techniques			
e. Teacher–pupil relations			
f. Classroom management and planning			
g. Individualized instruction			
h. Behavior modification			

IMPROVEMENT AREAS AND PRIORITIES	Needed for Students	Needed for Teachers	Priority
4. Classroom operation and teaching (cont'd.)			
i. Classroom morale/climate			
j. Inquiry—methods			
k. Learning centers			
l. Others (please specify)			
III. PROFESSIONAL RESPONSIBILITIES AND OPPORTUNITIES			
1. Teacher preparation and competence			
2. Supervision of instruction			
3. Coordination of instruction			
4. Leadership role of principal and teachers			
5. Staff motivation			
6. Professional attitudes			
7. Principal-teacher relations			
8. Instructional council			
9. Participation on school or system committees			
10. Classroom research			
11. Certification/degree work			
12. Improved communications			
13. Released time for in-service			
14. Policy clarification			
15. Visitation programs			
16. Participation in professional associations			
17. Individualized staff development			
18. Consortia—with schools or colleges			
19. Others (please specify)			
IV. COMMUNITY RELATIONS AND RESOURCES			
1. Community involvement (sites and personnel)			
2. Utilization of resources			
3. School-community relations			
4. Personal security and safety			
5. Agency participation			
6. Regional agencies—utilization			
7. School-university programs			

IMPROVEMENT AREAS AND PRIORITIES	*Needed for Students*	*Needed for Teachers*	*Priority*
IV. COMMUNITY RELATIONS AND RESOURCES			
8. Others (please specify)			
V. PHYSICAL PLANT IMPROVEMENTS			
1. Climate conditioning			
2. Cleanliness/attractiveness			
3. Sound control			
4. Light control			
5. Landscaping-grounds			
6. Building security			
7. Space—adequacy and use			
8. Others (please specify)			

	Indicate the highest priority numbers in each section	
	For Students	*For Teachers*
I. CURRICULUM IMPROVEMENT		
II. ORGANIZING FOR INSTRUCTION		
III. PROFESSIONAL RESPONSIBILITIES		
IV. COMMUNITY RELATIONS		
V. PHYSICAL PLANT		

COMMENTS:

APPENDIX B

Explicating Specific Program Objectives*

One problem evident in most staff development or educational improvement plans is the gap between identified student or staff needs and the program selected/developed to meet those needs. It is difficult to state overall project objectives and then spin these out into detailed and specific objectives that make program planning, monitoring, and evaluating more precise. The following discussion proposes that objectives can, and should be, developed to incorporate the basic district components, as well as the particular program elements that need to be addressed.

In this connection, the following matrix, Figure B–1, is proposed for study purposes. It is intended to facilitate a review of: (1) variables essential for a comprehensive plan, (2) the relationship to goals and objectives, and (3) various program levels or degrees of specificity. In the planning matrix, the horizontal axis is composed of four possible levels of objectives, moving from general goal statements to performance objectives. The vertical axis lists program components that are representative of those critical to any comprehensive educational plan. These include students, staff, curriculum or program, resources, and management. Others could be listed as needed, such as community or special support elements.

The following definitions may help clarify the concepts and items structured below. The various levels of objectives listed as the *horizontal axis* include considerations that include the degree of specificity, the delineation of responsibility, the portion of the total system that is involved, and the time requirements. These differences are as follows:

*This segment was developed in collaboration with Frank Gillespie, Program Planning Generalist, Northeast Georgia Cooperative Educational Service Agency, Athens, Georgia.

		Goals	Program Objectives	Interim or Enabling Objectives	Instructional or Performance Objectives
Program Components	Students				
	Staff				
	Curriculum				
	Resources				
	Management				

FIGURE B-1 Program Components and Levels of Objectives.

1. *Goal.* A statement of desired outcome that provides a general direction for a program, does not require accomplishment during a given time period, and does not indicate how achievement will be measured; it applies to the total experience and does not delineate areas of responsibility.

2. *Program Objectives.* A statement of desired outcome implying general performance to be accomplished during a specific period of time. Broad areas of responsibility are indicated.

3. *Interim or Enabling Objective.* A statement of observable outcome that focuses attention upon a specific area or task. Areas of responsibilities are clearly delineated, but the performance that is indicated can be applied to many related situations.

4. *Instructional or Performance Objective.* A statement of specific intent that clearly identifies observable outcome, including an indication of the condition imposed, the outcomes in terms of a person's actual performance, and an indication of the criteria that will be employed to determine achievement. In learning situations, these statements have test item equivalence.

The *vertical axis* is composed of the essential components of any comprehensive educational program. Unlike the various levels of objectives, these components do not differ with regard to any specific variable. Each component contained on the vertical axis is described below:

1. *Students.* This component refers to the general, implied, or specified learning outcomes that are the basic intent of the proposed educational program.

2. *Staff.* This component refers to all educational personnel who will be involved in the plan. It includes a description of the selection process employed, the procedures required for development of necessary competencies, and the delineation of specific competencies required for successful implementation of the proposed plan.

3. *Curriculum.* This component refers to the general or specific learning experiences that will be provided by the proposed plan. It includes a description of both the content and the instructional strategies to be employed in implementing the plan.

4. *Resources.* This component refers to the materials, texts, media, and physical facilities that will provide the necessary support for the successful implementation of the proposed plan.

5. *Management.* This component refers to the policy, leadership, and budgetary provisions that will be necessary for successful implementation of the proposed plan. It may also include a description of the monitoring and evaluation procedures to be employed.

HOW THE MATRIX CAN BE EMPLOYED

Through use of the proposed matrix, it becomes possible for educational planners to obtain a more complete view of the entire system, such a view being essential for comprehensive educational planning. For example, many current proposals suggest that systems base their staff development on identified student needs, but needs do not arise only from students. The staff, curriculum, resource, and management components also contribute to a system's needs. In order to obtain a more accurate picture of total system needs, all components of the program must be considered. Such a consideration results in the identification of areas of weaknesses, strengths, and relationships that are essential for effective and comprehensive educational planning.

Once the needs for the total system have been identified, planners have the task of developing goals; here again, attention must be given to all components. As student goals are defined, goals for all other components must also be developed because all are pieces of the same system. They are, therefore, interrelated.

Once the goals for each component of the program have been delineated, the basic parameters for the proposed innovation are established. What follows is the task of spinning out each goal contained within each component into increasing levels of specificity—by employing the three remaining levels of objectives that we have been suggested. Student, staff, curricular, resource, and management goals can be refined into *program*, *enabling*, and *performance* objectives as the following example illustrates.

An Example Utilizing the Proposed Matrix

This example is provided to demonstrate how a simultaneous consideration of all program components and levels of objectives can be utilized to develop a comprehensive educational plan.

In the example, the existing situation and related goals for each component of an *elementary science program* have been delineated; in addition, there are developed program objectives and examples of enabling and performance objectives for the staff component.

Figure B-2 indicates those *areas* developed for this example as well as the *steps* followed in the narrative describing the example.

		Levels of Objectives			
Program Component	*Existing Situation*	*Goals*	*Program Objectives*	*Enabling Objectives*	*Instructional Objectives*
Students					
Staff			Step 3	Step 4	Step 5
Curriculum	Step 1	Step 2			
Resources					
Management					

FIGURE B-2 Areas of Each Program Component Developed for the Elementary Science Example.

Step 1: Use of the Matrix to Examine the Existing Situation

Comprehensive educational planning generally begins with an identification of needs. As many current plans indicate, needs are defined as any discrepancy between desired levels of achievement and the current situation. Therefore, a need cannot be identified until the existing situation has been clearly defined.

For planning purposes, it may be helpful initially to set aside the task of developing statements of need, and instead, to focus on data relating to the existing situation. Once an accurate picture of the status quo, or existing situation, is determined, characteristics of the ideal situation can be developed and statements of system goals can be produced. This procedure streamlines the process of getting from the existing situation to goal statements.

Data employed in determining the existing situation can be obtained from a variety of sources, including general feelings as well as specific facts. It is usually desirable to document or indicate specific sources for the data presented. With specific facts, documentation is relatively easy; e.g., when standardized test scores, drop-out, or attendance figures are available.

General feelings are more difficult to document. However, educators often "know" some basic weaknesses of their system but may be unable to quantify this knowledge. When dealing with "felt needs," it is extremely important for planners to consider all system components because certain system needs are more likely to surface in specific aspects of the program.

In the example that follows, it is proposed that an examination of each component in terms of the existing situation indicates a reoccurring theme or basic shortcoming of the program. In the elementary science program, for example, learners have little opportunity to become actively involved in their own learning. This became evident only because all elements of the total program and all system components were examined. Each component area revealed the following in regard to the elementary science program:

A. Students (Component 1):
   1. Take little responsibility for their own learning.
   2. Have a negative attitude toward learning.
   3. Are exposed to primarily passive learning experiences.
   4. Cannot read science textbooks with comprehension.
   5. Find little in the science program to meet individual needs, interests, and abilities.

B. Staff (Component 2):
   1. Lack background or skills for teaching science.
   2. Are unable to utilize existing material and equipment.
   3. Lack skills for giving attention to a variety of interests, needs, and abilities.
   4. Show no incentive to change existing practices.

C. Curriculum (Component 3):
   1. Lacks coordination between and within levels.
   2. Is textbook and content-centered.
   3. Gives little attention to environmental education or metric system.
   4. Science area not included in standardized testing program.

D. Resources (Component 4):
   1. Limited materials and equipment in classrooms or library.
   2. Ineffective utilization of resources available.

E. Management (Component 5):
   1. Children grouped by I.Q. and grade level; no provisions for changing groups.
   2. Self-contained classrooms with little sharing among teachers.
   3. No opportunity for staff planning.
   4. No evident leadership to improve the program.

Step 2: Use of the Matrix to Assist in Determining Goals

After the existing situation has been clearly identified, goals could then be developed. The existing situation indicated those areas requiring improvement. Goal setting became essentially a determination of what "needs" should be given attention. It was clear that a consideration of all components was essential for goal development. In order to meet the needs or improve the situation in the student component, certain areas required changes in the other components.

In response to the analysis of the status quo described above, the following "goals" were proposed for each component of the elementary science program:

A. Students (Component 1):
   All students in the elementary science program will:
   1. Develop responsibility for their own learning.
   2. Develop a positive attitude toward learning through success oriented activities.
   3. Be involved in active, rather than passive, learning.
   4. Be given instruction in reading and comprehending science materials.
   5. Experience learning activities consistent with indivdual needs, interests, and abilities.

B. Staff (Component 2):
   All staff associated with the elementary science program will:
   1. Develop specific skills required for teaching process oriented science, including use of materials and resources.
   2. Provide a classroom environment that encourages the development of a positive attitude toward learning and stimulates student inquiry.
   3. Develop competencies required for implementation of active and inquiry learning; leadership and training will be provided.
   4. Be able to shift responsibility for learning to the learner.
   5. Design learning experiences consistent with individual needs, interests, and abilities.

C. Curriculum (Component 3):
   1. Be reorganized within and between existing levels.
   2. Become less textbook centered by the addition of improved resources and materials, and a process orientation.

3. Be strengthened with regard to environmental education and the metric system.
4. Appropriate evaluative measures will be developed.

D. Resources (Component 3):
The resources for the elementary science program will be:
1. Improved on basis of specific recommendations from staff.
2. Better utilized by staff and students.

E. Management (Component 3):
The administration for the elementary science program will:
1. Encourage grouping of learners by instructional levels related to individual needs, interests, and abilities.
2. Support development of necessary staff competencies, including time to plan.
3. Encourage development of a process oriented science program.
4. Assist in the coordination of science curriculum within and between levels.

Step 3: Using the Matrix to Develop Program Objectives

Because goals are essentially statements of general direction and of little value in specifying tasks and delegating responsibility, it was necessary to develop more specific statements of intent. The matrix, Figure B-2, proposed three additional stages, indicated as steps 3-5. These steps are essential to make the transition from statements of general direction (goals) to statements of specific performance (instructional objectives).

The first of these final three steps is the delineation of *program objectives.* During this step the goals for each component are expanded and refined in more specific terms, which also include broad areas of responsibility.

Since there is a considerable expansion that begins at the program objective level, *only the goals within the staff component are being considered for purposes of this discussion.* A similar process could be followed for goals contained within the other four program components.

Developing Program Objectives for the Staff Component Area

In order to accomplish the staff goals presented above, the following program objectives for elementary science teachers are proposed. As indicated, these illustrate an expansion of only one component area at the program objective level.

A. Competencies related to process skills (teaching):
1. Elementary school teachers will be able to employ and instruct students in the utilization of the following process skills:

Observing, classifying, predicting, inferring, measuring, identifying variables, constructing a table of data, constructing a graph, describing relationships between variables, acquiring and processing data, analyzing investigations, constructing hypothesis, designing investigations, experimenting, and constructing operational definitions.

B. Teacher competencies related to the classroom environment.
   Elementary science teachers will be able to provide a classroom environment that has the following characteristics:
   1. Freedom to explore.
   2. Time to explore.
   3. Use and acceptance of student input.
   4. Lesser concern for closure.
   5. Opportunity for success experiences.

C. Teacher competencies related to specific inquiry oriented instructional techniques. Elementary science teachers will be able to implement the following instructional techniques in their classrooms:
   1. Higher level questioning strategies.
   2. Alternative strategies for sequencing instruction.
   3. Alternative strategies for evaluation of student progress.

D. Teacher competencies related to self-paced or self-directed study.
   Elementary science teachers will be able to utilize the following self-instructional techniques in their classrooms:
   1. Learning centers.
   2. Student contracts.
   3. Learning packets.

E. Curriculum Development.
   In addition to the development of the teacher competencies mentioned above, the following activities are suggested:
   1. The development of a coordinated elementary science program.
   2. The identification and cataloging of local resources available for science education.
   3. The delineation of specific recommendations for the acquisitions of necessary materials and equipment.

Step 4: Using the Matrix to Develop Enabling Objectives

With the delineation of program objectives, educational planners have established specific areas of responsibility. Personnel within each component are now aware of the part they will play in achieving total program goals. Program objectives may be presented to specific task groups of consultants to provide parameters within which enabling and instructional objectives can be developed. This procedure provides for increased specificity and avoids unnecessary duplication.

As indicated earlier, because of the tremendous expansion that begins at the program objectives level and continues in the enabling and instructional objective levels, *only one program objective contained within the Staff Component area is being considered for illustrative*

	Program Objectives	*Enabling Objectives*	*Instructional Objectives*
	1.	1. Question classification systems	1.1
	2.		1.2 Indicate similarities and differences between specific question classification systems.
	3. Inquiry Techniques		
	a. Question asking		1.3
	b. Sequencing instruction		2.1 Classify a list of questions employing a classification system.
	c. Evaluation	2. Categorizing questions	
Staff Component	4.		2.2
	5.		2.3
			3.1
			3.2
		3. Rewriting questions	3.3 Rewrite a cognitive memory question as a divergent question.

FIGURE B-3 Selected Items for Development at Different Levels of Objectives.

purposes. This is a further focusing process; a similar process could be followed for program objectives contained within other components. The preceding diagram, Figure B-3, illustrates the expansion and increased specificity that can occur for one staff program objective in the enabling and instructional objective levels.

Examples of *enabling objectives* (Program level 3 in Figure B-3) that relate to one facet of inquiry oriented instructional techniques are those specific teacher competencies required for asking higher level questions (3.a of staff program level objectives). Selected examples of specific teacher competencies (staff enabling objectives) required for development of questioning strategies are:

1. All teachers will be able to indicate similarities and differences between various systems for classifying questions.
2. All teachers will be able to categorize questions according to the level of thinking that is stimulated by the questions.
3. All teachers will be able to rewrite questions so that they will stimulate a different level of thinking.

Step 5: Using the Matrix to Develop Instructional Objectives

For purposes of evaluation and accountability, it is necessary that specific criteria for measuring achievement be delineated. In order to meet this requirement, it is necessary that each of the enabling objectives (see step 4) be further refined into more specific instructional objectives; an illustration of this process follows. As defined, instructional objectives provide insight into the type of performance expected at the classroom level and relate to usually only one lesson or activity.

Some examples of *instructional objectives* that relate to higher level questioning strategies are indicated below. Enabling objectives contained within other components could be expanded in a similar manner.

1. Question classification systems:
   - 1.2 Participants will be able to list three differences between the Sanders and Aschner-Gallagher systems for classifying questions.
2. Categorizing Questions:
   - 2.1 Using one of five classification systems, the participants will be able to classify a list of 20 questions with 80% accuracy.
3. Rewriting Questions:
   - 3.3 Given a question designed to stimulate cognitive memory, the participant will rewrite the question so that it will stimulate divergent thinking, as defined.

CONCLUSION

Investigations of educational innovations over the past ten or fifteen years indicate that the success of a particular innovation depends to a large extent upon the degree of support given to the change. Many worthwhile projects failed because they did not receive total system support or adequate consideration during planning and implementing.

Through the utilization of the proposed two-dimensional matrix, it becomes possible for educational planners to: (1) examine the existing situation and (2) develop the necessary goals and objectives as they relate to particular system components. The latter is to provide insight into the total system support required for the successful implementation of the proposed program. Once the major types of system support have been identified in terms of objectives for the related components, the first step of a comprehensive educational plan is completed.

Following the delineation of system components, it is necessary that (3) each goal within each component be expanded and refined into increasing levels of specificity. To assist in this process, the proposed matrix suggests three levels of objectives (and three additional steps) that educational planners could follow to move from general to specific statements of performance as required by each system component. This process of delineating increasing levels of specificity through a consideration of levels of objective within each program component has certain advantages. For example, the process assists planners in clarifying and delegating specific roles or responsibility that must be assumed for the program to be a success. In addition, an indication is made as to how individual performance will be measured and how total program effects will be assessed.

In the example provided, it was shown how the matrix could be used in developing a comprehensive educational plan for improving an elementary science program. Because of space limitations, only one component of the elementary science program was refined and developed to any extent with regard to levels of objectives. Ideally, similar expansion should have occurred for other components.

To assist the reader in transferring the ideas presented to other situations, some additional outlines of comprehensive educational plans employing a consideration of essential system components and levels of objectives follow as Figures B-4 and B-5. Hopefully, these outlines will provide the reader with an understanding of the relationships that exist between system components and levels of objectives for a variety of possible educational changes leading to improved learner gain and related staff competencies.

	LEVELS OF OBJECTIVES			
Program Components	*Goals*	*Program Objectives*	*Interim or Enabling Objective*	*Instructional or Performance Objectives*
Students	Plans and policies essential to mastery of basic skills in use of words and numbers by learners	Student will demonstrate skill in reading comprehension	Student uses reading skills to understand written directions for science activities	Students use written instructions to successfully construct a balance that measures to the nearest gram
Staff	Facilitate the development of basic skills in the use of words and numbers	Teachers will aid students in the development of reading comprehension in all disciplines	Teacher asks student to rephrase sections of written directions for science activities in his own words	Teacher prepares written direction for balance construction and observed student performance
Curriculum	Includes an interdisciplinary approach to the teaching of words and numbers	The development of reading comprehension will be an ongoing objective for all subject areas within the school, and will be explicitly included in curriculum materials	Following written directions for science activities in appropriate curriculum areas	Construction of a balance from written instructions
Resources	Provide instructional materials that provide an interdisciplinary approach to the teaching of words and numbers	Materials provided to assist the development of skills in reading comprehension in all subject areas	Instructions provide for science activities written at level appropriate for individual students	Materials provided for balance construction, i.e., weights, beam, and pans, as well as written instructions
Management	Commitment to an interdisciplinary approach to the teaching of words and numbers. Schedule of activities essential to delivery of goals and objectives	Delegate responsibility for the development of reading comprehension to all subject area specialists. Provide personnel and schedule	Provide opportunities for skill development in reading instruction for science teachers	• Monitor student and teacher performance • Record observed performance • Recycle evaluation information, provide feedback to interested audiences

FIGURE B-4 Reading Comprehension—Program Components and Levels of Objectives.

Program Components	*LEVELS OF OBJECTIVES*			
	Goals	*Program Objectives*	*Interim or Enabling Objectives*	*Instructional or Performance Objectives*
Students	Students will experience an open learning environment	Students will accept responsibility for their own learning	Students will experience self-directed study based upon student contracts developed by themselves	Student will design a contract to guide individual investigation of the use of natural resources for energy production
Staff	Staff will provide transition from a closed to an open learning environment	Teachers will relinquish responsibility for learning to individual students	Provide learner with assistance in self-directed study through the planning implementation and evaluation of student contracts	Teachers will provide assistance to student developing contract to guide student investigation of the use of natural resources for energy production
Curriculum	Curriculum will focus on needs, interests and abilities of individual learners	Independent study designed to fit individual learner needs, interests, and abilities	Student will select a relevant problem area and design a contract to guide the investigation of this problem area	Use of natural resources in the production of energy
Resources	Resources will be related to needs, interests, and abilities of individual learners	Student will assume major responsibility for accumulation and production of resource materials	Student will gather or produce materials related to selected problem area and construct a "resource box"	Student will assemble resource material relevant to the use of natural resources in the production of energy
Management	Management will provide total commitment to transition to an open learning environment and communication with school board, parent, and community about transition	• Provide support to students and staff re student responsibility for own learning • Make all resources available to students and staff • Provide training activities for target staff • Establish evaluative measures	• Allow students to experience self-directed study • Provide teachers with opportunity to develop skills necessary for implementation of self-directed study	• Record student's development of contract to guide investigation of using natural resources for energy production • Monitor teacher performance

FIGURE B-5 Open Education—Components and Levels of Objectives.

APPENDIX C

A Monitoring Plan for Staff Development Projects*

Staff development and related program improvements will be a continuing effort in education. Means to this end are being developed by universities, state departments of education, and local school systems as they attempt to implement and support this approach. Accountability, credibility, and progress, all demand that the efforts being made are conceptually adequate and operationally sound. A major function of leadership is to establish a process by which it can stay informed of what is happening in regard to each project. This is in addition to providing leadership, making necessary changes, and keeping the activities productive.

The ideas that follow for monitoring and/or formative evaluation are designed to provide each local education agency with a series of possible agenda items that relate to standard elements in any comprehensive plan for staff development. It is proposed that these items could be modified to fit any project underway in a local school situation. Thus, this document is not proposed as an instrument for use, as it is; rather, it is presented as a framework and a series of sub-items that can be adapted to the unique needs, leadership, and program efforts of a school system. The emphasis has been placed on monitoring rather than on formative evaluation.

The actual use of these ideas will depend upon the school district style and its concepts of management, leadership, and personnel needs. The recommendation is to keep the implementation of such a scheme simple. It should be explained in detail to all who will be affected, and be related to the total program of the school district, not just to the "staff development" or in-service project. A qualitative program, learner gain, competent staff, and community support require some

*This segment was developed in collaboration with Dr. Lowell Ensey, Associate Director of Professional Development, Georgia Association of Educators, Atlanta, Georgia.

changes from past practices. Hopefully, the ideas suggested here can contribute to greater progress in these areas.

RATIONALE FOR MONITORING AND FORMATIVE EVALUATION

One basic challenge for educators is to develop schools with a built-in mechanism for constant renewal. It is obvious that any innovative arrangement will bear re-examination and require modification in light of new content and better educational methods. Within the educational structure, the need is to develop a process that can respond to today's needs and the different needs and situations of tomorrow.

The primary purpose of staff development is the educational improvement of the local school system. This approach can take as many forms as there are systems utilizing staff development. In exploring approaches to staff development, it is generally useful to consider the types of decisions to be made based upon data regarding: (1) a needs assessment, (2) possible programs that will meet the identified learner needs, (3) the competencies of the related educational personnel, and (4) the procedures, administrative leadership, and supportive mechanisms needed for successful staff development programs.

Decision making, in these instances, might be divided into two categories: one based upon antecedents and another based upon consequences. It is much easier to make decisions based upon *antecedents* (events that have already transpired or data that are already acquired) than it is to make decisions based upon *consequences* (events that occur as a result of the program implementation or in the process of gathering formative data.) In building effective new programs, school systems must establish creative ways to innovate, monitor, and, subsequently, to judge effectiveness. The required research and evaluation depends upon management's capability to use the new, pertinent, and reliable information as the basis for decisions to improve/reject new or ongoing programs.*

Multiple pressures to plan, evaluate, and improve staff development programs are not new concerns to the practicing educator. Monitoring can be a critical assist to the local school districts by providing a systematic approach to the decisions that will need to be made, and to the programs that will need to be developed. Through processes and data, this functioning will facilitate the responsibility for being "accountable."

Monitoring Defined

Monitoring is a process for "overviewing" the progress of a project or program; it designs the steps needed to "sense" or "check out" the

*Malcolm Provus, *Discrepancy Evaluation: For Educational Program Improvement and Assessment.* Berkeley, California: McCutchan Publishing Corporation, 1971, p. 9.

project or program as it operates. This process is undertaken in order to determine to what extent the program is actually operating as planned. Monitoring provides both data and opportunities for self-correction within the ongoing system. It provides a series of planned check points to determine whether the system is operating efficiently, or if corrective or preventive actions are indicated.

Concerns of the monitor in many procedures deal with efficiency and effectiveness as determined by instruments that indicate process and product outcomes. In this effort, feelings (identification, satisfaction, and commitment) are important elements to be ascertained and considered. Further, such a review is enhanced by developed and communicated program design elements such as those indicated below. Monitoring is closely allied with formative evaluation, although it will likely be a separate responsibility.

Thus, how closely monitoring is identified with ongoing evaluation is a result of both management decision making and design. A highly developed task analysis with specified events and performances standards is both informative and evaluative. The uses of such data and their incorporation into the functioning of staff personnel determine whether the monitoring function is identical, complementary, or separate from other systems and program operations.

A MONITORING PLAN

An application of the procedures just discussed can be both useful and informative. The monitoring plan presented in this section incorporates the basic phases identified as necessary to staff development, such as:

I. Organizing and coordinating staff development activities.
II. Conducting the needs assessment.
III. Developing statements of goals and objectives.
IV. Selecting educational improvement activities.
V. Determining the competencies of the target personnel.
VI. Conducting regular evaluation.
VII. Implementing the program.

A brief summary of each of these phases is included below and precedes the items in the monitoring plan. Each item incorporates a suggested task in staff development along with a four-step scale that indicates how far a school or school system has progressed in completing the determined task.

Example. The first task statement is:

A. Specific people and/or groups have been identified to coordinate the staff development project.

1. If this task statement is not applicable ("N/A") at this time or to the plan, the first scale point is checked.

N/A	B	P	C
X			

2. If the task identified is just starting ("B"—beginning) or is underway to a limited extent, the second scale point is checked.

N/A	B	P	C
	X		

3. If the task is underway ("P"—in process) but not yet completed, the third scale point is checked.

N/A	B	P	C
		X	

4. If the task is completed ("C"), the fourth scale point is checked.

N/A	B	P	C
			X

Obviously, the monitoring plan presented here does not include all the details of the procedures, responsibilities, and resources that a particular school or school system might use in the development and implementation of a staff development program. Rather, the proposed scheme provides general guidelines that can be followed as an initial effort. It can be rewritten subsequently by local districts into a comprehensive and developed task analysis that would include the necessary specified events, procedures, responsibilities, and performance standards.

Date:____

I. ORGANIZING AND COORDINATING STAFF DEVELOPMENT ACTIVITIES

A program for staff development requires an organizational plan and understanding by the related staff of the resources and procedures that facilitate the achievement of all program phases.

	N/A	B	P	C
1. Specific people and/or groups have been identified to coordinate the staff development project.				
2. A time schedule for the various staff development phases has been established.				

	N/A	B	P	C
3. Procedures have been determined for participation and involvement of all segments of the school community in the decision making process for the assessment of educational needs.	___	__	__	__
4. Procedures have been determined for participation and involvement of all segments of the school community in the decision making process for the identification and selection of goals and objectives.	___	__	__	__
5. Procedures have been determined for participation and involvement of all segments of the school community in the decision making process for the selection of an educational improvement activity.	___	__	__	__
6. Procedures have been determined for the participation and involvement of all segments of the school community in the decision making process required for the identification of staff competencies.	___	__	__	__
7. Procedures have been determined for participation and involvement of all segments of the school community in the decision making process for the evaluation of the staff development program.	___	__	__	__
8. A communication network for the dissemination and collection of data and information has been developed.	___	__	__	__
9. Resources have been identified in the following areas:				
a. Materials for staff.	___	__	__	__
b. Materials for students.	___	__	__	__
c. Allocations of funds.	___	__	__	__

10. What is the overall progress to date?

Comments:

11. Are there significant problems impeding the progress being made?

Comments:

12. What help is needed?

Comments:

Date:_____

II. CONDUCTING THE NEEDS ASSESSMENT

The staff development program is based on a comprehensive needs assessment conducted for the purpose of gathering data regarding students, school(s), school personnel, and community relative to the conditions in the school system.

	N/A	B	P	C
1. A time schedule for completion of the needs assessment has been established.	___	__	__	__
2. Consensus has been obtained regarding the procedures for the assessment of educational needs.	___	__	__	__
3. A determination of information to be collected has been made.	___	__	__	__
4. Procedures for collecting data are developed and written.	___	__	__	__
5. Needs assessment information has been collected.	___	__	__	__
6. Information has been processed and analyzed.	___	__	__	__
7. Statements of need have been written.	___	__	__	__

8. What is the overall progress to date?

   Comments:

9. Are there significant problems impeding the progress being made?

   Comments:

10. What help is needed?

    Comments:

Date:_____

III. DEVELOPING STATEMENTS OF GOALS AND OBJECTIVES

The staff development program requires statements of goals and objectives that are based upon data and upon shared consultation with teachers, parents, students, and community members.

	N/A	B	P	C
1. A time schedule has been made for the completion of goals assessing goals and writing objectives.	___	_	_	_
2. Consensus has been obtained regarding the procedures for the identification and selection of goals and objectives.	___	_	_	_
3. Instructional or system goals have been identified and written.	___	_	_	_
4. The method for ranking the goals has been determined.	___	_	_	_
5. A priority ranking of goals has been obtained.	___	_	_	_
6. The goals have been translated into program objectives.	___	_	_	_
7. Interim and/or enabling objectives have been written.	___	_	_	_
8. Performance objectives have been written.	___	_	_	_

9. What is the overall progress to date?

   Comments:

10. Are there significant problems impeding the progress being made?

    Comments:

11. What help is needed?

    Comments:

Date:_____

IV. SELECTING THE EDUCATIONAL IMPROVEMENT ACTIVITY

The program for staff development requires a decision as to the appropriate educational improvement activity that meets goal(s) and objective(s) already developed.

	N/A	B	P	C
1. The time schedule for selecting the educational improvement activity has been determined.	___	_	_	_

	N/A	B	P	C
2. A consensus regarding the procedures to be followed has been obtained regarding the selection of the educational improvement activity.	___	___	___	___
3. The advantages and disadvantages of existing LEA programs have been considered.	___	___	___	___
4. An appropriate exemplary improvement program has been located from the literature, as it exists in other LEA's, or has been locally developed.	___	___	___	___
5. Consideration has been given to the advantages and disadvantages of improvement activities under consideration that includes such concerns as compatibility with existing programs, financial cost, time, and space requirements, etc.	___	___	___	___
6. The educational improvement activity most appropriate to the developed objectives and constraints within the systems has been selected.	___	___	___	___
7. The adoption/adaptation process for the improvement program has been determined including such activities as organization for implementation, identification of resources for training, and the evaluation.	___	___	___	___
8. A training program has been planned for those who will direct and implement the proposed program.	___	___	___	___

9. What is the overall progress to date?

   Comments:

10. Are there significant problems impeding the progress being made?

    Comments:

11. What help is needed?

    Comments:

Date: ____

V. *DETERMINING THE COMPETENCIES OF THE TARGET EDUCATIONAL PERSONNEL*

The staff development program recognizes that knowledge, skills, and attitudes of staff are essential to the implementation and operation of the improvement activity.

	N/A	B	P	C
1. The time schedule has been determined for identifying staff competencies.	___	___	___	___
2. Consensus has been obtained on procedures for identifying staff competencies.	___	___	___	___
3. The specification and categorization of the critical competencies needed (knowledges, skills, and attitudes) for the improvement programs have been achieved.	___	___	___	___
4. The critical knowledges, skills, and attitudes of the target staff have been determined.	___	___	___	___
5. The knowledges required to implement and operate the improvement program have been specified.	___	___	___	___
6. The skills needed to implement and operate the improvement program have been specified.	___	___	___	___
7. The attitudes needed to implement and operate the improvement program have been specified.	___	___	___	___
8. The specified training for professional growth and competency attainment has been established including in-service activities, schedule of activities, personnel involved, materials required, etc.	___	___	___	___
9. Plans have been made for visitation, workshop experience, and course and consultant help that will be required.	___	___	___	___

10. What is the overall progress to date?

    Comments:

11. Are there significant problems impeding the progress being made?

    Comments:

N/A B P C

12. What help is needed?

    Comments:

Date:_____

VI. *CONDUCTING REGULAR EVALUATION*

The evaluation process is concerned with intermediate and terminal outcomes; also the use of data in the decision making, reporting, and feedback procedures as they relate to all phases of the program.

	N/A	B	P	C
1. The time schedule for completing the evaluation activities has been determined.	___	___	___	___
2. Concensus on the necessary evaluation procedures has been obtained.	___	___	___	___
3. Information sources have been identified. (They include such items as student target population, representation, and sampling procedure.)	___	___	___	___
4. Data collection devices have been specified. (They include operational items for criterion variables, such as a plan for achievement testing and/or interview schedules, observation instruments or process, and questionnaires for personal interaction.)	___	___	___	___
5. Conditions for data collection have been specified. (They include such items as an established time schedule, designated personnel responsibilities, and an orientation and climate for the administration of the data collection devices.)	___	___	___	___
6. The unit of analysis has been determined. (They include such items as the individual, classroom or group, grade level, and school or district to be assessed.)	___	___	___	___
7. The method for data analysis has been specified. (This includes such considerations as frequency distributions, summary statistics, percentages, means, medians, and the like.)	___	___	___	___
8. The necessary personnel and facilities for the evaluation have been specified. (These are such items as equipment, space, and personnel needs for the analysis.)	___	___	___	___

	N/A	B	P	C
9. The feedback and reporting audience has been identified. (This includes audience(s) identified to receive information and data—those persons who are to receive the evaluative data, such as students, teachers, superintendents, board, project director, supervisors, citizens, and others.)	___	___	___	___
10. The mode of reporting has been specified. (This includes such means as oral or written presentations, speeches, public meetings, reports, news releases, and year-end reports.)	___	___	___	___
11. The timing and frequency of the reports has been specified.	___	___	___	___

12. What is the overall progress to date?

    Comments:

13. Are there significant problems impeding the progress being made to date?

    Comments:

14. What help is needed?

    Comments:

Date:_____

VII. IMPLEMENTING THE PROGRAM

The implementation of a staff development program depends upon the quality of the planning and the preparations that have preceded the actual operation of the program. Continuous refinement and expansion of the procedures, structure, and evaluation components are essential.

	N/A	B	P	C
1. The time table for achieving full program operation has been established. Each program objective has been translated into a plan for operation.	___	___	___	___

	N/A	B	P	C
2. Procedures have been established for receiving and transmitting communication to and from every representative group within and outside the school system.	___	___	___	___
3. A procedure has been established for the continuous involvement of the staff in the implementation of the program.	___	___	___	___
4. A procedure has been established to account for the resources, materials, and funds used in the program operation.	___	___	___	___
5. The design and method have been established for the continuous, as well as the terminal, assessment of the program.	___	___	___	___
6. Staff duties and/or responsibilities have been delineated for central office, project manager(s), administrators, teachers, and other staff personnel.	___	___	___	___
7. A commitment has been obtained from school personnel directly responsible for program implementation and operation, and from the board and administration.	___	___	___	___
8. Procedures have been established to make the necessary adjustments in staff assignments, student schedules, budget, and school policies.	___	___	___	___
9. Field testing, simulations review panels, or other pilot efforts have been made to indicate likely problems and desirable revisions.	___	___	___	___
10. A clear relationship has been established between the project activity and the ongoing programs of the system.	___	___	___	___

11. What is the overall progress to date?

    Comments:

12. Are there significant problems impeding the progress being made?

    Comments:

13. What help is needed?

    Comments:

Date:_____

VII. IMPLEMENTING THE PROGRAM (CONT.)

Once the program is in operation, its adequacy and terminal and cumulative outputs need to be scrutinized; thus, monitoring continues. It is impossible to detail the sequence of tasks in the operational program, but a few suggested queries that can be answered YES or NO may be helpful.

1. Have the objectives been properly related to the necessary learning tasks? Yes _____ No _____

   Comments:

2. Do the learning tasks identify the basic gains that have to be made if the learners are to achieve the state program objectives? Yes _____ No _____

   Comments:

3. Are there a large number of tasks that do not directly contribute to the attainment of the specific program objectives? Yes _____ No _____

   Comments:

4. Are you satisfied that the basic functions and procedures needed to accomplish the learning tasks have been designated? Yes _____ No _____

   Comments:

5. In your estimation, are there adequate facilities, materials, and funds? Yes _____ No _____

   Comments:

6. Are you satisfied with the designated feedback and reporting efforts to keep everyone informed of the progress being made toward program objectives? Yes ____ No ____

   Comments:

7. Are there many necessary realignments of duties and responsibilities for the program to operate smoothly? Yes ____ No ____

   Comments:

8. Are staff members in departments and/or grade levels cooperating and working effectively? Yes ____ No ____

   Comments:

9. Are there significant problems impeding the progress being made? Yes ____ No ____

   Comments:

10. Are there records being kept of the overall progress? Yes ____ No ____

    Comments:

11. What help is needed?

    Comments:

As the project matures and runs its course, the data collected and the decisions made will facilitate the *summative evaluation*. This will be a judgment made as to the impact, efficiency, and adequacy of the total project. If the monitoring plan is used, each of the relevant items can be supported by documents (minutes, plans, and reports); and selected items can be researched in more detail using questionnaires, tests, and other instruments. In many instances, action will have been taken to change the situation, materials, leadership, organization, or activities; and these also can be indicated. Together, these data provide invaluable resources for program evaluation. These summative statements are useful for establishing baseline data regarding students, staff, organization, and procedures that will be helpful in regard to subsequent projects, and for making decisions as to the best procedures and techniques to employ in future programs. In this way each project builds a foundation of processes and products. These are essential to establish new objectives and new improvement efforts.

APPENDIX D

Implementing a Curricular or Instructional Change—Tasks, Functions, and Processes

IMPLEMENTATION–A DESIGN

One of the most difficult phases of any curricular or instructional change is the task of implementation. Because each situation is unique, most models for change do not attempt to develop a specific plan for this activity. The following guidelines are intended to provide a background for the specifications that follow.

1. *There is evident administration and board policy support;* the task to be undertaken must be clearly a priority. The power and project personnel must assist in the development of a climate and a commitment if the task is to be accomplished.
2. *The rationale and objectives are clear;* there must be an obvious relationship between what presently exists and what is to transpire. The change must be superior to the present program.
3. *Professional staff members will know how to participate and relate to the program;* a participatory (peer power), developmental approach is recommended. Multiple modes for involvement to accommodate different styles and different stages of development, different entry points, and varying achievement opportunities should be provided.
4. *There is adequacy, quality, and coordination in the materials to be used;* this is part of a support system that maximizes understanding and minimizes personal risk. Progress regarding support features such as equipment or building modifications should be explicit.
5. *Relevance and realism for professionals (as well as for learners) is apparent;* this relates to certification, status, attention, time, income, and especially to the ongoing tasks for which the staff member is accountable. These include content gain, skill acquisition, quality of work, professional role, and expertise.

6. *A reasonable plan for the achievement of the desired objectives has been developed;* it must include short and long range goals, time frames, management expectations and interventions, and processes for modification. Back-up support (such as help from consultants or clinic sessions) and/or alternative routes are helpful.
7. *Leadership and role responsibilities (performance expectations) for all staff members has been defined;* leadership should be determined on the basis of competency and accountability, rather than status per se. All segments of the system should contribute appropriately.
8. *Communication flow and feedback has been provided for as part of the process and program;* lack of feedback regarding performance, gain, or modification causes turbulence and reversion. This may affect learners and the community as well as the staff members who are involved. Communication is more difficult, but also more essential when interaction involves non-school agencies, businesses, or institutions.
9. *Time is essential for change, that is, time for development and accomodation, and time within the priority hours for activity.* If the program is an add-on or if it occurs only during "off" hours or days, then, all of the above elements including support and commitment are negated. Those involved must have opportunity to reconcile project objectives with individual commitments.
10. *Support and modification are observable in all components of the system.* A single change or thrust will be rejected or isolated by the routine, ongoing practices, and procedures. Instructional change and personalized staff development programs must be systemic as well as systematic.

This model makes certain assumptions:

1. The instructional or staff development area to be changed has already been identified, diagnosed, developed, and validated; also, some plan has been developed for its evaluation.
2. The visual model would operate as a work sheet to gain agreement on a two-phase implementation plan: (1) pre-operation and (2) operation.
3. Once explicated, this model would operate as general guidelines and task assignments for the implementation of a particular program.

Implicit in this approach is the desirability of wide participation and accountability. By acknowledging the tasks, functions, and processes to be performed by each person in the process, the implementation can be expected to occur with a minimum of error and a maximum of responsibility. Also, it should be possible to evaluate the effectiveness of the implementation process itself.

It will be noted that Figure D-1 shows a separation of personnel. Those on the left are *outside* the involved system, e.g., state department, regional education resources, university consultant, or other non-system personnel as well as external evaluators, program auditors, researchers, or agencies. Those on the right of the task listing are *within* the system. Only individual roles are shown, but groups, teams, or committees could be indicated; as well as other individuals such as counselors, media, or support persons.

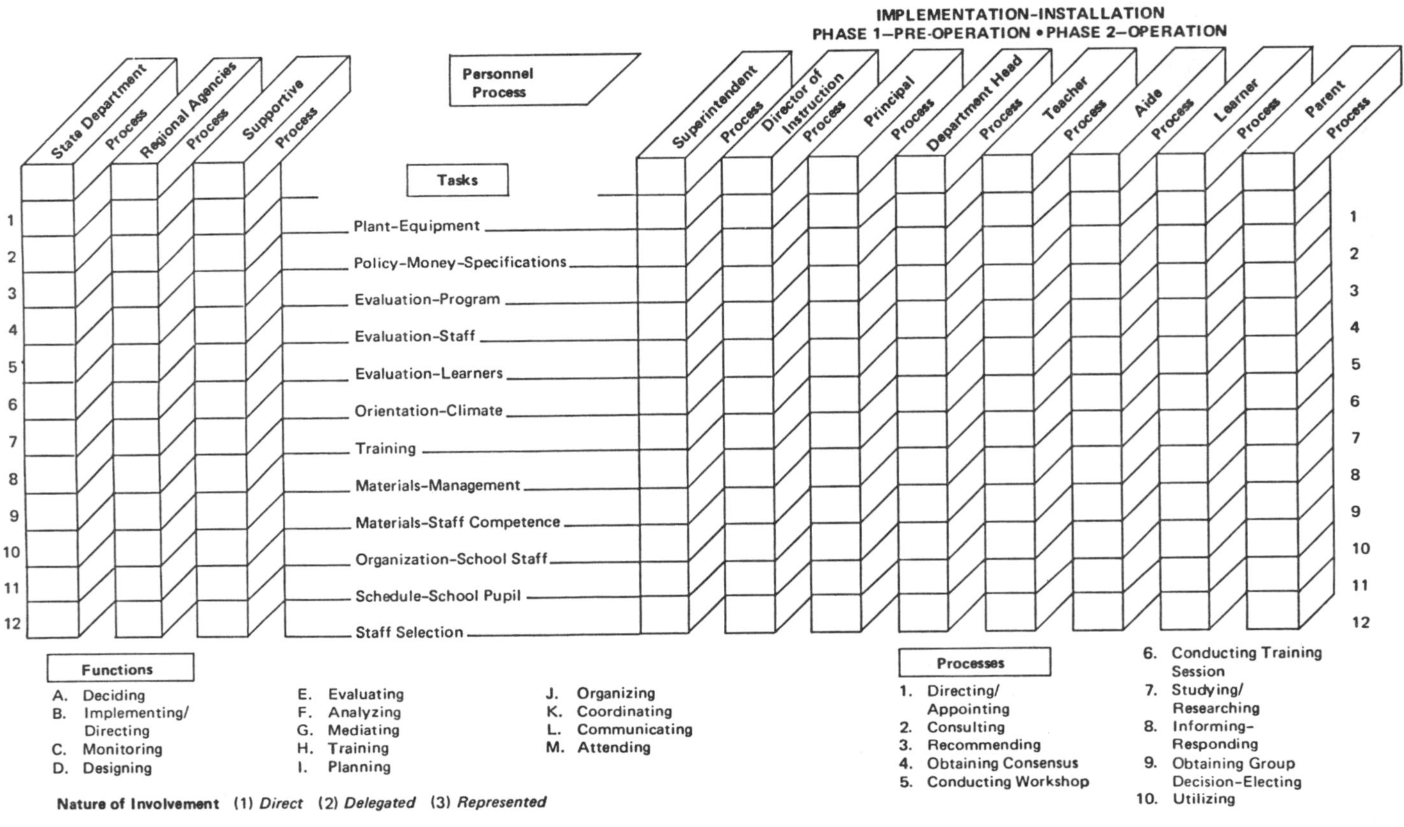

FIGURE D-1 Role Analysis and Accountability.

The design for implementation can be used for both pre-operation and operation planning; this would suggest the completion of the model *twice*, once for each phase, since many roles change in the two phases. Some persons, e.g., subject area consultants, may be active in the pre-operation design phase, less so in operation. Administrative personnel, on the other hand, tend to be consultants in the pre-operation, but implementors during the operation phase.

Implementation Tasks*

1. Plant-equipment—acquiring, building, or obtaining rights to large equipment (TV installations, computers, etc.) or significant building modifications; making necessary changes and maintenance.
2. Policy—specifications regarding program needs and objectives, designation of budget requirements, high level procedures to insure progress, and implementation; support of implementation procedures.
3. Evaluation-program—evaluation of overall program, concern for balance instrumentation procedures; utilizing standards and procedures and providing feedback.
4. Evaluation-staff—determining personnel competencies to effect particular curricular changes; ongoing evaluation.
5. Evaluation-learners—determining personnel competencies to effect particular curricular changes; ongoing evaluation.
6. Orientation-climate—establishing tone or climate for change; maintaining a high level of understanding and commitment.
7. Training—involving participants in specific tasks necessary for achieving a particular outcome; maintaining and improving competencies.
8. Materials-management—selecting, procuring, and distributing instructional materials; maintaining flow and coordination.
9. Materials-staff competencies—determining the performance levels of personnel for utilization of instructional materials; continuous evaluation of effectiveness of materials and use.
10. Organization-school-staff—determining criteria and patterns and organizing staff to implement curriculum; making necessary staff adjustments.
11. Schedule-school and pupil—developing or overseeing student schedules; making necessary changes and assignments to program areas.
12. Staff selection—selecting staff for specific assignments; making necessary adjustments.

Implementing Functions

A. Deciding —Making the critical judgment with respect to what is to be done in a particular situation or course of action.

*In regard to the following tasks, some items on the list are separated by semicolons. This punctuation separates those aspects of implementation that are pre-operation and those which are operation responsibilities.

B.	Implementing Directing	—Effecting previously determined decisions, policies, or procedures.
C.	Monitoring	—Active surveillance or supervision with authority to intervene.
D.	Designing	—Preparing plans that serve as guidelines for subsequent developments or actions.
E.	Evaluating	—Determining the value or worth, making an appraisal in order to find strengths and weaknesses.
F.	Analyzing	—Gathering evidence of and examining factors or parts in terms of the total.
G.	Mediating	—Working with contending parties in order to bring about a settlement or compromise.
H.	Training	—Helping others to become skillful or proficient in a particular task or process.
I.	Planning	—Forming a plan (scheme or method) for doing something specific.
J.	Organizing	—Making systematic or orderly arrangements for a program or activity.
K.	Coordinating	—Performing integrating tasks or processes.
L.	Communicating	—Relaying or conveying information.
M.	Attending	—Being informed with interest or commitment.

Implementation Process

1. Directing-Appointing.
   Taking action or putting a decision into effect.
2. Consulting.
   Judgments usually sought as to the most beneficial or worthy action; may propose alternatives.
3. Recommending.
   Being definitely involved but not the decision-maker.
4. Obtaining Consensus.
   Obtaining general agreement or collective opinion.
5. Conducting Workshop.
   Involving participants in activities designed for staff development.
6. Conducting Training Session.
   A limited involvement of participants designed to achieve specific objectives or skills.
7. Studying-Researching.
   Careful or disciplined inquiry directed toward the data collection, clarification, analysis, and/or recommendations for the resolution of a problem or for development.

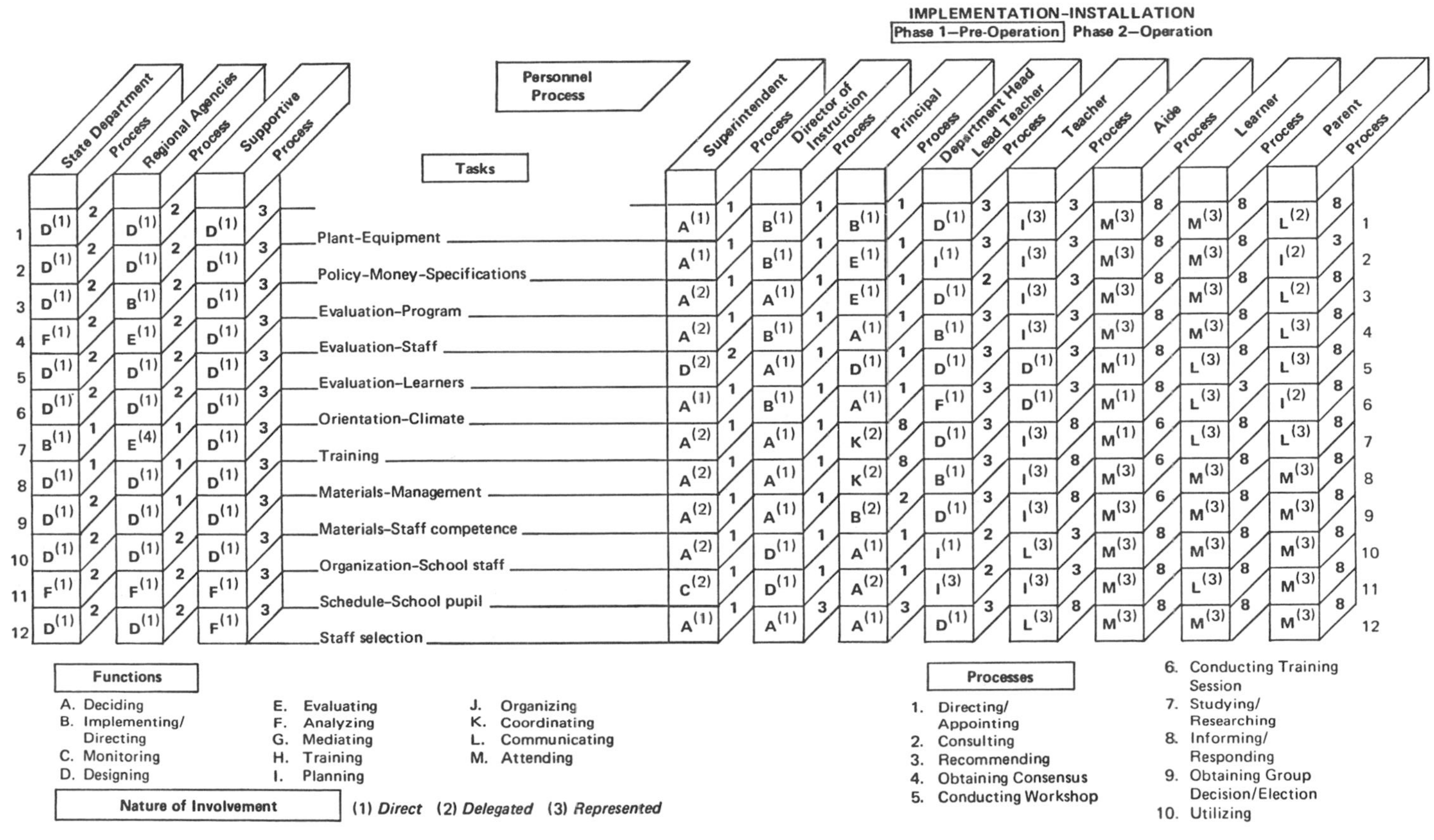

PLANNING-RESEARCH
MODEL

IMPLEMENTATION-INSTALLATION
Phase 1—Pre-Operation | Phase 2—Operation

	Tasks	State Department	Process	Regional Agencies	Process	Supportive	Process	Superintendent	Process	Director of Instruction	Process	Principal	Process	Department Head Lead Teacher	Process	Teacher	Process	Aide	Process	Learner	Process	Parent	Process	
1	Plant-Equipment	D(1)	2	D(1)	2	D(1)	3	A(1)	1	B(1)	1	B(1)	1	D(1)	3	I(3)	3	M(3)	8	M(3)	8	L(2)	8	1
2	Policy-Money-Specifications	D(1)	2	D(1)	2	D(1)	3	A(1)	1	B(1)	1	E(1)	1	I(1)	3	I(3)	3	M(3)	8	M(3)	8	I(2)	3	2
3	Evaluation-Program	D(1)	2	B(1)	2	D(1)	3	A(2)	1	A(1)	1	E(1)	1	D(1)	2	I(3)	3	M(3)	8	M(3)	8	L(2)	8	3
4	Evaluation-Staff	F(1)	2	E(1)	2	D(1)	3	A(2)	1	B(1)	1	A(1)	1	B(1)	3	I(3)	3	M(3)	8	M(3)	8	L(3)	8	4
5	Evaluation-Learners	D(1)	2	D(1)	2	D(1)	3	D(2)	2	A(1)	1	D(1)	1	D(1)	3	D(1)	3	M(1)	8	L(3)	8	L(3)	8	5
6	Orientation-Climate	D(1)	2	D(1)	2	D(1)	3	A(1)	1	B(1)	1	A(1)	1	F(1)	3	D(1)	3	M(1)	8	L(3)	3	I(2)	8	6
7	Training	B(1)	1	E(4)	1	D(1)	3	A(2)	1	A(1)	1	K(2)	8	D(1)	3	I(3)	8	M(1)	6	L(3)	8	L(3)	8	7
8	Materials-Management	D(1)	1	D(1)	1	D(1)	3	A(2)	1	A(1)	1	K(2)	8	B(1)	3	I(3)	8	M(3)	6	M(3)	8	M(3)	8	8
9	Materials-Staff competence	D(1)	2	D(1)	1	D(1)	3	A(2)	1	A(1)	1	B(2)	2	D(1)	3	I(3)	8	M(3)	6	M(3)	8	M(3)	8	9
10	Organization-School staff	D(1)	2	D(1)	2	D(1)	3	A(2)	1	D(1)	1	A(1)	1	I(1)	2	L(3)	3	M(3)	8	M(3)	8	M(3)	8	10
11	Schedule-School pupil	F(1)	2	F(1)	2	F(1)	3	C(2)	1	D(1)	1	A(2)	1	I(3)	2	I(3)	3	M(3)	8	L(3)	8	M(3)	8	11
12	Staff selection	D(1)	2	D(1)	2	F(1)	3	A(1)	1	A(1)	3	A(1)	3	D(1)	3	L(3)	8	M(3)	8	M(3)	8	M(3)	8	12

FIGURE D-2 Role Analysis—Pre-Operation.

PLANNING-RESEARCH MODEL

IMPLEMENTATION-INSTALLATION
Phase 1—Pre-Operation | Phase 2—Operation

Personnel Process

No.	Tasks	State Department	Process	Regional Agencies	Process	Supportive	Process	Superintendent	Process	Director of Instruction	Process	Principal	Process	Department Head Lead Teacher	Process	Teacher	Process	Aide	Process	Learner	Process	Parent	Process
1	Plant–Equipment	F(2)	3	C(1)	2	M(3)	10	E(1)	10	C(1)	3	C(1)	1	E(1)	3	K(1)	10	M(3)	8	M(3)	10	M(3)	10
2	Policy–Money–Specifications	F(2)	3	F(1)	2	M(3)	10	F(1)	10	B(1)	1	C(1)	1	K(1)	10	L(2)	10	M(3)	10	M(3)	10	M(3)	10
3	Evaluation–Program	D(2)	3	C(1)	2	F(1)	3	C(2)	4	A(1)	1	C(1)	1	C(1)	3	F(2)	3	M(3)	8	L(3)	8	M(3)	10
4	Evaluation–Staff	M(3)	8	C(1)	2	M(3)	8	K(2)	3	C(2)	2	A(1)	1	B(1)	3	M(3)	8	M(3)	8	L(3)	8	M(3)	10
5	Evaluation–Learners	M(3)	8	F(1)	2	M(3)	8	K(2)	4	F(1)	3	C(1)	1	B(2)	3	A(1)	1	K(3)	8	M(3)	10	M(3)	10
6	Orientation–Climate	F(1)	3	C(1)	2	F(1)	3	L(1)	8	B(1)	1	A(1)	1	C(2)	3	F(1)	8	L(3)	8	L(3)	8	M(3)	10
7	Training	M(3)	8	B(1)	1	B(1)	3	E(1)	3	A(1)	1	A(2)	8	B(1)	3	M(1)	10	M(3)	10	M(3)	10	M(3)	10
8	Materials–Management	M(3)	8	C(1)	2	F(1)	3	F(2)	3	C(2)	2	K(2)	8	B(1)	1	L(2)	10	M(3)	10	M(3)	10	M(3)	10
9	Materials–Staff competence	M(3)	8	C(1)	2	F(1)	3	F(1)	3	F(1)	2	D(2)	2	B(1)	3	M(2)	8	M(3)	10	M(3)	10	M(3)	10
10	Organization–School staff	F(1)	3	E(1)	3	F(1)	3	F(2)	4	F(1)	2	A(1)	1	B(1)	3	M(2)	8	M(3)	10	M(3)	10	M(3)	10
11	Schedule–School pupil	M(3)	8	F(1)	3	M(2)	8	F(2)	3	F(2)	3	A(2)	1	C(1)	3	L(1)	3	M(3)	10	M(3)	10	M(3)	10
12	Staff selection	M(3)	8	F(1)	3	M(3)	8	A(1)	3	F(2)	3	A(1)	3	E(1)	3	M(2)	8	M(3)	10	M(3)	10	M(3)	10

Functions

A. Deciding
B. Implementing/Directing
C. Monitoring
D. Designing
E. Evaluating
F. Analyzing
G. Mediating
H. Training
I. Planning
J. Organizing
K. Coordinating
L. Communicating
M. Attending

Nature of Involvement (1) *Direct* (2) *Delegated* (3) *Represented*

Processes

1. Directing/Appointing
2. Consulting
3. Recommending
4. Obtaining Consensus
5. Conducting Workshop
6. Conducting Training Session
7. Studying/Researching
8. Informing/Responding
9. Obtaining Group Decision/Election
10. Utilizing

FIGURE D-3 Rolè Analysis—Operation.

8. Informing-Responding.
   Relaying or conveying information; limited response to a particular communication or situation.
9. Obtaining Group Decision-Electing.
   Formal determination or selection of alternatives.
10. Utilizing.
    Using or implementing as previously determined.

The following lists provide another format for the same information contained in Figures D-2 and D-3. Note that both pre-operation and operation responsibilities are part of each role. These could be framed as specific or general role statements, or could be rewritten as job specifications or tasks to be monitored, or could be considered as guidelines for performance.

IMPLEMENTATION
(Pre-Operation)

STATE DEPARTMENT

Tasks	*Functions*	*Involvement*	*Process*
1. Plant-Equipment	Designing	Direct	Consulting
2. Policy-Money-Specifications	Designing	Direct	Consulting
3. Evaluation-Program	Implementing-Directing	Direct	Consulting
4. Evaluation-Staff	Evaluating	Direct	Consulting
5. Evaluation-Learners	Designing	Direct	Consulting
6. Orientation-Climate	Designing	Direct	Consulting
7. Training	Implementing-Directing	Direct	Directing-Appointing
8. Materials-Management	Designing	Direct	Directing-Appointing
9. Materials-Staff Competence	Designing	Direct	Consulting
10. Organization-School Staff	Designing	Direct	Consulting
11. Schedule-School Pupil	Analyzing	Direct	Consulting
12. Staff Selection	Designing	Direct	Consulting

IMPLEMENTATION
(Operation)

STATE DEPARTMENT

Tasks	*Functions*	*Involvement*	*Process*
1. Plant-Equipment	Analyzing	Delegated	Recommending
2. Policy-Money-Specifications	Analyzing	Delegated	Recommending
3. Evaluation-Program	Designing	Delegated	Recommending
4. Evaluation-Staff	Attending	Represented	Informing-Responding
5. Evaluation-Learners	Attending	Represented	Informing-Responding
6. Orientation-Climate	Analyzing	Direct	Recommending
7. Training	Attending	Represented	Informing-Responding
8. Materials-Management	Attending	Represented	Informing-Responding
9. Materials-Staff Competence	Attending	Represented	Informing-Responding
10. Organization-School Staff	Analyzing	Direct	Recommending
11. Schedule-School Pupil	Attending	Represented	Informing-Responding
12. Staff Selection	Attending	Represented	Informing-Responding

IMPLEMENTATION
(Pre-Operation)

REGIONAL AGENCY

Tasks	*Functions*	*Involvement*	*Process*
1. Plant-Equipment	Designing	Direct	Consulting
2. Policy-Money-Specifications	Designing	Direct	Consulting
3. Evaluation-Program	Implementing-Directing	Direct	Consulting
4. Evaluation-Staff	Evaluating	Direct	Consulting
5. Evaluation-Learners	Designing	Direct	Consulting
6. Orientation-Climate	Designing	Direct	Consulting
7. Training	Implementing-Directing	Direct	Directing-Appointing
8. Materials-Management	Designing	Direct	Appointing
9. Materials-Staff Competence	Designing	Direct	Directing-Appointing
10. Organization-School Staff	Designing	Direct	Consulting
11. Schedule-School Pupil	Analyzing	Direct	Consulting
12. Staff Selection	Designing	Direct	Consulting

IMPLEMENTATION
(Operation)

REGIONAL AGENCY

Tasks	*Functions*	*Involvement*	*Process*
1. Plant-Equipment	Monitoring	Direct	Consulting
2. Policy-Money-Specifications	Analyzing	Direct	Consulting
3. Evaluation-Program	Monitoring	Direct	Consulting
4. Evaluation-Staff	Monitoring	Direct	Consulting
5. Evaluation-Learners	Analyzing	Direct	Consulting
6. Orientation-Climate	Monitoring	Direct	Consulting
7. Training	Implementing-Directing	Direct	Directing-Appointing
8. Materials-Management	Monitoring	Direct	Consulting
9. Materials-Staff Competence	Monitoring	Direct	Consulting
10. Organization-School Staff	Evaluating	Direct	Recommending
11. Schedule-School Pupil	Analyzing	Direct	Recommending
12. Staff Selection	Analyzing	Direct	Recommending

IMPLEMENTATION
(Pre-Operation)

SUPPORTIVE PERSONNEL/CONSULTANT

Tasks	*Functions*	*Involvement*	*Process*
1. Plant-Equipment	Designing	Direct	Recommending
2. Policy-Money-Specifications	Designing	Direct	Recommending
3. Evaluation-Program	Designing	Direct	Recommending
4. Evaluation-Staff	Designing	Direct	Recommending
5. Evaluation-Learners	Designing	Direct	Recommending
6. Orientation-Climate	Designing	Direct	Recommending
7. Training	Designing	Direct	Recommending
8. Materials-Management	Designing	Direct	Recommending
9. Materials-Staff Competence	Designing	Direct	Recommending
10. Organization-School Staff	Designing	Direct	Recommending
11. Schedule-School Pupil	Analyzing	Direct	Recommending
12. Staff Selection	Analyzing	Direct	Recommending

IMPLEMENTATION
(Operation)

SUPPORTIVE PERSONNEL/CONSULTANT

Tasks	*Functions*	*Involvement*	*Process*
1. Plant-Equipment	Attending	Represented	Utilizing
2. Policy-Money-Specifications	Attending	Represented	Utilizing
3. Evaluation-Program	Analyzing	Direct	Recommending
4. Evaluation-Staff	Attending	Represented	Informing-Responding
5. Evaluation-Learners	Attending	Represented	Informing-Responding
6. Orientation-Climate	Analyzing	Direct	Recommending
7. Training	Implementing-Directing	Direct	Recommending
8. Materials-Management	Analyzing	Direct	Recommending
9. Materials-Staff Competence	Analyzing	Direct	Recommending
10. Organization-School Staff	Analyzing	Direct	Recommending
11. Schedule-School Pupil	Attending	Represented	Informing-Responding
12. Staff Selection	Attending	Represented	Informing-Responding

IMPLEMENTATION
(Pre-Operation)

SUPERINTENDENT

Task	*Functions*	*Involvement*	*Process*
1. Plant-Equipment	Deciding	Direct	Directing-Appointing
2. Policy-Money-Specifications	Deciding	Direct	Directing-Appointing
3. Evaluation-Program	Deciding	Delegated	Directing-Appointing
4. Evaluation-Staff	Deciding	Delegated	Directing-Appointing
5. Evaluation-Learners	Designing	Delegated	Consulting
6. Orientation-Climate	Deciding	Direct	Directing-Appointing
7. Training	Deciding	Delegated	Directing-Appointing
8. Materials-Management	Deciding	Delegated	Directing-Appointing
9. Materials-Staff Competence	Deciding	Delegated	Directing-Appointing
10. Organization-School Staff	Deciding	Delegated	Directing-Appointing
11. Schedule-School Pupil	Monitoring	Delegated	Directing-Appointing
12. Staff Selection	Deciding	Direct	Directing-Appointing

IMPLEMENTATION
(Operation)

SUPERINTENDENT

Task	*Functions*	*Involvement*	*Process*
1. Plant-Equipment	Evaluating	Direct	Utilizing
2. Policy-Money-Specifications	Analyzing	Direct	Utilizing
3. Evaluation-Progam	Monitoring	Delegated	Obtaining Consensus
4. Evaluation-Staff	Coordinating	Delegated	Recommending
5. Evaluation-Learners	Coordinating	Delegated	Obtaining Consensus
6. Orientation-Climate	Communicating	Direct	Informing-Responding
7. Training	Evaluating	Direct	Recommending
8. Materials-Management	Analyzing	Delegated	Recommending
9. Materials-Staff Competencies	Analyzing	Direct	Recommending
10. Organization-School Staff	Analyzing	Delegated	Obtaining Consensus
11. Schedule-School Pupil	Analyzing	Delegated	Recommending
12. Staff Selection	Deciding	Direct	Recommending

IMPLEMENTATION
(Pre-Operation)

DIRECTOR OF INSTRUCTION

Tasks	*Functions*	*Involvement*	*Process*
1. Plant-Equipment	Implementing-Directing	Direct	Directing-Appointing
2. Policy-Money-Specifications	Implementing-Directing	Direct	Directing-Appointing
3. Evaluation-Program	Deciding	Direct	Directing-Appointing
4. Evaluation-Staff	Implementing-Directing	Direct	Directing-Appointing
5. Evaluation-Learners	Deciding	Direct	Directing-Appointing
6. Orientation-Climate	Implementing-Directing	Direct	Directing-Appointing
7. Training	Deciding	Direct	Directing-Appointing
8. Materials-Management	Deciding	Direct	Directing-Appointing
9. Materials-Staff Competence	Deciding	Direct	Directing-Appointing
10. Organization-School Staff	Designing	Direct	Directing-Appointing
11. Schedule-School Pupil	Designing	Direct	Directing-Appointing
12. Staff Selection	Designing	Direct	Recommending

IMPLEMENTATION
(Operation)

DIRECTOR OF INSTRUCTION

Tasks	*Functions*	*Involvement*	*Process*
1. Plant-Equipment	Monitoring	Direct	Recommending
2. Policy-Money-Specifications	Implementing-Directing	Direct	Directing-Appointing
3. Evaluation-Program	Deciding	Direct	Directing-Appointing
4. Evaluation-Staff	Monitoring	Delegated	Consulting
5. Evaluation-Learners	Analyzing	Direct	Recommending
6. Orientation-Climate	Implementing-Directing	Direct	Directing-Appointing
7. Training	Deciding	Direct	Directing-Appointing
8. Materials-Management	Monitoring	Delegated	Consulting
9. Materials-Staff Competence	Analyzing	Direct	Consulting
10. Organization-School Staff	Analyzing	Direct	Consulting
11. Schedule-School Pupil	Analyzing	Delegated	Recommending
12. Staff Selection	Analyzing	Delegated	Recommending

IMPLEMENTATION
(Pre-Operation)

PRINCIPAL

Tasks	*Functions*	*Involvement*	*Process*
1. Plant-Equipment	Implementing-Directing	Direct	Directing-Appointing
2. Policy-Money-Specifications	Implementing-Directing	Direct	Directing-Appointing
3. Evaluation-Program	Implementing-Directing	Direct	Directing-Appointing
4. Evaluation-Staff	Deciding	Direct	Directing-Appointing
5. Evaluation-Learners	Designing	Direct	Directing-Appointing
6. Orientation-Climate	Deciding	Direct	Directing-Appointing
7. Training	Coordinating	Delegated	Informing-Responding
8. Materials-Management	Coordinating	Delegated	Informing-Responding
9. Materials-Staff Competence	Implementing-Directing	Delegated	Consulting
10. Organization-School Staff	Deciding	Direct	Directing-Appointing
11. Schedule-School Pupil	Deciding	Delegated	Directing-Appointing
12. Staff Selection	Deciding	Direct	Recommending

IMPLEMENTATION
(Operation)

PRINCIPAL

Tasks	Functions	Involvement	Process
1. Plant-Equipment	Monitoring	Direct	Directing-Appointing
2. Policy-Money-Specifications	Monitoring	Direct	Directing-Appointing
3. Evaluation-Program	Monitoring	Direct	Directing-Appointing
4. Evaluation-Staff	Deciding	Direct	Directing-Appointing
5. Evaluation-Learners	Monitoring	Direct	Directing-Appointing
6. Orientation-Climate	Deciding	Direct	Directing-Appointing
7. Training	Deciding	Delegated	Informing-Responding
8. Materials-Management	Coordinating	Delegated	Informing-Responding
9. Materials-Staff Competence	Designing	Delegated	Consulting
10. Organization-School Staff	Deciding	Direct	Directing-Appointing
11. Schedule-School Pupil	Deciding	Delegated	Directing-Appointing
12. Staff Selection	Deciding	Direct	Recommending

IMPLEMENTATION
(Pre-Operation)

DEPARTMENT HEAD, LEAD TEACHER

Tasks	Functions	Involvement	Process
1. Plant-Equipment	Designing	Direct	Recommending
2. Policy-Money-Specifications	Planning	Direct	Recommending
3. Evaluation-Program	Designing	Direct	Study-Researching
4. Evaluation-Staff	Implementing-Directing	Direct	Recommending
5. Evaluation-Learners	Designing	Direct	Recommending
6. Orientation-Climate	Analyzing	Direct	Recommending
7. Training	Designing	Direct	Recommending
8. Materials-Management	Implementing-Directing	Direct	Recommending
9. Materials-Staff Competence	Designing	Direct	Recommending
10. Organization-School Staff	Planning	Direct	Consulting
11. Schedule-School Pupil	Planning	Represented	Consulting
12. Staff Selection	Designing	Direct	Recommending

IMPLEMENTATION
(Operation)

DEPARTMENT HEAD, LEAD TEACHER

Tasks	*Functions*	*Involvement*	*Process*
1. Plant-Equipment	Evaluating	Direct	Recommending
2. Policy-Money-Specifications	Coordinating	Direct	Utilizing
3. Evaluation-Program	Monitoring	Direct	Recommending
4. Evaluation-Staff	Implementing-Directing	Direct	Recommending
5. Evaluation-Learners	Implementing-Directing	Delegated	Recommending
6. Orientation-Climate	Monitoring	Direct	Recommending
7. Training	Implementing-Directing	Direct	Recommending
8. Materials-Management	Implementing-Directing	Direct	Directing-Appointing
9. Materials-Staff Competence	Implementing-Directing	Direct	Recommending
10. Organization-School Staff	Implementing-Directing	Direct	Recommending
11. Schedule-School Pupil	Monitoring	Direct	Recommending
12. Staff Selection	Evaluating	Direct	Recommending

IMPLEMENTATION
(Pre-Operation)

TEACHER

Tasks	*Functions*	*Involvement*	*Process*
1. Plant-Equipment	Planning	Represented	Recommending
2. Policy-Money-Specifications	Planning	Represented	Recommending
3. Evaluation-Program	Planning	Represented	Recommending
4. Evaluation-Staff	Planning	Represented	Recommending
5. Evaluation-Learners	Designing	Direct	Recommending
6. Orientation-Climate	Designing	Direct	Recommending
7. Training	Planning	Represented	Informing-Responding
8. Materials-Management	Planning	Represented	Informing-Responding
9. Materials-Staff Competence	Planning	Represented	Informing-Responding
10. Organization-School Staff	Communicating	Represented	Recommending
11. Schedule-School Pupil	Planning	Represented	Recommending
12. Staff Selection	Communicating	Represented	Informing-Responding

IMPLEMENTATION
(Operation)

TEACHER

Tasks	*Functions*	*Involvement*	*Process*
1. Plant-Equipment	Coordinating	Direct	Utilizing
2. Policy-Money-Specifications	Communicating	Delegated	Utilizing
3. Evaluation-Program	Analyzing	Delegated	Recommending
4. Evaluation-Staff	Attending	Represented	Informing-Responding
5. Evaluation-Learners	Deciding	Direct	Directing-Appointing
6. Orientation-Climate	Analyzing	Direct	Informing-Responding
7. Training	Attending	Direct	Utilizing
8. Materials-Management	Communicating	Delegated	Utilizing
9. Materials-Staff Competence	Attending	Delegated	Informing-Responding
10. Organization-School Staff	Attending	Delegated	Informing-Responding
11. Schedule-School Pupil	Communicating	Direct	Recommending
12. Staff Selection	Attending	Delegated	Informing-Responding

IMPLEMENTATION
(Pre-Operation)

AIDE

Tasks	*Functions*	*Involvement*	*Process*
1. Plant-Equipment	Attending	Represented	Informing-Responding
2. Policy-Money-Specifications	Attending	Represented	Informing-Responding
3. Evaluation-Program	Attending	Represented	Informing-Responding
4. Evaluation-Staff	Attending	Represented	Informing-Responding
5. Evaluation-Learners	Attending	Represented	Informing-Responding
6. Orientation-Climate	Attending	Direct	Informing-Responding
7. Training	Attending	Direct	Informing-Responding
8. Materials-Management	Attending	Direct	Conducting Training Session
9. Materials-Staff Competence	Attending	Represented	Conducting Training Session
10. Organization-School Staff	Attending	Represented	Informing-Responding
11. Schedule-School Pupil	Attending	Represented	Informing-Responding
12. Staff Selection	Attending	Represented	Informing-Responding

IMPLEMENTATION
(Operation)

AIDE

Tasks	*Functions*	*Involvement*	*Process*
1. Plant-Equipment	Attending	Represented	Informing-Responding
2. Policy-Money-Specifications	Attending	Represented	Utilizing
3. Evaluation-Program	Attending	Represented	Informing-Responding
4. Evaluation-Staff	Attending	Represented	Informing-Responding
5. Evaluation-Learners	Coordinating	Represented	Informing-Responding
6. Orientation-Climate	Communicating	Represented	Informing-Responding
7. Training	Attending	Represented	Utilizing
8. Materials-	Attending	Represented	Utilizing
Management	Attending	Represented	Utilizing
9. Materials-Staff Competence	Attending	Represented	Utilizing
10. Organization-School Staff	Attending	Represented	Utilizing
11. Schedule-School Pupil	Attending	Represented	Utilizing
12. Staff Selection	Attending	Represented	Utilizing

IMPLEMENTATION
(Pre-Operation)

LEARNER

Tasks	*Functions*	*Involvement*	*Process*
1. Plant-Equipment	Attending	Represented	Informing-Responding
2. Policy-Money-Specifications	Attending	Represented	Informing-Responding
3. Evaluation-Program	Attending	Represented	Informing-Responding
4. Evaluation-Staff	Attending	Represented	Informing-Responding
5. Evaluation-Learners	Communicating	Represented	Informing-Responding
6. Orientation-Climate	Communicating	Represented	Informing-Responding
7. Training	Communicating	Represented	Informing-Responding
8. Materials-Management	Attending	Represented	Informing-Responding
9. Materials-Staff Competence	Attending	Represented	Informing-Responding
10. Organization-School Staff	Attending	Represented	Informing-Responding
11. Schedule-School Pupil	Communicating	Represented	Informing-Responding
12. Staff Selection	Attending	Represented	Informing-Responding

IMPLEMENTATION
(Operation)

LEARNER

Tasks	*Functions*	*Involvement*	*Process*
1. Plant-Equipment	Attending	Represented	Utilizing
2. Policy-Money-Specifications	Attending	Represented	Utilizing
3. Evaluation-Program	Communicating	Represented	Informing-Responding
4. Evaluation-Staff	Communicating	Represented	Informing-Responding
5. Evaluation-Learners	Attending	Represented	Utilizing
6. Orientation-Climate	Communicating	Represented	Informing-Responding
7. Training	Attending	Represented	Utilizing
8. Materials-Management	Attending	Represented	Utilizing
9. Materials-Staff Competence	Attending	Represented	Utilizing
10. Organization-School Staff	Attending	Represented	Utilizing
11. Schedule-School Pupil	Attending	Represented	Utilizing
12. Staff Selection	Attending	Represented	Utilizing

IMPLEMENTATION
(Pre-Operation)

PARENT

Tasks	*Functions*	*Involvement*	*Process*
1. Plant-Equipment	Communicating	Delegated	Informing-Responding
2. Policy-Money-Specifications	Planning	Delegated	Recommending
3. Evaluation-Program	Communicating	Delegated	Informing-Responding
4. Evaluation-Staff	Communicating	Represented	Informing-Responding
5. Evaluation-Learners	Communicating	Represented	Informing-Responding
6. Orientation-Climate	Planning	Delegated	Informing-Responding
7. Training	Communicating	Represented	Informing-Responding
8. Materials-Management	Attending	Represented	Informing-Responding
9. Materials-Staff Competence	Attending	Represented	Informing-Responding
10. Organization-School Staff	Attending	Represented	Informing-Responding
11. Schedule-School Pupil	Attending	Represented	Informing-Responding
12. Staff Selection	Attending	Represented	Informing-Responding

IMPLEMENTATION
(Operation)

PARENT

Tasks	*Functions*	*Involvement*	*Process*
1. Plant-Equipment	Attending	Represented	Utilizing
2. Policy-Money-Specifications	Attending	Represented	Utilizing
3. Evaluation-Program	Attending	Represented	Utilizing
4. Evaluation-Staff	Attending	Represented	Utilizing
5. Evaluation-Learners	Attending	Represented	Utilizing
6. Orientation-Climate	Attending	Represented	Utilizing
7. Training	Attending	Represented	Utilizing
8. Materials-Management	Attending	Represented	Utilizing
9. Materials-Staff Competence	Attending	Represented	Utilizing
10. Organization-School Staff	Attending	Represented	Utilizing
11. Schedule-School Pupil	Attending	Represented	Utilizing
12. Staff Selection	Attending	Represented	Utilizing

APPENDIX E

Representative Impact Strategies and Techniques

Throughout the text mention has been made of various styles, approaches, and technologies for change. Each of these impact strategies has a developed structure, related processes, techniques, and competencies. Each has been the subject of many publications and research efforts.

Since only selected elements from these resources were used in the body of the book, the following section has been included to provide some starting points for further study. The following sketches are not presumed to describe the range, depth, or style of these strategies adequately. Rather, it is hoped that the descriptions will provide an introduction to possibilities, making it possible to proceed on the basis of interest or intent.

In such a reference section*, a question always arises as to which organizing principle will be most useful. In this case, an attempt is made to cluster the techniques for a similarity in approach or in the related utilizations (see Figure E-1). Some tend to suggest a task orientation; others, a human relations orientation. The placement may reflect the author's bias rather than accurately interpreting the position desired by the various authorities cited. With that caveat in mind, the reader is encouraged to make his own decisions as to orientation, style, and utility.

1. *Individual Growth Modes:*

    Transcendental Meditation
    Interpersonal Relations
      Parent Effectiveness Training
      Transactional Analysis

*This section has been developed in collaboration with Dr. Martina Bryant, Staff Assistant, Curriculum and Supervision Department, University of Georgia, Athens, Georgia.

Helping (Carkhuff)
Self-Actualization
Mock Reality Techniques
Role Playing
Simulation–Gaming
Clinical Supervision
Competency Based Instruction

2. *Instructional Improvement Techniques:*

Programmed Instruction
Computer Technology
Computer Managed Instruction
Computer Assisted Instruction

IMPACT STRATEGIES

1. Individual growth modes.
2. Instructional improvement techniques.
3. Organizational approaches.
4. Operational procedures.
5. Assessment alternatives.

FIGURE E–1

The Voucher Plan
Performance Contracting
Microteaching
Behavioral Objectives
Systematic Observation and Interaction Analysis
Force Field Analysis

3. *Organizational Approaches:*

Organizational Behavior
  Organizational Health
  Organizational Climate
  Organizational Development
Group Processes
  Group Dynamics
  Sensitivity Training and "T" Groups
Management Philosophy—Theory X and Theory Y
Curriculum Council

4. *Operational Procedures:*

Systems Approach
Management by Objectives
Program, Planning, Budgeting, and Evaluating System
Educational Futures

5. *Assessment Alternatives:*

Formative and Summative Evaluation
Accountability
Action Research

SCIENCE OF CREATIVE INTELLIGENCE (SCI) OR TRANSCENDENTAL MEDITATION (TM)

The science of creative intelligence or transcendental meditation is a thought process by which individuals meditate and achieve restful alertness and self-realization. TM is one of many Eastern philosophical imports, which include Yoga, Zen, and Sufi. The chief proponent of SCI–TM, Maharishi Mahesh Yogi, a college physics major, believes that TM alleviates stress and allows creative intelligence to flow from the inner person to a level of conscious awareness from which the individual perceives it and acts. Through the reduction of stress and a growth of conscious awareness, one possibly may become more at ease, energetic, healthy, creative, clear-minded, and perceptive.

Scientific data establish the fact that TM can lower the heart rate, oxygen consumption, and brain wave patterns. Evidence indicates that TM reduces the chance of stress, sickness, and cravings for alcohol, tobacco, and drugs. Research in TM is being carried on throughout the world—with some study here in the United States by the National Institute of Health, the Pentagon, Harvard Medical School, and the Stanford Research Institute.

When applied to educational uses, claims are made that TM can aid in the reduction of drug abuse and social tension within a classroom. It can improve attitudes and behavior and offer a chance for achieving stated goals for the education of students without sacrificing performance goals. For school personnel, TM can lead to a more effective, creative, and rewarding working opportunity. For many, TM, through intellectual analysis and direct experience of the field from which all knowledge springs, may provide a means for achieving individual self-realization or actualization, a goal espoused by many systems. In order to facilitate individual attainment of this potential, TM is being furthered through formalized training of SCI teachers, preparation of syllabi and teaching aids, and the offering of TM as a course at all educational levels and through many agencies.

REFERENCES

Driscoll, F., "TM as a Secondary School Subject." *Phi Delta Kappan*, 54 (1972) pp. 236-237.

Levine, P., "Transcendental Meditation and the Science of Creative Intelligence," *Phi Delta Kappan*, 54 (1972) pp. 231-235.

Narango, C., and Ornstein, R. E., *On the Psychology of Meditation.* New York: Viking Company, 1971.

INTERPERSONAL RELATIONS

The following, presented as summaries of ideas and writings, offer insights into the relationships that develop as two or more individuals interact. The latter four summaries are especially useful in presenting techniques that may be used for achieving healthy human relations.

In *Games People Play*, Berne asserts that people go through life playing certain games in their interpersonal relationships. Games are played to avoid confronting reality, to conceal ulterior motives, to rationalize activities, or to avoid actual participation. Berne analyzes seven categories of games: life, marital, sexual, party, underworld, consulting room, and "good" games that ascertain how people achieve new self-awareness.

Gordon purports that Parent Effectiveness Training (P.E.T.) provides effective conflict management methods in order to encourage children to accept responsibilities for solving their own problems. Parents may be winners (conflict resolution won by parents with the child as a loser), losers (the child wins as the parent loses), and oscillators (strict and lenient, tough and easy, restrictive and permissive, and winning and losing). The alternative to the "win-lose" method is the no-lose method of resolving conflict, helping parents to learn how to use the techniques of active listening. In Parent Effectiveness Training, techniques are prescribed as to how one should listen to children, how to talk to kids, and how to modify unacceptable behavior. A discussion of parental power also is presented.

Harris clarifies and extends the concept of transactional analysis that was outlined by Berne. Transactional analysis confronts an individual with the fact that he is responsible for what happens in his future, no matter what has happened in the past. Three active elements make up an individual's personality role: The Parent, the Adult, and the Child (P–A–C). The Parent personifies the "do's" and "do not's," which are implanted in the individual during his earliest years and then automatically accepted as truth. The Child represents spontaneous emotion. Both the Parent and the Child must be kept in proper relation to the Adult, whose function is that of grinding out decisions after computing information. The Adult's information is derived from three sources: the Parent, the Child, and the data that the Adult has gathered and is gathering. Through transactional analysis, one seeks to strengthen and free the Adult from the archaic recordings in Parent and Child in order to make free choice and the creation of new options possible.

Klopf realizes that changes are facilitated by individuals who are prepared to accept them. He has categorized the major processes of interactions that enable people to meet change successfully. The four processes are consultation, dialogue, encounter, and confrontation. Consultation helps a consultee to understand a situation, his position, strategies, and needs, and to help himself. Dialogue and exchange, which involves two to four individuals, is a mutual exploration of an idea important to the group. Encounter is a meeting of two or more individuals who purposely face a situation in terms of themselves and their roles as different individuals in the situation. No facades are allowed. Confrontation is a planned activity, initiated by someone based on the understandings of the persons, the conflict, and the quality of the relationships.

Robert R. Carkhuff in *Helping and Human Relations*, Volumes I and II, deals with all phases of effective helping relations programs in terms of identifiable and repeatable communications operations. Carkhuff's helping process is guided by "Four R's for Helping": (1) The right of an individual to intervene in another person's life. (2) The responsibility the helper must assume when he intervenes. (3) The role a helper plays in the process of helping. (4) The realization by the person of his own resources for helping.

The effective helper is personally committed to his own emergence, which frees him to make personal commitments to others. The helper must be self-actualized; for, if he is not, he can not enable a helpee to become so. Training then focuses upon the change or gain of the trainee himself. Systematic human resource development is the aim of the training process. Systematic programs are developed to equip people with training techniques necessary for them, and which, in turn, are necessary to produce effective people. Helpees are transformed into helpers, forming a system of developed human resources.

Volume I of Carkhuff's book is concerned with the selection and training of helpee's through the use of a comprehensive model of the helping relationship or process. Volume II reviews the helping process treatment literature, elaborates on modes of treatment, and presents issues and problems involved in making systematic inquiries into effective treatment.

The concerns of supervision demand that changes occur constantly. Supervisors, consequently, should have a personal openness to the idea of change. Such an openness will help them to engage in their tasks more completely and also to assist other educational personnel in accepting change.

REFERENCES

Berne, Eric, *Games People Play.* New York: Grove Press, Inc., 1964.

________________, *What Do You Say After You Say Hello?* New York: Bantam Books, 1974.

Carkhuff, R. R., *Helping and Human Relations.* Volumes I and II, New York: Holt, Rinehart, and Winston, 1969.

Gordon, T., *P.E.T.—Parent Effectiveness Training.* New York: Peter H. Wyden, Inc., 1970.

Harris, T., *I'm OK—You're OK: A Practical Guide to Transactional Analysis.* New York: Harper and Row, 1969.

Klopf, G., "Interaction Processes and Change," *Educational Leadership,* 27:(1970) pp. 334-338.

SELF-ACTUALIZATION

The following are descriptions of self-actualization theories as offered by four leading psychologists. Combs, in his writings, describes four characteristics of the perceptual field that underlies the behavior of one who is a truly adequate or self-actualized person. These characteristics are as follows:

1. The self-actualized person has a positive view of self that is learned from the ways in which he is treated by those in his environment.
2. The self-actualized person has the capacity to identify with his fellow human beings. Such an expanded feeling of the self allows him to identify with great blocks of mankind without references to race, creed, color, or personality.
3. The self-actualized person possesses perceptual fields constantly open to experience, thus making change and adjustment possible.
4. The self-actualized person has a rich and extensive perceptual field that provides an understanding of the events in which he is involved.

From a belief that all perceiving is learned, Combs implies that individuals can be taught how to perceive and, thus, how to become self-actualized beings. Combs says that educators, often unknowingly, have been effecting changes in perception since teaching was begun.

Jourard (1971) feels that man can attain health and full personal development only in so far as he gains courage to be himself with others and only when he finds goals that have meaning for him. These goals must include the reshaping of society so that it is fit for all to live and grow. Man will permit himself to be known when he believes his audience is one of goodwill. Self-disclosure follows an attitude of love and trust and is the key to self-actualization.

Maslow's organismic psychology, called by him a holistic dynamic point of view, results in a need hierarchy that considers five levels of human needs in relation to each other and classifies and arranges them in a hierarchy. For example, Need B can be satisfied only after one has satisfied Need A, a more powerful, "prepotent" need. Further, no need can be treated as if it were isolated or discrete; every drive is related to the state of satisfaction or dissatisfaction of other devices. When a need is fairly well satisfied, the next prepotent need emerges and tends to dominate the individual's concern.

Maslow's "Need Hierarchy" follows and is listed from most potent to least potent:

1. Physiological Needs—need for food and water.
2. Safety Needs—need for protection against danger, threat, and deprivation.
3. Social Needs—need for belongings, association, acceptance, for giving and receiving, friendship, and love.
4. Ego or Egotistic Needs—need which relates to one's self-esteem, self-confidence, independence, achievement, competence, need for knowledge, and those related to one's reputation, status, recognition, appreciation, and respect.
5. Self-actualization Needs—need for realizing one's own potentialities for continued self-development, for being creative in the broadest sense of the term.

Rogers views the self-actualized individual as one who becomes a fully functioning person. Noted for his concept on non-directive counseling, he believes that human beings are always striving for, or moving toward, an implicit goal of becoming a fully functioning person.

As he describes the fully functioning person, Rogers has identified three principles at work:

1. Individuals move toward being open toward their experiences.
2. Each person moves toward a more acceptant and existential being.
3. The individual increases trust in his organism as a means of arriving at the most satisfying behavior in each existential situation.

In sum, a fully functioning person is one who has good psychological health, is dynamic, is sensitive to all his experiences, lives with the immediate, trusts his being, is creative, and views life as a wide variety of experiences.

REFERENCES

Association for Supervision and Curriculum Development, *Perceiving, Behaving, Becoming.* Yearbook. Washington, D.C.: author, 1961.
Avila, D. L., Combs, A. W., and Purkey, W. W., *The Helping Relationship Sourcebook.* Boston: Allyn and Bacon, Inc., 1972.
Combs, A. W., Avila, D. L., and Purkey, W. W., *Helping Relationships: Basic Concepts for the Helping Professions.* Boston: Allyn and Bacon, Inc., 1972.
Combs, A. W., and Snygg, D., *Individual Behavior: A Perceptual Approach to Behavior.* New York: Harper and Brothers, 1959.
Jourard, S. M., *The Transparent Self.* New York: D. Van Nostrand Company, 1971.
Maslow, A. H., *Motivation and Personality.* New York: Harper, 1954.
_____, *New Knowledge in Human Values.* New York: Harper, 1959.
_____ *Self-Actualizing People: A Study of Psychological Health.* New York: Brooklyn College Bookstore, 1951.
_____, *Toward a Psychology of Being.* Princeton: D. Van Nostrand Company, 1962.
Rogers, C. R., *Client-Centered Therapy: Its Current Practice, Implications, and Theory.* Boston: Houghton Mifflin Company, 1951.
_____, *Freedom to Learn.* Columbus, Ohio: Charles E. Merrill Publishing Company, 1969.
_____, *On Becoming a Person.* Boston: Houghton Mifflin Company, 1961.

MOCK-REALITY TECHNIQUES

Education strategists are producing an abundance of techniques that will contribute to an understanding of the dynamics that occur during educational tasks, such as decision making, goal setting, and judging products. Two such techniques employing a "mock-reality" approach will be discussed. Both allow a group to confront a hypothetical problem, experience the perplexities of solving it, and offer possible solutions for it. The hypothetical problem or need situation is one that corresponds to what may be a "real-life" dilemma in education.

Role Playing

Role playing takes place when a group watches "actors" enact roles for the purpose of analyzing some real life situation in which the group is interested. The performance is usually followed by discussion. The skit may present a situation so that the audience can be helped to understand what happens or happened in a given circumstance. The main point is that role playing is used to make a situation, problem, or incident real; and thereby, makes it possible for the group to understand it and to discuss or cope with it.

Role playing can be a powerful method that provides a close-to-reality base for personal understanding and insights and for group discussion and training. Used in human relations, leadership, and sensitivity training after Dr. J. L. Moreno of the Psycho-Dramatic Institute in New York introduced methods that he called "Psychodrame" and "sociodrame," role playing allows the trainee to identify with the role playing participants. Thus, the trainee is enabled to appraise his/her own actions towards others and their reactions to him/her.

Simulation or Gaming

Simulation or gaming is a miniature representation or symbolic model of a large-scale system or process. Simulations are real, dynamic, and operating situations, as opposed to static or pictorial representations. Simulation and games usually imply use of replicas of events in phased sequences, and opportunities for change and development to reach a desired goal during the sequences. Thus, these are educational tools that can involve and motivate participants quickly and intensely into a learning process. They can provide useful opportunities for experience in problem solving, planning, analyzing, communicating, negotiating, and using of resources. Participants can develop intellectual, emotional, and social capabilities through the use of simulations and games.

REFERENCES

Adult Education Association, *How to Use Role Playing* (leadership pamphlets). Washington, D.C.: author, 1955.

Bavelas, A., "Role Playing in Management Training." *Social Sciences,* M.I.T., Department of Economics and Social Science, 2:21 (1947).

Bradford, L. P., and Lippitt, R., "Role Playing in Supervisory Training." *Personnel,* 22:(1946) pp. 358-369.

Broodbeth, S., "Simulation in the Social Studies: An Overview." *Social Education,* 33:(1969).

Burgess, P. M., Peterson, L. E., and Frantz, C. D., "Organizing Simulated Environments." *Social Education,* 33:(1969) pp. 185-192.

Chesler, M., and Fox, R., *Role Playing in the Classroom.* Chicago: Science Research Associates, 1966.

Coleman, J. S., "Academic Games and Learning." *The Bulletin of the National Association of Secondary School Principals,* 52:325 (1968) pp. 62-67.

Cruickshank, D. R., "The Use of Simulation in Teacher Education: A Developing Phenomenon." *Journal of Teacher Education,* 20:1 (1969) pp. 23-26.

Hyman, R. T., "The Name of the Game is Teaching." *Teaching: Vantage Points for Study,* New York: J. B. Lippincott Company, 1968.

Klein, A., *Role Playing in Leadership Training and Group Problems.* New York: Associates Press, 1966.

Macdonald, J. B., "Gamesmanship in the Classroom." In *Teaching: Vantage Points for Study* by R. T. Hyman, editor. New York: J. B. Lippincott Company, 1968.

Maier, N. R. F., Salem, A. R., and Maier, A. F., *Supervisory and Executive Development: A Manual for Role Playing.* New York: Wiley, 1957.
Miles, M. B., *Learning to Work in Groups.* New York: Teachers College, Columbia University, 1959.
Moreno, J. L., *Psychodrama,* Volume 1, New York: Beacon House, 1946.
Rasmussen, G. R., and Hughes, L. W., "Simulation: It's the Real Thing." *The Bulletin of the National Association of Secondary School Principals,* 56:(1972) pp. 76-81.

CLINICAL SUPERVISION

Clinical supervision focuses upon the improvement of a teacher's classroom instruction through direct observation. It encourages a close relationship between a supervisor and a classroom teacher as they work cooperatively in planning and evaluating the observation period. As the two work together, their ultimate aim is to improve the teacher's performance in the classroom. The supervisor and teacher use a variety of data to provide them with information regarding the classroom behavior of the teacher. The data include, principally, records of classroom events supplemented by information about the teacher's and student's perceptions, beliefs, attitudes, and knowledge relevant to instruction.

The analysis of the classroom events and the relationship between the teacher and supervisor are important features of the clinical supervision approach. From this approach, a teacher is able to confront instructional problems with the aid of someone trained especially for the task. It is hoped that a feeling of mutual trust is developed between the teacher and supervisor as they plan improvement strategies. Out of this relationship and from data secured primarily through a planned observation period should come suggestions for the teacher to use in improving his/her instructional behavior. The basic model for clinical supervision consists of five stages:

1. A *pre-observation conference* between the teacher and supervisor.
2. An *observation* of the teacher in an instructional setting by the supervisor.
3. An *analysis of data* obtained by the supervisor and an *outline of conference strategy* by both parties.
4. A *supervision conference.*
5. A *post-conference analysis.*

REFERENCES

Cogan, M. L. *Clinical Supervision.* Boston: Houghton Mifflin Company, 1973.
Goldhammer, R., *Clinical Supervision: Special Methods for the Supervision of Teachers.* New York: Holt, Rinehart, and Winston, Inc., 1969.
Lewis, A. J., and Miel, A., *Supervision for Improved Instruction.* Belmont, California: Wadsworth Publishing Company, Inc., 1972.

COMPETENCY BASED INSTRUCTION

Competency based instruction is often referred to as a byproduct of the behavioral objectives movement as well as concern for accountability and cost. It is one of a cluster of "competency" concepts with which educational reformists hope to provide an answer to the public's call for increased learning outputs. The nucleus of competency based instruction involves the provision of opportunities for a learner to reach a pre-specified objective.

In a competency based instructional program, an attempt is made to base instructional strategies and measurements of behavior upon competencies that have been predetermined. The process of competency based instruction entails: (1) The identification and translation of desired competencies into precise behavioral objectives. (2) A pre-assessment of learner behavior in regard to the desired competency. (3) The development of content. (4) The formulation of multi-options that will enable the learner to attain the pre-specified competency. (5) The utilization of procedures to assess the learner's achievement of the objective in accordance with stated criteria. Evaluation procedures generally make provisions for the sampling of learner behavior at several times during the instructional experience. As a formative evaluative measure, this sampling indicates the need for improvement to the learner.

Howsam and Houston (1972) identify two other characteristics of competency based instruction. First, they suggest that there is a public sharing of the objectives, criteria for meeting them, assessment procedures, and alternative activities in competency based instruction. Second, this type of instruction, they indicate, places the accountability for meeting the criteria on the learner.

Related to this indication is the generally accepted notion that a program of competence based instruction is ideally a program of individualized instruction. Such a notion embraces the belief that competency based instruction allows a learner to work according to his/her particular mode of learning and at whatever rate is most suitable to him/her. A competency based program of instruction should also make allowances for the learner to assist in determining what competencies he/she is expected to acquire.

REFERENCES

Burns, Richard W., and Klingstedt, Joe Lars, editors, *Competency-Based Education: An Introduction.* Englewood Cliffs, New Jersey: Educational Technology Publications, 1973.

Davies, Ivor K., *Competency-Based Learning: Technology, Management, and Design.* New York: McGraw-Hill, 1973.

Howsam, Robert B., and Houston, W. Robert, "Change and Challenge." In *Competency-Based Education: Progress, Problems, and Prospects*, edited by Robert B. Howsam and W. Robert Houston. Chicago: Science Research Associates, 1972.

Popham, W. J., and Baker, Eva L., *Systematic Instruction.* Englewood Cliffs, New Jersey: Prentice-Hall, 1970.

Schmieder, Allen, *Competency-Based Education: The State of the Scene.* Washington, D.C.: American Association of Colleges for Teacher Education and the ERIC Clearinghouse on Teacher Education, 1973.

PROGRAMMED INSTRUCTION

Programmed instruction is one of numerous technologies developed to facilitate learning. One important feature is that it is based on principles from studies in behavioral psychology. The ideas of shaping behavior through specific objectives, providing feedback, and giving reinforcement (characterized by the technique of programmed instruction) were derived from the basics of behaviorist writings.

Instruction using programmed material refers to the use of carefully constructed information units presented in a sequential manner. The learner, using the material, is guided through the sequence until he/she has reached a performance level specified in the objectives of the programmed material. Upon completion of each unit, the learner is given directions for the next move. If, for instance, the unit was successfully completed, it is indicated that he/she should proceed. A wrong response for a unit, however, may require restudying the unit before moving to subsequent ones.

Programmed instruction is of two basic types. The linear type has the learner making responses that are reinforced immediately. In constructing this type, planners give care to each frame so that a correct response is almost certain. The branching type, on the other hand, has the learner's responses determine the next units. For example, if he/she answers incorrectly, he/she is guided to branches that will enable learning the concept required for the correct response. Once this is accomplished, the student returns to the main line.

A real benefit of programmed instruction is that it fosters the idea of individualized instruction and independent study. It provides a means for a learner to work at a personally convenient pace and it offers constant feedback regarding progress. Also, the teacher who makes use of programmed material is in a better position to guide and direct the individual learner's particular learning needs.

As programmed materials become accessible, the supervisor's responsibility may be to provide basic information about them to teachers. The supervisor may also wish to clarify the concept of programmed instruction and to translate their uses into those that are applicable to a particular teaching–learning situation.

REFERENCES

Glaser, R., ed., *Teaching Machines and Programmed Learning.* Washington, D.C.: National Education Association, 1965.

Lumsden, D. B., "Individualizing Instruction Through the Use of Programmed Instruction." *Educational Forum,* 38:(1974) pp. 145-52.

Scherman, A., and Scherman, M., "Free Choice, Final Performance, and Attitudes Toward Different Types of Programmed Instruction." *Journal of Education,* 155:(1973) pp. 56-63.

Schramm, W., *Programmed Instruction Today and Tomorrow.* New York: Fund for Achievement of Education, 1962.

Skinner, B. J., "The Science of Learning and the Art of Teaching." *Harvard Educational Review,* 24:(1954) pp. 86-97.

COMPUTER TECHNOLOGY

A derivative of the electronic machine age, the computer has been utilized most frequently in military, industrial, and scientific organizations. In recent years, various segments of the educational arena have adapted the computer for their purposes. Two current educational innovations that involve computer technology make available systems for facilitating the instructional process.

Computer-Managed Instruction

Computer-managed instruction is conceived to aid the teacher in planning, implementing, and evaluating an instructional process. When a specific instructional experience is desired for a specified group and/or student, computer-managed instruction can be of immense value. It offers a means for: (1) choosing objectives, (2) identifying alternative learning strategies, (3) compiling instructional materials, and (4) engaging in management techniques necessary for the particular teaching-learning experience. The evaluation phase of the experience is considered in the provision of procedures for making diagnostic, intermediate, and terminal evaluations. Both students and the instructional program can be objects, "subjects," for the evaluative measures.

A well-designed system of computer-managed instruction allows teachers to prescribe instructional programs that are: (1) varied, (2) individualized in a way similar to Glaser's IPI, (3) well monitored, and (4) supported by the necessary instructional materials. Because of the pluralistic American society, the non-rigidness implied in the concept of computer-managed instruction is beneficial to those concerned.

The Westinghouse Learning Corporation, together with the American Institute for Research, has developed perhaps the best known system for computer-managed instruction. Called PLAN, for *P*rogram for

*L*earning in *A*ccordance with *N*eeds, the system has been operating in schools across the country since the late sixties.

Computer-Assisted Instruction

In computer-assisted instruction, the student becomes involved with the computer during the instructional process. This innovation embodies the idea that the computer will present to a student carefully prepared units that have been selected especially for him. The computer units for instruction are designed in regard to specific objectives, activities, and outcomes that are related to student variables. The choice of an instructional unit for use with a student and/or group then will be dependent upon the student/group variables operative in the learning situation.

The possibilities that computer-assisted instruction offers are manifold. As computer technology becomes more practical and accessible, the student might be one of the first to reap the rewards.

REFERENCES

Anderson, G. E., "Computer-Assisted Instruction: State of the Art." *Technology in Education: Challenge and Change*, by F. J. Pula and R. J. Gaff (Editors). Worthington, Ohio: Charles A. Jones Publishing Company, 1972.

Brudner, H. J., "Computer-Managed Instruction." *Technology in Education: Challenge and Change*, by F. J. Pula and R. J. Gaff (Editors). Worthington, Ohio: Charles A. Jones Publishing Company, 1972.

Cooley, W. W., and Glaser, R., "The Computer and Individualized Instruction." *Science*, 166:1969) pp. 574-582.

Eisele, J. E., *Computer-Assisted Planning of Curriculum and Instruction*. Englewood Cliffs, New Jersey: Educational Technology Publications, 1970.

Flanagan, J. C., "Functional Education for the Seventies." *Phi Delta Kappan*, 49:(1967) pp. 27-32.

McMullen, D. W., "Generative CAI: Procedures and Prospects." *Educational Technology*, 14:2 (1974) pp. 27-30.

Reed, F. C., et al., "Model for the Development of Computer-Assisted Instruction Programs." *Educational Technology*, 14:3 (1974) pp. 12-20.

Schoen, H. L., "CAI Development and Good Educational Practice." *Educational Technology*, 14:4 (1974) pp. 54-56.

THE VOUCHER PLAN

The voucher plan is one of a number of educational reform strategies that have been proposed to ameliorate growing discontent among citizens with school systems across the country and to provide an alternative or choice in education. The basic concept of the voucher plan is not complicated; it may be considered in terms of a three stage design:

1. Parents of a school age child receive vouchers usually worth an amount equal to the average per child expenditure of a school system.
2. The parents then enroll their child in a school commensurate with their value system; the vouchers are given to the school in which the child enrolls.
3. The school receives remittance for the vouchers from the educational funding agency.

The basic voucher plan may have unlimited variations that usually emanate from the particular situations in which the plan is used. Two illustrative voucher plans that are frequently discussed in the literature may clarify this point.

The Jencks plan, advanced by Christopher Jencks, is characterized by variations that include the following:

1. Vouchers cannot be supplemented by parents.
2. Vouchers can be supplemented for low-income pupils by the funding agencies.
3. Both public and private schools may participate in the plan.
4. Schools cannot indulge in discriminatory practices.

Another plan at Alum Rock, California has the following features:

1. Parents are given guidance in making decisions about educational choices.
2. Only public school programs are available.
3. Program choices include the traditional as well as the more innovative offerings.

The voucher concept is still in the early stages of development. While numerous proposals have been made, they yet have to be implemented, evaluated, and revised. Only through larger-scale experimentation can the real benefits or defects of the concept be discerned.

Von Haden and King (1971) have attempted to make some determination about the use of voucher plans. They feel that, in one respect, voucher plans offer a way to increase educational provisions for all students. But, in another respect, they may create nothing more than a "splintering" effect on the system of public education in America.

REFERENCES

Jencks, C., "Educational Vouchers." *The New Republic*, 163:1 (1970) pp. 19-21.

——, *Educational Vouchers: Report on Financing Education by Payment to Parents.* Cambridge, Massachusetts: Center for the Study of Public Policy, 1970.

Mecklenburgen, J., "Vouchers at Alum Rock," *Phi Delta Kappan*, 54:1 (1972).

Sizer, T., and Whitten, P., "A Proposal for a Poor Children's Bill of Rights." *Psychology Today*, 2:3 (1968) pp. 59-63.

Spears, H., "Please Get in Line for Your Voucher." *The School Administrator*, Washington, D.C.: American Association of School Administrators, 1970.

Von Haden, H. I., and King, J. M., *Innovations in Education: Their Pros and Cons.* Worthington, Ohio: Charles A. Jones Publishing Company, 1971.
"Voucher Test for Schools Working Well." *The Atlanta Journal and Constitution,* July 7, 1974, p. 15.

PERFORMANCE CONTRACTING

Performance contracting is an educational idea that utilizes concepts from the world of industry and business. It occurs when a school system engages the services of outside agencies to perform certain instructional opportunities for a group of learners. The performance contract is usually based on a proposal submitted by a school system to an agency being considered to undertake an educational learning task. The proposal has among its contents an explanation of the services desired, the expected results, and reimbursement details. The terms for reimbursement, generally, depend upon the expected results and the achieved results.

When a firm signs a contract with a school system, it takes responsibility for designated phases of the instructional program. For example, it may contract to supply the curriculum designs, devise instructional strategies, obtain materials, locate audio-visuals and computer hard- and software, and organize staff personnel. In many instances, the staff will consist of persons who enter the situation with the firm and others who are already employed by the school system.

Financing performance contracts may be the responsibility of several organizations. The U.S. Office of Economic Opportunity has taken a lead in sponsoring some experimental programs. If performance contracts prove effective as an educational innovation, additional funds for financing may come from the federal government, state boards of education, or local school systems.

Programs involving performance contracting may extend for one year or more. It is desirable, however, that more than one year is allowed for the operation. Blaschke, a noted proponent of performance contracts, has offered the turnkey concept in order to keep successful programs operating. The turnkey concept means that a "program" will be turned over to the contracting school officials at the end of the contract. The school system, in receiving all components of the contract program, utilizes them in an effort to continue the program that was initiated by the "commercial" agency.

REFERENCES

Berson, M., " 'Texarkana and Gary,' A Tale of Two Performance Contracts." *Childhood Education,* 47:(1971) pp. 339-343.

Blaschke, C., *Performance Contracting: Who Profits Most?* Bloomington, Ind.: Phi Delta Kappa Educational Foundation, 1972.

Blaschke, C., Brings, P., and Martin, R., "The Performance Contract—Turnkey Approach to Urban System Reform," *Educational Technology*, 10:9 (1970) pp. 45-48.

Bratten, D., Gillin, C., and Roush, R., "Performance Contracting: How It Works in Texarkana." *School Management*, 14:8 (1970) pp. 8-10.

Campbell, R. F., and Larion, J. E., *Performance Contracting in School Systems.* Columbus, Ohio: Charles E. Merrill Publishing Company, 1972.

Gillis, J. C., "Performance Contracting." *Educational Technology*, 11:5 (1969) pp. 17-20.

Performance Contracting in Education. Washington, D.C.: Education Turnkey Systems, 1970.

Schwartz, R., "Performance Contracting." *Nation's Schools*, 86:3 (1970), pp. 53-55.

MICROTEACHING

A recently developed technique, microteaching, is useful in teacher preparation and in-service training programs. Because of its emphasis on skill development for teachers, the technique can be a valuable asset in supervisory practice. The microteaching idea may be summarized as follows:

> A person participating in the training program teaches minilessons to small groups of students. The "teacher" is observed, given feedback on the performance, and allowed to react. Students are also encouraged to contribute in the feedback process.

A video tape unit is highly desirable for recording the proceedings during the minilessons. The spontaneity, objectivity, and comprehensiveness that it provides can facilitate the analysis of the performance. The ease with which the tape can be stored for future use is beneficial. The "teacher" has an instant record for comparing teaching behaviors that may be demonstrated in the future.

Von Haden and King (1971) cite the following as some advantages of microteaching:

1. Attention is given to the teacher's specific behavioral acts.
2. Less time is required in microteaching than in student teaching.
3. All aspects of teaching can be considered.
4. Supervisors who monitor a microteaching exercise can make comments that are definite, understandable, and relevant because they refer to precise acts.
5. The technique can be adopted for use in any college course.

REFERENCES

Allen, D., and Ryan, K., *Microteaching.* Reading, Massachusetts: Addison-Wesley, 1969.

Fortune, J., Cooper, J., and Allen, D., "The Stanford Summer Microteaching Clinic." *Journal of Teacher Education.* 18:4 (1965) p. 389^{+}.

Gage, N. L., "An Analytical Approach to Research on Instructional Methods." *Technology in Education: Challenge and Change,* by F. J. Pula and R. J. Goff (Editors). Worthington, Ohio: Charles A. Jones Publishing Company, 1972.

Langer, P., "Minicourse: Theory and Strategy," *Educational Technology,* 9:9 (1969) pp. 54-59.

Von Haden, H. I., King, J. M., *Innovations in Education: Their Pros and Cons.* Worthington, Ohio: Charles A. Jones Publishing Company, 1971.

Wilhems, F., *Supervision in a New Key.* Washington, D.C.: Association for Supervision and Curriculum Development, 1973.

Young, D. B., "The Modification of Teacher Behavior Using Videotaped Models in a Microteaching Sequence." *Educational Leadership,* 26:4 (1969) pp. 394-403.

BEHAVIORAL OBJECTIVES

The identification of educational goals and objectives is a major task for educational workers. Once identified and stated, they cover a wide range, extending from broad statements of national or system goals to specific objectives for one lesson in a particular educative setting. Many statements of the latter are written in behavioral terms in a manner that is specific, clear, and concise.

A general definition of behavioral objectives describes them as statements of the behaviors a student should have after a learning event, whether it be a lesson, unit, course, or term. The specificity of the behavioral objective allows the learner to know: (1) what the learning task is, (2) when the objective has been achieved, and (3) what the constraints are surrounding the performance. Thus, a behavioral objective is characterized by three traits:

1. A *performance* to be attained is identified.
2. The *conditions* under which the behavior is to occur are cited.
3. The *criteria* for judging the performance are set forth.

A sample behavioral objective with its component parts is written as follows:

conditions	performance	criteria
Given a book of poems,	the student will identify	at least five that are sonnets.

When used in the classroom situation, teachers may discover that behavioral objectives are particularly useful because of their specificity. They assist a teacher in determining exactly what a student needs, what instructional actions are needed, and what the evaluation standard is.

REFERENCES

Esbensen, T., "Writing Instructional Objectives." *Phi Delta Kappan*, 48:(1967) pp. 246-247.

Mager, R., *Preparing Instructional Objectives.* Palo Alto, California: Fearon Publishers, 1962.

Popham, J. W., "Probing the Validity of Arguments against Behavioral Goals." Symposium presented at the annual American Education Research Association, Chicago, February, 1968.

Popham, T. W., "Must All Objectives be Behavioral?" *Educational Leadership*, 29:(1972) pp. 605-608.

SYSTEMATIC OBSERVATION AND INTERACTION ANALYSIS*

The importance of knowing actually what transpires during a teaching-learning situation has been discussed by educators for years. However, acceptable and worthwhile procedures for accomplishing the task have not been readily available. The possibilities presented by systematic observation techniques may provide the desired means for discovering more about what occurs in the classroom. More specifically, systematic observation offers a plethora of techniques that can be used ultimately to improve instruction. Through it, the teacher can become aware of the behaviors he utilizes in the classroom and the consequences of them in terms of learner reactions. The teacher may then utilize the information so as to enhance the teaching-learning experience.

Murray lists five areas of classroom behavior that have received attention in systematic observation research: verbal interaction, nonverbal interaction, subject matter/content areas, general content dimension, and teacher practices. Interaction analysis is one systematic observation technique. It is a procedure for identifying, qualifying, and quantifying the verbal interactions in a classroom. Through a knowledge of these interactions, it is hoped that some statements regarding effective teacher behavior can be generalized.

The Flanders' system of interaction analysis is, perhaps, the most well-known system. The system has ten categories with three segments that focus on teacher talk, student talk, and silence or confusion. The ten category observation guide for recording is accompanied by a scheme for interpreting the recordings made.

In the practice of supervision, skepticism abounds regarding classroom observations. The cause probably stems from the misuse of the visitation concept; too often it results in threats and criticisms to teachers. Supervisors and researchers who use techniques of systematic observation might provide them in a diagnostic context rather than an evaluative one. They should supply a model for the use of systematic observation in helping teachers know who they are and who their students are. Such use of systematic observation may be an initial step in

*Other strategies that relate to this category include the use of logs, anecdotal records, observational data, and critical incidents.

eliminating undesirable connotations for observations of teachers and classroom experiences.

REFERENCES

Amidon, E. and Flanders, N., *The Role of the Teacher in the Classroom.* Minneapolis: Amidon and Associates, 1963.

Amidon, E. J., and Haugh, J. B., *Interaction Analysis: Theory, Research, and Application.* Reading, Massachusetts: Addison-Wesley, 1967.

Beegle, C. W., and Brandt, R. M., *Observational Methods in the Classroom.* Washington, D.C.: Association for Supervision and Curriculum Development, 1973.

Brown, B., Ober, R., and Soar, R., *The Florida Taxonomy of Cognitive Behavior.* Gainesville, Florida: University of Florida, 1967.

Flanders, N. A., *Analyzing Teacher Behavior.* Reading, Massachusetts: Addison-Wesley, 1970.

Medley, D. M., and Mitzel, H. E., "Measuring Classroom Behavior by Systematic Observation." *Handbook of Research on Teaching,* by N. L. Gage (ed.). Chicago: Rand-McNally, 1963.

Murray, C. K., "The Systematic Observation Movement." *Journal of Research and Development in Education,* 4:1 (1970) pp. 3-9.

Rosenshine, B., "Interaction Analysis: A Tardy Comment." *Phi Delta Kappan,* 51:(1970) pp. 445-446.

Ryans, D. G., and Wandt, E. A., "A Factor Analysis of Observed Teacher Behaviors in the Secondary School." *Educational Psychological Measurement,* 12:(1950).

FORCE FIELD ANALYSIS

Force field analysis can be considered as a problem-solving technique wherein forces, both positive and negative, affecting a task are diagrammed and weighted. Derived from physics and applied as Lewin's vector psychology as a means of describing psychological phenomena, force field analysis has planning implications for supervisors and curriculum workers.

Lewin, a field theory psychologist, contends that one's equilibrium was maintained by a balance of driving and restraining forces that are present in an individual's field of references. In explaining the dynamics of the personality, Lewin proposes that altering the equilibrium through changes to certain weighted forces or vectors can enable the personality to develop into a total, adjusted entity. When total personality balance is achieved, the individual then becomes capable of responding appropriately in an organization, thus making possible the attainment of organizational goals. The procedures involved in force field analysis are as follows:

1. Define the goal to be reached.
2. On one side of the field of the goal, list all data (facts, attitudes, feelings, etc.) that facilitate attainment of the goal.
3. On the opposite side of the field, list all forces as data that restrain or hinder attainment of the goal.
4. Assess the differing strengths of each facilitating and hindering force.

5. Determine those forces, both positive (facilitating-augmenting) and negative (hindering-restraining) that can be either increased or decreased or changed in direction, in order to efficiently and effectively reach the goal.

When applied to supervision, force field analysis provides a tool that the supervisor may use to plan strategies for change by considering the restraining forces that need to be minimized and the facilitating forces that need to be reinforced.

REFERENCES

Benne, K. D., and Muntyan, B., *Human Relations in Curriculum Change*. Illinois Secondary School Curriculum Program Bulletin, Circular Series A, 7:51 (1949).

"Force Field Analysis." *Journal and Handbook of Staff Development*, Washington, D.C.: NTL-NEA, March, 1968, pp. 105-111.

Hall, C. S., and Lindzey, G., *Theories of Personality*. New York: John Wiley and Sons, Inc., 1957.

Lewin, K., *A Dynamic Theory of Personality*. New York: McGraw-Hill, 1935.

________, *Field Theory in Social Science*. New York: Harper and Row, 1951.

Smith, B. O., Stanley, W. O., and Shores, J. H., *Fundamentals of Curriculum Development*. New York: World Book Co., 1957.

ORGANIZATIONAL BEHAVIOR

In a general context, an organization has been defined by Griffiths as a collection of people who perform different but interrelated functions so that one or more tasks may be completed. Organizations currently are being studied vigorously in connection with the systems approach to management. The accumulating body of organizational theory attempts to delineate those purposes, environmental forces, human interactions, and hierarchal structures that give commonality to organizations.

Educational organizations have found that concepts from organizational theory can apply to their purposes and can contribute to their operations. The following descriptions of three such concepts relate to organizations in education. Supervisors may readily discover their value in assisting and planning a proper environment in which changes may occur.

Organizational Health

A broad approach to understanding the sentiment, attitude, and orientation of a given school is embodied in a concept of organizational health. Miles, who contributed to a body of knowledge regarding organizational health, sees the healthy organization as one that can continuously maintain itself in its environment. It is constantly developing and engaging in coping activities so that it can further extend its usefulness.

Miles's concept of a healthy organization is presented in a discussion of ten dimensions that resulted from an orientation to industrial organizations. According to Miles, the healthy organization:

1. Exhibits clear, achievable, and appropriate goals.
2. Has a distortion-free environment that makes possible an open communication network.
3. Has a distribution of influence that is rather equitable.
4. Utilizes all human and material resources effectively and efficiently.
5. Encourages its members to feel a part of the organization, thus developing cohesiveness.
6. Promotes a healthy morale among its individual members.
7. Has a tendency to be innovative.
8. Maintains a degree of autonomy.
9. Can make adaptions.
10. Can adequately solve problems when confronted with them.

Recognizing that these ten dimensions did not come directly from observations of school organizations, Miles believes that they can be applied to them. Caution must be taken in application because school organizations do have certain properties that make them distinctive.

Organizational Climate

Organizational climate, as defined by Halpin, refers to the feeling that exists in a given school and the variability of the feeling as one moves from school to school within a system. Halpin and Croft have developed the *O*rganizational *C*limate *D*escription *Q*uestionnaire (OCDQ) to measure and chart the differences in feelings that characterize individual schools. The questionnaire examines eight dimensions of organizational climate, four of which focus on teacher behavior, and four, on that of the principal: for the teacher, *disengagement, hindrance, espirit, intimacy;* for the principal, *aloofness, production, trust,* and *consideration.* As measured by the instrument, an open climate school is characterized by low disengagement, hindrance, aloofness, and production; and high espirit, intimacy, trust, and consideration. The closed school exhibits high disengagement, hindrance, intimacy, aloofness, and production emphasis; and low espirit, trust, and consideration.

Organization Development (OD)

Organization development involves someone entering an organization for the expressed purpose of making improvements within it. Through intervention strategies, the designated members of the organization engage in structured activities that can bear upon, directly or indirectly, organizational improvement.

Interventions constitute the action thrust of organization development; they make things happen. The intervener, usually an outside consultant, brings to the system a set of values, assumptions, and goals that are implemented through a set of structured activities. Interventions may be classified by families; e.g., diagnostic, team-building, intergroup, survey-feedback, education and training, process consultation, grid organization, third-party peacemaking, coaching and counseling, life and career planning, and planning and goal setting activities. They also may be classified by thematic interventions; e.g., discrepancy, theory, procedural, relationship, experimentation, dilemma, perspective, organization, and cultural interventions.

REFERENCES

Argyris, C., *Intervention Theory: A Behavioral Science View.* Reading, Massachusetts: Addison-Wesley Publishing Company, 1970.

———, *Intervention Theory and Method.* Reading, Massachusetts: Addison-Wesley Publishing Company, 1970.

Bennis, W., *Organization Development: Its Nature, Origins, and Prospects.* Reading, Massachusetts: Addison-Wesley Publishing Company, 1969.

Carver, F. D., and Sergiovanni, T., "Source Notes on the OCDQ." *Journal of Educational Administration,* 7:(1969) pp. 78-81.

Griffiths, D. E., "Administrative Theory and Change in Organizations." *Educational Administration and the Behavioral Sciences: A Systems Perspective,* by M. M. Milstein and J. A. Belasco (Editors). Boston: Allyn and Bacon, 1973.

Halpin, A., *Theory and Research in Administration.* New York: Macmillian, 1967.

Miles, M. B., "Planned Change and Organizational Health: Figure and Ground." *Change Process in the Public Schools,* Eugene, Oregon: University of Oregon, Center for the Advanced Study of Educational Administration, 1965.

Schmuck, R. A., and Miles, M. B., *Organization Development in Schools.* Palo Alto, California: National Press Books, 1971.

Watkins, J. F., "The OLDQ—An Application and Some Implications." *Educational Administration Quarterly,* 4:(1968) pp. 46-60.

GROUP PROCESSES

Supervision often requires that people come together to accomplish specified tasks. It also has a responsibility for assisting teachers in providing an optimum educative environment for the pupils that come to them. Because supervision is concerned with people working and/or learning together, theories and concepts from group behavior research offer numerous suggestions of interest to supervisors. The following items describe concepts and techniques that can be beneficial when people need to function as a collectivity.

Group Dynamics

Group dynamics is the interaction process that distinguishes a group (two or more individuals who are aware of one another and are interrelated) from an aggregate of individuals. The group is not only interactive, but it is also dynamic—continuously changing and adjusting relationships with reference to each individual's changes. As individuals change, the group changes, hopefully becoming more flexible and adaptable. Consequently, group changes are dependent on the degree of organization of a group. Group dynamics investigates the formation and change in structure and functions of the psychological grouping of people as they seek to solve their problems and satisfy their individual needs as well as those of the group. It is also concerned with the nature of groups, the laws of their development, and their interrelations with individuals, other groups, and larger institutions.

Sensitivity Training and T-Groups

The T-group is an experience in social creativity. In a usual sensitivity session, ten to fifteen individuals, with a professional trainer who acts as a catalyst and facilitator for the group, face a task within a relatively short but concentrated period of time. The session involves creating, developing, and maintaining a small social organization under unusual conditions. This emerging social organization (group) faces real, hard-headed problems of social formation, individual relationships, and work achievement. Conceptual material that relates to interpersonal relations, individual personality theory, and group dynamics is a part of the program. The process of developing a group is the means of achieving the purpose of helping individuals to learn, improve, and change insights, understandings, sensitivities, and skills.

REFERENCES

Argyris, C., "T-Groups for Organizational Effectiveness." Reprinted from *Harvard Business Review*, Washington, D.C.: National Training Laboratories, National Education Association, (March-April, 1954).

Benne, K. D., Bennis, W. G., and Chin, R., eds., *The Planning of Change.* New York: Holt, Rinehart, and Winston, 1961.

Bennis, W. G., and Schein, E. H., *Interpersonal Dynamics.* Homewood, Illinois: Richard D. Irwin, 1964.

Blake, R. R., Mouton, J., and Fructer, B., "A Factor Analysis of Training Group Behavior," *Journal of Social Psychology*, 58:(1962) pp. 121-130.

Bonner, H., *Group Dynamics: Principles and Application.* New York: Ronald Press, 1959.

Bowers, N. D., and Soar, R. S., *Evaluation of Laboratory Human Relations Training for Classroom Teachers—Studies of Human Relations in the Teaching-Learning Process: V. Final Report.* U. S. Office of Education Contract No. 8143, Columbia, S.C.: University of South Carolina, 1961.
Bradford, L. P., ed., *Group Development.* Washington, D.C.: National Training Laboratories, National Education Association, 1961.
Burke, R., and Bennis, W., "Changing in Perception of Self and Others during the Human Relations Training." *Human Relations,* II(1961) pp. 165-182.
Cartwright, D., and Zander, A., eds., *Group Dynamics.* Evanston, Illinois: Harper and Row, 1968.
Fox, R., Lippitt, R., and Schmuck, R., *Pupil-Teacher Adjustment.* Washington, D.C.: U.S. Office of Education, 1964.
Gibb, J. R., Platts, G., and Miller, L., *Dynamics of Participative Groups.* St. Louis: Swift, 1951.
Hare, A. P., *Handbook of Small Group Research.* New York: Free Press of Glencoe, 1962.
Klein, J., *Working with Groups: The Social Psychology of Discussion and Decision.* New York: Hillary House, 1961.
Miles, M. B., ed., *Innovation in Education.* New York: Bureau of Publications, Teachers College, Columbia University, 1964.
Mill, C. R., "A Theory for the Group Dynamics Laboratory Millieu." *Adult Leadership,* II(1962) pp. 133-134.
Olmsted, M., *The Small Group.* New York: Random House, 1961.
Schein, E. H., and Bennis, W. G., eds., *Personal and Organizational Change through Group Methods: The Laboratory Approach.* New York: Wiley, 1965.
Tannebaum, R., and Bugental, T. F. T., "Dyads, Clans, and Tribe: A New Design for Sensitivity Training." *Human Relations Training News,* 7:1 (1963).
Underwood, W. J., "Evaluation of Laboratory Method Training." *Training Directors Journal,* 19:(1965) pp. 34-40.
Watson, G., *Social Psychology· Issues and Insights.* Philadelphia: Lippincott, 1966.

MANAGEMENT PHILOSOPHY—THEORY X AND THEORY Y

Douglas McGregor has offered two management theories that are being discussed widely in terms of their applicability to educational organizations. The two theories are usually graphically depicted as bipolar variants on a continuum: X____________Y. The X theory is a management philosophy that embraces control and direction. The Y theory espouses the view that management, if it is to function successfully, can benefit from a more humane reaction to the persons that support it.

The X position, according to McGregor, is based on assumptions that dictate a manipulative control of individuals. It is assumed that man is passive, inherently lazy, resistant to progress, and unresponsive to the organization. Theory X, thus, proposes that management must take all responsibility in directing the organization, its resources, and the people that it employs. External motivation provided by management is what individuals need who work for an organization.

The opposite of Theory X is found in Theory Y at the other end of the continuum. Based on more humane assumptions, it holds that management has to provide an environment where people can be motivated to pursue organizational ends. Through fulfilling the higher order needs of its workers, the organization then has in its employ workers who are self-directed, self-controlled, and ready for growth. The result is a reciprocal interaction of mutual benefit.

REFERENCES

Bennis, W. G., and Schein, E. H., *Leadership and Motivation: Essays of Douglas McGregor.* Cambridge, Mass.: Massachusetts Institute of Technology Press, 1966.

Carver, F. D., and Sergiovanni, T. J., *Organizations and Human Behavior: Focus on Schools.* New York: McGraw-Hill, 1969.

McGregor, D., *The Human Side of Enterprise.* New York: McGraw-Hill, 1960.

Sergiovanni, T. J., and Starratt, R. J., *Emerging Patterns of Supervision: Human Perspectives.* New York: McGraw-Hill, 1971.

CURRICULUM COUNCIL

The curriculum council is a decision making agency for curriculum or change; it encourages all persons affected by curriculum decisions to have a representative voice in planning the general policies for the curriculum of the district.* The literature suggests that the council, whether elected or appointed, be comprised of students, parents, teachers, representatives of the school board, the school superintendent and/or associates, curriculum specialists, and representatives of industry, business, and the community. The primary concern of the curriculum council, the coordination of the curriculum renewal and policy making activities for a school district, is accomplished through regular meetings in which the council: (1) screens problems or recommendations, (2) assigns problems to committees, (3) hears progress reports and provides guidance to the called committees, (4) considers and approves or rejects the committee recommendations, and (5) forwards the recommendations to the superintendent for authorization.

*Other strategies for this grouping include designs involving teacher centers, professional media centers, program steering committees, and school-community advisory councils.

REFERENCES

American Association of School Administrators and Association for Supervision and Curriculum Development, *Organizing for Improved Instruction.* Washington, D.C.: The Association, 1963.

Caswell, H. L., *Curriculum Improvement in Public School Systems.* New York: Bureau of Publications, Teachers College, Columbia University, 1950.

Doll, R. C., *Curriculum Improvement: Decision-Making and Process.* Boston: Allyn and Bacon, 1970.

Feyereisen, K. V., Fiorino, A. J., and Nowak, A. J., *Supervision and Curriculum Renewal: A Systems Approach.* New York: Meredith Corporation, 1970.

Jackson, S., "The Curriculum Council: New Hope, New Promise." *Educational Leadership,* 29:(1972) pp. 690-694.

Neagley, R. L., and Evans, N. D., *Handbook for Effective Supervision of Instruction.* Englewood Cliffs, N.J.: Prentice-Hall, 1970.

Saylor, J. G., and Alexander, W. M., *Planning Curriculum for Schools.* New York: Holt, Rinehart, and Winston, 1974.

Smith, B. O., Stanley, W., and Shores, J. H., *Fundamentals of Curriculum Development.* New York: World Book Company, 1957.

THE SYSTEMS APPROACH

Business enterprises have long made use of the systems approach to help solve operational problems more efficiently and effectively. As education enterprises become more complicated, the systems approach has been proposed as a technology to facilitate their operations, expecially when educational processes are considered an open system with an array of forces contributing to its total functioning.

The systems approach is a method of analyzing a set of operations as a goal is moved from conception to actualization. The organization and administration of a process/program is facilitated through the delineation of the necessary elements for accomplishing a goal. The analytic quality of the approach is to be discovered, scrutinized, and remedied. The desired outcome is a product free from defects that may have arisen from a faulty system.

The basic system model contains three phases: input, process, and output. The input phase focuses on the identification of needs and, hence, goals for the operation. It also focuses on the strategies that are required to meet the needs. During the process phase, the proposed strategies will be implemented, managed, and monitored. Finally, the output phase involves the evaluation of the product effectiveness based on the goals identified during the input phase. If modifications must be made in the system, they become known through a feedback network, another part of the output phase. The three phases are usually presented in the manner below.

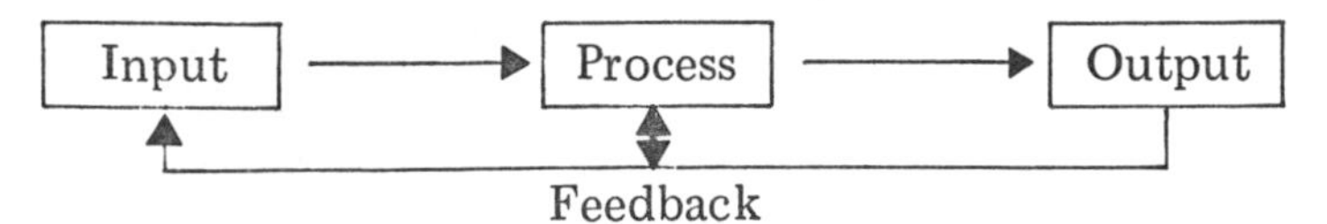

In educational undertakings, the systems concept is applied to various operations in the educational process. It is being used in the development of change models, decision making processes, administrative functions, planning, instructional processes, evaluation, and budgeting resources.

Recognizing that supervisory tasks are expanded considerably, Feyereisen, Fiorino, and Nowak apply the systems concept to supervision and curriculum undertakings. Their supervisory system consists of three basic functions: designing curriculum, providing advice to teachers, and working with the instructional staff on problems that relate to teaching.

According to them, supervision characterized by a systems approach has integrated all its elements into a single conceptual scheme. Because of this, it is possible to take a comprehensive view of the total operation. The use of systems methods provides better personnel, increased technical competence, and better use of available resources.

REFERENCES

Churman, C., *The Systems Approach.* New York: Delta Publishing Co., 1968.

Corgan, V., "Systems Concept: A Practical Application. *Business Education Forum,* 28:2 (1974) pp. 17-21.

Edney, Philip J., *A Systems Analysis of Training.* New York: Pitman Publishing Corporation, 1972.

Feyereisen, K., Fiorino, A., and Nowak, A., *Supervision and Curriculum Renewal: A System Approach.* New York: Appleton-Century-Crofts, 1970.

Granger, Robert L., *Educational Leadership: An Interdisciplinary Perspective.* Scranton: Intext Educational Publishers, 1971.

Hill, J., *How Can Schools Apply Systems Analysis?* Bloomington, Indiana: Phi Delta Kappa Educational Foundation, 1972.

Hussain, Khateeb M., *Development of Information Systems for Education.* Englewood Cliffs, New Jersey: Prentice-Hall, 1973.

Kast, Fremont Ellsworth, and Rosenzweig, James E., *Organization and Management: A Systems Approach.* McGraw-Hill, 1970, reprinted 1974.

McManama, J., *Systems Analysis for Effective School Administration.* West Nyack, New York: Parker Publishing Co., 1971.

Quade, E. S., *Analysis for Military Decisions.* New York: American Elsevier Publishing Company, 1970.

Romiszowski, A. J., ed., *A Systems Approach to Education.* London: Kogan Page, 1970.

Sabine, Creta D., ed., *Accountability: Systems Planning in Education.* Leon Lessinger and Associates. Creta D. Sabine, Editor. Homewood, Illinois: ETC Publications, 1973.

Silvern, Leonard C., *Systems Engineering of Education I: The Evolution of Systems Thinking in Education.* Los Angeles: Education and Training Consultants Company, 1965.

Thompson, Robert B., *A Systems Approach to Instruction.* Hamden, Connecticut: Shoe String Press, 1971.

Von Bertalanffy, L., *General System Theory.* New York: Braziller Press, 1968.

MANAGEMENT BY OBJECTIVES

Educational literature is replete with claims that objectives are the foundation of instructional activities. Whether broad or specific, they have long been considered as the blueprints for action in the classroom. As the educational organization expands, objectives are being utilized in areas other than instruction.

Management By Objectives (MBO) is a management approach that stresses a detailed listing of objectives in operating large organizations. Used initially in the business world, MBO is now being applied to the educational organization. Specifically, the approach can be used to facilitate the operation of the administrative, instructional, curricular, and supervisory segments of an educational system.

Knezevich defines MBO as a management system that seeks to encourage change and improvement in an organization by focusing on desirable results. The objectives identified are instrumental in moving the organization from the status quo to higher levels. In a more specific definition, Boston calls MBO an organized system that allows personnel for all management levels to enter into the planning for their areas of responsibility and the general management of the organization. MBO, in this context, encourages a general concern for the health of the entire organization. It creates a situation where no one person should be held singly accountable for any problem that may arise in the organization.

In operation, an MBO system requires that clear objectives first be derived for an operation. These then will propose certain resources that are necessary in order to attain the objectives. The objectives are as a means for: (1) planning, (2) operating, and (3) evaluating the desired results. They provide the criteria by which the results are to be judged. As a management and control technique, MBO allows for the evaluation of people as well as processes.

Boston has offered a five-step model that describes a management process using the MBO principles. The process is as follows:

1. Goals must be interpreted.
2. Clearly stated objectives have to be constructed.
3. Programs to attain the objectives have to be designed.
4. Evaluations of the program processes and the outcomes are necessary. A base for the evaluations is the objectives.
5. The system is recycled, giving attention to improvement dictated by the evaluations.

REFERENCES

Boston, R. E., "Management by Objectives: A Management System for Education." *Educational Technology*, 1972.

Campbell, J. C., "Harmonizing Decisions: Management by Objectives." *Educational Technology*, 13:6 (1973).

Drucher, P. F., *The Practice of Management.* New York: Harper and Row, 1954.

Knezevich, S. J., "MBO—Its Meaning and Application to Educational Administration." *Education*, 93:(1972) pp. 12-21.

Odiorne, G. S., "Management by Objectives." *College and University Journal*, 10:2 (1971) pp. 13-15.

PLANNING, PROGRAMMING, BUDGETING, AND EVALUATION SYSTEM (PPBES)

PPBES is one example of a management science concept that has taken hold in education. Developed initially as PPBS, the approach was primarily used in industry; then, during World War II, it was revised by the U.S. government for planning and budgetary purposes. In the sixties, it was employed in developing weapons systems and then became of general use. PPBS, during this evolution, has been expanded by the inclusion of an evaluation component, and as PPBES, it is widely being implemented for educational purposes.

When applied to education, PPBES can be briefly described as a group of procedures for coordinating usually independent activities that are involved in an educational program and the financial operations that support it. It is the structure established: (1) to determine policy regarding resource allocation, (2) to identify and achieve high priority objectives with emphasis on long-range planning, (3) to bring economic considerations into the process of program determination, (4) to evaluate program alternatives and outcomes, and (5) to use goals and objectives as the focal elements in decision making.

PPBES has many implications for staff development, instructional improvement programs, and organizational changes. While in PPBES, the emphasis is on objectives and long-range planning rather than crises planning; there is also a shift from input to outcome considerations. School leaders are expected to *plan* and anticipate rather than react and remediate; they are required to show effectiveness in identifying program outcomes as well as quality in studying the resources and staff. Responsiveness and responsibility are to be built into program planning as well as in public relations.

Programming is the designation for the process whereby alternative activities plus cost and effectiveness measures, which are expected to accomplish the designed objectives, are delineated. The process stresses multi-year planning that includes program reviews and analysis of alternatives. Suggested program efforts—be they in staff development, instructional change, or renewal—will need to be related specifically to ongoing efforts and programs if they are to assume their rightful place, have budget adequacy, and witness public support.

The allocation of resources, *budgeting*, is expected to be achieved in relationship to stated program objectives and plans. As such, it will be subject to more open decision making; it will require more precise data regarding program structure and cost; and it will make more visible curricular and instructional expenditures. Problems in budgeting may arise as new configurations of power and decision making insist that programs for staff learners be integral and specific entities, not "add on" or general cost allotments.

Evaluation consists of a review of performance and product. As the use of evaluation procedures is increased, more monitoring, process evaluation, and auditing will be necessary to make in-process decisions and program modifications and corrections. Such feedback may result in redesigning the objectives, recycling program efforts, or reallocating resources. The need for goal and policy clarification is likely to increase as more persons are required to understand and relate to the operations and outcomes expected of a particular program.

If fully implemented, the PPBE System requires that educational workers become involved in the total scheme of educational planning, implementing, and evaluating. Their usual tasks will be altered as the PPBE System is put into operation. The system requires more delineated goals and program strategies. New priorities and projects will emerge as it becomes necessary to eliminate diffused institutional goals and generalized approaches. Role responsibilities and operational modes may need new specifications. Current practices will need to be analyzed to determine critical components and discrepancies. Program objectives will need instruments and procedures to identify, validate, develop, and deliver.

In brief, concerns for cost and purpose, and the emphasis on proposed planning and budgeting have reinforced the application of PPBES to educational purposes. Likewise, the delineation of objectives, priorities, and program cost alternatives has made it attractive to school boards, legislatures, and decision-makers. Consequently, some form of PPBES is operational or anticipated in most school systems as they respond to an increased emphasis on professional stewardship, efficiency, and effectiveness. The emphasis has been so widespread that some form of Management by Objectives (MBO) is now an expected competency for all leadership or management personnel.

REFERENCES

Alioto, R. J., and Jungher, J. A., *Operational PPBS for Education: A Practical Approach to Effective Decision Making.* New York: Harper and Row, 1971.

Avedisian, C. T., "Planning, Programming, Budgeting Systems." *Journal of Health, Physical Education, and Recreation,* 43:8 (1972) pp. 37-39.

Farlies, R. H., "Cost-Effectiveness Analysis: Primer and Guidelines." *Educational Technology*, 14:3 (1974) pp. 21-27.

Hartley, H. J., *Educational Planning, Programming, Budgeting.* Englewood Cliffs, N.J.: Prentice-Hall, 1968.

_____, "PPBS: Status and Implications." *Educational Leadership*, 29:(1972) pp. 658-661.

Ross, R. J., "You and the Common Sense of PPBS." *Educational Technology*, 13:12 (1973) pp. 57-59.

Sesson, R. L., Brewin, C. E., and Renshaw, B. H., "An Introduction to the Educational-Planning-Programming-Budgeting System." *Educational Technology*, 12:2 (1972) pp. 54-60.

Weiss, E. H., "PPBES in Education." *Journal of General Education*, 25:(1973) pp. 17-27.

EDUCATIONAL FUTURES

Educational futurism is education's response to increased concern with the acceleration of change and the direction of that change. Rather than simply reacting to change, education futurists advocate, indeed implore, professional educators to attend to the possibilities of the future. "What are alternative futures?" and "How are these futures brought about?" are two major questions that futurists urge educators to explore for implications in educational planning and in determining content for teaching. The purpose of such action is to anticipate possible future situations before they are encountered.

On the educational planning level, it is possible to identify alternative futures and plan change in a desired direction. Forecasting is a major process or methodology used for hypothesizing about the future and is often equated with prediction. It helps to predict the rate, quality, and degree of change. Roger Ravelle has identified three kinds of forecasting; namely, (1) the projection of trends, which involves the extrapolation of present trends, (2) the development of models and the study of the consequences of such future models, and (3) normative forecasting, which develops normative models of desirable futures. Other kinds of forecasting are possible using a combination of the above three.

Various techniques are available for forecasting the future. Delphi studies, scenarios, simulations, and trend analysis seem to be the more popular techniques. Other possible techniques include matrix forecasting, relevance tree and contextual map forecasting, Monte Carlo analysis, Bayesian statistical forecasting, force analysis, Markov Chain forecasting, and assessment.

Educational futurism also has implication for the curriculum and for teaching techniques. The intent of educational futurism at this level is to help students in anticipating what they may face in the future and to assist them in developing the skills and attitudes necessary to cope with the future. Moreover, present day students are the decision makers of the future. Hence, they ought to have a way of thinking about the future and dealing with many possible futures. The number of "futures" courses are increasing in universities, colleges, and elementary and high schools. Already established courses are including "futuristics" as an added element. Some of the techniques mentioned above as ways of forecasting can be adapted to the classroom, thereby becoming exciting teaching tools. Delphi studies, scenarios simulations, and trend analysis also lend themselves to instructional planning.

REFERENCES

Anderson, Robert H., Almy, Millie, Shane, Harold, and Tyler, Ralph, *Education in Anticipation of Tomorrow.* Worthington, Ohio: Charles A. Jones, 1973.

Barnes, Ron, *Learning Systems for the Future.* Bloomington, Indiana: Phi Delta Kappa Educational Foundation, 1972.

Beckwith, Burnham P., *The Next 500 Years.* New York: Beckwith Press, 1967.

Bell, Daniel, *Toward the Year 2000: Work in Progress.* American Academy of Arts and Sciences. Boston, Mass.: Houghton Mifflin Company, 1967.

Hack, W. G., et al., *Educational Futurism 1985.* Berkeley, California: McCutchan Publishing Corporation, 1971.

Harman, Willis W., *Alternative Futures and Educational Policy.* Menlo Park, California: Stanford Research Institute, 1970.

Hencley, Stephen P., and Yates, James R., eds., *Futurism in Education: Methodologies.* Berkeley, California: McCutchan Publishing Corporation, 1974.

Hipple, Theodore W., ed., *The Future of Education: 1975-2000.* Pacific Palisades, California: Goodyear Publishing Company, Inc., 1974.

Kahn, Herman, and Wiener, Anthony J., *The Year 2000: A Framework for Speculation.* New York: MacMillan, 1967.

Leonard, George B., *Education and Ecstasy.* New York: Dell Publishing Company, 1968.

Marien, M., and Zeigler, W. L., eds., *The Potential of Educational Futures.* Worthington, Ohio: Charles A. Jones Publishing Company, 1972.

Marien, Michael, *Alternative Furtures for Learning: An Annotated Bibliography.* Syracuse: Educational Policy Research Center, 1971.

Meeker, Robert J., and Weiler, Daniel M., *A New School for the Cities.* Santa Monica, California: System Development Corporation, 1970.

Morphet, Edgar L., and Ryan, Charles O., eds., *Designing Education for the Future, Number 2: Implications for Education of Prespective Changes in Society.* New York: Citation Press, 1967.

———, *Designing Education for the Future, Number 3: Planning and Effecting Needed Changes in Education.* New York: Citation Press, 1967.

Shane, Harold, "Looking to the Future: Reassessment of Educational Issues of the 1970's." *Phi Delta Kappan,* 54:(January, 1973) pp. 326-337.

Toffler, Alvin, ed., *Learning for Tomorrow: The Role of the Future in Education.* New York: Vintage Books, 1974.

Toffler, Alvin, *Future Shock*. New York: Random House, 1970.
Van Til, W., ed., *Curriculum: Quest for Relevance*. Boston: Houghton Mifflin Company, 1974.
Williams, Charles, and Nusberg, Charlotte, *Anticipating Educational Issues over the next Two Decades: An Overview Report of Trends Analysis*. Menlo Park, California: Stanford Research Institute, 1973.

FORMATIVE AND SUMMATIVE EVALUATION

Scriven, a theoretician in educational evaluation, has proposed that evaluation has only one goal, but several roles. In delineating the roles of evaluation, he has offered the concept of formative and summative evaluation as a means of clarifying them. Formative evaluation is the continuous feedback of information during the intermediate stages of a process. The feedback is done so that alterations can be made if any deficiencies are found to exist in the process. Thus, formative evaluation is concerned with program improvement; it is obtaining information while a program is in process and making decisions that may contribute to the overall effectiveness of the program.

In considering formative evaluation in more specific terms, Bloom, et al., calls it a technique that provides for diagnostic measures of performance and produces data to be analyzed. The results of the data analysis can provide the intelligence necessary for redesigning the instructional program, if needed. Formative evaluation can occur during the initial, intermediate, or later stages of a process, program, or performance.

The educational worker can employ formative evaluation for numerous purposes. In doing so, he uses intermediate assessments for eliminating deficiencies that are discovered in an educational undertaking prior to any terminal evaluation procedures. These assessments may be made in order to: (1) ascertain whether or not instructional procedures or materials are effective, (2) discover the adequacy of various learning modes in regard to individual students, (3) point out areas of weakness in a master budgeting plan, (4) find salient points in an in-service training program, or (5) make decisions about the revision of a new curriculum design.

The counterpoint of formative evaluation, which Scriven has identified, is summative evaluation. While the former is primarily concerned with evaluation for improvement, the latter emphasizes evaluation procedures that provide an indication of overall effectiveness. As the name suggests, summative evaluation occurs at the end of a term, course, or program. It is the collection of data to determine the effectiveness of a specific curriculum design, course of study, or innovative technique. The results of summative evaluation may become known through various means; i.e., grades, ratings, certifications, and definitive statements that indicate the general effectiveness of that which was evaluated. The results are useful in providing base-line data in decision making processes.

In an instructional situation, for example, a judgment is made through summative evaluation about a student, teacher, or curriculum activity with regard to the effectiveness of learning or instruction after it has taken place. Summative evaluation may be short-term, intermediate, or long-range and may employ absolute or comparative standards of measurement.

The nature of formative and summative evaluation requires some distinct technical competencies of evaluators. Evaluators who guide formative evaluation procedures should be fully aware of the goals and operations of the program under consideration. Scriven believes that they are handicapped if they are less than fully familiar and fully sympathetic with the arms of the program. It is not desired, however, that summative evaluators be as attached to the program as formative evaluators. Their autonomy, void of any emotional or economic binders, is necessary to insure the most objective judgments possible.

REFERENCES

Association for Supervision and Curriculum Development, *Evaluation as Feedback and Guide.* Yearbook. Washington, D.C.: author, 1967.

Bloom, B. S., Hastings, J. T., and Maduns, G. F., *Handbook of Formative and Summative Evaluation of Student Learning.* New York: McGraw-Hill Book Company, 1971.

National Study for the Study of Education, The Sixty-Eight Yearbook, *Educational Evaluation: New Roles, New Means, Part II.* Chicago: The University of Chicago Press, 26:50 (1969) pp. 221-241.

Payne, D. A., ed., *Curriculum Evaluation: Commentaries on Purpose, Process, Product.* Lexington, Massachusetts: D. C. Heath Co., 1974.

_____, "Some Old and New Wives' Tales Concerning Curriculum Evaluation." *Educational Leadership,* 30:(1973) pp. 343-347.

Provus, M., *Discrepancy Evaluation.* Berkeley, California: McCutchan Publishing Corp., 1971.

Scriven, M. S., "The Methodology of Evaluation." *Readings in Curriculum Evaluation,* P. A. Taylor and D. M. Cowley, Editors. Dubuque, Iowa: William C. Brown Company, 1972.

Walburg, H. J., ed., *Evaluating Educational Performance.* Berkeley, California: McCutchan Publishing Corporation, 1974.

Weiss, C. H., *Evaluating Action Programs: Readings in Social Action and Evaluation.* Boston: Allyn and Bacon, Inc., 1972.

ACCOUNTABILITY

For the past few years, the term *accountability* has increased in use and impact in educational circles. School personnel, politicians, educational leaders, and laymen have joined to proclaim the importance of the accountability concept. While not really a new idea in education, accountability has bombarded the current educational scene under a multiplicity of guises, all aimed at improving the schools.

Educational accountability has been defined in many ways. Lessinger, a leader in the movement, defines it as the ability to deliver on promises. Lewis and DeNovellis extend that idea when they define educational accountability as "reporting the congruence between agreed-upon goals and their realization." Wildavsky discusses accountability as a means of holding someone responsible for the levels of achievement reached by students.

Regardless of how accountability is defined, it is a concept comprised of a variety of factors as educationists seek to report the results of their work to citizens, legislators, funding agencies, and the higher echelon of the educational hierarchy. Dyer thinks, for instance, that accountability programs may emphasize one of four concerns: accountability for cash, accountability for things, accountability for deeds, and accountability for results. The last factor has been the major focus of many accountability programs. It is the factor relating directly to student performance and levels of attainment. Involved in a program of accountability for results are questions of who is to be responsible, how levels of attainment are to be determined and measured, and how to judge them.

Lessinger, however, has discussed accountability in more extensive terms by proposing accountability programs that take into consideration the total functioning of the school. Comprehensive accountability involves more than accounting for the products of education; it seeks to discover the adequacy of the processes involved in the total operation. Thus, management designs, cost analysis systems, needs assessment, and goal identification are important elements of the total accountability programs. The rationale for comprehensiveness rests on a sound base as the educational enterprise is viewed more and more as a system. The net result is the involvement of many interested parties in accounting for the total educational system.

REFERENCES

DeNovellis, R. L., and Levis, A. J., *Schools Become Accountable: A PACT Approach*. Washington, D.C.: Association for Supervision and Curriculum Development, 1973.

Dyer, H., *How to Achieve Accountability in the Public Schools.* Bloomington, Ind.: Phi Delta Kappa Educational Foundation, 1973.

Lessinger, L. M., *Every Kid a Winner: Accountability in Education.* New York: Simon and Schuster, 1970.

Sabine, Creta D., ed., *Accountability: Systems Planning in Education.* Leon Lessenger and Associates. Homewood, Illinois: ETC Publications, 1973.

Sciara, F. J., and Jantz, R. F., eds., *Accountability in American Education.* Boston: Allyn and Bacon, Inc., 1972.

Wildavsky, A., "A Program of Accountability for Elementary Schools." *Phi Delta Kappan,* 53:(1970) pp. 212-216.

ACTION RESEARCH

Action research is the process of systematically collecting research data about an ongoing system or problem relative to some objectives of the system, feeding these data back into the system, taking actions by altering selected variables within the system, and evaluating the results of actions by collecting more data. Another strategy for action research is monitoring, the details of which were explicated in Chapter 8.

Several authors have noted the importance of viewing action research as a process. Stephen Corey, an early advocate of action research, states:

> The process by which practitioners attempt to study their problems scientifically in order to guide, correct, and evaluate their decisions and actions is what a number of people have called action research. Corey also defines the term more in terms of a practitioner's tool: Action research in education is research undertaken by practitioners in order that they may improve their practice.

The following are suggested steps to be taken in action research:

1. Determine the clear need for the proposed research activity.
2. Define the problem or problems with realistic limitations.
3. Review the literature to help set the design and hypotheses for the proposed study.
4. Design and evaluate the study or research process.
5. Build in to the design progress reports to be sent to appropriate persons.
6. Keep accurate records of data and notes of meetings.
7. Analyze the data for meaningful principles.
8. Accept or reject the established hypotheses.
9. Delineate recommendations for further study.

REFERENCES

Chein, I., Cook, S., and Harding, J., "The Field of Action Research." *American Psychologist,* 3:(1948) pp. 43-50.

Corey, S. M., *Action Research to Improve School Practices.* New York: Bureau of Publications, Teachers College, Columbia University, 1953.

Franseth, J., "Improving the Curriculum and Teaching Through Action Research." *School Life*, 42:(1959) pp. 8-9.

Good, C. V., *Introduction to Educational Research 2nd ed.* New York: Appleton-Century-Crofts, 1963.

Neagley, R. L., and Evans, N. D., *Handbook for Effective Supervision of Instruction.* Englewood Cliffs, N.J.: Prentice-Hall, Inc., 1970.

Shepard, H. A., "An Action Research Model." *An Action Research Program for Organization Improvement,* Ann Arbor. The Foundation for Research on Human Behavior, University of Michigan, 1960.

Index

A

B

C

H

I

J

K

L

Q

R

S